The Pastoral Companion

The Pastoral Companion

A Canon Law Handbook
for Catholic Ministry

New Series, Second Edition
Revised, Updated, and Expanded

by

John M. Huels, O.S.M., J.C.D.

Franciscan Press

The Pastoral Companion: A Canon Law Handbook for Catholic Ministry
John M. Huels, O.S.M., J.C.D.

Franciscan Press
Quincy University
1800 College Avenue
Quincy, IL 62301
217.228.5670
fax 217.228.5672

©1995 Franciscan Press

Book design, typesettting by Laurel Fitch, Chicago, IL

Printed in the United States of America
First Printing: August 1995
1 2 3 4 5 6 7 8 9 0

Library of Congress Cataloging-in-Publication Data
Huels, John M.
      The pastoral companion: a canon law handbook for Catholic ministry
      / by John M. Huels. -- New ser., 2nd ed., rev., updated and expanded.
            p. cm.
            Included bibliographical references and index.
            ISBN 0-8199-0968-8 (alk. paper)
      1. Canon law--outlines, syllabi, etc. 2. Catholic Church--Clergy-
      Handbook, manuals, etc. I. Title
      LAW   95-31178
      262.9'4--dc20   cip

acknowledgements

Excerpts from the English translation of documents in the *Canon Law Digest* edited by T. Bouscaren and J. O'Connor (vols. 1-6, Milwaukee/New York: Bruce Publishing Co., 1934-1969; vols. 7-10, Chicago: Canon Law Digest, Chicago Province S.J., 1975-1986; vol. 11, Washington: Canon Law Society of America, 1991, used with permission.

Excerpts from the English translation of *Lectionary for Mass* © 1969, International Committee on English in the Liturgy, Inc. (ICEL); excerpts from the English translation of *The Roman Missal* © 1973, ICEL; excerpts from *Pastoral Care of the Sick: Rites of Anointing and Viaticum* © 1982, ICEL; excerpts from the English translation of *Documents on the Liturgy, 1963-1979: Conciliar, Papal, and Curial Texts* © 1982; excerpts from the *Order of Christian Funerals* © 1985, ICEL; excerpts from the *Rite of Christian Initiation of Adults* © 1985, ICEL; excerpts from the English translation of *Ceremonial of Bishops* © 1989, ICEL. All rights reserved ICEL. All rights reserved.

Excerpts from *National Statutes for the Catechumenate* Copyright © 1988 United States Catholic Conference, Washington, D.C. Used with permission. All rights reserved.

contents

abbreviations

ICEL   International Committee on English in the Liturgy
LFM   Lectionary for Mass
NCCB   National Conference of Catholic Bishops of the United States
NCCC   National Catholic Cemetery Conference
NSC   National Statutes for the Catechumenate, approved by the NCCB and appended to U.S. editions of the RCIA.
OCF   Order of Christian Funerals, approved for use in the dioceses of the U.S.A. by the NCCB (1989)
PCS   Pastoral Care of the Sick: Rites of Anointing and Viaticum, approved for use in the dioceses of the U.S.A. by the NCCB (1983)
RA   Rite of Anointing
RB   Rite of Blessings
RBaptC Rite of Baptism of Children
RCIA   Rite of Christian Initiation of Adults
RConf   Rite of Confirmation
RDCA   Rite of Dedication of a Church and an Altar
RF   Rite of Funerals
RFC   Rite of Reception of Baptized Christians into Full Communion with the Catholic Church
RM   Rite of Marriage
RO   Rite of Ordination (1990 revised edition)
RP   Rite of Penance
US   The version of a liturgical book approved for use in the dioceses of the United States, e.g., the U.S. version of the Rite of Christian Initiation of Adults.
USCC   United States Catholic Conference

Series 2: Commentaries

Abbo/Hannan — J. Abbo and J. Hannan. *The Sacred Canons.* 2 vols. St. Louis: B. Herder, 2nd ed., 1960.

Alford — C. Alford. *Jus Matrimoniale Comparatum.* Rome: Anonima Libraria Cattolica Italiana, 1938.

Capello — F. Capello. *Tractatus Canonico-Moralis de Sacramentis.* 5 vols. Rome: Marietti, 1949-1958.

CCLA — *Code of Canon Law Annotated.* Ed. E. Caparros, M. Thériault, J. Thorn. Montréal: Wilson & Lafleur Limitée, 1993.

CDC — *Código de Derecho Canónico: Edición bilingüe comentado por los profesores de la facultad de derecho canónico de la Universidad Pontificia de Salamanca.* Ed. L. de Echeverria. Madrid: Bibiloteca de Autores Christianos, 1983.

Chiappetta — L. Chiappetta, *Il Codice di Diritto Canonico: Commento giuridico-pastorale.* 2 vols. Naples: Edizioni Dehoniane, 1988.

CLSA Comm. — *The Code of Canon Law: A Text and Commentary.* Ed. J. A. Coriden, T. J. Green, and D. E. Heintschel. New York/Mahwah: Paulist, 1985.

Coronata — M. Conte a Coronata. *Institutiones Iuris Canonici ad usum utriusque cleri et scholarum.* 2nd ed. 5 vols. Rome: Marietti, 1939-1947.

Gasparri — P. Gasparri, *Tractatus Canonicus de Matrimonio.* Ed.post Codicem. 2 vols. Rome: Vatican Press, 1932.

Genicot — E. Genicot, J. Salsmans, and A. Gortebeck. *Institutiones Theologiae Moralis.* 17th ed. 2 vols. Brussels: 1951.

Handbuch — *Handbuch des katholischen Kirchenrechts.* Ed. J. Listl, H. Müller, and H. Schmitz. Regensburg: Friedrich Pustet, 1983.

Matthis/Bonner — M. J. Mathis and D. W. Bonner, *The Pastoral Companion: A Handbook of Canon Law,* 14th ed. Chicago: Franciscan Herald, 1976.

Noldin — H. Noldin, A. Schmitt, and G. Heinzel, *Summa Theologiae Moralis,* 3 vols. Oeniponte: Typis et Sumptibus Feliciani Rauch, 1953-54. Vol. 2, 30th ed., 1954; vol. 3, 30th ed., 1954; vol. 1, 31st ed., 1953.

Pospishil — V. J. Pospishil. *Eastern Catholic Church Law.* Brooklyn: Saint Maron Publications, 1993.

Pospishil/Faris — V. J. Pospishil and J. D. Faris. *The New Latin Code of Canon Law and Eastern Catholics.* Brooklyn: Diocese of Saint Maron, 1984.

Regatillo — E. F. Regatillo, *Ius Sacramentarium,* 3rd ed. Santander: Sal Terrae, 1960.

Sipos/Galos — S. Sipos and L. Galos. *Enchiridion Iuris Canonici.* 6th ed. Rome: Herder, 1954.

Vermeersch/Creusen — A. Vermeersch and J. Creusen. *Epitome Iuris Canonici.* 3 vols. Mechlinia and Rome: H. Dessain. Vol. 1, 7th ed., 1949; vol. 2, 7th ed., 1954; vol. 3, 6th ed., 1946; 7th ed., 1956.

Vlaming/Bender — T. Vlaming and L. Bender. *Praelectiones Iuris Matrimonii.* 4th ed. Bussum: Paul Brand, 1950.

Woestman — W. H. Woestman, *Sacraments: Initiation, Penance, Anointing of the Sick: Commentary on Canons 840-1007.* Ottawa: Faculty of Canon Law, St. Paul University, 1992.

Wrenn — Lawrence G. Wrenn. *Annulments.* 5th ed. rev. Washington: CLSA, 1988.

Woywod — S. Woywod and C. Smith. *A Practical Commentary on the Code of Canon Law.* New York: Joseph F. Wagner, 1962.

preface

to the Second Edition, New Series

The revised *Code of Canon Law* was promulgated in 1983. Since then significant new legislation has been promulgated, warranting a thorough revision and updating of the first edition of the new series of *The Pastoral Companion* published in 1986. Among the documents of major consequence are *The Code of Canons of the Eastern Churches* (1990), the revised *Directory for the Application of Principles and Norms on Ecumenism* (1993), and the apostolic constitution *Pastor bonus* (1988) by which the Roman curia was reorganized.

Changes in law have also come about by the promulgation of several revised liturgical books, including *The Rite of Ordination* (1990) and *The Rite of Marriage* (1991) for the universal Latin church and, for the church in the United States, revised and adapted versions of the *Order of Christian Funerals* (1989), *Book of Blessings* (1989), and *Rite of Christian Initiation of Adults* together with the National Statutes for the Catechumenate (1988). These new books and documents have not only introduced many new laws, but have also in some cases derogated from existing laws in the code and the liturgical books.

Other decrees and documents affecting pastoral ministry have also been published by various dicasteries of the Holy See and by the National Conference of Catholic Bishops of the United States. In addition, more than 25 authentic interpretations have been issued to clarify the meaning of various canons of the code, in some cases changing the meaning of the canons. All of this has created a body of hundreds of new laws, many of which are related to pastoral ministry and are noted in this handbook.

Since the first edition of the new series in 1986, other canonical commentaries have appeared in various languages, and many scholarly

and pastoral articles, books, and canonical opinions have been published, enriching the science of canon law and pastoral studies with
new insights for both scholarship and praxis. One feature of this
revised edition is an appendix with a select bibliography of canonical
publications related to the themes treated in this volume and arranged
in twelve categories. There are five other new appendices: the
approved English translation (1991) of the Profession of Faith and Oath
of Fidelity on Assuming Office; a schematic overview of the consultative and legislative offices and bodies of the Roman Catholic churches
sui iuris, both Latin and Eastern; a summary outline of the principal
dicasteries of the Roman curia as reorganized in 1988; a glossary of
canonical terms, particularly those used in this work; and an index of
the canons cited from the code of the Eastern Catholic churches.

Because many seminarians and clergy use this handbook, a new
chapter on holy orders has been added. Other new sections are: in the
first chapter on the faithful and their rights and obligations; in the
fourth chapter on Communion outside Mass; in the thirteenth chapter
on sacramentals; in the fourteenth chapter on sacred places; in the fif-
teenth chapter on ecumenical and interfaith marriage liturgies.
Moreover, much of the commentary has been revised, updated, and
expanded for this new edition.

Users of this handbook have found that one of its chief advantages
is its citation of other relevant sources of law in addition to the canons
of the code, notably the liturgical laws, authentic interpretations and
decrees of the Holy See, and the particular laws of the United States. All
of these are truly legislative in nature and bind those for whom they
were made. Other documents that have executory rather than legislative force, such as instructions, declarations, directories, etc. are also
cited when they help to shed light on the law's meaning and observance.

The commentary is everywhere indented on the page to distinguish it from the legal texts and the citations from other binding documents, except when the commentary introduces a chapter or a major
section of a chapter, or in the case of an extended treatment of a topic
not directly based on a cited law. The legal texts are identified by a
canon number or other citation in parentheses following the texts.
They are direct translations of the law or other document unless the
citation begins with the word "See," in which case they are either a
paraphrase of the law or, more commonly, a partial citation of it.
Where there are noteworthy differences in law between the Latin
code and the Eastern code, the Eastern law is also quoted or is mentioned in the commentary. Particular laws from the NCCB are clearly
indicated so that they can be easily identified by American readers,
and just as easily ignored by those who are not.

The longstanding purpose of *The Pastoral Companion* is to provide ministers and students with a handy reference of Church laws and brief commentary on topics pertinent to Catholic ministry, especially parish and liturgical ministry. As in past editions, the format is topical, not a canon-by-canon approach. This permits the reader to find more readily the relevant laws from various sources treated under the same heading. Not all canons under each heading are always given, but mainly those with greater relevance and importance to the pastoral ministry. Likewise, while there are many citations from the liturgical books, these are but selected norms that are of greater canonical significance. A more complete understanding of the rites requires a direct reading of the introductions and rubrics of the liturgical books themselves.

Prior to this new series begun in 1986, fourteen editions of *The Pastoral Companion* were published from 1929-1976 by Franciscan canonists Honoratus Bonzelet, Marcian Mathis, Clement Leahy, Nicholas Meyer, and Dismas Bonner. This new edition is dedicated in their memory.

John Huels, O.S.M.
June 29, 1995

I Fundamental Laws and General Norms

one
The Faithful

A. The Baptized

The faithful (*christifideles*) are those who, incorporated by baptism in Christ, are constituted as the people of God, and for this reason, have been made participants in their own way in the priestly, prophetic, and governing roles of Christ. In accord with their proper condition, they are called to exercise the mission which God entrusted the Church with fulfilling. (Can. 204, §1)

> This is mainly a theological description of the members of the Church, called in the code *christifideles*, the faithful of Christ. All who are baptized, Catholic and non-Catholic, are members of Christ's Church.

B. The Catholic Faithful

The Church, constituted and ordered as a society in this world, subsists in the Catholic Church, governed by the successor of Peter and the bishops in communion with him. (Can. 204, §2) The baptized who are in full communion with the Catholic Church on this earth are those who are united with Christ in his visible body by the bonds of profession of faith, the sacraments, and ecclesiastical governance. (Can. 205)

> Not all the baptized are members of the Catholic Church. Catholics, also called Roman Catholics, are those in full communion with the Catholic Church, namely, those who are united in its visible structure by the bonds of the Catholic faith and sacraments, and in ecclesiastical governance under the authority of the

3

bishop of Rome and the bishops in communion with him. The members of the separated Eastern churches and the Protestant ecclesial communities are members of Christ's Church, but not in full communion with the Catholic Church. Catholics themselves can become separated from full communion with the Catholic Church by apostasy, heresy, or schism. However, they always remain Catholics and can return to the Church at any time through the sacrament of penance and, when necessary, by the remission of the penalty of excommunication.

C. The Catholic Churches

A church *sui iuris* is a group of the faithful which is united by a hierarchy according to the norm of law and which is expressly or tacitly recognized as *sui iuris* by the supreme authority of the Church. (CCEC, can. 27)

The Roman Catholic Church consists of 22 distinct churches *sui iuris*, which roughly translates as "autonomous" churches. The Latin church and the 21 Eastern Catholic churches each have their own hierarchy in communion with the bishop of Rome. (See Appendix II.) The canons of the *Code of Canon Law* of the Latin church affect only the Latin church. (See can. 1.) The Eastern Catholic churches have a common code of law, the *Code of Canons of the Eastern Churches* (CCEC), which affect only the Eastern churches unless it is expressly stated otherwise. (See CCEC, can. 1.)

A rite is the liturgical, theological, spiritual, and disciplinary patrimony, which is distinguished by the culture and the historical circumstances of peoples, and which is expressed in its own manner of living the faith by each church *sui iuris*. (CCEC, can. 28, §1.)

In the past, the churches *sui iuris* used to be called "rites"–the Latin rite, the Ukrainian rite, the Ruthenian rite, etc. This use of the term is still found in various canons of the Latin code, which also uses the term "ritual church *sui iuris*." With the promulgation of the Eastern code in 1990, the use of "rite" in this sense is obsolete. Now one must distinguish between a "rite" and a "church *sui iuris*." A rite is a whole tradition of a group of Christian people, including its liturgy, its laws and customs, its theological heritage and its spirituality; a church *sui iuris* is a juridically distinct community of the faithful which has its own hierarchy and which, in fact, may share its rite with others, e.g., the Byzantine rite which is common to thirteen churches *sui iuris*. There are six rites: the

Roman, Constantinopolitan (Byzantine), Alexandrian, Antiochene, Armenian, and Chaldean.

D. Membership in a Church *Sui Iuris*

1. By baptism

If both parents belong to the Latin church, their child becomes a member in it by receiving baptism. If one of the parents does not belong to the Latin church, they may decide by common agreement to have their child baptized in the Latin church; but if they are unable to agree, the child should become a member of the church *sui iuris* to which the father belongs. (See can. 111, §1.)

> Under the former law, the children had to be baptized in the church *sui iuris* of the father. Under the revised legislation, parents of different Catholic churches may choose the church *sui iuris* of either for the baptism of their children. If they are unable to agree, the children are baptized in the church *sui iuris* of the father.
>
> *Eastern law.* The code of the Eastern Catholic churches favors baptism in the church *sui iuris* of the father. However, the child may be baptized in the church of the mother, if the father is not Catholic, or if both parents agree to it and freely request it. (See CCEC, can. 29, §1.)

(1) If children under fourteen are born of an unwed mother, they become a member in the church to which the mother belongs. (2) If they are born of unknown parents, they become a member of the church of those who are legitimately entrusted with their care; (3) If they are adopted, they become a member of the church of the father, or of the mother when the father is not Catholic or when they both agree to the mother's church; (4) If they are born of non-baptized parents, they become a member of the church of the person who is in charge of their upbringing in the Catholic faith. (See CCEC, can. 29, §2.)

> Although these rules are found only in the Eastern code, they can be taken as suppletory law for the Latin church, observing the difference that in the Latin church a child may become a member of the church *sui iuris* of either parent.
>
> It is not the liturgical rite of baptism celebrated that determines one's membership in a church *sui iuris*, but rather the church to which the parents belong. If, e.g., Eastern Catholic parents have their baby baptized in a Latin parish because they have no parish of their own, the child is still a member of their Eastern

church. Baptism is the beginning of one's membership in a church. The precise church is determined by the rules above regarding parents or those who take their place, not by the place or liturgy of baptism.

Anyone to be baptized who is at least fourteen may freely choose to be baptized in the Latin church or in some other church *sui iuris.* In such a case the person belongs to that church which he or she has chosen. (Can. 111, §2)

2   By transfer

After baptism one can become a member of another church *sui iuris* if one:

    a)   obtains the permission of the Apostolic See;

    b)   is a spouse who, when getting married or during the marriage, declares that he or she is transferring to the church *sui iuris* of the other spouse; if the marriage is terminated, however, he or she may freely return to the Latin church;

    c)   is a child under fourteen of those mentioned in a or b; or, in a mixed marriage, is a child under fourteen of the Catholic party who has legitimately transferred to another church *sui iuris,* but when the children have completed their fourteenth year they may choose to return to the Latin church. (Can. 112, §1)

> The permission of the Apostolic See is necessary for the liceity of transfer by a Latin Catholic to an Eastern Catholic church. For an Eastern Catholic to transfer, the permission is necessary for the validity of the transfer. (See CCEC, can. 32.)
>
> In a marriage of a Latin and Eastern Catholic, either spouse may freely transfer to the church of the other simply by making a declaration, whether orally or in writing. The oral declaration should be made before, or a written declaration sent to, the pastor of the church to which one is transferring, and he should then notify the pastor of baptism so that the transfer can be recorded in the person's baptismal register. (See can. 535, §2.) The transfer may take place at the time of the marriage or anytime during the marriage.
>
> *In the Eastern law,* the wife may transfer to the church of the husband, but the husband may not transfer to the church of the wife. (See CCEC, can. 33.) The Eastern code requires that the transfer be declared before the local hierarch or the pastor of the church to which one is transferring, or a priest delegated by either of them, and before two witnesses. (See CCEC, can. 36; see also can. 37 on recording the transfer.)

In a marriage where one spouse has transferred, when the marriage ends due to death, annulment, dissolution, or permanent separation, the spouse who transferred may freely return to his or her own original church. This new transfer should also be declared before the pastor (or other minister) of the parish to which one is returning, and notification sent to the parish of baptism for recording in the baptismal register.

When anyone transfers to another church *sui iuris,* their children under fourteen automatically transfer with them. The transfer must be noted in the baptismal register of each of them. When the children turn fourteen, or anytime thereafter, they are free to transfer back to their original church, again with notification to the parish of baptism for proper recording.

In the Eastern law, if both parents are Catholic and only one parent transfers, the consent of both parents is needed for the children under fourteen to transfer. (See CCEC, can. 34.) In the Latin law, the children under fourteen transfer along with the parent who is transferring even without the consent of the other parent.

In a mixed marriage between a Catholic and a non-Catholic, if the Catholic transfers to another church *sui iuris* with the permission of the Apostolic See, the children under fourteen also are transferred. For example, the father is Russian Orthodox and the mother is Latin Catholic, and she wishes to transfer to the Russian Catholic church to share in the ecclesial tradition of her husband. She may transfer with the permission of the Apostolic See. Permission would not be needed for the transfer of her children under fourteen.

If a Latin Catholic wishes to transfer to an Eastern Catholic church *sui iuris* that has an eparchy within the boundaries of the Latin diocese, he or she may transfer with the written permission of the bishops of both dioceses without permission of the Apostolic See. (See Secretary of State, rescript, Nov. 21, 1992, *Communicationes* 24 (1992) 200; see also CCEC, can. 32, §2.)

This is a derogation from the *Code of Canon Law.* Whenever anyone wishes to transfer to another church *sui iuris,* they need only the permission of the bishops of both dioceses, provided the territories of the two dioceses are overlapping and the persons transferring reside in that territory.

The custom, no matter how longstanding, of receiving the sacraments in the rite of another church *sui iuris,* does not bring about membership in that church. (Can. 112, §2; see also CCEC, can. 38.)

It sometimes happens that an Eastern Catholic has been raised in a Latin Catholic parish and is registered there, having gone to the parish school, having made first Communion, attending Mass weekly, etc. However, this does not bring about a change in their membership in their own Eastern church. This fact has important consequences. In the case of confirmation, the Eastern Catholics have likely already been confirmed as infants and may not be confirmed again. In the case of marriage, they may not validly marry in the Latin parish, unless they are marrying a Latin Catholic.

3. By reception into full communion

Baptized non-Catholics coming into full communion with the Catholic Church should retain their own rite and practice it everywhere in the world and should observe it to the extent of their capability. They should join the church *sui iuris* of that same rite without prejudice to the right of petitioning the Apostolic See in special cases of persons, communities, or regions. (CCEC, can. 35)

Although this law of the Eastern code is not found in the Latin code, it is the practice of the entire Church. (See Vatican II, decree *Orientalium Ecclesiarum,* 4, CLD 6:9.) When non-Catholic Christians are received into full communion with the Catholic Church, they must become members of the church *sui iuris* indicated by their baptism. Thus, Protestants must become members of the Latin church; a Greek Orthodox must become a member of the Greek Catholic church; a Syrian Orthodox must become a member of the Syrian Catholic church, etc. Exceptions constitute a transfer, requiring the permission of the Apostolic See or of the two Catholic bishops whose jurisdictions overlap.

t w o

Physical Persons

A. Subjects of the Law

Those bound to observe merely ecclesiastical law are those baptized into the Catholic Church or received into it, who enjoy a sufficient use of reason and, unless the law expressly states otherwise, have reached the age of seven. (Can. 11)

> *Divine law* is the law revealed by God in scripture and tradition. Only the supreme authority of the Church, the pope or the college of bishops, can define a matter of divine law. Divine law binds everyone, Catholic and non-Catholic alike. *Ecclesiastical* law binds only Catholics who have the use of reason and are at least seven. For example, the law requiring attendance at Mass on Sundays and holy days begins to bind a Catholic child at the age of seven.

The canons of the *Code of Canon Law* pertain only to the Latin Church. (Can. 1)

> Although the Latin code does not bind Catholics who belong to the Eastern Catholic churches, there are times when it does; e.g., when an Eastern Catholic marries a Latin Catholic, the parties are subject to the marriage laws of both churches.

An *adult* is a person who has completed the eighteenth year of age; a *minor* is one below this age. A minor younger than seven is called an *infant* and is considered *non sui compos* [legally incompetent]; but after the seventh birthday the use of reason is presumed. (Can. 97)

Whoever habitually lacks the use of reason is considered *non sui compos* and is equated with infants. (Can. 99)

> In canon law, one completes a year of life at midnight at the end of the day of one's birthday. Thus, one becomes an adult at midnight at the end of one's eighteenth birthday; one is presumed to have the use of reason and begins to be bound by canon law at midnight at the end of one's seventh birthday. This is the way all canonical age requirements are to be reckoned. (See can. 203.)

Adults have the full exercise of their rights. Minors remain subject to their parents or guardians in the exercise of their rights, with the exception of those areas in which minors are exempt from parental control either by divine law or by canon law. In reference to the designation of guardians and their authority, the civil law should be observed unless canon law establishes something else, or if, in certain cases and for a just reason, the diocesan bishop has decided to provide otherwise by the appointment of another guardian. (Can. 98)

B. Subjects of Universal and Particular Law

Everyone, for whom universal laws are made, is bound to observe them everywhere on the earth. However, when universal laws are not in force in a certain territory, all who are actually in that territory are exempt from them. (Can. 12, §§ 1, 2)

> Universal laws are established for members of the Church everywhere. For example, the *Code of Canon Law* is universal law binding Latin Catholics everywhere as applicable. Thus, the laws on clergy bind all clergy; the laws on religious bind all religious, etc. When there are exemptions for a particular territory, all those actually in the territory are exempt.
>
> *Exempting causes* are those in virtue of which one ceases to be a subject of the law. One form of exempting cause is mentioned in canon 12, namely, those which actually remove the subject from the jurisdiction of a superior. For example, one who goes from a diocese where there exists an obligation to attend Mass on a certain holy day into a diocese in a foreign country where such an obligation does not bind, has placed an exempting cause by leaving the territory of the superior. There are other causes that create exemptions from certain laws. Those who profess vows in religious institutes of pontifical right place a cause which gives them greater autonomy from the jurisdiction of the local Ordinary than do those who enter institutes of diocesan right. Or, a change in age may amount to an exempting cause, e.g.,

the completion of one's fifty-ninth year exempts from the obligation imposed by the law of fasting. (See Mathis/Bonner, 18-19.)

Bound to laws established for a particular territory are those for whom they were enacted, and those who have either domicile or quasi-domicile and likewise are actually staying there, with due regard for canon 13. (Can. 12, §3)

Particular laws bind only in the territory or only the persons for whom they were made. In order to be bound by the particular laws of a territory—e.g., some diocese, province, or region—it is required that one be both of the territory and actually in the territory. In other words, the subject of particular law not only has a domicile or quasi-domicile in the territory, but is actually present in the diocese, province, or region and is not travelling elsewhere. Exceptions are given in canon 13.

Particular laws are not presumed to be personal but rather territorial, unless otherwise evident. (Can. 13, §1)

Personal laws bind persons wherever they go. For example, religious are bound by the constitutions of their institute wherever they go. Laws are presumed to be territorial unless it is clear that they are personal. Thus, the laws of the code are territorial, binding Catholics everywhere. Particular laws are also presumed to be territorial, binding only those who are both of the territory and in the territory.

Travelers (peregrini) are not bound by particular laws of their own territory as long as they are absent from it, unless the transgression of the laws would cause harm in their own territory, or unless the laws are personal. (Can. 13, §2, 1°)

Examples of laws which cannot be violated without doing harm to one's own territory would be a law requiring the pastor's presence in his parish on a certain day, a law requiring his presence at the diocesan synod, or restricting his absence from the diocese. Particular laws concerning these and similar matters must be observed even when one is outside the territory. Moreover, the lawgiver may make personal particular laws which must be observed even when a subject is outside the territory. Thus, a diocesan bishop may make certain disciplinary rules and norms for his clergy, clearly indicating the personal character of these norms. However, this personal character must be quite evident and clear; in doubt, the presumption of territoriality takes precedence.

Travelers are not bound to the laws of a territory in which they are staying except for those which pertain to public order, which determine the formalities of legal acts, or which pertain to immoveable things located in the territory. (Can. 13, §2, 2°)

> Laws which concern the public order are those which are enacted to avert harm, scandal, and other evils, to prevent crimes and disturbances, to guard and protect peace and tranquility, and to promote the public welfare. Some of them may be especially made to include outsiders. For example, there might be certain particular laws restricting clerics and religious in the matter of engaging in business, politics, etc., and such laws may pertain to the public order. In doubt whether a given law is one which pertains to the public order, freedom on the part of the traveler is favored. Laws which concern legal formalities are those which determine the acts and procedures required in the drafting of wills and contracts, the conduct of trials, etc. Laws pertaining to immoveable things refer to buildings and property which cannot be moved.

Transients (*vagi*) are bound to both universal and particular laws which are in force in the place where they are staying. (Can. 13, §3)

> Transients are those who have no domicile or quasi-domicile anywhere, e.g., homeless people, migrants, itinerants.

C. Excusing Causes

Ignorance or error about invalidating or incapacitating laws do not impede their effectiveness unless the contrary is expressly stated. Ignorance or error is not presumed about a law or a penalty, or a fact concerning oneself or a notorious fact concerning another person. (Can. 15)

> Invalidating laws are those which establish criteria for the validity of legal acts. Incapacitating laws are those which establish the qualifications which enable a person to perform validly certain legal acts. Ignorance is lack of knowledge. Error is mistaken judgment. A notorious fact about another is one which is publicly known. Akin to ignorance is inadvertence, where a person knows about a law, a penalty, or some fact, but does not advert to it at a specific time and unwittingly violates a law.
> Excusing causes render the observance of the law impossible or extremely difficult. In such a situation a person remains a sub-

ject of the law but is not bound to observe it. Ordinarily, ignorance, inadvertence, and error constitute excusing causes from moral guilt and from full legal imputability for a violation of the law. Since these factors render an act involuntary, at least to some extent, they prevent a true violation of law with its consequent effects.

Canon 15 states a notable exception to the general rule on excusing causes: ignorance of invalidating and incapacitating laws does not excuse from their observance and effects, unless the law expressly declares otherwise. For example, ignorance does not excuse one from incurring impediments to matrimony, because all matrimonial impediments are incapacitating laws; ignorance also does not excuse from irregularities and impediments to holy orders, even though they are not incapacitating laws, because the law expressly states that ignorance does not excuse. (See can. 1045.)

Physical and moral impossibility are other excusing causes. *Physical impossibility* exists when compliance with the law is simply beyond human capability; such impossibility certainly excuses from the observance of law, since no one can be obliged to perform what is not possible.

Moral impossibility arises when the observance of the law is rendered very difficult by reason of grave fear, serious harm, or inconvenience which may be connected with the fulfillment of the law in question. Moral impossibility sometimes excuses from ecclesiastical law, because the legislator is not presumed to impose his law on his subjects when its observance results in notable negative consequences. The grave fear, serious harm, or inconvenience must be accidental, i.e., not fostered deliberately to create moral impossibility. These factors must also be extrinsic to the law itself; if they are intrinsically bound up with its observance, they must be regarded as foreseen by the lawgiver, and therefore borne by the subjects. Note that not even danger of death excuses in cases where violation of the law harms the common good, inflicts extreme spiritual harm on a given person, results in hatred of God or contempt of the Church. The common good is always to be preferred to the private good of an individual.

Outside of the above cases, moral impossibility can excuse from law. In the case of ecclesiastical law, when its observance entails relatively serious fear, harm, or inconvenience, it becomes by that very fact an impossible law, since human law must be observable by the application of the ordinary capacities of people. In any given case, in order to determine how much harm or inconvenience is necessary to excuse, one must look to the seriousness of the precept and the strictness with which it is enjoined.

In general, negative laws oblige more strictly than affirmative ones; those which are expressions of divine natural or positive law more strictly than those which are merely ecclesiastical laws. In any event, the opinions of authors can be of great assistance in determining what constitutes an excusing cause in a given instance. Note that, in the case of invalidating or incapacitating laws, moral impossibility on the part of a private person does not excuse, since such laws are intended to safeguard the common good.

An example: A priest has spent a good part of the night in the hospital ministering to a dying parishioner. He awakens for morning Mass very tired and groggy. He needs a cup of coffee to make him alert enough to celebrate the Eucharist with fitting devotion and attention. However, the law requires him to fast at least one hour. Since his fasting could lead to a kind of spiritual harm to the people due to a poorly celebrated liturgy, this would be sufficient cause to excuse from the observance of the law of fast.

D. Domicile and Quasi-Domicile

Domicile is acquired by residence in the territory of some parish or at least of a diocese which is conjoined with either the intention of remaining there perpetually if nothing calls one away, or the completion of residence for five years. (Can. 102, §1)

Quasi-domicile is acquired by residence in the territory of some parish or at least of a diocese which is conjoined with either the intention of staying there three months if nothing calls one away, or the completion of residence for three months. (Can. 102, §2)

> When domicile or quasi-domicile is acquired by actual residence for a period of five years or of three months respectively, the time need not be absolutely continuous; moral continuity suffices. Hence, brief absences do not break the continuity of the time period.

A domicile or quasi-domicile in the territory of a parish is called parochial; in the territory of a diocese, even if not in a parish, is called diocesan. (Can. 102, §3)

Spouses may have a common domicile or quasi-domicile; for reason of legitimate separation or for another just cause, either can have one's own domicile or quasi-domicile. (Can. 104)

A person is called a *resident* in the place where one has domicile; a *temporary resident* in the place of quasi-domicile; a *traveler* (*peregri-*

nus) if outside one's domicile or quasi-domicile while still retaining it; a *transient* (*vagus*) if one has neither a domicile nor a quasi-domicile anywhere. (Can. 100)

Minors necessarily retain the domicile or quasi-domicile of those who have authority over them. Those who are beyond infancy [seven or older with the use of reason] are able to acquire their own quasi-domicile; and those who have been legitimately emancipated according to the norm of civil law may also acquire their own domicile. Whoever has been placed legally under the guardianship or care of another for some reason other than minority [under eighteen] has the domicile or quasi-domicile of the guardian or curator. (Can. 105)

Members of religious institutes and societies of apostolic life acquire domicile in the place where the house to which they belong is located; they acquire quasi-domicile in the house where they are living in accord with canon 102, §2. (Can. 103)

One acquires a pastor and Ordinary through both one's domicile and quasi-domicile. The proper pastor or Ordinary of a transient is the pastor or Ordinary of the place in which the transient is actually staying. The proper pastor of those who have only a diocesan domicile or quasi-domicile is the pastor of the place in whey they are actually staying. (Can. 107)

> The proper parish is determined by the parish territory of domicile or quasi-domicile, unless it is a personal parish, such as one established for a certain ethnic group. A Catholic has a right to the sacraments and other liturgical rites in his or her territorial parish, including baptism, marriage, and funeral rites. This right is not dependent on one's registration in the parish. The right to the liturgical rites of the Church is not lost by failure to register in a parish.

> While the Catholic faithful have a right to liturgical celebrations in their own territorial (or personal) parish, they do not have that right in any other parish. Thus, e.g., a pastor may celebrate the baptism or assist at the marriage of non-parishioners, or he can refuse them. The pastor of the parish where they reside cannot refuse them, as long as the other requirements of the law are met.

> It frequently occurs that a person has several proper Ordinaries and pastors by reason of domicile in one place and quasi-domicile in one or more other places. Which proper Ordinary or pastor is to be preferred in various cases (as for baptism or burial) is sometimes determined either by law or legal custom. In other cases one has the liberty to choose which ever proper Ordinary or pastor one prefers.

Domicile and quasi-domicile are lost by departing from a place with the intention of not returning, the prescript of canon 105 remaining intact. (Can. 106)

Mere absence, even for a number of years, does not cause loss of domicile or quasi-domicile as long as the intention to return exists.

Legal (necessary) domicile of minors is not lost by departure even with the intention never to return; it is lost only when subjection to the authority of parents or guardian ceases. (Cf. can. 105.)

E. Consanguinity and Affinity

Consanguinity is computed by lines and degrees. In the direct line there are as many degrees as there are generations, that is, as there are persons, not counting the common ancestor. In the collateral line there are as many degrees as there are persons in both lines, not counting the common ancestor. (Can. 108)

Consanguinity, or blood relationship, exists in the direct line if one person is the direct ancestor of the other, e.g., grandfather, father, son, etc. It exists in the collateral line if neither person is the direct ancestor of the other but both are descended from a common ancestor, e.g., brothers and sisters, cousins, uncles and nephews and aunts and nieces, etc.

Since carnal generation is the basis of consanguinity, the relationship arises from both legitimate and illegitimate generation. A degree of relationship indicates the measure of distance of two related persons. In the direct line there are as many degrees as there are generations or persons, not counting the common ancestor. Thus, the relationship between parent and child is first degree; that between grandparent and grandchild is second degree; etc.

In the collateral line there are as many degrees as there are persons in both lines together, not counting the common ancestor. Thus, brothers and sisters are related in the second degree; uncle or aunt and nephew or niece in the third degree; first cousins in the fourth degree; great aunt or uncle and grand nephew or niece in the fifth degree; second cousins in the sixth degree, etc.

To compute the degree of relationship one must always identify the common ancestor. For example, the common ancestor of first cousins is the common grandparents. It is helpful to diagram the relationship.

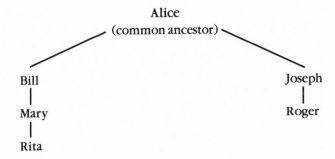

Alice
(common ancestor)

Bill   Joseph

Mary   Roger

Rita

In this example, Bill and Joseph are brothers, related in the second degree, the sons of Alice. Mary is Bill's daughter and Roger is Joseph's son. Joseph is Mary's uncle (third degree) and Bill is Roger's uncle (third degree). Mary and Roger are first cousins (fourth degree), the grandchildren of Alice. Rita is Mary's daughter, Bill's granddaughter. She is related by consanguinity to Joseph, her great uncle, in the fourth degree collateral line, and to Roger in the fifth degree collateral line.

The rule for determining the degree is to count the number of persons taken together on both lines but without counting the common ancestor. The first line is that from Alice through Rita; the other line is that from Alice through Roger. Also, descendants who are not relevant are not counted. For example, in determining that Rita is related to Joseph in the fourth degree, Joseph's descendant, Roger, is not counted—he is irrelevant to determining the relationship between Rita and Joseph.

Affinity arises from a valid marriage, even if not consummated, and it exists between a man and the blood relations of his wife and also between a woman and the blood relations of her husband. It is computed such that those who are blood relatives of the man are related by affinity to his wife in the same line and degree as they are related by consanguinity to the man, and vice versa. (Can. 109)

Affinity arises from valid marriage, whether ratified only or both ratified and consummated. It is the "in-law" relationship, i.e., father-in-law, daughter-in-law, brother-in-law, etc. It exists only between the husband and the blood relatives of the wife and the between the wife and the blood relatives of the husband.

Affinity is computed as follows: The blood relatives of the husband are related by affinity to the wife in the same line and degree as they are related by consanguinity to the husband, and vice versa.

To compute affinity, therefore, one need only determine the line and degree of consanguinity, because it is exactly the same line and degree for affinity. Thus, a man is related to his mother by consanguinity in the first degree of the direct line; his wife is related to his mother (her mother-in-law) by affinity also in the first degree of the direct line.

Some other examples: a man's brother is related by affinity to his wife in the second degree of the collateral line; the wife's first cousin is related by affinity to the husband in the fourth degree of the collateral line.

three

The Power of Governance

A. Division

The power of governance, also called the power of jurisdiction, exists in the Church by divine institution. (See can. 129, §1.) The power of governance is normally exercised in the external forum, but sometimes it is exercised in the internal forum only, but in such a way that the effects which its exercise is supposed to have in the external forum are not recognized in this forum, with the exception of those cases determined in the law. (Can. 130)

The power of governance, also called "jurisdiction," in the *external forum* provides primarily and directly for the common and public good of the Church; it regulates the social action of the faithful, their relationship to the external and visible society of the Church. Therefore, it is exercised publicly and has juridical effects.

Enacting laws, exercising judgment in ecclesiastical courts, establishing censures, and appointing pastors are examples of the exercise of governance in the external forum. Such actions as the remission of certain censures and dispensations from vows and matrimonial impediments usually are acts of the external forum but may, in a proper case, fall within the internal forum.

Governance in the *internal forum,* the forum of conscience, provides primarily and directly for the private welfare of the faithful; it regulates their private actions and their moral relationship to God. Therefore it is exercised privately and confidentially, often in complete secrecy, and has no public juridical effects unless these are expressly granted by the law or by the action of some competent superior. (See can. 130.) Some examples of governance exercised in the internal forum include dispensations from occult impediments to marriage in accord with canon 1079, §3; secret marriages treated in canons 1130-1133; the remission of reserved censures in accord with canon 1357. The dicastery of the Roman curia that handles matters of the internal forum is the Apostolic Penitentiary.

The power of governance in the internal forum is *sacramental* when it can be exercised only in the administration of the sacrament of penance, e.g., when a penitent requests absolution for a sin for which he or she has incurred an automatic censure that has not been declared. (See can. 1357). Governance in the internal forum is *extra-sacramental* when it can be exercised apart from any relation to the administration of the sacrament of penance, though still in a private manner.

Ordinary power of governance is that which is connected with some office by the law itself; delegated power is that which is granted to a person not by means of an office. (Can. 131, §1)

Ordinary power. For governance to be classified as ordinary, it must be attached to an office by the law itself, i.e., either by the universal law or particular law, or by legal custom. For example, the power of pastors and clerical superiors to dispense from fast and abstinence is ordinary governance since it is granted by the code, canon 1245.

Delegated power. The power of governance which is granted to a person not by means of an office is delegated power. For example, some dioceses delegate to parish priests and deacons the faculty to permit mixed marriages, a power which the universal law reserves to the local Ordinary. (See can. 1125.) Rules for delegation are given below.

Ordinary power of governance can be either proper or vicarious. (Can. 131, §2)

Proper and vicarious power. Proper power is that which is exercised in one's own name in virtue of the office one has. For example, when the diocesan bishop exercises the power of his office, he does it in his own name. When the vicar general or episcopal vicar exercise the power of their office, they do it vicariously, that is, in the name of the bishop. Likewise, when a pastor is impeded from exercising his pastoral office and a parochial vicar exercises the power of the pastor, the parochial vicar exercises vicarious power in the name of the pastor. (See can. 541.) On the other hand, when the pastor exercises the power of his office, he does so in his own name, and thus he exercises proper power.

The power of governance is distinguished as legislative, executive, and judicial. Legislative power is exercised in the manner prescribed by law; legislative power in the Church possessed by a legislator below the supreme authority cannot be validly delegated unless the law explicitly so provides. A law from a lower level legislator that is contrary to a higher level law may not be validly enacted. (Can. 135, §§ 1, 2)

Legislative power cannot be validly delegated by anyone other than the pope or ecumenical council, unless the law explicitly provides otherwise. For example, diocesan bishops, particular councils, episcopal conferences, and general chapters of religious institutes cannot delegate their law-making powers to others. Furthermore, a lower level legislator is unable validly to enact a law contrary to the law of a superior. For example, a diocesan bishop could not enact a law contrary to a canon of the code, since the *Code of Canon Law* is papal law.

Judicial power, which judges or judicial colleges enjoy, must be exercised in the manner prescribed by law and it cannot be delegated except to carry out acts which are preparatory to a decree or sentence. (Can. 135, §3)

The manner of exercising judicial power is treated in Book VII of the code.

Executive power is enjoyed by various ecclesiastical authorities, such as diocesan bishops and their vicars, pastors, religious superiors. Executive power can be delegated in accord with the following rules.

B. Delegation

The following rules on delegation apply to any kind of delegation of executive power of governance. Priests and deacons in pastoral ministry will find these rules most useful in respect to delegating the faculty to assist at marriage. Although the faculty to assist at marriage is not technically considered an exercise of the power of governance, the delegation of this faculty follows the same rules as for the delegation of executive power of governance.

1. Ordinary executive power can be delegated both for a particular act or for all cases unless the law expressly provides otherwise. (Can. 137, §1)

Power delegated for a particular act is called *special delegation;* that granted for any number of cases of the same kind is called *general delegation.* For example, a pastor, who has ordinary power, is going on vacation, and he delegates a visiting priest to perform the six marriages scheduled in the parish during his absence. This is special delegation and can be used only for those six marriages. If the pastor had granted general delegation, the visiting priest could have assisted at all marriages celebrated in the parish, even those that had not been scheduled.

Pastors have the faculty in virtue of their office to assist at marriages within their parish of any couple, provided at least one of the parties is a Latin rite Catholic. (See can. 1109.) They can grant this faculty either by way of general or special delegation to any priest or deacon. (See can. 1111.)

Although pastors have the faculty in virtue of their office to hear confessions in their territory, they may not delegate this faculty to others. The faculty to hear confessions is granted by the local Ordinary or clerical superior in accord with canons 968-969.

Pastors and other priests with an office of pastoral care, such as parochial vicars and chaplains, have the faculty of confirming after baptism an initiate who is seven years of age or older as well as a baptized non-Catholic who is being received into the full communion of the Catholic Church. However, they could not delegate this to another priest; the faculty must be given by the diocesan bishop. (See cans. 883, 2°; 884, §1.)

2. Subdelegation.

Executive power delegated by another authority having ordinary power, if it was delegated for all cases, can be subdelegated only in individual cases; but if it was delegated for a particular act or acts, it cannot be subdelegated unless by express grant of the one delegating. (Can. 137, §3)

For example, a parochial vicar or a deacon has general delegation to assist at marriages in the parish. With general delegation, he could subdelegate another priest or deacon to assist at marriages in individual cases, that is, for specified weddings. He could not grant general delegation to another priest or deacon. General delegation can only be granted by the authority having ordinary power, the pastor or local Ordinary.

If a priest or deacon has only special delegation, he could not subdelegate another to assist at the marriage or marriages for which he was delegated unless the one who delegated him had granted him the power to subdelegate. For example, a pastor who is going on vacation delegates a visiting priest to assist at the six scheduled marriages during his absence, but he does not mention that the visitor may subdelegate this power. In such a case, the visiting priest could not subdelegate this power to another priest or deacon even in a case of necessity; the delegation would have to come from the pastor or local Ordinary (or from a parochial vicar or deacon in the parish with general delegation, if there is one).

3. No subdelegated power can be subdelegated again unless this was expressly granted by the one delegating. (Can. 137, §4)

C. Use

Those who have executive power of governance may exercise it on behalf of their subjects even if they themselves or their subjects are outside the territory, unless something else is evident by the nature of the matter or by prescript of law. They may also exercise this power on behalf of travelers who are in the territory, provided it is a question of granting favors or of enforcing either universal or particular laws to which they are bound by canon 13, §2, n. 2. (Can. 136)

> An example of this rule for pastoral ministry is a dispensation from the law of fast and abstinence or from the Sunday or holy day obligations which the pastor can grant even for visitors in his parish, or for his parishioners even when he or they are outside the parish boundaries. (See can. 1245.)
> There is an exception to this general principle regarding the faculty for assisting at marriages and the faculty for presbyters to confirm. Marriages performed outside one's territory (usually the parish) without special delegation are invalid, as are confirmations by presbyters outside their territory (unless they are baptizing someone from an Eastern Catholic church or someone in danger of death). (See cans. 1109-11; 887; CCEC, can. 696, §2.)
> Canon 13, §2, n. 2 exempts travelers from all particular laws except for those laws which provide for the public order, which determine legal formalities, or which deal with immoveable goods situated in that territory.

D. Cessation

1. Ordinary power is lost by the loss of the office to which it is connected. (Can. 143, §1) An ecclesiastical office is lost by the end of a predefined term limit, by reaching an age defined in the law, by resignation, transfer, removal, and privation. (Can. 184, §1)

For example, if a pastor's term expires, or he is transferred or removed from office, or his resignation is accepted by the bishop, he loses the ordinary power of a pastor.

Unless the law provides otherwise, ordinary power is suspended if one legitimately appeals or makes recourse against a privation or removal from office. (Can. 143, §2)

For example, if a diocesan bishop decrees the removal of a certain pastor and the pastor makes recourse against this decision to the Holy See, his ordinary power is not lost but he cannot exercise it until the case is resolved in his favor.

2. Delegated power is lost: (a) when the mandate for which it was given is fulfilled; (b) when the time of delegation or the number of cases for which it was given has run out; (c) when the motivating cause of the delegation has ceased; (d) by revocation on the part of the delegating authority, upon direct notice thereof to the delegate; (e) by renunciation on the part of the delegate, upon direct notice to and acceptance thereof by the delegating authority. Delegated power is not lost, however, by the expiration of the authority of the one delegating, unless this is apparent from clauses appended to it. (Can. 142, §1)

E. Supplied Jurisdiction

In case of inadvertence. An act of delegated power which is exercised only in the internal forum is valid if it is done inadvertently after the grant has expired. (Can. 142, §2)

For example, a priest from a religious institute has been transferred from his house in diocese X to a new assignment in diocese Y. Before arriving at his new domicile, he takes a summer course for two months in diocese Z and receives the faculty to hear confessions in that diocese for two months. At the end of the course, someone asks to go to confession to him and he hears the confession, not adverting to the fact that his temporary faculty has just expired. Although he lacks the faculty, the Church supplies it *(ecclesia supplet)* in the internal forum in the case of inadvertence.

In common error, whether of fact or of law, and also in positive and probable doubt of law or of fact, the Church supplies executive power of governance both for the external and internal forum. This same norm applies to the faculties for confirmation, penance, and marriage. (See can. 144.)

When the Church supplies jurisdiction, it is not a matter of sanating an invalid act, but of the law actually delegating the executive power of governance where it is lacking. The reasons for this provision of canon law are the protection of the spiritual welfare of the faithful, the common good of the Church, and legal certainty.

According to canon 144, there are two general situations in which the Church supplies executive power of governance. The first is common error. *Common error of fact* occurs when all the faithful of a place, or at least the majority of them, believe a person to have the power of governance when in fact he or she does not. *Common error of law* occurs when the circumstances are such that the great part of the community could be in error about a person's possession of the power of governance, even though the community does not in fact make this error.

The Church also supplies executive power of governance where it is lacking in *positive and probable doubt of law or fact.* While common error occurs on the part of the community, doubt occurs on the part of the individual who performs some act requiring executive power of governance. Objectively, the person lacks the power of governance, but subjectively he or she is doubtful about its possession.

Positive doubt is that which is founded upon one or more reasons. A negative doubt is mere ignorance. The Church does not supply the power of governance for a negative doubt. The doubt must be not only one that is positive but also is *probable* in that the reason or reasons for it have a certain degree of validity or sincerity leading to the conclusion on the part of the individual that the power may very well be possessed, even though the individual is not certain that it is possessed. The doubt may be a *doubt of law,* that is, about a law which would confirm or deny the existence of the power in question. The doubt may concern the existence of the law, its interpretation, its application, its extension. A *doubt of fact* is a doubt whether the power of governance actually has been granted, either by means of office or delegation, or if the power had been granted whether it has now expired.

The principle of supplied jurisdiction extends also to the faculties necessary for the valid administration of confirmation, penance, and marriage. For examples and further discussion on its application to these sacraments, see pages 74, 133, and 259.

four
Dispensations

A. Power to Dispense

A dispensation, which is the relaxation of a merely ecclesiastical law in a particular case, can be granted by those who enjoy executive power within the limits of their competence, and also by those to whom the power of dispensing has been given explicitly or implicitly whether by the law itself or in virtue of legitimate delegation. (Can. 85)

> Dispensations can be granted only for ecclesiastical laws, not for divine laws. Thus, e.g., a dispensation from the marital impediment of prior bond is never given because the law against divorce and remarriage is divine law.
> Dispensations are granted only for particular cases, either for an individual or for a group. The particular case may involve many repetitions of the same circumstances for which a dispensation is given. For example, a person who for good reason must miss Sunday Mass repeatedly could be given one dispensation for as long as that reason lasts, or the Sunday obligation could be commuted to other forms of prayer or charitable deeds.

Laws are not subject to dispensation insofar as they define those things which are essentially constitutive of juridical institutes or acts. (Can. 86)

> Constitutive laws may not be dispensed because they regulate matters that are essential to a juridical institute or act. Some constitutive laws affect the validity of acts, e.g., the essential

26

requirements for the valid celebration of the sacraments. Some other examples of constitutive law are: canon 767, §1 defining the essential aspects of a homily; canon 492 requiring a finance council in each diocese; canon 521 requiring that the pastor of a parish be a priest; canon 607, §2 stating that members of religious institutes must profess public vows.

One who has the power of dispensing can exercise it on behalf of his subjects even when he is outside his territory and even when they are absent from the territory. Unless the contrary be expressly established, he also can dispense travelers who are actually in his territory, and he can dispense himself. (Can. 91)

A dispensation is an act of executive power of governance. Therefore the above rules follow the general rules for executive power of governance. The dispensing power can be exercised in one's own territory not only for one's subjects but also for outsiders who are temporarily staying in or travelling through the territory. It can also be exercised outside one's territory on behalf of one's subjects or on one's own behalf.

The diocesan bishop, as often as he judges it to be for the spiritual good of the faithful, can dispense them from disciplinary laws, both from universal laws and from particular laws established by the supreme authority of the Church for his territory or for his subjects. However, he cannot dispense from procedural or penal laws nor those laws whose dispensation is specially reserved to the Apostolic See or another authority. (Can. 87, §1)

The diocesan bishop may dispense from universal and particular laws that are disciplinary in nature. He may not dispense from divine laws or constitutive laws. He may not dispense from procedural laws, such as the laws of Book VII of the code on the Church's judicial and administrative procedures. He may not dispense from penal laws, the laws given in Book VI of the code dealing with canonical crimes and penalties. Nor may he dispense from a law whose dispensation is reserved to the Apostolic See or another authority, for example, the marriage impediments of crime, holy orders, and a public perpetual vow of chastity in a religious institute of pontifical right. (See can. 1078, §2.)

Ordinaries. If recourse to the Holy See is difficult and likewise there is danger of serious harm in delay, any Ordinary can dispense from these same laws, even if the dispensation is reserved to the Holy

See, provided it is a question of a dispensation which the Holy See is accustomed to grant in these same circumstances, with due regard for canon 291. (Can. 87, §2)

> The following are considered Ordinaries in canon law besides the pope and diocesan bishops: territorial prelates, territorial abbots, apostolic vicars, apostolic prefects, apostolic administrators, diocesan administrators when the see is vacant, vicars general, episcopal vicars, and major superiors of clerical religious institutes of pontifical right and of clerical societies of apostolic life of pontifical right. (See cans. 134 and 368.)
>
> Canon 291 states that a dispensation from the obligation of clerical celibacy is granted by the pope alone.

In doubt of fact, an Ordinary can dispense from the law, even from a law whose dispensation is reserved, provided the dispensation is usually granted by the authority to whom it is reserved. (See can. 14.)

> If one is not certain about some fact after making serious attempts to discover the truth of the matter, there is a doubt of fact. For example, the law requires that a married man be at least 35 years old in order to be ordained a permanent deacon. (See can. 1031, §2.) In a certain mission territory, the local civil authorities do not keep birth records, and a man wishing to be ordained a deacon was baptized as an adult, so there is no documentary record of his age in his baptismal record. However, he looks to be a person who is in his mid-thirties and has been married for about the time that a person 35 years old typically would have been married in that culture. If, after hearing whatever evidence may be available from witnesses about the date of his birth, a doubt still remains about his age, the Ordinary may dispense from the age requirement, in case the candidate might not be old enough, and permit his ordination. (Note that the Ordinary had the power to dispense for up to a year in any case. See can. 1031, §4.)

Local Ordinaries, [all Ordinaries except clerical major superiors] can dispense from diocesan laws and, as often as they judge it to be for the good of the faithful, from laws established by a plenary or provincial council or by the episcopal conference. (Can. 88)

> In addition to the diocesan bishop, the vicar general and episcopal vicar can dispense from particular laws of the diocese, plenary and provincial councils, and the episcopal conference.

The pastor and other presbyters or deacons may not dispense from

universal or particular law unless this power has been expressly granted to them. (Can. 89)

Presbyters and deacons should consult their diocesan faculties
to determine what dispensations they may give. The law itself
allows the pastor and clerical superiors to dispense in individual
cases from the obligations to rest from labor and attend Mass on a
Sunday or holy day and from fast and abstinence on a day of
penance; and to dispense from private vows and promissory oaths.
(See cans. 1245; 1196, 1°; 1203.) Parochial vicars and deacons could be
delegated to give these dispensations. Pastors, presbyters and deacons who have delegation to assist at marriages, and confessors
may dispense from certain marital impediments in danger of
death and in urgent cases in accord with canons 1078-1081.

B. Just Cause for Dispensation

A dispensation from an ecclesiastical law should not be given without a just and reasonable cause, bearing in mind the circumstances of
the case and the importance of the law being dispensed. Otherwise the
dispensation is illicit and, unless it was given by the legislator himself
or his superior, it is also invalid. In doubt whether the cause is sufficient, a dispensation is validly and licitly granted. (Can. 90)

The spiritual good of the faithful is always a legitimate cause
for a dispensation.

Intrinsic reasons for granting a dispensation arise from a difficulty in observing the law (e.g., sickness with regard to fast and
abstinence, bad eyesight with regard to the obligation to celebrate
the liturgy of the hours, foul weather with regard to attendance at
Sunday Mass). Extrinsic reasons may arise: (1) from the condition
of the person who is dispensed (e.g., his or her special merits or
great dignity, a special benefit for a particular person arising from
the dispensation); (2) from the status of the person dispensing (e.g.,
to manifest his kindness or liberality); or (3) from the desire to promote the common good (e.g., avoidance of many transgressions
against the law, the seeking of alms for a pious cause, increase of
the common joy). (See Mathis/Bonner, 12-13.)

Doubt concerning the reason for a dispensation may concern
the sufficiency of a reason which is known to exist, or even the
very existence of a reason itself. In any case, a dispensation granted
in circumstances of doubt is valid, even though it be later discovered that the reasons alleged were insufficient or completely non-
existent. The doubt, however, must be positive, i.e., there must be a
reason for the doubt. If there is no reason, one is in a state of ignorance rather than doubt.

C. Cessation of Dispensation

A dispensation that has successive applications ceases in the same ways as a privilege; it also ceases by the certain and total cessation of the motivating cause. (Can. 93)

> A dispensation which is granted for a single act, once it has been put into effect, produces a situation where the law which was relaxed can never again be effective in the same case, e.g., a dispensation from today's fast, from the impediment of consanguinity, etc. However, as long as the dispensation has not been used, it can be revoked by the legislator.
>
> A dispensation which has recurring application (e.g., from abstaining on Fridays or from the obligation to celebrate the liturgy of the hours) expires: (1) by revocation, provided the dispensed person is notified of this; (2) by renunciation, provided the renunciation is accepted by the dispensing superior; (3) when the period of time for which the dispensation was granted has run out, or the lapse of the number of times that the dispensation could be given; (4) by the certain and complete cessation of the motivating cause for the dispensation. (Cf. also cans. 47, 79, 80, 83.)
>
> A motive or motivating cause is one which is of itself sufficient to ask and grant a dispensation. It is distinguished from a subsidiary cause which adds its influence to the motivating cause, but does not of itself suffice for the dispensation. The cessation of subsidiary causes does not affect a dispensation. Moreover, for a dispensation to cease, it is required that all (not only some) of the motivating causes cease certainly (not only probably or doubtfully) and completely (not only partially). (See Mathis/Bonner, 14.)
>
> A dispensation which has recurring application does not expire: (1) on the expiration of the authority of the person who granted the dispensation, unless he gave it *ad beneplacitum nostrum*, at my good pleasure, e.g., as long as I am bishop; (2) by the death of the person dispensed, provided the dispensation was given to the ecclesiastical office the person held, rather than to the particular individual holding that office; (3) by non-use or by contrary use, provided the dispensation is not burdensome to others (e.g., a dispensation from abstinence in no way affects others). However, should the dispensation place a burden on others (e.g., a dispensation which would involve exemption from some jurisdiction of the local Ordinary), it ceases through legitimate prescription. (Cf. cans. 93, 81, 78, 82.)

five

Rights and Obligations
of the Faithful

Among all the faithful, by their rebirth in Christ, there exists a true equality as to their dignity and activity by which all cooperate, in accord with the condition and duty of each, in building up the body of Christ. (Can. 208)

This canon establishes the fundamental dignity of all the faithful and equality among them. The following rights and duties are common to all the faithful—clergy, laity, and members of institutes of consecrated life and societies of apostolic life.

A. Rights of the Faithful

1) *Evangelization.* All the faithful have the duty and right to work so that the divine message of salvation may increasingly reach the whole of humanity in every age and every land. (Can. 211)

2) *Expression of needs.* They have the freedom to make known their needs, especially their spiritual needs, and their desires to the pastors of the Church. (Can. 212, §2)

3) *Expression of opinions.* In accord with their knowledge, competence, and position, they have the right and even at times the duty to manifest to the sacred pastors their opinion on matters which pertain to the good of the Church, and to make their opinion known to other faithful, with due regard for the integrity of faith and morals and with respect for their pastors, and taking account of the common good and the dignity of persons. (Can. 212, §3)

4)   *Word of God and sacraments.* They have the right to receive assistance from their pastors from the spiritual goods of the Church, especially from the word of God and the sacraments. (Can. 213)

5)   *Worship and spirituality.* They have the right to worship God in accord with their own rite approved by the lawful pastors of the Church, and to follow their own form of spirituality consistent with the teaching of the Church. (Can. 214)

6)   *Association.* They have the freedom freely to establish and direct associations which serve charitable or pious purposes or the promotion of the Christian vocation in the world, and the freedom to hold meetings to pursue these purposes in common. (Can. 215)

7)   *Apostolate.* Since they participate in the mission of the Church, they have the right to promote and support apostolic action on their own initiative, in accord with their own state and condition. No initiative, however, may be called Catholic without the consent of the competent ecclesiastical authority. (Can. 216)

8)   *Christian education.* Since they are called by baptism to lead a life in harmony with the gospel teaching, they have the right to a Christian education which genuinely teaches them to strive for the maturity of the human person and at the same time to come to know and live the mystery of salvation. (Can. 217)

9)   *Academic freedom.* Those who are engaged in the sacred sciences have due freedom of inquiry and freedom to express their views prudently on matters in which they are expert, having observed that respect (*obsequium*) owed to the ecclesiastical magisterium. (Can. 218)

10)   *Choice of vocation.* All the faithful have the right to be immune from any kind of coercion in the choice of their state of life. (Can. 219)

11)   *Good reputation and privacy.* No one may unlawfully damage the good reputation which a person enjoys, nor violate the right of people to safeguard their own privacy. (Can. 220)

12)   *Procedural rights.* The faithful may lawfully vindicate their ecclesial rights and defend them, in accord with the norm of law, before the competent ecclesiastical forum. The faithful also have the right, if they are called to judgment before the competent authority, to be judged in accord with the prescripts of law applied with equity. They have the right not to be inflicted with canonical penalties except in accord with the norm of law. (Can. 221)

Regulation of rights. It is the competence of ecclesiastical authority, in the interest of the common good, to regulate the exercise of rights which are proper to the faithful. (Can. 223, §2)

B. Obligations of All the Faithful

1) *Communion with the Church.* The faithful are bound always to maintain communion with the Church, even in their external actions. (Can. 209, §1)

2) *Duties to the Church.* They are to fulfill with diligence the duties they have to the Church, both universal and particular, in accord with the prescripts of law. (Can. 209, §2)

3) *Holiness.* All the faithful, in accord with their own condition, must do all they can to lead a holy life and promote the growth of the Church and its continual sanctification. (Can. 210)

4) *Evangelization.* All the faithful have the duty and the right to work so that the divine message of salvation may increasingly reach the whole of humanity in every age and every land. (Can. 211)

5) *Obedience.* The faithful, conscious of their own responsibility, are obliged to show Christian obedience to what the sacred pastors, as representatives of Christ, declare as teachers of the faith and to what they establish as leaders of the Church. (Can. 212, §1)

6) *Expression of opinions.* In accord with their knowledge, competence, and position, they have the right and even at times have the duty to manifest to the sacred pastors their opinion on matters which pertain to the good of the Church, and to make their opinion known to other faithful, with due regard for the integrity of faith and morals and with respect for their pastors, and taking account of the common good and the dignity of persons. (Can. 212, §3)

7) *Church support.* The faithful are obliged to provide for the needs of the Church so that it has available to it those things that are necessary for divine worship, for works of the apostolate and of charity, and for the decent support of its ministers. (Can. 221, §1)

8) *Social justice.* They are also obliged to promote social justice and, mindful of the Lord's commands, to support the poor from their own resources. (Can. 222, §2)

9) *The common good.* In exercising their rights, the faithful both as individuals and in associations must keep in mind the common good of the Church and the rights of others as well as their responsibilities to others. (Can. 223, §1)

C. Rights of the Laity

By divine institution, there are among the faithful sacred ministers in the Church who are called clerics in the law; the others are called the laity. (Can. 207, §1)

The Church holds that the distinction between clergy and

laity is of divine law because Christ established the ordained ministry by appointing the apostles for a special role. The specific rights and obligations of clergy are given in chapter seven.

1) *Evangelization.* Since the laity like all the faithful are deputed by God to the apostolate through their baptism and confirmation, they are bound by the general obligation and have the right, whether as individuals or in associations, to strive so that the divine message of salvation may be known and accepted by all people throughout the world. This obligation is all the more forceful in those circumstances in which people can hear the gospel and know Christ only through them. (Can. 225, §1)

2) *Parents.* Since they have given life to their children, parents are obliged by the strictest obligation and they enjoy the right to educate them. Therefore it is primarily Christian parents who are to see to the Christian upbringing of their children according to the teaching handed down by the Church. (Can. 226, §2)

3) *Freedom in secular affairs.* It is the right of the lay faithful to have acknowledged as theirs that freedom in secular affairs which belongs to all citizens; when they exercise such freedom, however, they are to take care that their actions are imbued with the spirit of the gospel and they are to heed the teaching of the Church proposed by the magisterium, but they must avoid proposing their own view as the teaching of the Church in matters of opinion. (Can. 227)

4) *Offices and functions.* Qualified lay persons are capable of assuming from their sacred pastors those ecclesiastical offices and functions which, in accord with the prescripts of law, they are able to discharge. (Can. 228, §1)

5) *Experts and advisors.* The laity who excel in the necessary knowledge, prudence, and integrity are capable of assisting the pastors of the Church as experts and advisors, even at councils in accord with the norm of law. (Can. 228, §2)

6) *Christian education.* Lay people have the obligation and right to acquire the knowledge of Christian teaching which is appropriate to their capacity and condition so that they can live in accord with that teaching, announce it, defend it if need be, and be enabled to assume their role in exercising the apostolate. (Can. 229, §1)

7) *Study of sacred sciences.* Lay persons also possess the right to acquire that deeper knowledge of the sacred sciences which is taught in ecclesiastical universities or faculties or in institutes of religious sciences, attending lectures there and acquiring academic degrees. (Can. 229, §2)

8) *Teaching sacred sciences.* Likewise, having observed the pre-

scripts as to the required suitability, they are capable of receiving from the lawful ecclesiastical authority a mandate for teaching the sacred sciences. (Can. 229, §3)

9) *Lector and acolyte.* Lay men, who meet the age and qualifications determined by the conference of bishops, can assume the stable ministries of lector and acolyte; however, the conferral of these ministries does not bring with them the right to obtain sustenance or remuneration from the Church. (Can. 230, §1)

10) *Temporary ministries.* Lay persons can fulfill the function of lector in liturgical celebrations by temporary deputation. Likewise, all lay persons can function in the roles of commentator, cantor, and other ministries in accord with the norm of law. (Can. 230, §2)

11) *Extraordinary ministries.* Where the need of the Church urges it and ministers are lacking, lay persons, even if they are not lectors or acolytes and in accord with the prescripts of law, can also supply certain of their duties, namely, to exercise the ministry of the word, to preside at liturgical prayers, to confer baptism, and distribute holy Communion. (Can. 230, §3)

12) *Wages and benefits.* Without prejudice to the prescript of canon 230, §1, lay persons have the right to adequate remuneration suited to their condition, also observing the prescripts of civil law, so they are able to provide for their own and their families' necessities. Likewise, they have the right to have duly provided their insurance, social security, and health benefits. (Can. 231, §2)

D. Obligations of the Laity

1) *Evangelization.* Since the laity like all the faithful are deputed by God to the apostolate through their baptism and confirmation, they are bound by the general obligation and have the right, whether as individuals or in associations, to strive so that the divine message of salvation may be known and accepted by all people throughout the world. This obligation is all the more forceful in those circumstances in which people can hear the gospel and know Christ only through them. (Can. 225, §1)

2) *Christian witness.* All lay persons, in accord with their own condition, are obliged by a special duty to imbue and perfect the order of temporal affairs with the spirit of the gospel. In this way, particularly in conducting secular business and exercising secular functions, they give witness to Christ in a special way. (Can. 225, §2)

3) *Spouses.* Those who are married are obliged by a special obligation, in accord with their own vocation, to work toward the building up of the people of God through their marriage and family. (Can. 226,

§1)

4)   *Parents.* Since they have given life to their children, parents are obliged by the strictest obligation and they enjoy the right to educate them. Therefore it is primarily Christian parents who are to see to the Christian upbringing of their children according to the teaching handed down by the Church. (Can. 226, §2)

5)   *Christian education.* Lay people have the obligation and right to acquire the knowledge of Christian teaching which is appropriate to their capacity and condition so that they can live in accord with that teaching, announce it, defend it if need be, and be enabled to assume their role in exercising the apostolate. (Can. 229, §1)

6)   *Formation.* Lay persons who are committed to a special service of the Church either permanently or for a time are obliged to acquire a suitable formation that their ministry requires and to fulfill that ministry conscientiously, earnestly, and diligently. (Can. 231, §1)

E. Consecrated Life

Among both the clergy and laity there are members of the faithful who, by profession of the evangelical counsels through vows or other sacred bonds recognized and approved by the Church, are consecrated to God in their own special way and serve the saving mission of the Church. Although their status does not pertain to the hierarchical structure of the Church, it does belong nevertheless to the Church's life and holiness. (Can. 207)

The rights and obligations of members of religious institutes are treated in canons 662-672. For members of secular institutes, see canon 719. For members of societies of apostolic life, see canons 739-740.

II Baptism

one
Fundamental Norms

A. Necessity of Baptism for Reception of Other Sacraments

No one may validly be admitted to the other sacraments without having first received baptism. (Can. 842, §1)

B. Relation to Full Initiation

The sacraments of baptism, confirmation, and Eucharist are so related to each other that all are required for full Christian initiation. (Can. 842, §2) Thus the three sacraments of Christian initiation closely combine to bring the faithful to the full stature of Christ and to enable them to carry out the mission of the entire people of God in the Church and in the world. (CIGI, 2)

C. Matter and Form

1. The water.

For validity, baptism must be conferred with true water. (See can. 849.) Except in a case of necessity, the water to be used in conferring baptism must be blessed according the norms of the liturgical books. (Can. 853) Baptism is to be conferred either by immersion or by pouring, observing the prescripts of the episcopal conference. (Can. 854)

> True water is that which is understood as water in the common estimation of persons, whether the water be natural or chemically made. The water can be from any source, including rivers, seas, lakes, rain, melted snow or ice, condensation, distilled, etc. Invalid matter would include sweat, saliva, tears, liquid strained from plants, wine, beer, and the like. (See Regatillo, 34.)
>
> For liceity, in ordinary circumstances, the water must be

39

blessed. The water is blessed during the rite itself, except during the Easter season when water blessed at the Easter Vigil is to be used. (See CIGI, 21.) A priest, deacon, or catechist may bless the water. Another minister should use blessed water, unless none is available. (See RBaptC 142, 157.)

Although three infusions or immersions are prescribed, one suffices for validity. The bishops of the United States urge the use of immersion as the fuller and more expressive sign of the sacrament; they also commend partial immersion, namely, immersion of the candidate's head. (See NSC, 17.) Sprinkling, although illicit, is a valid form of baptism, provided the water touches the person being baptized while the minister pronounces the Trinitarian formula.

2. *The anointings.*

The baptismal anointings are for liceity only. The anointing with the *oil of catechumens* on the breast in infant baptism may be omitted for serious reason in the judgment of the episcopal conference. In the United States, it may be omitted when the minister of baptism judges that it is pastorally necessary or desirable to omit it (See RBaptC, 51.) The anointing of the catechumens in adult baptism is also optional. (See RCIA, 103, 127; US, 79, 98.) If it is used, the oil may be blessed by the priest during the rite itself. (See RCIA, 129; US, 101; NSC, 16.) In adult baptism, confirmation is the post-baptismal anointing.

3. *The form.*

The form of the sacrament in the Latin church is the Trinitarian formula: "N., I baptize you in the name of the Father, and of the Son, and of the Holy Spirit."

The formula, for validity, must express the one baptizing, the one being baptized, the present act of baptizing, and the three divine persons and their unity. (See Regatillo, 38.) If the name of the one being baptized is not known, it suffices to say "I baptize you ...." The minister who pronounces the words must be the same one who pours or immerses; otherwise the baptism is invalid. The formula cannot be altered in any way, as this may affect the validity of the sacrament. (See can. 841.) For example, the substitution of other words for "Father" or "Son" would be invalid. The addition of words to the formula would be gravely illicit, as for example: "N., I baptize you in the name of God who is Father and Mother, Son and Holy Spirit." In the Latin rite it is not valid to use the passive voice in baptizing, for example, "You are baptized in the name ...." The one who is baptizing (the "I") must be expressed as well as the present act of baptizing.

D. Intention

For validity, the minister of baptism must have the intention of baptizing. The intention must be to do what the Church does when it baptizes. Even non-Christians may validly baptize if they have this minimal intention.

The recipient of baptism, if an adult, must have the intention of receiving baptism. This applies to anyone who has sufficient use of reason to choose baptism on one's own. A baptism performed against the will of a person would be invalid. The intention is a positive act of the will to choose Christian baptism. A habitual intention suffices, that is, an intention given and not withdrawn. (See CCLA, 566.)

Adults who fall into a coma, suffer brain damage, etc. such that they lose the use of reason, may not be baptized unless they had previously manifested a desire for baptism. If they previously had the use of reason and had not asked for baptism, it is presumed they did not intend to be baptized.

E. Non-repeatability

Any person not yet baptized is capable of being baptized. (Can. 864) The sacrament of baptism cannot be repeated because it imparts a character. (See can. 845, §1.) Because of that unchangeable effect (signified in the Latin liturgy by the anointing of the baptized person with chrism in the presence of God's people), the rite of baptism is held in highest honor by all Christians. It may never lawfully be repeated once it has been validly celebrated, even if by fellow Christians from whom we are separated. (CIGI, 4)

The council of Trent taught that baptism, as well as confirmation and holy orders, imprint an indelible "character" on the soul. Contemporary theologians explain this to mean that these sacraments have a permanent effect.

F. Conditional Baptism

If there is a doubt whether someone was baptized, or whether the baptism was validly conferred, and this doubt remains after a serious investigation, then baptism should be administered conditionally. (Can. 869, §1; see can. 845, §2.)

The formula for conditional baptism is: "N., if you are not baptized, I baptize you in the name of the Father, and of the Son, and of the Holy Spirit." Regarding the doubtful baptism of non-Catholics, see pp. 340-43.

t w o
Adult Initiation

A. The RCIA

For adults to be baptized, they must manifest the desire to receive baptism, be sufficiently instructed in the truths of the faith and in the Christian obligations, and be tested in the Christian life through the catechumenate. They also are to be admonished to be sorry for their sins. (Can. 865, §1)

All these requirements are for liceity. For validity, the adult must have the intention of receiving baptism. The *manifestation* of the intention is a requirement for liceity which serves to demonstrate the interior desire which is necessary for validity.

The prescripts of canon law on adult baptism refer to all who are no longer infants and have the use of reason. (Can. 852, §1.)

Anyone who is seven years old and older and has the use of reason is to observe all the requirements of the RCIA unless there are exceptional circumstances, especially danger of death.

Baptism is to be administered according to the rite prescribed in the approved liturgical books. (See can. 850.)

Preparation for adult baptism must follow the catechumenal process as prescribed in the *Rite of Christian Initiation of Adults.* The RCIA may be adapted by the episcopal conferences in accord with the norms established by and with the approval of the Apostolic See. An adapted rite for the dioceses of the United States was approved by the Apostolic See in 1988. Because many readers of *The Pastoral Companion* come from outside the United States, the citations to the RCIA in this book will first indicate the paragraph number of the norm as found in the 1972 edition for the universal Church followed by the number in the 1988 adapted version for the U.S. church. The bishops of the United States, in accord with canon 788, §3, also approved particular laws governing the catechumenate, called "The National Statutes for the Catechumenate" (NSC).

The RCIA consists of several rites of adult initiation: the *Rite of the Catechumenate Arranged in Stages,* the *Simple Rite for the Initiation of an Adult, the Short Rite for the Initiation of an Adult in Danger of Death or at the Point of Death,* and *the Rite of Initiation for Children of Catechetical Age.*

An adult who intends to receive baptism should be admitted to the catechumenate and, as far as possible, should be gradually led to sacramental initiation through the various stages. (See can. 851, 1°.)

The various stages are: evangelization and precatechumenate, catechumenate, period of purification and enlightenment (Lenten preparation), sacraments of initiation, and period of post-baptismal catechesis or mystagogy. Ordinarily, adult baptism is celebrated only after the completion of the catechumenal process.

Catechumens

Catechumens are connected with the Church in a special way; moved by the Holy Spirit they have the explicit desire to be incorporated in the Church, and therefore by this very desire, as well as by a life of faith, hope, and charity, they are joined with the Church, which already cherishes them as its own. The Church has a special care for catechumens, inviting them to lead the evangelical life and introducing them to celebrations of sacred rites; it already grants them various prerogatives which are proper to Christians. (Can. 206)

The two most important privileges of catechumens are (1) the right to a church wedding, whether to a Catholic or a non-Catholic; and (2) the right to the funeral rites of the Church. (See RCIA, 47; can. 1183, §1; NSC, 8, 10.)

The term "catechumen" should be strictly reserved for the unbaptized who have been admitted into the order of catechumens; the term "convert" should be reserved strictly for those converted from unbelief to Christian belief and never used of those baptized Christians who are received into the full communion of the Catholic Church. (NSC, 2)

Thus, the catechumenate proper lasts from the rite of admission into the order of catechumens until sacramental initiation.

Irregular marriages. Persons who are invalidly married because they or their present spouse or both had previously been married may become catechumens. However, they may not receive the sacraments of initiation unless they are free to marry by obtaining annulments of previous marriages or dissolutions in favor of the faith. (See CDF, private reply, July 11, 1983; CLD 10:139.)

B. Abbreviated Catechumenate

In extraordinary circumstances, when a catechumen has been unable to go through all the stages of initiation, or when the local Ordinary, convinced that the candidate's Christian conversion is sincere and that he or she is religiously mature, decides that the candidate may receive baptism without delay, the bishop can allow the use of the *Simple Rite for the Initiation of an Adult.* (See RCIA, 240.)

The U.S. version refers to the rite as "Christian Initiation of Adults in Exceptional Circumstances," which clarifies by its very title that it can be used only in limited situations. (See US, 331.)

The simple rite, whether in its expanded form or abbreviated form, is exceptional. Permission for its use must be obtained from the diocesan bishop. There are two general reasons for permitting its use. The first is when the catechumen has been unable to go through all the stages of the catechumenate. Some examples of justifying circumstances are sickness, old age, change of residence, and long absence for travel. However, the catechumenate of those who move from one parish to another should not be abbreviated for that reason alone, unless the circumstances justify it. (See RCIA, 274; US, 332; NSC, 20.)

The second general reason for using the simple rite of adult initiation is when the catechumen already demonstrates sincere Christian conversion and is religiously mature, as judged by the local Ordinary. This may happen, e.g., when someone has spent a long time in personal preparation for conversion to Christianity before seeking admission as a catechumen.

C. Children of Catechetical Age

The Rite of Initiation for Children of Catechetical Age is intended for children, unbaptized as infants, who have reached the age of reason and are of catechetical age. They are brought by their parents or guardians for Christian initiation or they request it of their own accord with parental permission. (See RCIA, 306; US, 252.)

The children in question are in the age range of about seven to thirteen. It is possible to admit children somewhat younger than seven to the children's catechumenate, provided they have attained the use of reason, that is, they are able to pursue the children's catechumenate without great difficulty, understanding the meaning of Christian initiation and freely choosing it for themselves. Children may also be enrolled in the adult catechumenate for good reason, as when there is no children's catechumenate, or they are accompanying a parent in the catechumenal process.

D. Necessity of Full Initiation

Unless a serious reason prevents it, an adult to be baptized is to be confirmed immediately after baptism and is to participate in the Eucharistic celebration and receive Communion. (Can. 866; see also NSC, 14, 18.)

This is the normative pattern of sacramental initiation which shows the interrelatedness of the three sacraments required for full Christian initiation. (See can. 842, §2.)

The requirement applies to *all* who receive adult baptism, including children seven and older who have the use of reason. An example of a serious reason that would prevent full initiation of an adult would be danger of death when the adult is baptized and the sacred chrism is not available for confirmation or the Blessed Sacrament is not available for Communion. Another example is when a deacon or lay minister baptizes in an emergency; only a priest has the power to confirm.

E. Christian Name

The RCIA contains a rite for choosing a baptismal name that may be celebrated on Holy Saturday or at the rite of acceptance into the order of catechumens. The elect may choose a new name, which is either a traditional Christian name or a name in use in that part of the world, provided it is not a name that is offensive to Christians. (See RCIA, 203; US, 200; can. 855.)

three
Infant Baptism

A. Those Baptized as Infants

A minor under the age of seven is an infant in canon law, as is anyone who habitually lacks the use of reason. (See cans. 97, 99.)

> Habitual lack of the use of reason may be for any cause, including mental retardation, insanity, brain damage, or senility. The baptism of children under seven and of anyone who habitually lacks the use of reason is celebrated according to the *Rite of Baptism for Children*. Those who lack the use of reason due to insanity, brain damage, or senility are not to be baptized unless their condition has existed from birth, or from a time preceding their attaining the use of reason.

Abandoned infants are to be baptized, but first there should be a diligent investigation to determine whether the infant already had been baptized. *Aborted fetuses* are to be baptized insofar as possible, provided they are still living. (See cans. 870, 871.)

B. Rite of Baptism for Children

Baptism should be administered according to the rite prescribed in the approved liturgical books. (See can. 850.)

> *The Rite of Baptism for Children* consists of several rites of infant baptism: *the Rite of Baptism for Several Children,* the *Rite of Baptism for One Child,* the *Rite of Baptism for a Large Number of Children,* the *Rite of Baptism for Children Administered by a Catechist when no Priest or Deacon is Available,* and the *Rite of Baptism for Children in Danger of Death when no Priest or Deacon is Available.*

C. Preparation of Parents and Godparents

The parents of an infant to be baptized, as well as those who will be the godparents, should be suitably instructed about the meaning of this sacrament and about the obligations that go with it. The pastor personally or through others should ensure that the parents are duly instructed through pastoral exhortations and also by common prayer; bringing several families together for this purpose and, where possible, visiting them. (Can. 851, 2°)

> The requirement of suitable preparation for baptism is more important in the case of parents than of godparents since parents are the primary educators in the faith of their children. (See cans. 774, §2; 793, §1.) Godparents may more readily be excused from this obligation, while parents should have compelling reasons to be excused, e.g., they already had the same instruction program for a previous child; or one or both of them has to work at the time of the sessions. Pastoral ministers and catechists should try to accommodate the parents on the time of the preparation sessions so that at least one parent can participate, even if a special session may be necessary to accomplish this. Failure to participate in preparation sessions, however, is in itself not sufficient cause for delay of baptism.

D. Delay of Baptism

For an infant to be baptized licitly, it is necessary that: (1) at least one of the parents consents to it, or the person who lawfully takes their place; (2) there is a well founded hope that the child will be brought up in the Catholic religion. If this hope is utterly lacking, the baptism should be deferred according to the prescripts of particular law, and the reason for the deferral is to be explained to the parents. (Can. 868, §1)

> It often happens that young parents who request the sacrament of baptism are not registered in the parish and/or do not attend Sunday Mass. This alone is not a ground for deferral of baptism. The preparation for baptism as well as its celebration are excellent opportunities to instruct or remind the parents of their obligations as Christians and as parents. Sunday Mass attendance and registration in the parish by the parents are not requirements for infant baptism. Nor does either guarantee that the parents will continue to practice the faith once the baby is baptized. The best pastoral approach is to welcome the parents and during the course of preparation help them to realize what baptism means and

entails so that they know how and can responsibly choose to be proper role models in the faith for their child. "Forced conversion" never works.

Baptism may be delayed only when there is no "founded hope" that the child will be raised in the Catholic faith. For example, both parents are non-Catholics and they want the child baptized merely for later enrollment in a Catholic school where the education is superior. Another example: the parents are non-practicing Catholics themselves and will not guarantee that they will raise the child in the Catholic faith but intend to let the child make up his or her own mind later, and want the child baptized now merely to please their own parents. In such a case, baptism should be delayed until at least one parent will agree to the child's Catholic upbringing, or at least until the parents agree to allow someone else to assume this responsibility.

It may happen that the godparents, or a grandparent, or some other person will see to the child's Catholic upbringing, and the parents do not object. In such a case there is a founded hope, a hope based on a reason, that the child will be brought up Catholic.

In 1970 the Congregation for the Doctrine of the Faith established some guidelines for the case of parents who are not Christian or who are irregular Christians. By irregular Christians, the Congregation means "polygamous Christians, concubinaries, lawful spouses who have abandoned all regular practice of the faith, or who request baptism of the infant for the sole reason of social propriety." Although these guidelines do not have the same force as the canons of the code, they may be helpful in handling a case where there is lacking a well founded hope that the child will be brought up in the Catholic religion.

1) It is important to make the parents become conscious of their responsibilities.

2) Further, it is important to pass judgment on the sufficiency of the guarantees regarding the Catholic education of the infants—guarantees given by some member of the family, or by the godfather or godmother, or by the support of the community of the faithful. (By guarantees we mean that there is founded hope of Catholic education.)

3) If the conditions are sufficient in the judgment of the pastor, the Church can proceed to the baptism because the infants are baptized in the faith of the Church.

4) If the conditions are not sufficient, one will be able to propose to the parents:
—enrollment of the infant with a view to baptism later;
—continuance of pastoral contacts with them as a way of preparing them for the rite of reception of their child for baptism. (See

CDF, reply, July 13, 1970, *Notitiae* 7 (1971) 64-69; CLD 7:593-94.)

Also helpful on this issue is an instruction of the Congregation for the Doctrine of the Faith of October 20, 1980 which discusses the historical, theological, and pastoral issues at some length. In speaking of the "well founded hope," the instruction states: "If sufficient assurances are given, for example, by the selection of godparents who will sincerely undertake the care of the child, or by the assistance of the faithful in the community, then the priest cannot refuse to celebrate the baptism without delay, exactly as he would do with regard to children of Christian families."

The instruction also clarified what it means to enroll the infant for later baptism. "Enrollment in a future catechumenate, if it should take place, should not be celebrated with any ritual set up for that purpose since it could easily be considered as the equivalent of the sacrament itself. It should also be clear that enrollment of this kind is not actual entrance into a catechumenate, nor are the children who are thus enrolled, connected with this state. At a later time they will have to be presented for a catechumenate suited to their age." (See CDF, reply, Oct. 20, 1980, AAS 72 (1980) 1137; CLD 9:508-27, esp. pp. 524-25.)

E. Baptismal Name

The parents, godparents, and pastor are to see that the name given is not foreign to Christian sensibilities. (Can. 855)

> The law does not require that the child be given a saint's name, but forbids a name that would be offensive to Christians. This may vary according to the culture and traditions of the people.

four
Offices and Ministries

A. Ordinary Ministers

The ordinary minister of baptism is a bishop, presbyter, or deacon. (See can. 861, §1.)

The bishop. The baptism of adults, at least of those who are fourteen and older, should be referred to the diocesan bishop so that he may administer it if he considers it expedient. (Can. 863)

> *In the United States.* The diocesan bishop is the proper minister of the sacraments of initiation for adults, including children of catechetical age, in accord with canon 852, §1. If he is unable to celebrate the sacraments of initiation with all the candidates of the local church, he should at least celebrate the rite of election or enrollment of names, ordinarily at the beginning of Lent, for the catechumens of the diocese. (NSC, 11)

The pastor. The administration of baptism is a function especially entrusted to the pastor. (See cans. 861, §1 and 530, 1°.)

> Although the pastor is especially entrusted with the celebration of baptism, it is not a function reserved exclusively to him. Nevertheless, other ministers should not celebrate baptism in the parish without at least the presumed permission of the pastor. (See CCLA, 390.)

Priests who do not exercise a pastoral office but participate in a catechumenal program require a mandate from the diocesan bishop if they are to baptize adults; they then do not require any additional mandate or authorization in order to confirm, but have the faculty to confirm from the law, as do priests who baptize adults in the exercise of their pastoral office. (NSC, 12)

> Unlike the pastor and parochial vicar, priests who do not have a pastoral office do not have the faculty to confirm by law at adult initiation but must receive a mandate to baptize an adult. The mandate to baptize an adult carries with it the faculty to confirm, because confirmation and first Eucharist must follow baptism at adult initiation, even of young children who have reached the age of reason.

B. Extraordinary Ministers

If the ordinary minister is absent or impeded, a catechist lawfully confers baptism as does another person deputed for this ministry by the local Ordinary; in a case of necessity, anyone with the proper intention may baptize. Pastors of souls, especially pastors of parishes, are to be solicitous in seeing that the faithful are taught how to baptize correctly. (Can. 861, §2; see also can. 230, §3.)

> The proper intention of the minister is to do what the Church does when it baptizes.
> *In the Eastern Catholic churches,* baptism is ordinarily administered by a priest (bishop or presbyter) and not by a deacon because baptism is followed by chrismation with holy myron (confirmation) which only a priest can validly administer. However, in a case of necessity a deacon, another cleric, a member of an institute of consecrated life, or any member of the faithful who knows how to baptize, including the mother or father, may do it. (See CCEC, can. 677.)

C. Godparents

There should be a godparent for the person to be baptized insofar as this is possible. In adult baptism the godparent assists in Christian initiation. In infant baptism the godparent, together with the parents, presents the child for baptism and helps the baptized to lead the Christian life in harmony with baptism and to fulfill faithfully the obligations inherent to it. (Can. 872)

Number of godparents. There may be one godfather, one godmother, or one of each. (Can. 873)

> If there are two godparents, one must be male and the other female. A single godparent may be of either sex. It may happen that parents want two persons of the same sex to be godparents

and they have good reasons for this. A possible solution to such a case is to register one as the official godparent, while the other would assume only the cultural and familial customs connected with the role.

Qualifications of godparents. The qualifications of godparents at baptism given in canon 874, §1 also apply to the godparent (sponsor) for confirmation, as follows:

1)   The godparents are to be chosen by the adult who is to be baptized or, at infant baptism, by the parents or the person who takes their place. When this is not possible, the pastor or other minister should choose the godparent or godparents.

2)   The godparents must have the qualifications for and intention of carrying out this duty.

> The godparents' duty is not only to be present for the celebration of the sacrament, but it is a lifelong responsibility to help the baptized lead a Christian life in harmony with baptism, and to fulfill faithfully the obligations connected with it. (See can. 872.)

3)   They are to be at least sixteen years of age, unless the diocesan bishop shall have established another age or unless in an exceptional case it seems to the pastor or minister that there is just cause to admit a younger person.

4)   They must be Catholics who are already confirmed and have received the holy Eucharist.

5)   They should be leading a life of faith in harmony with the duty they are undertaking.

6)   They may not be under a lawfully imposed or declared canonical penalty.

7)   They may not be the father or mother of the one to be baptized.

> It is often difficult for the pastor or other minister to be assured that those who seek permission to be a godparent have met all these requirements, particularly the requirement that they lead a life of faith in harmony with the duty they are undertaking. To satisfy this requirement, it is helpful to instruct the parents that it is their responsibility to choose godparents who are suitable role models in the faith. This removes the burden from the minister or catechist in judging the worthiness of individuals about whose faith lives little is known.
>
> Concerning the age for the godparent, parents should be reminded that this is an adult role and that sixteen is typically the

minimal age. For good reasons someone younger may be chosen, but not so young that the person is not capable of adequately fulfilling the responsibilities of this adult role.

Additional duties for adult initiation. Godparents for adults are chosen on the basis of example, good qualities, and friendship. They accompany the candidate on the day of election, in the celebration of the sacraments, and during the period of postbaptismal catechesis. They show the catechumens in a friendly way the place of the gospel in their own life and in society, help them in doubts and anxieties, give public testimony for them, and watch over the progress of their baptismal life. The public office of godparent begins from the day of election when the godparents give their testimony about the catechumens before the community. The godparental responsibilities remain important when the neophytes have received the sacraments and need to be helped to remain faithful to their baptismal promises. (See RCIA, 43; US, 11.)

> The duties of the godparent are considerably greater during preparation for adult initiation than for infant initiation. After being chosen by the candidate, the godparent is approved by the priest and delegated by the Christian community. (See RCIA, 43, 136; US, 11, 123.) The meaning of delegation by the community should be understood in keeping with particular law or local custom. In the absence of local custom or law, approval by the priest suffices since the priest represents the community.

Godparent by proxy. If the godparent cannot be present in person, he or she may appoint another person to serve as a proxy, but the appointment must be made in such a way that there is certainty as to the person who takes the responsibility as godparent. Ordinarily the appointment of the proxy should be made by the godparent in writing or before two witnesses, in order that there be certainty as to who is the responsible person. The custom of leaving the appointment of the proxy to the parent of the infant or to the baptizing priest tends to make sponsorship doubtful, and is to be reprobated. The real godparent must give a mandate directly or indirectly (through the agency of others but with his or her consent) to the proxy. In the record of baptism the names of both the godparent and the proxy should be entered. (See CSacr, instruction, Nov. 25, 1925; AAS 18 (1926) 43; CLD 1:338-44.)

D. Sponsor

The sponsors accompany the candidates when they ask to be admitted as catechumens. The qualifications of sponsor are: to know the candidate, to help him or her, and be a witness to the candidate's faith, morals, and intention to be a Christian. (See RCIA, 42; US, 10.)

The RCIA distinguishes between the canonical godparent and the sponsor. The same person may assume both roles, or they may be distinct.

E. Non-Catholic Witness

A baptized person belonging to a non-Catholic ecclesial community may be admitted as a witness to baptism but only along with a Catholic godparent. (Can. 874, §2)

Although a Protestant may only be admitted as a witness, a member of an Eastern non-Catholic church may be admitted as a godparent together with a Catholic godparent. Further discussion of this rule is found in chapter fifteen, page 339.

F. Other Roles and Ministries in Adult Initiation

Presbyters. Besides the usual ministry exercised in any celebration of baptism, confirmation, and the Eucharist, presbyters have the responsibility of attending to the pastoral and personal care of the catechumens, especially those who seem hesitant and weak, in order to provide for their catechesis with the help of deacons and catechists. They also are to approve the choice of godparents and gladly listen to them and help them. Finally, presbyters should be diligent in the correct celebration and adaptation of the rites throughout the entire rite of Christian initiation. (RCIA, 45; US, 13)

Deacons. Deacons who are available should be ready to help. If the episcopal conference judges it opportune to have permanent deacons, it should make provision that their number is adequate to permit the stages, periods, and exercises of the catechumenate to take place everywhere when required by pastoral needs. (RCIA, 47; US, 15)

Catechists. The office of catechist is important for the progress of the catechumens and for the growth of the community. As often as possible, catechists should have an active part in the rites. When they are teaching, they should see that their instruction is filled with the spirit of the gospel, adapted to the liturgical signs and the course of the Church year, and enriched by local traditions as far as possible. When so delegated by the bishop, they may perform minor exorcisms and blessings. (RCIA, 48; US, 16)

five
Time and Place of Celebration

A. Time of Baptism

Day of celebration. Although baptism may be celebrated on any day, it is commendable to celebrate it ordinarily on Sundays or, if possible, at the Easter Vigil. (Can. 856) On Sunday baptism may be celebrated during Mass, so that the entire community may be present and the relationship between baptism and Eucharist may be clearly seen; but this should not be done too often. (RBaptC, 9)

Adult baptism. Ordinarily pastors should make use of the rite of initiation in such a way that the sacraments will be celebrated at the Easter Vigil and the election will take place on the First Sunday of Lent. (RCIA, 49; US, 17) Because of unusual circumstances and pastoral needs, however, the rite of election and the period of purification and enlightenment or illumination may be held outside Lent and the sacraments may be celebrated outside the vigil or Easter Sunday. (RCIA, 58; US, 26)

> For further details on the times of the stages of the catechumenate and the celebration of the sacraments of initiation for adults, see RCIA, 49-62; US, 17-30. For children of catechetical age, see RCIA, 310; US, 256.

Infant baptism. Parents are bound by obligation to ensure that infants are baptized within the first weeks after birth. As soon as possible after birth, or even before it, they should go to the pastor to ask for the sacrament for their child and be prepared for it. (Can. 867, §1) As for the time of baptism, the first consideration is the welfare of the child, that it may not be deprived of the benefit of the sacrament; then the health of the mother must be considered, so that, as far as possible she too may be present. Then, as long as they do not interfere with the greater good of the child, there are pastoral considerations such as allowing sufficient time to prepare the parents and for planning the actual celebration to bring out its paschal character. (RBaptC, 8)

The phrase, "within the first weeks after birth," may be broadly interpreted to allow adequate time for preparation for baptism and arrangements for its celebration. Special family considerations may sometimes necessitate a longer delay, for example, to await the return of a family member who lives out-of-town. Pastoral ministers should respect the wishes of parents in this regard, but if the delay is too long they should remind the parents of their serious obligation to have their child baptized. It is not simply the fear of a child dying that is at stake, but also the delay in welcoming the child into the Christian community through its rebirth in the waters of baptism.

As far as possible, all recently born babies should be baptized at a common celebration on the same day. Except for a good reason, baptism should not be celebrated more than once on the same day in the same church. (CIGI, 27)

B. Place of Baptism

Except in a case of necessity, no one may administer baptism in another territory, even to one's own subjects, without the proper permission. (Can. 862)

Permission to baptize in another parish must be obtained from the pastor of that parish or from the local Ordinary. The reason for this requirement is to stress the significance of baptism as entrance into the local community that will be one's own, or that of one's parents. It also assures the proper recording of the baptism. (See CLSA Comm., 624.)

Outside a case of necessity, the proper place for baptism is a church or oratory. As a rule, the baptism of adults is held in their own parish church, and the baptism of infants takes place in the parish church of their parents, unless there is a just reason for having it elsewhere. (Can. 857)

An example of a just reason for celebrating baptism in a church or oratory other than one's parish is the convenience of the faithful, as when most of the family members live a great distance from the parish of the one to be baptized. The pastor of the one to be baptized as well as the local Ordinary are competent to grant this permission. If the church where the baptism is held is a parish church, the baptism is recorded there. If not, it should be recorded in the parish of the baptized.

If on account of distance or other circumstances, the person to be baptized cannot without grave inconvenience go or be brought to the parish church or another church or oratory in the parish boundaries that has a baptismal font, baptism may and must be conferred in a closer church or oratory, or even in another suitable place. (See can. 859.)

Except in a case of necessity, baptism may not be conferred in private homes, unless the local Ordinary has permitted it for a serious reason. Except in a case of necessity or for another pressing pastoral reason, baptism may not be celebrated in hospitals unless the diocesan bishop has decreed otherwise. (Can. 860)

Since baptism is an incorporation into the Church, it is an ecclesial event, not a private family celebration. Therefore it ordinarily must take place in church, especially in one's own parish.

Emergency Baptism

A. Urgent Necessity

Baptism is to be administered according to the rite prescribed in the approved liturgical books except in the case of urgent necessity, in which case only those things must be observed that are required for the validity of the sacrament. (Can. 850)

The official rites of baptism (the *Rite of Christian Initiation of Adults* and the *Rite of Baptism of Children*) must be fully observed in ordinary circumstances. However, in urgent necessity only the requirements for validity need be observed, namely, the use of water (blessed or unblessed) and the Trinitarian formula, along with the requisite intention on the part of the minister and on the part of the one being baptized, if an adult. If there is time, the minister should use as much of the appropriate rite of baptism as circumstances allow, e.g., as found in the *Short Rite of Adult Initiation in Proximate Danger of Death or at the Point of Death* or the *Rite of Baptism for Children in Danger of Death when no Priest or Deacon is Available.* Some examples of urgent necessity are danger of death, religious persecution, and serious family disagreement about the baptism.

In necessity, baptism need not be celebrated in a church or oratory, and it may be celebrated in a home or hospital. The minister may confer baptism even outside his territory in such cases. Also, in necessity, any person with the proper intention may baptize.

B. Danger of Death

Adults. An adult in danger of death can be baptized if he or she has some knowledge of the principal truths of the faith, manifests in some way the intention to receive baptism, and promises to observe the requirements of the Christian religion. (Can. 865, §2) Persons who have already been accepted as catechumens must make a promise that upon recovery they will complete the usual catechesis. Persons who are not catechumens must give serious indication of their conversion to Christ. They must also promise that upon recovery they will go through the complete program of initiation as it applies to them. (RCIA, 279; US, 371)

> If possible, the minister should observe the short rite of adult initiation in danger of death which provides specific questions addressing the principal truths of the faith. (See RCIA, chapter III; US, Part II, section 2.) In doubt whether the person has manifested sufficient intention to be baptized, conditional baptism may be given using the formula: "N., if you intend to be baptized, I baptize you in the name of the Father, and of the Son, and of the Holy Spirit."

Infants. If an infant is in danger of death, it should be baptized without delay. (Can. 867, §2) In danger of death, an infant of Catholic parents, and even of non-Catholic parents, may lawfully be baptized even if the parents are against it. (Can. 868, §2)

> When no priest or deacon is available, anyone with the proper intention may baptize using water and the Trinitarian formula or, if it is prudently judged that there is sufficient time, the *Rite of Baptism for Children in Danger of Death when no Priest or Deacon is Available.* The priest or deacon may also use this shorter form if necessary. (RBaptC, 22) The pastor or any priest should confirm after baptism, even of a newly born infant. In this case he omits the postbaptismal anointing with chrism. (See RBaptC, 22; can. 883, 3°.) The holy Eucharist may be administered to children in danger of death if they are able to distinguish the body of Christ from ordinary food and receive Communion reverently. (Can. 913, §2)
>
> Infants may be baptized in danger of death even against the positive objections of the parents, provided one can prudently judge that the infant will not live to attain the use of reason, and that the baptism can be administered in such a manner as to avoid scandal or hatred of the faith. The baptism can be conferred secretly without the parents' knowledge of it.

seven
Proof and Recording
of Baptism

A. Proof of Baptism

To prove the conferral of baptism, if there is no conflict of interest, it suffices to have a declaration from one witness who is above suspicion or the oath of the baptized person, provided he or she received
baptism as an adult. (Can. 876) Unless a godparent is present, the one
who administers baptism should see to it that at least one witness is
present by whom the conferral of baptism can be proved. (Can. 875)

Baptism is ordinarily proved by means of a baptismal certificate or a letter from the minister of the church where baptism was
celebrated. This kind of documentary evidence is preferred, but
sometimes is impossible to obtain, e.g., if the church's records were
destroyed in a fire, or the person was baptized in a foreign country and attempts to get information from the church there are not
successful. In the absence of documentary evidence, it suffices to
have the testimony of one reliable witness. If the person whose
baptism is to be proved was at least seven years old and had the
use of reason when baptized, the oath of the baptized person suffices as proof. However, neither of these would constitute proof if
there is a possibility of a conflict of interest. For example, in a certain marriage annulment case the proof of baptism in the Catholic
Church is necessary to prove the invalidity of a marriage. In such a
case more evidence to prove baptism would be needed than the
allegedly baptized person's own word, since that person's testimony would be prejudicial to his or her own case.

The witness must be someone who actually witnessed the
baptism taking place, or who can give reliable evidence that it did
take place. For example, the witness attended a party after the

baptism and the people there talked about the baptism; or the witness once saw the person's baptismal record or baptismal certificate. Such evidence carries more weight when other circumstances confirm it, e.g., the person was raised in a Christian denomination, has always been considered a Christian, perhaps has been admitted to confirmation and holy Communion, etc.

B. Recording of Baptism

The pastor of the place where baptism is celebrated must carefully and without any delay record in the baptismal register the names of the baptized, the minister of baptism, the parents, godparents and, if there were any, the witnesses, and the place and day that baptism was administered. He should also note the day and place of birth. (Can. 877, §1; see also CIGI, 29.)

> This canon applies both to adult and infant initiation. Since the baptismal register is an important source of historical information, the names of parents, whether living or deceased, and the day and place of birth should be recorded even of adults.

Illegitimate children. In the case of a child born of an unwed mother, the mother's name is recorded if there is public proof of her maternity or if she freely requests this in writing or before two witnesses. Likewise the name of the father is to be recorded if his paternity is proven by some public document or he himself makes a declaration of his paternity before the pastor and two witnesses. In other cases, the name of the baptized is recorded without any mention of the name of the father or the parents. (Can. 877, §2)

Adopted children. In the case of an adopted child, the names of the adopting parents are recorded and also, at least if this should be done in the civil records of the region, the names of the natural parents in accord with §§ 1 and 2 [as above], and observing the statutes of the episcopal conference. (Can. 877, §3)

If baptism was administered neither by the pastor nor in his presence, the minister of baptism, whoever that may be, must notify the pastor of the parish in which baptism was administered so that it may be recorded in accord with the norm of canon 877, §1. (Can. 878)

> The pastor of the territorial parish in which baptism was administered should be notified and he should record the baptism. Notification must also be sent to the territorial pastor in the case of emergency baptism.

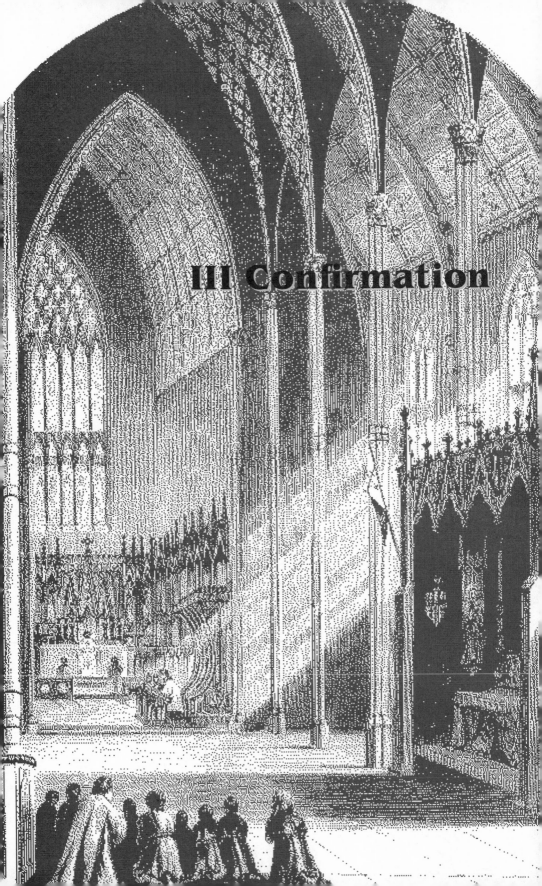

III Confirmation

one
General Norms

A. Juridical Consequences

By confirmation the baptized are joined more perfectly to the Church, are strengthened, and are more strictly obliged to be witnesses to Christ by word and deed and to spread and defend the faith. (See can. 879.)

By baptism and confirmation the faithful are deputed to the apostolate. (See can. 225, §1.)

Those who are confirmed may licitly enter the novitiate of a religious institute (can. 645, §1), be admitted to a society of apostolic life (can. 735, §2), receive holy orders (can. 1033), or marry (can. 1065, §1), provided all other requirements of law have been met.

B. Relation to Full Initiation

The sacraments of baptism, confirmation, and the holy Eucharist are so related to each other that all are required for full Christian initiation. (Can. 842, §2) Confirmation is a continuation of the journey of Christian initiation. (See can. 879.) Unless a serious reason stands in the way, an adult who is baptized should be confirmed immediately after baptism and should participate in the Eucharistic celebration, also receiving Communion. (Can. 866)

Since children who have reached the use of reason are considered, for purposes of Christian initiation, to be adults (canon 852, §1), their formation should follow the general pattern of the ordinary catechumenate as far as possible, with the appropriate adaptations permitted by the ritual. They should receive the sacraments of baptism, confirmation, and Eucharist at the Easter Vigil, together with the older catechumens. (NSC, 18; see also RCIA, 344; US, 305; RConf, 11.)

As in adult initiation, children of catechetical age who are baptized must also be confirmed and receive first holy Communion all in the same ceremony. This applies to everyone seven and older with the use of reason. Only a serious reason excuses from this obligation, such as danger of death when a priest does not have the sacred chrism when he baptizes, or when a deacon or lay person baptizes in an emergency.

C. Non-repeatability

The sacrament of confirmation cannot be repeated because it imparts a character. If, after a diligent investigation, a doubt still remains whether confirmation was actually or validly conferred, it should be conferred conditionally. (See can. 845.)

In the Eastern churches, both Catholic and non-Catholic, the sacrament of confirmation is always conferred immediately after baptism, even of infants. It is enough to establish the fact of baptism to prove that confirmation was also conferred. It often happens that no mention is made of confirmation in the canonical testimony of baptism. This does not give grounds for doubting that this sacrament was also conferred. (See DE, 145.)

D. Matter and Form

The sacrament of confirmation is administered by the anointing with chrism on the forehead which is done by the imposition of hands using the words prescribed in the approved liturgical books. The chrism used in the sacrament of confirmation must be consecrated by a bishop, even if the sacrament is administered by a presbyter. (Can. 880) In the Latin church, the sacramental form is: "Be sealed with the gift of the Holy Spirit." (See RConf, 9.)

These words are necessary for validity. The matter of the sacrament, necessary for validity, is the anointing on the forehead with the sacred chrism. The chrism is consecrated by the bishop in the Chrism Mass that is ordinarily celebrated on Holy Thursday or some other day in Holy Week. (See RConf, 10.) Although only a bishop ordinarily consecrates the chrism, the Holy See has granted the faculty to some apostolic administrators to consecrate it, even though they were presbyters. (See Congregation for the Evangelization of Peoples, rescript, Feb. 17, 1973, CLD 8:472.)

Even though the laying of hands on the candidates with the prayer **All-powerful God** does not pertain to the valid giving of the sacrament, it is to be strongly emphasized for the integrity of the rite and the fuller understanding of the sacrament. (RConf, 9)

The minister need not actually impose his hand on the head of the one being confirmed since the anointing with chrism on the forehead sufficiently expresses the laying on of hands. (See Pontifical Commission for the Interpretation of the Decrees of the Second Vatican Council, June 9, 1972, AAS 64 (1972) 526; DOL 2529; CLD 7:611.)

> While the imposition of hands is an integral part of the rite, it is not necessary for the validity of the sacrament.

E. Time and Place

The sacraments for the initiation of adults ordinarily are to be celebrated at the Easter Vigil. (See RCIA, 55; US, 23.)

> When confirmation is celebrated apart from baptism, it can be administered on any day, but the Easter season is especially appropriate.

It is desirable that the sacrament of confirmation be celebrated in a church and also within Mass. However, for a just and reasonable cause it may be celebrated outside Mass and in any fitting place. (Can. 881)

> A just cause for celebrating confirmation outside a church would be, e.g., if there are too many people for the celebration to be accommodated in the church. The minister of the sacrament would be competent to make this judgment, unless particular law determines something else.

$t\,w\,o$
Subjects of Confirmation

A. Capability for and Age of Confirmation

Capability. All and only the baptized who are not yet confirmed are capable of receiving confirmation. (Can. 889, §1)

Age. The sacrament of confirmation should be conferred on the faithful around the age of discretion, unless the conference of bishops has determined another age, or if there is danger of death, or in the judgment of the minister a serious reason suggests otherwise. (Can. 891)

> Confirmation in the Latin church is delayed until about the seventh year for those baptized in infancy. The proper sequence of Christian initiation should be followed, if possible, with confirmation preceding first Communion. In danger of death any baptized Catholic, even an infant, should be confirmed. Confirmation may also be administered below the age of seven for other serious reasons, in the judgment of the minister, e.g. in a remote area where the bishop is not able to visit regularly. In some countries an immemorial custom permits the confirmation of children below the age of reason.
>
> *In the United States.* The National Conference of Catholic Bishops decreed "that the sacrament of confirmation in the Latin rite shall be conferred between the age of discretion, which is about the age of seven, and eighteen years of age, within the limits determined by the diocesan bishop and with regard for the legitimate exceptions given in canon 891, namely, when there is danger of death or, where in the judgment of the minister grave cause urges otherwise." This decree was approved by the Congregation for Bishops for a period of five years from July 1, 1994 through

July 1, 1999. (See *BCL Newsletter* 30 (May, 1994), 17.)

The diocesan bishop may determine certain limits, e.g., he may establish a general policy for confirmation regarding catechesis, frequency of administration in each parish, who may be ministers, and the like. He may not, however, determine a specific age for confirmation because it has been established by higher authority as being between seven and eighteen. A comparable situation occurred under the former law when a local Ordinary forbade confirmation of any children under ten. The Holy See ruled that this was beyond the bishop's powers. (CodCom, interpretation, Mar. 26, 1952, AAS 44 (1952) 446; CLD 3:314-15.)

It must be stressed that the faithful have a fundamental right to the sacraments (can. 213). If both the universal law and the law of the episcopal conference permit confirmation at the age of seven, it does not seem that a diocesan bishop can refuse the sacrament, for reason of age alone, to a seven year old child who requests the sacrament and is suitably instructed according to his or her capacity.

B. Requirements for Liceity

To receive confirmation licitly, apart from danger of death, one must be suitably instructed, properly disposed, and be able to renew one's baptismal promises. Those who are in danger of death, or those who do not have the use of reason, are exempted from these requirements. (See can. 889, §2.)

The proper disposition includes being in the state of grace and, for those with the use of reason, the intention to receive the sacrament. Those without the use of reason are presumed to be in the state of grace because they have insufficient capacity of will to commit mortal sin.

Persons who lack the use of reason due to a developmental disability such as mental retardation should be confirmed at age seven or at the age that other children are confirmed. Although they are not required to have any previous instruction, special catechetical programs designed for them are helpful in their spiritual preparation according to their capacity.

The faithful are obliged to receive confirmation at the proper time. Parents, pastoral ministers, and especially pastors should see to it that the faithful are properly instructed for receiving this sacrament and that they come for it at the appropriate time. (Can. 890)

The proper time to receive confirmation in the Latin rite, outside the danger of death, is at about the age of discretion, or seven years of age. The proper instruction will depend upon the maturity of the candidate. Strictly speaking, no instruction is necessary for the fruitful reception of the sacrament, since even infants can be confirmed. If a seven year old child requests the sacrament of confirmation, the catechesis should be geared to the level of a seven year old.

Uncatechized adults. Adult Catholics who were baptized as infants, or baptized in danger of death or similar cases, and who did not receive further catechetical formation, should be confirmed according to the *Rite of Christian Initiation of Adults,* chapter IV (in the U.S., Part II, Section 4): "Preparing Uncatechized Adults for Confirmation and Eucharist." Any confusion between such baptized persons and catechumens must be avoided.

Some of the rites belonging to the catechumenate, suited to the condition and spiritual needs of these adults, can be used to advantage. Among these are the presentation of the Creed, the Lord's Prayer, and the gospels. (See RCIA, 302; US, 407.) Other liturgical rites for the catechesis of the baptized are described in a March 8, 1973 document of the Congregation for Divine Worship. (See *Notitiae* 9 (1973) 274-78; DOL 2489.) Uncatechized adult Catholics should not, however, be indiscriminately treated like catechumens. Above all, they should not be dismissed after the liturgy of the word along with the catechumens. Not only do they have the right to attend the full Eucharist, they also have the obligation to participate at Mass on Sundays and holy days. (See cans. 213; 1247.)

Before marriage. Sometimes the preparation of a baptized adult for confirmation is part of the preparation for marriage. In such cases, if it is foreseen that the conditions for a fruitful reception of confirmation cannot be satisfied, the local Ordinary will judge whether it is better to defer confirmation until after the marriage. (RConf, 12)

Danger of death. It is of the greatest importance that baptized persons complete their Christian initiation before death through the sacraments of confirmation and Eucharist. Confirmation should be administered before Viaticum is given. Confirmation ordinarily is not celebrated in the same rite with the anointing of the sick. (See RConf, 52.)

three

The Minister

The ordinary minister of confirmation is a bishop. A presbyter also validly confers this sacrament if he has this faculty by virtue of the universal law or a special concession of the competent authority. (Can. 882)

> *In the Eastern churches,* presbyters as well as bishops are ordinary ministers of the chrismation with holy myron, which is the Eastern name for confirmation. (See CCEC, can. 694.) In the Eastern churches the chrismation is conferred immediately after baptism, even of infants. (See CCEC, can. 695.)

A. Presbyters with the Faculty by Law

1) Within the boundaries of their jurisdiction, those presbyters may confirm who are equated in law with the diocesan bishop. (See can. 883, 1°.)

> These are the territorial prelate, territorial abbot, vicar apostolic, prefect apostolic, apostolic administrator, and diocesan administrator.

2) Those presbyters may confirm who, by virtue of office or a mandate of the diocesan bishop, baptize someone beyond infancy [seven or older with the use of reason], or who admit someone already baptized into full communion with the Catholic Church. (See can. 883, 2°.)

> The law does not grant the faculty to every presbyter to confirm at adult baptism or reception into full communion of the Church, but only to one who has an office, e.g., the pastor,

parochial vicar, chaplain. Presbyters without an office of pastoral care must have a special mandate from the diocesan bishop. The mandate does not have to be specifically for confirming, so long as it is a mandate for baptizing an adult or receiving a baptized person into full communion, but it must come from the diocesan bishop or his delegate. (See NSC, 12; CLSA Comm., 665.) The faculty of a presbyter to confirm is territorially limited, as noted below.

3)   Presbyters with an office of pastoral care who receive apostates from the faith back into the Church may confirm them using the *Rite of Receiving Baptized Christians into the Full Communion of the Catholic Church.* This also applies in the case of those baptized as Catholics who without fault were brought up in a non-Catholic religion or adhered to a non-Catholic religion. (See Pontifical Commission for the Interpretation of the Decrees of the Second Vatican Council, interpretation, Dec. 21, 1979, AAS 72 (1980) 105; CLD 9:527-28; NSC, 28.)

N.B. The law does not give presbyters with a pastoral office the faculty to confirm unbaptized Catholics who have not practiced the faith. Only on behalf of those who left the Church, or who were brought up in or adhered to another faith, does the law grant this faculty to presbyters in the case of adult Catholics. Others must be treated as Catholics, even if they have never practiced their baptismal faith. To confirm in such cases, presbyters need the delegated faculty. Particular law in the U.S. requires the presbyter to seek the faculty to confirm uncatechized adult Catholics in order to maintain the interrelationship and sequence of confirmation and Eucharist. (See NSC, 29.)

4)   The pastor, or any presbyter, may confirm someone in danger of death. (See can. 883, 3°.)

This includes even presbyters who are laicized or suspended.

5)   *Inter-ecclesial faculties.* All presbyters of the Eastern churches can validly administer the chrismation with holy myron, along with baptism or separate from it, to all members of the faithful of any ritual church, including the Latin church. The faithful of the Eastern Catholic churches may validly receive confirmation also from presbyters of the Latin church according to the faculties that they have. For liceity, a presbyter ordinarily administers this sacrament only to members of his own church *sui iuris.* (See CCEC, can. 696.)

If a Latin presbyter has the faculty to confirm, he may also validly confirm a Catholic of an Eastern church *sui iuris.* If Eastern Catholic parents have no parish or priest of their own and they attend a Latin church, the Latin pastor should get the faculty from the appropriate Eastern hierarch or from the Latin diocesan bishop to confirm the infants of an Eastern family immediately after baptism so that they can be faithful to the observance of their Eastern traditions and discipline. The presbyter should, however, observe the liturgical rites of the Latin church, unless he has a bi-ritual faculty. (See can. 846, §2.) Baptism and confirmation by the Latin priest does not constitute a change of membership from the Eastern church to the Latin church.

If the Eastern church has the practice of infant Communion, the infant should also be fully initiated by administering first holy Communion. If the infant cannot take solid food, the priest may dip his finger in the precious blood and insert his finger in the infant's mouth.

6) The chaplain, or the priest who takes his place, entrusted with the pastoral care of emigrants, seamen and seafarers, nomads, circus people, merchants, travelers, and strangers may administer confirmation to them after they have been duly instructed and if they are properly disposed. (Pontifical Commission for the Spiritual Care of Migrants and Travellers, decree, Mar. 19, 1982, AAS 74 (1982) 742; CLD 10:36.)

B. Presbyters with Delegated Faculty

The diocesan bishop should administer confirmation personally or should see that it is administered by another bishop. If need requires, he may concede the faculty to one or several specified presbyters who may administer this sacrament. (Can. 884, §1)

> Cases of need would include the illness of the bishop, his necessary absence from the diocese for an extended period, or a large number of parishes where confirmation is celebrated. (See CLSA Comm., 637.) Another case is the need to maintain the interrelatedness and sequence of initiation when uncatechized adult Catholics are to be confirmed and receive holy Communion. (See NSC, 29.) In doubt whether there is a true need, the bishop can validly grant the faculty anyway. (See Woestman, 82.)

The presbyter who has the faculty to confirm must use it for those in whose favor the faculty was granted. (Can. 885, §2)

> For example, a presbyter who by law or mandate baptizes an adult, including children of catechetical age, must also confirm. (See CLSA Comm., 637; NSC, 13.)

Ad hoc delegation. For a serious reason, the bishop and also the presbyter who by law or special concession of the competent authority has the faculty to confirm, may choose presbyters, in particular cases, to help with the administration of the sacrament. (See can. 884, §2.)

> A serious reason for using this provision of the law is the large number of those to be confirmed. (See RConf, 8.) In doubt about the gravity of the cause, the faculty may be validly granted.

C. Extent of Faculty

A presbyter who has the faculty to administer confirmation may also licitly confer the sacrament in his designated territory on outsiders, unless their own Ordinary has forbidden it. However, he may not validly confer the sacrament outside his territory except in the case of danger of death. (Can. 887)

> The faculty, whether conceded by law or delegation, is territorially limited. A presbyter cannot *validly* confirm outside his territory except: (1) in danger of death; (2) if he is confirming a member of an Eastern church in accord with his faculties (CCEC, can. 696, §2); or (3) if he receives a new faculty for that territory, including "*ad hoc* delegation." For example, a pastor or parochial vicar who confirms an adult after baptism can do so validly only within the boundaries of the parish, with the exceptions noted above.

D. Supplied Faculty

In common error of fact or of law and also in positive and probable doubt, whether of law or of fact, the Church supplies executive power of governance both for the external and the internal forum. This also applies to the faculty for confirmation. (See can. 144.)

> See the discussion on supplied jurisdiction in general terms in chapter one, page 24, as background to the following cases.
>
> *Common error.* Supplied jurisdiction for confirmation in the case of common error should be interpreted in the same way as that for marriage. Therefore, the error must concern the "status" of the presbyter in question who lacked the faculty to confirm. For example, a priest is only in residence in a parish and does not celebrate baptisms, receive Christians into full communion, etc. On a given Sunday the pastor is away on an emergency call and the resident priest is asked to celebrate the Sunday Eucharist at which

there is going to be an adult baptism. The resident priest celebrates the Eucharist with the baptism, and confirms the initiate in accordance with the rite.

The community is not at all surprised by this, because the priest resides in the rectory and regularly celebrates the parish Eucharist. It is not necessary that the community actually make a mistake in thinking that the priest has the faculty (error of fact); it suffices that the situation exists such that the faithful could make that erroneous judgment (error of law). Although he has no mandate to celebrate adult initiation, nor any pastoral office, the Church supplies the faculty to confirm because the community errs, or could err, regarding the status of the priest, supposing him to be regularly mandated to confirm when he is not.

The reason the Church supplies the faculty is not for the private good of this one individual being confirmed, but for the common good of the potentially many who could approach the priest under similar circumstances. On the other hand, the Church does not supply the faculty to confirm when the common good is not at stake. For example, a priest who is not in residence at the parish receives an adult into full communion and confirms her, and only later notifies the pastor to have it recorded. The confirmation is invalid because of the lack of a pastoral office or a mandate from the diocesan bishop. The community would not err concerning the status of this priest, nor is there a danger to the common good.

Positive and probable doubt. The Church also supplies the faculty to confirm when the minister has a positive and probable doubt, whether of law or fact, that he has the faculty, when in fact he does not have it. Example of doubt of fact: A presbyter who has just been appointed a dean is asked by a neighboring pastor on short notice to confirm the children in his parish because the auxiliary bishop who was going to celebrate the sacrament has suddenly become ill. The dean has not yet received his list of faculties and is unsure whether he has the faculty to confirm. In the past the deans of the diocese were regularly mandated to confirm, but the dean is doubtful if this will continue since two new auxiliary bishops have just been appointed. He has a positive and probable doubt of fact, the fact being whether he has been granted the faculty by virtue of his appointment as dean. Even when he learns later that he does not have the faculty, the confirmations are valid because the law itself supplies the faculty in this situation.

Another example: A religious order priest, who is a teacher without a pastoral office, confirms a baptized person during the rite of reception into full communion in the high school chapel. He is doubtful whether the law includes him as having a pastoral office and decides that the Church will supply the faculty.

However, this is not a positive doubt of law, but a negative doubt, or ignorance. The priest simply does not know whether the law applies to him or not. Since there is no positive and probable doubt of law or fact here, and since he does not have a pastoral office, the confirmation is invalid.

$$four$$
Other Roles

A. The Sponsor

Insofar as possible, there should be a sponsor for the person to be confirmed. The sponsor's duty is to see that the one confirmed acts as a true witness to Christ and faithfully fulfills the duties inherent in this sacrament. (Can. 892)

It is desirable that one's baptismal godparent also serve as one's sponsor for confirmation. (Can. 893, §2) This expresses more clearly the relationship between baptism and confirmation and also makes the function and responsibility of the sponsor more effective. Nonetheless, the choice of a special sponsor for confirmation is not excluded. (See RConf, 5.)

> Although the law speaks only in the singular, the possibility of having two sponsors, one male and one female, is not excluded, especially when they are the baptismal godparents. (See CSacr, reply, Nov. 13, 1984; CLD 11:193.)
>
> *Parents.* The qualifications of the sponsor at confirmation are the same as for the godparent at baptism. (See cans. 893, §1 and 874.) This excludes a parent from serving as sponsor. A parent may "present" the child for confirmation, but this is not the same thing as being the sponsor. (See RConf, 5.) The Congregation for Sacraments and Divine Worship explained the difference: "This presentation, which is defined less extensively in the rite, occurs in this way: With the gospel having been proclaimed when confirmation is conferred during Mass, or the readings having been finished when the confirmation is conferred outside of Mass, 'each one to be confirmed ... approaches the sanctuary, if they are in fact

children they are to be accompanied by one of the godparents or by one of the parents, and stand in front of the celebrant' (RConf, 21, 38)." *(Notitiae* 20 (1984) 211; CLD 11:203)

B. Ministries for Adult Confirmation

Adult catechumens, who are to be confirmed immediately after baptism, have the help of the Christian community and, in particular, the formation which is given to them during the catechumenate, catechesis, and common liturgical celebrations. Catechists, sponsors, and members of the local church should participate in the catechumenate. The steps of the catechumenate will be appropriately adapted to those who, baptized in infancy, are confirmed only as adults. (RConf, 3)

C. Parents

The initiation of children into the sacramental life is for the most part the responsibility and concern of Christian parents. They are to form and gradually increase a spirit of faith in the children and, with the help of catechism classes, prepare them for the fruitful reception of the sacraments of confirmation and the Eucharist. The role of the parents is also expressed by their active participation in the celebration of the sacraments. (RConf, 3)

five
Proof and Recording

A. Proof of Confirmation

To prove conferral of confirmation, if there is no conflict of interest, it suffices to have a declaration of one witness who is above suspicion or the oath of the confirmed person, provided he or she was confirmed in adulthood [seven or older with the use of reason]. (See cans. 876; 894.)

See the commentary in chapter two, page 61.

B. Recording of Confirmation

The names of the confirmed, the minister, the parents and sponsors, and the place and date of confirmation should be recorded in the confirmation register of the diocesan curia or, where it is prescribed by the bishops' conference or the diocesan bishop, in a register in the parish archives. The pastor must notify the pastor of the place of baptism that confirmation was conferred so that he might record it in the baptismal register in accord with the norm of can. 535, §2. (Can. 895)

If the pastor of the place was not present, the minister either personally or through another should notify him as soon as possible of the conferral of confirmation. (Can. 896)

s i x
Receiving a Baptized Christian into Full Communion

A. Eastern Christians

In the case of Eastern Christians who enter into the fullness of Catholic communion, nothing more than a simple profession of Catholic faith is required, even if they are permitted, upon recourse to the Apostolic See, to transfer to the Latin rite. (RCIA, Appendix, 2; US, 474)

> An Eastern non-Catholic who wishes to become a Catholic must join the respective Catholic rite. If the person was Russian Orthodox, e.g., he or she should join the Russian Catholic church *sui iuris.* To join the Latin church, or a different Eastern Catholic church, permission of the Apostolic See is necessary. (See CCEC, can. 35.)
>
> The one to be received joins the community in the recitation of the Nicene Creed, and then adds the words: "I believe and profess all that the holy Catholic Church believes, teaches, and proclaims to be revealed by God." (See RCIA, Appendix, 15; US, 491.)

B. Other Baptized Christians

The rite. Those baptized in a separated ecclesial community are received into full communion by the *Rite of Receiving Baptized Christians into the Full Communion of the Catholic Church.* The rite should be seen as a celebration of the Church, with its climax in Eucharistic communion. For this reason the rite of reception is generally celebrated within Mass. (RCIA, Appendix, 3; US, 475) Any confusion between catechumens and candidates for reception into communion should be absolutely avoided. (Ibid., 5; US, 477)

U.S. law. It is preferable that reception into full communion not take place at the Easter Vigil lest there be any confusion of such baptized Christians with the candidates for baptism, possible misunderstanding of or even reflection upon the sacrament of baptism celebrated in another church or ecclesial community, or any perceived triumphalism in the liturgical welcome into the Catholic Eucharistic community. (NSC, 13)

The minister. It is the office of the bishop to receive baptized Christians into full communion. But the presbyter to whom he entrusts the celebration of the rite has the faculty of confirming the candidate during the rite of admission, unless the latter has already been validly confirmed. (RCIA, Appendix, 8; US, 481)

The sponsor. At the reception, candidates should be accompanied if possible by a sponsor, that is, the person who has had the chief part in bringing them into full communion or in preparing them. Two sponsors may be permitted for each candidate. (Ibid., 10; US, 483)

Recording. The names of those received into full communion should be recorded in a special register, with the date and place of baptism also noted. (Ibid., 13; US, 486)

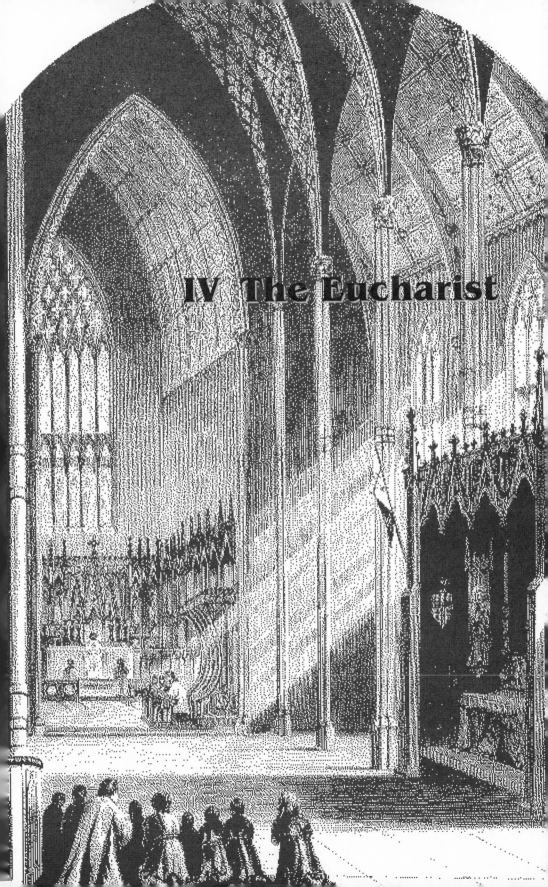

IV The Eucharist

one

Ministries

A. The Celebrant

In the *Code of Canon Law* the term "celebrant" includes concelebrants as well as the presider.

Within the community of believers, the presbyter is another [besides the bishop] who possesses the power of orders to offer sacrifice in the person of Christ. He therefore presides over the assembly and leads its prayer, proclaims the message of salvation, joins the people to himself in offering the sacrifice to the Father through Christ in the Spirit, gives them the bread of eternal life, and shares it with them. At the Eucharist he should, then, serve God and the people with dignity and humility; by his bearing and by the way he recites the words of the liturgy he should communicate to the faithful a sense of the living presence of Christ. (GIRM, 60)

For validity. Only a validly ordained priest may validly bring about the sacrament of the Eucharist. (See can. 900, §1.) Also for validity, the priest must say the words of consecration and intend to consecrate. If a lay person attempts the liturgical action of the Eucharistic sacrifice, he incurs automatically the penalty of interdict; if a deacon, the penalty of suspension. (See can. 1378, §2, 1°.)

It does not seem that a woman who pretends to celebrate the Eucharist can incur the penalty of interdict since the apparent purpose of the law is to protect the faithful from impostors; and no one would likely be deceived into thinking that a woman was a validly ordained Catholic priest. (See can. 1024.)

For liceity. A priest who is not canonically impeded licitly celebrates the Eucharist. (See can. 900, §2.)

> Priests can be deprived of their right to celebrate Mass in virtue of a canonical penalty (cf. cans. 1331, §1, 2°; 1332; 1333, §1, 1°; 1338, §2); or if they have lost the clerical state (cf. cans. 290; 292; 1336, §1, 5°); or if they have incurred an irregularity or impediment to the exercise of their orders (cf. can. 1044).

B. The Deacon

Among ministers, the deacon, whose order has been held in high honor since the early Church, has first place. At Mass he has his own functions: he proclaims the gospel, sometimes preaches God's word, leads the general intercessions, assists the priest, gives Communion to the people (in particular, ministering the chalice), and sometimes gives directions regarding the assembly's moving, standing, kneeling, or sitting. (GIRM, 61)

C. The Reader

The liturgical assembly needs readers, even if they are not instituted for this function. Therefore, one should see to it that there are some qualified lay persons who have been prepared to fulfill this ministry. When there is more than one reader and more than one reading, it is desirable to distribute the readings among them. (LFM, 52; see also LFM, 51-55; GIRM, 34; 66.) Readers have their own proper function in the Eucharistic celebration and should exercise this even though ministers of a higher rank may be present. (GIRM, 66)

> Readers may be commissioned on a stable basis by a special liturgical rite of institution. In most dioceses in North America this stable ministry is limited to seminarians and candidates for the diaconate since it is a requirement for ordination and is not open to women. (See can. 230, §1.) Lay persons also can fulfill the function of reader at the liturgy by means of a temporary deputation. (See can. 230, §2.)

D. The Acolyte and Altar Server

The acolyte is instituted to serve at the altar and to assist the priest and deacon. In particular it is for him to prepare the altar and the vessels and, as a special minister of the Eucharist, to give Communion to the faithful. (GIRM, 65)

> This norm pertains to the stable ministry of acolyte, not to be confused with the temporary ministry of altar server. Like the sta-

ble ministry of reader, this ministry is conferred only rarely on anyone in North America except for seminarians preparing for the priesthood and candidates for the permanent diaconate.

A July 11, 1992 authentic interpretation of the Pontifical Council for the Interpretation of Legislative Texts clarified that canon 230, §2 of the 1983 *Code of Canon Law* permits females as well as males to exercise the liturgical function of altar server. (See AAS 86 (1994) 541; *BCL Newsletter* 30 (April, 1994) 13.) Regarding the use of female servers, the Holy See respects the policy of each diocesan bishop, after the bishop has heard the opinion of the episcopal conference.

In the United States the National Conference of Catholic Bishops decreed on June 16, 1994: "It is the opinion of the National Conference of Catholic Bishops (NCCB) that the option of having women and girls serve at the altar is a welcome one, subject always to the guidance of the diocesan bishop...." (See *BCL Newsletter* 30 (1994) 29.) The Bishops' Committee on the Liturgy issued suggested guidelines to be used as a basis for developing diocesan policy. (See *BCL Newsletter* 30 (1994) 21.)

E. Eucharistic Ministers

The ordinary minister of holy Communion is a bishop, presbyter, or deacon. When ordinary ministers are lacking and the needs of the Church require it, an acolyte or other deputed lay person may serve as a special minister of holy Communion. (See cans. 910 and 230, §3.)

In virtue of their liturgical institution, acolytes are commissioned special ministers of the Eucharist on a permanent basis. Other special ministers are commissioned for a set period by the local Ordinary or his delegate according to the *Rite of Commissioning Special Ministers of Holy Communion*. (For the U.S. church this rite can be found in the *Book of Blessings*, chapter 63, which states in n. 1873 that the pastor is the usual minister of this rite.)

Special ministers may distribute Communion at Mass only when there are insufficient ordinary ministers present in the church, provided the ordinary ministers are not otherwise impeded. It is not necessary that the ordinary ministers be participating in that Mass. (See CodCom, interpretation, Feb. 20, 1987, AAS 80 (1988) 1373; *BCL Newsletter* 24 (1988) 104.)

The authentic interpretation reinforces the extraordinary nature of this ministry, that it is to be exercised only when there are not enough clergy who are physically or morally available for this ministry. They are physically unavailable if they are not present in the church at the time of Communion. They would be morally unavailable, even if physically present, if, e.g., they are not properly vested in alb and stole (or surplice and stole), or if they are too ill or infirm to distribute Communion.

Ad hoc appointment. Local Ordinaries may permit priests to appoint a qualified person to distribute Communion for single occasions in a case of necessity. (See CSacr, instruction *Immensae caritatis* 2, 6; AAS 65 (1973) 264-71; DOL 2076, 2080.)

A case of necessity occurs when there are too many communicants and insufficient ordinary and special ministers to distribute Communion without delaying the Mass. With this faculty the priest may designate one or more special ministers of Communion for that Mass only. During the breaking of the bread the person or persons who have been designated are to come before the celebrant. The celebrant then blesses them, saying: "Today you are to distribute the body and blood of Christ to your brothers and sisters. May the Lord bless ✠ you, N. R. Amen."

In the Eastern Catholic churches a priest is the minister of Communion; a deacon may administer Communion if permitted by particular law of the church *sui iuris.* The synod of bishops of the patriarchal church or the council of hierarchs can decide whether laity may serve as Eucharistic ministers. (See CCEC, Can. 709.)

F.   The Cantor or Psalmist

To fulfill the task of the psalmist, or cantor, it is expedient to have in each ecclesial community lay persons who are talented in the art of singing and have a facility for speaking and pronouncing words correctly. (LFM, 56; see also n. 53; GIRM, 36, 37, 47, 64, 67.)

G.   The Choir and Musicians

The *schola cantorum* or choir exercises its own liturgical function within the assembly. Its task is to ensure that the parts proper to it, in keeping with the different types of chants, are carried out becomingly and to encourage active participation of the people in the singing. What is said about the choir applies in a similar way to other musicians, especially the organist. (GIRM, 63)

H.   The Commentator

This minister provides explanations and commentaries with the purpose of introducing the faithful to the celebration and preparing them to understand it better. The commentator's remarks must be meticulously prepared and marked by a simple brevity. In performing this function the commentator stands in a convenient place visible to the faithful, but it is preferable that this not be at the lectern where the Scriptures are read. (GIRM, 68a; see also LFM, 57.)

t w o
Preaching

A. Faculty for Preaching

Without prejudice to canon 765, presbyters and deacons enjoy the faculty of preaching everywhere, with at least the presumed consent of the rector of the church, unless the same faculty has been restricted or taken away by the competent Ordinary, or unless express permission is required by particular law. (Can. 764)

> Canon 765 states that permission of the competent superior, in accord with the Constitutions, is necessary to preach to religious in their churches and oratories. If a priest is invited to celebrate Mass for a religious community, he may presume permission to give a homily, unless the contrary is evident.
>
> Presbyters and deacons, in virtue of their ordination, have the faculty to preach everywhere. No other permission is needed unless one or more of the exceptions mentioned in canon 764 above are applicable. The faculty applies to all forms of preaching, not only the homily at Mass.

Bishops have a right to preach everywhere, including the churches and oratories of religious institutes of pontifical right, unless the bishop of the place has expressly denied it in particular cases. (Can. 763; see also cans. 762, 768-772.)

> If a bishop is invited to preside at a Eucharist, he has the right to give the homily. His permission would be needed for someone else to preach at a Mass at which he presides.

B. The Homily

Among the forms of preaching the homily is preeminent; it is a part of the liturgy itself, and it is reserved to the priest or deacon. In the homily the mysteries of the faith and the norms of the Christian life are proclaimed from the sacred text throughout the course of the liturgical year. (Can. 767, §1)

> This is a constitutive law, defining the three constitutive elements of a homily. A homily is: (1) that form of preaching (2) which is part of the liturgy itself and (3) is reserved to a priest or deacon. Thus, a homily is only one form of preaching, namely, preaching at liturgy by a cleric. Preaching outside liturgy cannot be called a homily, nor can preaching during the liturgy by a lay person be called a homily, but must be called a reflection, an instruction, an exhortation, or the like. The diocesan bishop may not dispense from this norm, evidently because it is a constitutive law. (See CodCom, interpretation, May 26, 1987, AAS 79 (1987) 1249; *BCL Newsletter* 24 (1988) 103.)

There must be a homily at all Sunday and holy day Masses which are celebrated with a gathering of people. It may not be omitted except for a serious reason. (Can. 767, §2)

> Some examples of serious reasons for omitting the homily are: when the priest does not speak the language of the congregation; when the priest is too old and infirm to preach effectively; when the needs of the Church require another form of preaching, e.g., an instruction by a lay religious on the missionary works of the institute.

It is highly desirable, if there is a sufficient gathering of people, that there also be a homily on weekdays, especially during Advent and Lent or on some feast or occasion of mourning. (Can. 767, §3)

> The homily is optional on weekdays but is recommended if there is a sufficient number of people present, especially during the seasons of Advent and Lent, at funerals, and on special feasts and occasions.

The pastor or rector of a church is to see that the rules of canon 767 on preaching are zealously observed. (See can. 767, §4.)

C. Lay Preaching

Lay persons may be admitted to preach in a church or oratory if in certain circumstances necessity requires it or in particular cases it is useful. The norms of the episcopal conference are to be observed and also canon 767, §1. (Can. 766)

Mass with children in which only a few adults participate. With the consent of the pastor or rector of the church, one of the adults may speak to the children after the gospel, especially if the priest finds it difficult to adapt himself to the mentality of children. (DMC, 24)

Lay persons may not give a homily which is reserved to a priest or deacon at liturgy, but they may preach, even during the liturgy, for example, at liturgies of the word, the liturgy of the hours, and other celebrations at which they may preside. They may also preach at the Eucharistic liturgy at times, for example, at Masses for children. The universal law assumes that lay preaching will be regulated by the conference of bishops. However, in the absence of a policy from the episcopal conference, the diocesan bishop is competent to enact norms and regulate lay preaching for his diocese. (See cans. 756, §2; 772, §1.)

three
Participation in the Eucharist

A. The Assembly

The intimate connection between the liturgy of the word and the liturgy of the Eucharist in the celebration of Mass should lead the faithful to be present in the celebration from the beginning and to participate attentively. As far as possible they should be prepared for listening, especially by acquiring beforehand a more profound knowledge of sacred scripture. Moreover, the connection between liturgies of word and Eucharist should arouse in them the desire to attain a liturgical understanding of the texts which are read and the will to respond in song. (LFM, 48; see also 44–47.)

The faithful should hold the holy Eucharist in highest honor. They should take part actively in the celebration of the most august sacrifice, receive the sacrament very devoutly and frequently, and worship it with great devotion. (See can. 898.) They should become one body, whether by hearing the word of God, joining in prayers and song, and above all by offering the sacrifice together and sharing together in the Lord's table. (GIRM, 62)

In the office of sanctifying the laity have their proper role by actively participating in their own way in liturgical celebrations, especially the Eucharist. (See can. 835, §4.) In the celebration of the Eucharist, deacons and lay persons are not permitted to say prayers, especially the Eucharistic prayer, or perform actions which are proper to the celebrating priest. (Can. 907)

B. Right to the Eucharist

Anyone baptized, who is not prohibited by law, may and must be admitted to holy Communion. (Can. 912)

93

The baptized have a right to the sacraments which they are capable of receiving according to the norm of law. Besides requirements of age and use of reason, the law requires the recipient of the Eucharist to be in the state of grace and not have any penalty of excommunication or interdict. The restrictions on the reception of the Eucharist by non-Catholic Christians are discussed in chapter fifteen.

C. Prohibition of Eucharist to Manifest Sinners

Those who have been excommunicated or interdicted after an imposed or declared sentence as well as others who obstinately persevere in manifest, grave sin are not to be admitted to holy Communion. (Can. 915)

> A manifest sin is one which is publicly known. Obstinate perseverance in such a state of sinfulness is indicated when a person persists in the sinful state and does not heed the teachings of the Church or the warnings of Church authorities. Those who have been publicly excommunicated or interdicted are expressly prohibited from receiving the Eucharist and other sacraments. (See cans. 1331, §1, 2°; 1332.)
>
> This provision is intended to be applied by the minister in individual cases where the community would be scandalized if a manifest, grave sinner received holy Communion. Before refusing Communion the minister must have verified that the person is in a state of serious sin, is obstinately persevering in it, and that this state is publicly known. Since a fundamental right to the sacrament is involved, a doubt about the existence of any of the conditions of the law should be resolved in favor of the right of the person who wishes to receive Communion.
>
> For example, in a certain area a Catholic doctor owns an abortion clinic where he regularly performs abortions. This is commonly known and is a source of scandal. Even if this doctor had not been declared excommunicate, he could still be prevented from receiving holy Communion on the basis of this canon. On the other hand, it would not be proper to apply this canon to someone who has taken a political stance in favor of legalized abortion because it is at least doubtful that this political opinion in itself is necessarily a mortal sin. Regarding persons in irregular marriages, see page 294.

The Congregation for the Doctrine of the faith has declared that the faithful who enroll in Masonic associations are involved in serious sin and may not approach holy Communion. (See declaration, Nov. 26, 1983, AAS 76 (1984) 300; CLD 10:285.)

A committee of the American bishops recognized two problems with regard to the Masonic question: (1) A pastoral problem for those who have become or continue to be Masons in good faith on the basis of a previous, less restrictive interpretation. (2) A public relations problem resulting from the common American perception of Masonry as a purely social and philanthropic organization. (See NCCB Committee on Pastoral Research and Practices, Apr. 19, 1985, CLD 11:323.) It is clear, therefore, that pastors must continue to teach that good Catholics may not join the Masons. On the other hand, it is not certain that all American Catholics who may have joined the association in good faith are necessarily persevering obstinately in manifest, grave sin.

In the Eastern Catholic churches those who are publicly unworthy are to be prohibited from receiving the divine Eucharist. (See CCEC, can. 712.)

D. State of Grace

One who is conscious of serious sin should not celebrate Mass or receive the body of the Lord without previous sacramental confession unless there is a grave reason and there is no opportunity to confess. In this case the person is bound to make an act of perfect contrition which includes the intention of confessing as soon as possible. (Can. 916)

One who is *conscious* of serious sin is one who is *certain* of it. If a priest is in serious sin, he may not celebrate the Eucharist without first going to confession unless there is a grave reason and there is no opportunity to confess. An example of a grave reason is when the priest cannot omit Mass (even a weekday Mass) without infamy or scandal arising, or when he must celebrate a Mass for the faithful. Likewise, the necessity to communicate must be grave, e.g., to avoid infamy or scandal which can arise if one does not go to Communion at a wedding Mass, a family celebration, etc. (See Mathis/Bonner, 69, 87.)

The *lack of opportunity* to confess may arise from various sources: e.g., there is no confessor at hand and one cannot get to a confessor without grave inconvenience (which is prudently judged from the distance to go, the time one has, one's age and physical condition, etc.) or, e.g., because of extraordinary shame one cannot confess before a certain priest; or, e.g., one cannot go to a confessor who is present without danger of infamy, as when going to confession immediately before Mass is, according to the circumstances, an admission to others that one has committed a mortal sin.

E. Children and Persons with Developmental Disabilities

In order that the holy Eucharist may be administered to children, it is required that they have sufficient knowledge and careful preparation so that they can understand the mystery of Christ according to their capacity and receive the body of the Lord with faith and devotion. However, the holy Eucharist can be given to children in danger of death if they can distinguish the body of Christ from ordinary food and receive Communion reverently. (Can. 913)

Parents, primarily, and those who take the place of parents, as well as the pastor have the duty to see that children with the use of reason are suitably prepared for and are refreshed by this divine food as soon as possible, having first made sacramental confession. The pastor also is to be vigilant lest children come to the holy banquet who do not have the use of reason or whom he judges are not sufficiently disposed. (Can. 914)

> *First penance.* The law presumes that a child reaches the use of reason at age seven. Hence, children should be prepared for first Communion at this age so that they may receive the sacrament "as soon as possible." Canon 914 implies that there also should be some preparation for the sacrament of penance before first Communion so that the children may realistically avail themselves of the sacrament of penance. However, if the parents believe their child is not ready for the sacrament of penance, first Communion should not be denied the young child on the presumption that the child is not in a state of mortal sin.
>
> *Children who are in danger of death* may receive Viaticum even if they lack the knowledge and preparation needed for first Communion. All that is required is that they be able to differentiate the body of Christ from ordinary food and be able to receive Communion reverently. When Viaticum is given during Mass, as is optimal, the sacred character of the liturgical action and the reverent participation of family and friends enables the child to make this distinction more easily, at least on a symbolic and intuitive level if not on the cognitive level. In other words, the child may not be able to conceptualize and articulate the difference between the body of Christ and ordinary food in abstraction of the Eucharistic action, but may well intuitively appreciate this difference during the celebration itself.
>
> *Persons with developmental disabilities.* The universal law makes no specific provisions for persons whose use of reason is impaired due to developmental disabilities such as mental retardation. However, some episcopal conferences and dioceses have policies and programs for the preparation of such persons for the

reception of the sacraments, including the Eucharist. Where such local policies are lacking, it falls to the pastor and parents (or guardians) to see that persons with developmental disabilities are prepared for the Eucharist according to their capacity and that they receive it. (See can. 777, 4°.)

In the Eastern Catholic churches, infants may receive Communion when they are baptized and chrismated provided this is permitted in the liturgical books of each church *sui iuris.* (See CCEC, can. 710.)

F.   Eucharistic Fast

1)   Before receiving holy Communion one should abstain for at least one hour from all food and drink except water and medicine. (Can. 919, §1)

Medicine is whatever is taken to cure, ease, or prevent illness, whether prescribed by a physician or commonly recognized as medicine. It is not necessary to avoid a medicine which contains alcohol, as long as it is truly and properly called a medicine. Other food and beverages, although they could be said to have a medicinal effect, cannot be taken unless the communicant is elderly or ill. (See Mathis/Bonner, 90.)

2)   Those who are advanced in age or suffer from some illness, as well as those who care for them, may receive the holy Eucharist even if they have taken something during the preceding hour. (Can. 919, §3)

The sick, elderly, and those who care for them are not bound to any Eucharistic fast. The typical situation addressed by this norm is Communion given outside Mass in a home or institution. A person who is too sick or too old to go to church does not have to fast. However, even the sick or elderly who are able to attend Mass need not fast if their condition requires some nourishment. *Those who care for the sick and elderly* include not only their attendants who provide physical care but also family and friends insofar as they are providing emotional and spiritual care by visiting the sick or elderly person.

3)   A priest who celebrates the holy Eucharist twice or three times on the same day may take something before the second or third celebration, even if the interval of one hour has not elapsed. (Can. 919, §2)

It does not matter when the bination or trination occurs. For example, a priest who celebrates the Eucharist in the morning and again in the evening is not bound to fast for the second celebration even though it is later in the day.

G. Paschal Precept

All the faithful, after they have been initiated into the Eucharist, are obliged to receive holy Communion at least once a year. This precept must be fulfilled in paschal time, but for a just cause it may be fulfilled at another time during the year. (Can. 920)

> Those bound to the paschal precept, or law of the Easter duty, are all who have been initiated into the Eucharist, i.e., those who have made their first Communion. They must receive Communion at least once a year during the Easter season, which in this context means from Passion (Palm) Sunday to Pentecost Sunday inclusive. In the United States, by special concession of the Holy See, the time for fulfilling one's Easter duty extends from the first Sunday of Lent to Trinity Sunday inclusive, unless the Ordinary restricts the time. (See Second Council of Baltimore, n. 257.) The paschal precept may be fulfilled at some other time during the year for a just cause, e.g., in a remote area when a minister is lacking to celebrate Mass or give Communion. Those in serious sin are also bound to go to confession at least once a year. (See can. 989.)

H. Communion Twice a Day

Those who have already received the holy Eucharist may receive it again on the same day but only during the Eucharistic celebration at which they are participating. Those in danger of death may receive Viaticum even outside Mass, even if they have already received Communion that day. (See cans. 917; 921, §2.)

> In order to receive Communion a second time on the same day, one must receive it only during the Mass at which one is participating, i.e., attending. It is not lawful simply to enter Mass at Communion time in order to receive a second time. One must be participating in the whole celebration. Those who are in danger of death may receive Viaticum during or outside Mass, even if they have already received Communion that day. Reception of Communion a third time in one day is illicit, except in the case of a priest who must trinate. (See CodCom, interpretation, June 26, 1984, AAS 76 (1984) 746; *BCL Newsletter* 24 (1988) 103.)

f o u r
Different Forms
of Celebration

A. Mass With a Congregation

Mass with a congregation means a Mass celebrated with the people taking part. As far as possible, and especially on Sundays and holydays of obligation, this Mass should be celebrated with song and with a suitable number of ministers. But it may be celebrated without music and with only one minister. (GIRM, 77)

B. Concelebration

1. *Occasions for concelebration*

Concelebration is *required* at the ordination of bishops and presbyters and at the Chrism Mass.

> Although the Mass must be concelebrated on these occasions, it is not required that every priest in attendance concelebrate.

Concelebration is *recommended*, unless the good of the faithful should require or suggest otherwise, at:

> a) the evening Mass of the Lord's Supper on Holy Thursday;
> b) the Mass for councils, meetings of bishops, and synods;
> c) the Mass for the blessing of an abbot;
> d) the conventual Mass and the principal Mass in churches and oratories;
> e) the Mass of any kind of meeting of priests, whether secular or religious. (See GIRM, 153.)

Concelebration is *optional* at other times. It may take place provid-

ed the needs of the faithful do not require or suggest individual cele-
bration. It is forbidden to have an individual celebration of the
Eucharist in the same church or oratory during a concelebrated Mass.
(See can. 902.)

2   General discipline of concelebration

Where there is a large number of priests, the authorized superior
may permit concelebration several times on the same day, but either at
different times or in different places. (GIRM, 154)

No one is ever to be admitted into a concelebration once Mass has
already begun. (GIRM, 156)

> This means that *no priest* may join the ranks of the concele-
> brants once Mass has begun in order to ensure proper decorum.
> The Mass begins with the initial sign of the cross and the greeting;
> hence, it is not required that all the concelebrants be in the
> entrance procession.

In the sacristy or other suitable place, the concelebrants put on the
vestments usual for individual celebrants. For a good reason, however,
as when there are more concelebrants than vestments, the concelebrants may omit the chasuble and simply wear the stole over the alb;
but the principal celebrant always wears the chasuble. (GIRM, 161)

> In some regions, including the United States and Canada, the
> chasuble-alb may be worn at concelebrations. The stole is worn
> over the chasuble-alb and should be the color appropriate to the
> Mass being celebrated. (See CLD 8:528.)

3   Regulation of concelebration

The right to regulate, in accord with the law, the discipline for concelebration in his diocese, even in churches and oratories of exempt
religious, belongs to the bishop. (GIRM, 155)

> The bishop may establish rules governing the external con-
> duct of concelebration held in his diocese. This is merely an appli-
> cation and recognition of the general right and duty of the bishop
> to moderate the liturgy in his diocese. (See can. 838, §1.) The dioce-
> san bishop has the right to regulate the *public* exercise of the litur-
> gy in his diocese, that is, liturgical celebrations that are open to the
> faithful. (See can. 678, §1.) The community liturgies of clerical reli-
> gious which are not open to the faithful are subject to the supervi-
> sion of the competent religious superiors.

4. Interritual concelebration

Catholic priests are prohibited from concelebrating the Eucharist with priests or ministers of churches or ecclesial communities which do not have full communion with the Catholic Church. (Can. 908) However, concelebration between priests of different Catholic churches *sui iuris* can be done with the permission of the Eastern eparchial bishop, observing the liturgical books of the presider and wearing the appropriate vestments and insignia of one's own church *sui iuris*. (See CCEC, can. 701.)

> Canon 908 excludes interdenominational concelebration, but not concelebration with Catholics of other churches *sui iuris*. Permission for interritual concelebration can be obtained from the Eastern bishop. Such permission is necessary in view of canon 846, §2 which states that ministers are to celebrate the sacraments according to their own rite. Some authors maintain it is an accepted custom that no permission is needed for interritual concelebration on an occasional basis. (See Pospishil/Faris, 35.) At such concelebrations only one rite may be followed, that of the presider, and incompatible elements from another rite are not permitted. The concelebrants may retain the vestments and insignia of their own churches, as well as other elements which will not offend the unity of the concelebration or amount to a confusion of rituals. For a just cause and removing any wonderment by the faithful, Eastern Catholic priests may use the liturgical vestments of another church *sui iuris*. (See CCEC, can. 707, §2.)

C. Mass with Elderly, Infirm or Blind Celebrant

A priest who is infirm or elderly and is unable to stand may celebrate the Eucharistic sacrifice while seated, observing the liturgical laws. He may not celebrate in this way before the people unless he has the permission of the local Ordinary. A blind priest or one who has some other infirmity may lawfully celebrate the Eucharistic sacrifice using the text of any approved Mass. If need be, he should have the assistance of another priest or deacon or even a properly instructed lay person. (Can. 930)

D. Mass Without a Congregation

The priest should not celebrate the Eucharist without the participation of a server or at least some member of the faithful except for a just and reasonable cause. (See GIRM, 211 and can. 906.) By their very nature liturgical actions are communal celebrations and when possible should be celebrated with the presence and active participation of the faithful. (See can. 837, §2.)

The presence of a server is not required, but ordinarily there must be at least some, i.e., at least one member of the faithful present to respond to the priest and represent the Christian people who celebrate sacraments as a community. A just and reasonable cause for celebrating alone would be demonstrated whenever a member of the faithful is unavailable and when the priest is unable to participate in a communal celebration, e.g., as a result of illness, infirmity, or travel. The mere convenience of the priest or his preference for celebrating alone would not be sufficient cause. The liturgical law governing such a celebration is found in GIRM, 209-231 and the *Order of Mass Without a Congregation* in the *Roman Missal.* N.B. On Holy Thursday Mass without a congregation is prohibited.

$$five$$

Rites and Ceremonies

A. Eucharistic Bread and Wine

It is absolutely forbidden, even in extreme necessity, to consecrate the bread or wine alone without the other element, or to consecrate them both outside the Eucharistic celebration. (See can. 927.) If the priest notices after the consecration or as he receives Communion that water instead of wine was poured into the chalice, he pours the water into another container, then pours wine with water into the chalice and consecrates it. He says only the part of the institution narrative related to the consecration of the chalice, without being obliged to consecrate the bread again. (GIRM, 28)

> The priest may not, however, consecrate additional bread or wine if, once they are validly consecrated, he finds at Communion time that there is not enough for all the faithful. (See Woestman, 167.) It would be valid and probably also licit, however, to give unconsecrated hosts to the faithful that are intincted in the chalice, since Communion under the form of wine alone is permitted in a case of necessity.

The bread must be merely wheat and recently made so that there is no danger of corruption. (Can. 924, §2)

> For *validity*, the bread must be made substantially of wheat flour. If there are any additives in it, they cannot be such that the bread would no longer be considered wheat bread *according to the common estimation*. (See CSacr, instruction, Mar. 26, 1929, AAS 21 (1929) 631; CLD 1:355.) If the bread has become so corrupt that its

103

nature is substantially altered and can no longer be considered bread, it constitutes invalid matter. The judgment concerning the validity of the substance to be used as Eucharistic bread must be based on the bread's contents, not on its appearance. Thus, knowing the composition of the bread, if the common estimation of persons would judge that it is wheat bread it would be valid matter even if there are other additives. However, it is illicit to use any additives at all to the wheat flour and water.

In accord with the ancient tradition of the Latin church, the priest should use unleavened bread for the Eucharistic celebration whenever he offers Mass. (Can. 926) The nature of the sign demands that the material for the Eucharistic celebration truly have the appearance of food. Accordingly, even though unleavened and baked in the traditional shape, the Eucharistic bread should be made in such a way that in a Mass with a congregation the priest is able actually to break the host into parts and distribute them to at least some of the faithful. (When, however, the number of communicants is large or other pastoral needs require it, small hosts are in no way ruled out.) The action of the breaking of the bread, the simple term for the Eucharist in early times, will more clearly bring out the force and meaning of the sign of the unity of all in the one bread and of their charity, since the one bread is being distributed among the members of one family. (GIRM, 283) It is most desirable that the faithful receive the Lord's body from hosts consecrated at the same Mass. (See GIRM, 56h.)

All of these requirements are for liceity. Leavened bread is used in many Eastern churches.

The wine must be natural from the fruit of the vine and not corrupt. (See can. 924, §3 and GIRM, 284.)

Wine made from any fruit other than grapes is invalid matter, as is wine which is made chemically, although it may have the color of wine and may be said in a sense to contain its elements, or wine to which water has been added in a greater or equal quantity. (See CSacr, instruction, Mar. 25, 1929, AAS 21 (1929) 631; CLD 1:355.) The criterion for what constitutes natural wine is the common estimation of persons. The wine must be a natural product from the juice of grapes and not an artificial product of chemical synthesis. Wine would be altered or corrupted when it has lost those qualities by which the common estimation of people identify wine.
Care must be taken so that the wine does not turn to vinegar.

(See GIRM, 285.) If it is so sour that the common estimation of persons would regard it as vinegar rather than wine, it is invalid matter. Or if other substances are added, such as water, to such an extent that it loses the qualities of wine, it is likewise invalid.

A small amount of water is to be mixed with the wine. (See can. 924, §1.)

The ritual mixing of water and wine by the deacon or celebrant at the preparation of the gifts is for liceity only. It need be observed only for the principal vessel in order to preserve the symbol of the one cup. Other cups should be kept on a separate table until Communion time when they are filled with the consecrated wine. (See BCL, *Environment and Art in Catholic Worship,* Washington: NCCB (1978), n. 96.)

Priests recovering from alcoholism who are unable to consume wine may receive by intinction when concelebrating or, when celebrating alone, again by intinction but leaving it to an assistant to consume the consecrated wine. (See CDF, letter, Sept. 12, 1983; CLD 11:208-09.) Those who concelebrate need no further permission to receive by intinction. Those who preside without concelebration must receive permission from the local Ordinary to receive by intinction. (CDF, response, Oct. 29, 1982, AAS 74 (1982) 1298; CLD 10:158.)

Those desiring the indult to use grape juice instead of wine when they preside, or to receive the consecrated bread alone when they concelebrate, must petition for an indult. The practice of the Holy See has been for the priest's proper superior (the bishop or superior general) to send the petition of the recovering priest. The petition is to be accompanied by testimony from a doctor verifying that even the minimal amount of alcohol ingested by intinction would endanger the priest's health or recovery. (See CDF, letter, Sept. 12, 1983, CLD 11:208-10.)

B. Communion Under Both Kinds

Holy Communion has a more complete form as a sign when it is received under both kinds. For in this manner of reception a fuller light shines on the sign of the Eucharistic banquet. Moreover there is a clearer expression of that will by which the new and everlasting covenant is ratified in the blood of the Lord and of the relationship of the Eucharistic banquet to the eschatological banquet in the Father's kingdom. (GIRM, 240)

Four distinct methods of ministering the consecrated wine are possible: (1) the communicant drinks from the cup; (2) Communion is given by intinction, i.e., part of the host is dipped in the consecrated wine and placed on the recipient's tongue; (3) the precious blood is taken through a tube; (4) the consecrated wine is given to the communicant by spoon. (See GIRM, 244-51.) The method of drinking from the cup is preferred. (See Congregation for Divine Worship, instruction *Sacramentali Communione*, n. 6, June 29, 1970, AAS 62 (1970) 664-66; DOL 2115.)

In the United States. The particular law governing the dioceses of the United States notes that the three options other than direct reception from the chalice are not customary in the United States and adds: "Reception of the precious blood through a tube, in a spoon or by intinction may remove the communicant's legitimate option to receive Communion in the hand or, for valid reasons, not to receive the consecrated wine. However, if Communion is given by intinction the communicant may never dip the Eucharistic bread into the chalice. Communion under either the form of bread or wine must always be given by a minister with the usual words." (See NCCB, *This Holy and Living Sacrifice: Directory for the Celebration and Reception of Communion Under Both Kinds*, 51-52.)

The occasions on which Communion under both kinds may be distributed are regulated by particular law as well as by the universal law found in the *General Instruction of the Roman Missal*, n. 242. The conferences of bishops have the power to decide to what extent and under what conditions Ordinaries may allow Communion under both kinds on occasions that are of special significance in the spiritual life of any community or group of the faithful.

In the United States the Ordinary may permit Communion under both kinds at all Masses, with the following exceptions:

1) not at Masses celebrated in the open with a great number of communicants (e.g., in a stadium);

2) not at other Masses where the number of communicants is so great as to make it difficult for Communion under both kinds to be given in an orderly and reverent way (e.g., Masses celebrated in a civic square or building that would involve the carrying of the sacred species up and down a number of steps);

3) not at Masses where the assembled congregation is of such a diverse nature that it is difficult to ascertain whether those present have been sufficiently instructed about receiving Communion under both kinds;

4) not when circumstances do not permit the assurance that due reverence can be maintained towards the consecrated wine

both during and after the celebrations. (See NCCB, *This Holy and Living Sacrifice: Directory for the Celebration and Reception of Communion Under Both Kinds,* 22.)

C. Communion Under the Species of Wine Only

In a case of need, holy Communion may be given under the species of wine alone. (See can. 925.)

A case of need is demonstrated when a person is unable to consume the consecrated bread as a result of any kind of medical condition. One might judge another situation of need to be a situation when there are not enough consecrated hosts for all the communicants.

D. Communion in the Hand

Episcopal conferences may decree that Communion may be given in their territories by placing the consecrated bread in the hands of the faithful provided there is no danger of irreverence or false opinions about the Eucharist. (See HCW, 21.)

In the United States the local Ordinary may permit the faithful to have the *option* of receiving Communion in the hand. (See Appendix to the GIRM for the Dioceses of the U.S., 240.)

E. Language of the Eucharist

The Eucharist may be celebrated in Latin or another language provided the liturgical texts have been lawfully approved. (Can. 928)

Whether the Eucharist is celebrated in Latin or the vernacular, only the liturgical books approved by the Apostolic See may be used, in particular the 1970 Roman Missal of Pope Paul VI.

The *Tridentine rite* Mass according to the 1962 edition of the *Roman Missal* may only be used with the permission of the diocesan bishop or the Pontifical Commission *Ecclesia Dei.* (See John Paul II, apostolic letter, Mar. 27, 1988, AAS 80 (1988) 1495-98, *Origins* 18 (1988) 149; and Pontifical Commission *Ecclesia Dei,* letter, Origins 21 (1991) 144-45.)

Sign language. Sign language may be used with and by deaf people throughout the liturgy whenever it is judged to be pastorally suitable. (See Consilium for the Implementation of the Constitution on the Liturgy, reply, Dec. 10, 1965, CLD 6:552.)

F.   Vestments

For Mass. The vestment common to ministers of every rank is the alb, tied at the waist with a cincture, unless it is made to fit without a cincture. An amice should be put on first if the alb does not completely cover the street clothing at the neck. A surplice may not be substituted for the alb when the chasuble or dalmatic is to be worn or when a stole is used instead of the chasuble or dalmatic. (GIRM, 298)

> The General Instruction of the Roman Missal contains other norms governing vestments for Mass. (See GIRM, 299-310.) In several countries, including the United States and Canada, the chasuble-alb may be used in concelebrations, in Masses for special groups, in celebrations which are carried on outside of a sacred place, and in similar cases in which considerations of place or persons advise it. The stole, which is worn over the chasuble-alb, is to be the color appropriate to the Mass being celebrated. (See Congregation for the Sacraments and Divine Worship, decree, June 14, 1976, *Notitiae* 12 (1976) 312-13; CLD 8:528.)
>
> In the United States the color of vestments for funeral services and at other offices and Masses for the dead is white, violet, or black. (See Appendix to the GIRM for the Dioceses of the U.S., 308.)

For holy Communion. When a priest or deacon distributes Communion in a church or oratory, he wears an alb and stole, or a surplice and stole over a cassock or habit. Special Eucharistic ministers are to wear whatever is customary or approved by the Ordinary. For Communion outside a church or oratory, the vesture of the minister should be suitable and in accord with local circumstances. (See HCW, 20.)

Frequency, Time and Place of Celebration

A. Bination and Trination

A priest may not licitly celebrate or concelebrate Mass more than once a day except on those occasions when the law permits it. (Can. 905, §1)

Occasions permitted by law. For a particular reason, having to do either with the meaning of the rite or of the liturgical feast, to celebrate or concelebrate more than once on the same day is permitted as follows:

1) One who has celebrated or concelebrated the chrism Mass on Holy Thursday may also celebrate or concelebrate the evening Mass.

2) One who has celebrated or concelebrated the Mass of the Easter Vigil may celebrate or concelebrate the second Mass of Easter.

3) All priests may celebrate or concelebrate the three Masses of Christmas, provided the Masses are at their proper times of day.

4) One who concelebrates with the bishop or his delegate at a synod or pastoral visitation, or concelebrates on the occasion of a meeting of priests, may celebrate another Mass for the benefit of the people. This holds also, in analogous circumstances, for gatherings of religious. (GIRM, 158; see also GIRM, 76.)

> Priests who have the faculty to trinate on all Sundays and holy days need not observe the requirement that the three Masses on Christmas be at the proper times of the day. On Christmas the Mass offerings may be kept by the priest for all three Masses.

Faculty from local Ordinary. If there is a scarcity of priests, the local Ordinary may allow priests to celebrate Mass twice a day for a just cause; in pastoral necessity he can allow priests to celebrate Mass even three times on Sundays and holy days of obligation. (Can. 905, §2)

Generally the permission to binate on weekdays and trinate on Sundays and holy days is given to priests in their diocesan faculties. If the faculty is given only to parish clergy, other priests who substitute for the pastor or the parochial vicar should also be understood as having this permission for the duration of their service in the parish.

A *just cause* is required for a priest to celebrate two Masses on a weekday. Although canon 905 makes no mention of the good of the faithful, the just cause must have some relation to it. If a purely private reason of the priest would suffice (e.g., devotion) there would hardly be reason to require a scarcity of priests before the faculty could be used. Therefore the just cause must have some public character, e.g., weddings, funerals, Lenten Masses, renewal of the reserved Eucharist in houses of lay religious, etc. (See Mathis/Bonner, 71.)

In order for a priest to trinate on Sundays or holy days, there must be a genuine *pastoral necessity.* The mere convenience of the faithful would not be adequate reason to trinate unless a sufficient number of them could not otherwise attend Mass as, e.g., when a priest has the care of more than one church or when the church is unable to accommodate all the faithful who wish to attend. The Apostolic See discourages a priest from celebrating more Masses than necessary for the faithful because "the pastoral effort is weakened" by multiple Masses, i.e., the participation of the people in a scattered congregation is diminished and the effectiveness of overworked priests is reduced. (See Congregation of Rites, instruction *Eucharisticum mysterium,* 26, May 25, 1967, AAS 59 (1967) 539; CLD 6:533.)

When reckoning binations and trinations, it should be noted that the vigil Mass on Saturday evening is considered a Mass of that Saturday, not of Sunday. If pastoral need requires priests to trinate regularly on Saturdays or other days, or to celebrate more than three Masses on Sundays and holy days, the bishop should seek an indult from the Holy See to permit this. (See *Communicationes* 15 (1983) 192.) One may not presume permission to exceed the number of Masses permitted by canon 905, nor may the local Ordinary grant the faculty orally. (See CCLA, 583.)

B. Time of Celebration

Ordinarily, the celebration of the Eucharist and the distribution of Communion can take place on any day and at any hour. (See can. 931.)

Anticipated evening Masses on days before a day of precept may be held only in the evening. (See can. 1248, §1.)

The anticipated Mass should not begin earlier than 4:00 p.m. (See Piux XII, apostolic constitution *Christus Dominus,* n. VI, Jan. 6, 1953, AAS 45 (1953) 14; CLD 4:275-76.)

During Holy Week there are additional regulations for the time of the Eucharist, as follows:

1) *The Mass of the Lord's Supper* is to be celebrated in the evening at a convenient hour. Where true pastoral reasons require it, the local Ordinary may permit another Mass in churches or oratories and, in case of true necessity, even in the morning, but only for the faithful who find it impossible to participate in the evening Mass. Such Masses must not be celebrated for the advantage of private persons or prejudice the principal evening Mass. Holy Communion may be distributed only during Mass, except for the sick. (See *Roman Missal* for the Evening Mass of the Lord's Supper.)

2) *On Good Friday* holy Communion is distributed only during the celebration of the passion of the Lord which takes place at 3:00 in the afternoon, unless for a pastoral reason a later hour is selected. For the sick who are unable to participate in this celebration, it may be given at any hour of the day. (See *Roman Missal* for the Celebration of the Lord's Passion, n. 3.)

3) The *Easter Vigil* takes place at night. It should not begin before nightfall and should end before daybreak. It is never permitted to anticipate the Mass of Easter before the Easter Vigil or celebrate more than one Easter Vigil service in the same church. On *Holy Saturday,* holy Communion may be given only as Viaticum for those in danger of death. (See *Roman Missal* for Holy Saturday.)

In the United States, for pastoral reasons the local Ordinary may permit an additional anticipated Mass of Easter after the Easter Vigil. (See *The Sacramentary Approved for Use in the Dioceses of the USA,* Introduction to the Easter Vigil, n. 3.)

C. Place of Celebration

The Eucharist should be celebrated in a sacred place, unless in a particular case necessity requires otherwise. In such a case, the celebration must occur in a decent place. (Can. 932, §1)

A particular case includes not only a single occasion but also an individual priest who must celebrate outside a sacred place on a regular basis. Cases of necessity include sickness, old age, distance from a church, and pastoral advantage such as Masses for children and other particular groups. The priest himself can judge whether the place is suitable for Mass, unless this is regulated by particular law.

The Eucharistic sacrifice should take place on a dedicated or blessed altar. Outside a sacred place a suitable table may be used, always with a cloth and corporal. (Can. 932, §2) Mass may not be celebrated on an altar under which a corpse is buried. (See can. 1239, §2.)

In a non-Catholic church. For a just cause and with the express permission of the local Ordinary, and having avoided scandal, a priest may celebrate the Eucharist in the place of worship of some church or ecclesial community which does not have full communion with the Catholic Church. (Can. 933)

> The local Ordinary's permission is not needed to celebrate the Eucharist in an interdenominational chapel, such as at a hospital, prison, or military installation, since the canon refers only to the place of worship of some Christian denomination which is not in full communion with the Catholic Church, such as a Protestant or Orthodox church.

In a church where the celebrant is unknown. A priest should be allowed to celebrate the Eucharist even if he is unknown to the rector of a church provided he has a letter of recommendation from his Ordinary or his superior which is dated at least within the year. If he lacks such a letter he can still be allowed to celebrate if it is prudently judged that he should not be prevented. (Can. 903)

> This is the law of the *celebret.* A celebret is a letter from a priest's local Ordinary or religious superior, including local superior, which testifies that the priest is in good standing so that he might celebrate the Eucharist in places where he is not known. The letter must have been dated at least within a year of its presentation to the rector, namely, to the pastor, superior, or other person in charge of the church. The celebret is not absolutely required; the rector of a church can safely admit a visiting priest provided there is no reason for suspicion.

s e v e n
Mass Intentions
and Offerings

A. Mass Intentions

Priests may apply Mass for anyone, whether living or dead. (Can. 901)

> A priest may accept a Mass offering for the intention of anyone, whether living or deceased, Catholic or non-Catholic. However, ancient Christian liturgical and ecclesiological tradition permits the specific mention in the Eucharistic Prayer only of the names of persons who are in full communion with the Church celebrating the Eucharist. (See DE, 121.)

It is highly recommended that priests celebrate Mass for the intention of the faithful, especially of the poor, even if they receive no offering. (Can. 945, §2)

Missa pro populo. The diocesan bishop and the pastor have the duty of applying a Mass for their people on all Sundays and holy days. (See cans. 388 and 534.)

In the Eastern Catholic churches a priest may accept offerings not only for the celebration of the Divine Liturgy but also for the Liturgy of the Presanctified and for commemorations in the divine liturgy if this is established by legitimate custom. (See CCEC can. 715.)

B. Individual and Collective Intentions

In accord with the approved custom of the Church, each priest, whether presider or concelebrant, may accept an offering to apply Mass for a certain intention. (Can. 945, §1) Once the offerings are accepted, separate Masses are to be applied for the intentions of those who gave individual offerings, even though they be small in amount. (Can.

948) Whoever has the obligation to celebrate and apply a Mass for the intention of those who gave an offering is bound to fulfill this obligation even if without fault he has lost the offering. (Can. 949)

The rule is stated in canon 948 that ordinarily there may be no more than one offering conjoined with an intention accepted by each priest for a single Mass. By exception, offerings can be received from more than one donor for a collective intention.

Collective intentions. In 1991 the Congregation for the Clergy issued a decree that derogated from canon 948 by permitting the practice of taking more than one offering for a single Mass. (See Congregation for the Clergy, decree, Jan. 22, 1991, AAS 83 (1991) 443-46; *BCL Newsletter* 27 (1991) 13-16.) The principal rules governing this practice are:

1) The donors of the Mass offerings must be informed and agree to combine their offerings with others in a single Mass.

2) The time and place for the celebration of the Mass are to be made public.

3) Masses for collective intentions may not be celebrated by a priest more than twice a week.

4) If the total amount of the offerings given for a collective intention exceeds the amount of the usual offering, the priest may only keep for himself the amount of the usual offering; the excess is to be given to the Ordinary for the purposes he has specified in virtue of canon 951, §1.

This fourth point is an exception to the rule that priests ordinarily may accept an offering that is larger (or smaller) than the amount established by the bishops of the province. (See can. 952, §1.) Evidently the legislator wants to ensure that the practice of collective intentions is not to be used for the purpose of increasing the income of an individual priest.

C. Additional Masses the Same Day

A priest who presides at more than one Mass on the same day may apply each one for an intention for which an offering is given. On Christmas a priest may keep offerings for three Masses celebrated. On all other days he may keep only one offering, and give the others to purposes prescribed by the Ordinary. However, some compensation by virtue of an extrinsic title is admissible. (Can. 951, §1)

The offerings from binations and trinations go to the Ordinary for the purposes established by him. The Ordinary is the personal Ordinary of the priest. In the case of religious, the major superior receives the offerings from binations and trinations. However, in the case of pastors and parochial vicars, the Ordinary here refers to the local Ordinary, even if the pastor or parochial vicar is not a secular priest. (See Pontifical Commission for the Authentic Interpretation of Canon Law, interpretation, Apr. 23, 1987, AAS 79 (1987) 1132.)

An example of an extrinsic title is the compensation owed to a priest for his services in celebrating the Mass over and above the amount of the Mass offering. Those who must celebrate a Mass *pro populo* on Sundays and holy days may keep the offering from a second Mass that day.

A priest concelebrating another Mass on the same day may not accept an offering for it under any title. (Can. 951, §2)

> A priest who is concelebrating may not accept an offering for that Mass unless it is the only Mass he is offering that day.

D. Amount of Offering

The provincial council or the meeting of the bishops of a province is to define by decree the amount that is to be offered in the whole province for the celebration and application of Mass. A priest may not ask for an amount higher than this. However, a priest is free to accept an offering voluntarily given which is higher or lower than the established amount. In the absence of such a decree, the custom of the diocese is to be observed. Also the members of every kind of religious institute must observe the amount defined by the above-mentioned decree or custom. (Can. 952)

If a sum of money is offered for the application of Masses and there is no indication of the number of Masses to be celebrated, the number is reckoned on the basis of the amount of the offering established in the place where the donor lives, unless the donor's intention legitimately ought to be presumed to have been otherwise. (Can. 950)

> If the Mass offerings have come from a legacy or foundation of any kind, and the amount of each is less than the current offering, the diocesan bishop or the supreme moderator of clerical institutes of pontifical right can reduce the number of Masses. (See can. 1308.) For example, a woman left a thousand dollars in her will for 200 Masses, but the will was written when the Mass offering was five dollars in that diocese. Since then the offering has doubled to ten dollars. Accordingly, the competent authority could reduce the number of Masses to 100.

E. Excess Mass Obligations

No one is allowed to accept more Mass offerings to be applied by himself than he is able to satisfy within a year. (Can. 953) If in certain churches or oratories the number of Masses requested to be celebrated is greater than can be celebrated there, the Masses may be celebrated elsewhere unless the donors shall have expressly indicated the contrary. (Can. 954) Eastern Catholic priests who accept offerings for the Divine Liturgy from the faithful of another ritual church are bound by a grave obligation to observe the norms of that church, unless otherwise established by the donor. (See CCEC, can. 717.)

Whoever intends to commit to others the celebration of Masses for intentions should do so as soon as possible, sending them to priests of his own choice, provided he is certain that they are trustworthy. He must send the entire offering received unless it is certain that the excess of the amount established in the diocese was given to him personally. His obligation to see that the Masses are celebrated remains until such time as he has received evidence that both the obligations were accepted and the offerings were received. The time within which a priest has to celebrate these Masses begins on the day on which he has received them, unless established otherwise. (See can. 955, §§ 1, 2.)

All administrators of pious causes or those in any way obliged to see to the celebration of Masses, whether cleric or lay, should send to the Ordinary, in the manner defined by him, all Mass obligations not satisfied within a year. (Can. 956)

F. Record and Supervision

Those who transfer to others any Masses to be celebrated should record without delay both the Masses which were received and those which were given to others. The amount of the offerings is also to be noted. (Can. 955, §3) Each priest must accurately record the Masses he has agreed to celebrate and those which he has satisfied. (Can. 955, §4)

The pastor or rector of some church or other pious place in which Mass offerings are customarily received should have a special book in which they accurately record the number of Masses to be celebrated, the intention, the offering received, and also the fact of their celebration. (Can. 958, §1)

The duty and right of ensuring that Mass obligations are satisfied belong to the local Ordinary in churches of the secular clergy and to superiors in churches of religious institutes or societies of apostolic life. (Can. 957) The Ordinary is obliged either personally or through another to inspect every year the Mass offering books. (Can. 958, §2)

Even the appearance of trafficking or commercialism in regard to Mass offerings is strictly prohibited. (Can. 947) One who unlawfully profits from a Mass offering is to be punished with a censure or another just penalty. (Can. 1385)

eight

Reservation and Veneration of the Eucharist

A. Purpose of Reservation

The primary and original reason for reservation of the Eucharist outside Mass is the administration of Viaticum. The secondary ends are the giving of Communion and the adoration of our Lord Jesus Christ present in the sacrament. (HCW, 5)

B. Place of Reservation

The holy Eucharist *must* be reserved in a cathedral church or its equivalent, in every parish church, and in the church or oratory attached to the house of a religious institute or society of apostolic life. (Can. 934, §1, 1°) In the house of a religious institute or some other pious house, the holy Eucharist is reserved only in the church or principal oratory connected with the house. Nevertheless, for a just cause the Ordinary may permit it to be reserved in some other oratory of the same house. (Can. 936)

> An example of a just cause would be when there is more than one distinct community living under the same roof; each may have its own oratory with the reserved Blessed Sacrament.

The holy Eucharist *may* be reserved in a bishop's chapel and, with the permission of the local Ordinary, in other churches, oratories, and chapels. (Can. 934, §1, 2°)

In sacred places where the holy Eucharist is reserved, there must always be someone who cares for it and, as far as possible, a priest should celebrate Mass there at least twice a month. (Can. 934, §2)

No one may have personal possession of the Eucharist or take it on a journey unless there is urgent pastoral necessity and the regulations of the diocesan bishop are observed. (Can. 935)

Unless there is a serious reason, the church in which the holy Eucharist is reserved should be open for at least some hours every day so that the faithful may pray before the Blessed Sacrament. (Can. 937)

An example of a serious reason for not opening the church each day would be the unavailability of someone to guard it together with a reasonable fear of burglary or vandalism.

C. The Tabernacle

The holy Eucharist should be reserved on a regular basis in only one tabernacle in a church or oratory. (Can. 938, §1)

Every encouragement should be given to the practice of Eucharistic reservation in a chapel suited to the faithful's private adoration and prayer. If this is impossible because of the structure of the church, the sacrament should be reserved at an altar or elsewhere, in keeping with local custom, and in a part of the church that is worthy and properly adorned. (GIRM, 276; see also HCW, 9.)

Further regulations on the tabernacle are found in canon 938, §§ 2-5, the *Rite of Holy Communion and Worship of the Eucharistic Mystery Outside Mass,* nn. 10-11, and the *General Instruction of the Roman Missal,* n. 277.

D. The Lamp

Before the tabernacle in which the holy Eucharist is reserved there should be a special lamp continually lit which indicates and honors the presence of Christ. (Can. 940) According to traditional custom, an oil lamp or a lamp with a wax candle is to be used as far as possible. (HCW, 11)

Although the law prefers the traditional oil lamp or wax candle, other kinds of lamps are not excluded if there is a just cause for using them.

E. Renewal of the Sacred Species

Consecrated hosts in sufficient quantity for the needs of the faithful should be kept in a pyx or ciborium. They are to be renewed frequently, with the old ones being properly consumed. (Can. 939)

A sufficient number of hosts is that required for the Communion of the sick and others outside Mass. (See HCW, 7.)

On the grounds of the sign value, it is more in keeping with the nature of the celebration that, through reservation of the sacrament in the tabernacle, Christ not be present eucharistically from the beginning on the altar where Mass is celebrated. That presence is the effect of the consecration and should appear as such. (See HCW, 6.) It is most desirable that the faithful receive the Lord's body from hosts consecrated at the same Mass. (See GIRM, 56 h.)

F. Exposition of the Blessed Sacrament

In churches or oratories in which it is permitted to reserve the holy Eucharist, exposition may be done using a pyx or a monstrance, observing the norms of the liturgical books. The exposition of the Blessed Sacrament should not be held in the same part of a church or oratory in which Mass is being celebrated. (Can. 941)

Extended exposition. It is recommended that in churches and oratories that have the reserved Eucharist there be an annual solemn exposition of the Blessed Sacrament extended for a suitable period even if not continuous, so that the local community might more attentively meditate on and adore the Eucharistic mystery. However, such an exposition should take place only if it is foreseen that it will attract a suitable number of the faithful, and established norms are observed. (Can. 942)

For any serious and general need, the local Ordinary is empowered to order prayer before the Blessed Sacrament exposed for a more extended period of time in those churches to which the faithful come in large numbers. (HCW, 87)

If exposition of the Blessed Sacrament goes on for a day or for several successive days, it should be interrupted during the celebration of Mass, unless it is celebrated in a chapel separate from the area of exposition and at least some of the faithful remain in adoration. (HCW, 83)

Brief exposition. Shorter expositions of the Eucharist are to be arranged in such a way that the blessing with the Eucharist is preceded by a reasonable time for readings of the word of God, songs, prayers, and a period for silent prayer. Exposition merely for the purpose of giving benediction is prohibited. (HCW, 89)

Ministers. The priest or deacon is the minister of exposition and benediction. In particular circumstances and observing the norms of the diocesan bishop, an acolyte, special minister of holy Communion, or other person deputed by the local Ordinary may be the minister of exposition and reposition, but not the benediction. (Can. 943) Such ministers may open the tabernacle and also, as required, place the ciborium on the altar or place the host in the monstrance. At the end of the period of adoration, they replace the Blessed Sacrament in the tabernacle. It is not lawful, however, for them to give the blessing with the sacrament. (HCW, 91)

nine
Communion Outside Mass

A. Communion for the Sick and Elderly

It is strongly recommended that the faithful receive Communion during the Eucharistic celebration. Nevertheless, if they ask for it for a just reason, it should be administered to them outside Mass, observing the liturgical rites. (Can. 918) In fact it is proper that those who are prevented from being present at the community's celebration should be refreshed with the Eucharist. In this way they may realize that they are united not only with the Lord's sacrifice but also with the community itself and are supported by the love of their brothers and sisters. Pastors should take care that the sick and elderly be given the opportunity, even if they are not gravely ill or in imminent danger of death, to receive the Eucharist often, even daily, especially during the Easter season. It is lawful to minister Communion under the form of wine alone to those who cannot receive the consecrated bread. (See HCW, 14.) Holy Communion may be given to the sick at any time and on any day except on Holy Saturday when it may only be given to the dying. (See *Roman Missal* for Holy Saturday.)

Ordinarily Communion is administered during Mass but, by exception, it can be given outside Mass for a just cause, e.g., Communion for the sick and elderly. The minister of Communion follows the *Rite of Distributing Holy Communion Outside Mass* from the *Roman Ritual*. There are two forms, a long rite and a short rite, both with a celebration of the word. The short rite is used when the longer form is unsuitable, especially when there are only one or two communicants and a truly communal celebration is impossible. (HCW, 42)

B. Communion for the Dying

Viaticum. The faithful who are in danger of death from any cause should be refreshed by holy Communion in the form of Viaticum. Even if they have already received holy Communion that same day, it is highly recommended that those who are in danger of death communicate again. As long as the danger of death lasts, it is recommended that holy Communion be administered a number of times, but on separate days. Holy Viaticum should not be delayed too long. Those involved in pastoral care are to be especially vigilant that the dying receive Viaticum while they are fully conscious. (Cans. 921; 922)

> The cause for the danger of death must be proximate, not remote. For example, a person who is about to undergo open heart surgery is in proximate danger; a person taking an airplane trip is only in remote danger.

All baptized Christians who are able to receive Communion are bound to receive Viaticum by reason of the precept to receive Communion when in danger of death from any cause. (RA, 27)

> All the baptized who are eligible by law to receive Communion are obliged to receive Viaticum in danger of death. Children who have not reached the age of reason may receive Viaticum provided they can distinguish the body of Christ from ordinary food and receive Communion reverently. (See can. 913, §2.)

Whenever possible Viaticum should be given during Mass and under both species of bread and wine. If Mass is not celebrated in the presence of the dying person, the blood of the Lord should be kept in a properly covered chalice which is placed in the tabernacle after Mass. It should be carried in a vessel which is closed in such a way as to eliminate all danger of spilling. All who take part in the celebration may receive Communion under both kinds. (See RA, 26, 95, 96; PCS, 26, 181.)

Ministers of Viaticum. The administration of Viaticum is a function especially committed to the pastor. (See can. 530, 3°.) Pastors, parochial vicars, and chaplains have the duty and right to bring Viaticum to the dying. In the house of a clerical religious institute or society of apostolic life, this duty and right belongs to the superior of the house who may exercise it on behalf of all staying in the house. (See can. 911, §1.) In case of need or with at least the presumed permission of the pastor, chaplain, or superior, any priest or other minister of holy Communion must give Viaticum and should notify the proper authority afterwards. (See can. 911, §2.)

Ordinary ministers of the sick or dying are bishops, presbyters, and deacons. Extraordinary ministers are acolytes and extraordinary lay ministers appointed for this function. (See cans. 909 and 230, §3.) A priest or deacon administers Communion or Viaticum to the sick in the manner prescribed by the *Rite of Anointing and Pastoral Care of the Sick.* When an acolyte or a special minister gives Communion to the sick or Viaticum to the dying, he or she uses the *Rite of Holy Communion and Worship of the Eucharistic Mystery Outside Mass* under the title, "Administration of Communion and Viaticum to the Sick by a Special Minister." (HCW, 54)

C. Communion Services

Among the forms of celebration found in liturgical tradition when Mass is not possible, a celebration of the word of God is particularly recommended, and also its completion, when possible, by Eucharistic communion. In this way the faithful can be nourished by both the word of God and the body of Christ. (See Congregation for Divine Worship, *Directory for Sunday Celebrations in the Absence of a Priest,* n. 20, June 2, 1988; English translation by ICEL, USCC publication n. 251-9.)

Communion services on Sundays may be permitted by the diocesan bishop, after hearing the presbyteral council. They are prohibited in any place where Mass has been or will be celebrated that day or on the preceding evening, nor may there be more than one such celebration on any given Sunday. They should not be celebrated when the faithful are able to go to a church nearby for the Eucharist. The celebration takes place in the context of a liturgy of the word or the liturgy of the hours. It is to be led by a deacon or, in his absence, by an instituted acolyte, reader, or a lay minister appointed and instructed for this role. (See *Directory for Sunday Celebrations in the Absence of a Priest,* 18, 21, 23, 30, 33.)

Communion services may replace Mass also on weekdays when no priest is available for Mass. Moreover, the faithful may gather for the liturgy of the hours, a liturgy of the word, or another form of prayer or devotion without the administration of holy Communion.

V Penance

one

Celebration
of the Sacrament

The *Roman Ritual* provides three sacramental rites of penance and a non-sacramental penitential service. Among the sacramental rites are two rites for individual confession of sins—the *Rite of Reconciliation of Individual Penitents* and the *Rite of Reconciliation of Several Penitents with Individual Confession and Absolution*—and a rite using general absolution—the *Rite for Reconciliation of Several Penitents with General Confession and Absolution.*

A. Individual Confession

Individual and integral confession and absolution constitute the only ordinary way by which the faithful who are conscious of serious sin are reconciled with God and the Church. Only physical or moral impossibility excuses from this kind of confession, in which case there also may be reconciliation in other ways. (Can 960)

To obtain the saving remedy of the sacrament of penance, according to the plan of our merciful God, the faithful must confess to a priest each and every grave sin that they remember after an examination of conscience. (RPen, 7a)

> The Council of Trent solemnly taught that for complete and perfect remission of sins three acts are required on the part of the penitent as the matter of the sacrament, namely, contrition, confession, and satisfaction. It also taught that absolution by a priest is a judicial act and that by divine law it is necessary to confess to a priest each and every mortal sin and the circumstances which change the species of the sin insofar as the memory can recall them after a diligent examination of conscience. (See CDF,

125

Pastoral Norms, *Sacramentum Paenitentiae,* AAS 64 (1972) 510; June 16, 1972, CLD 7:668.)

The ordinary way that sacramental reconciliation occurs is by individual and integral confession and absolution. The extraordinary ways are by general absolution and by an act of perfect contrition. An act of perfect contrition includes the intention to confess as soon as possible. (See can. 916)

Reconciliation with God and the Church for those in venial sin can also take place through other means, especially through the Eucharist as well as non-sacramental penance and contrition.

Shorter rite of individual confession. When pastoral need dictates, the priest may omit or shorten some parts of the rite but must always retain in their entirety the penitent's confession of sins and acceptance of the act of penance, the invitation to contrition (RPen, 44), and the formularies of absolution and dismissal. In imminent danger of death, it is sufficient for the priest to say the essential words of the form of absolution, namely: "I absolve you from your sins in the name of the Father, and of the Son, and of the Holy Spirit." (RPen, 21)

> Individual penance should be scheduled so that the complete rite may be used properly with all penitents without haste or delay. However, pastoral need, such as the great number of penitents, may sometimes suggest that the complete rite be shortened as indicated in the ritual.

B. General Absolution

Absolution may not be imparted in a general fashion to many penitents at the same time without previous individual confession, unless: (1) danger of death is imminent and there is not time for the priest or priests to hear the confessions of each penitent; (2) there is a serious need such as when, due to the number of penitents, there are not enough confessors to hear properly the confessions of individuals within a suitable time such that the penitents, through no fault of their own, would be forced to go for a long time without sacramental grace or holy Communion. However, the need is not considered sufficient if confessors cannot be present for the sole reason of the great number of penitents such as may happen on some great feast or pilgrimage. (Can. 961, §1)

> The availability of a sufficient number of confessors is a relative matter depending on various circumstances, especially the period of time necessary for properly celebrating the individual rite. It could even involve a relatively small number of penitents

in a remote area which might deny freedom of choice of confessors or desired anonymity to penitents. (See CLSA Comm., 679.)

Another condition for the use of general absolution is that the faithful, through no fault of their own, would be forced to go without sacramental grace or holy Communion for a long time. The sacramental grace refers to the grace of the sacrament of penance. This applies to those in venial sin as well as mortal sin who may wish to have the sacramental grace, even though it is not required to have venial sins absolved by the sacrament.

In the United States, the NCCB has interpreted the "long time" *(diu)* to go without sacramental grace or holy Communion as "one month." This decision was not given the approval of the Apostolic See since it was not considered a decree. (See *The Jurist* 53 (1993) 404.) Therefore, it has a persuasive rather than properly juridic force, akin to a guideline or recommendation for the policies of each diocese.

It pertains to the diocesan bishop to make the judgment whether the conditions are fulfilled for the use of general absolution. He may establish such cases of need in view of criteria agreed upon with other members of the episcopal conference. (See can. 961, §2.)

In the absence of such criteria, the diocesan bishop can act on his own authority. (See can. 838, §4.)

That the faithful may receive a valid absolution given to many at the same time it is required not only that they be properly disposed but likewise have the intention in due time to confess individually their serious sins which at present they are unable to confess. The faithful are to be taught this requirement insofar as possible, even on the occasion of the reception of general absolution. There is to be an exhortation preceding general absolution that each person is to make an act of contrition, even in the case of danger of death if there is time. (Can. 962)

The law requires, for validity of the general absolution, that anyone in serious sin must not only be suitably disposed but also intend to confess individually those serious sins in due time. This due time is explained in canon 963 as meaning "as soon as possible when there is the opportunity." Minimally, this must be before another general absolution, unless there is a just reason, or within a year from one's last confession. (See can. 989.)

Unless a just cause prevents it, one whose serious sins are remitted by a general absolution should go to individual confession as soon as possible when there is the opportunity before receiving another general absolution. The obligation of canon 989 remains in force. (Can. 963)

Canon 989 is the precept to confess serious sins annually.
Thus, since those who receive a general absolution are bound to
confess their serious sins individually as soon as there is opportunity before they receive a second general absolution, this could
well be even before they would be required to confess their mortal sins annually. They are excused from this requirement if they
are impeded by a just cause. An example of a just cause would be
serious inconvenience to the penitent or the confessor. Hence, if
the penitent is unable to approach individual confession at a regularly scheduled time at a church in the area, this would be sufficient cause to excuse from this requirement. Another example is
the case of a remote area where sufficient confessors are not available to guarantee desired anonymity or freedom of choice of confessors.

On the other hand, only physical or moral impossibility
would excuse from the requirement to confess mortal sins annually. (See RPen, 34.) Examples would include physical illness; lack
of a confessor; a psychological reason, such as a deep fear of confessing individually.

C. Time and Place of Celebration

The reconciliation of penitents may be celebrated in all liturgical
seasons and on any day. But it is right that the faithful be informed of
the day and hours at which the priest is available for this ministry.
They should be encouraged to approach the sacrament of penance at
times when Mass is not being celebrated and preferably at the scheduled hours. Lent is the season most appropriate for celebrating the
sacrament of penance. (See RPen, 13.)

All to whom the care of souls is committed by virtue of office are
obliged to provide for the hearing of the confessions of the faithful
entrusted to them when the faithful reasonably request it. They are to
provide for the faithful the opportunity for individual confession at
days and hours established for the faithful's convenience. In urgent
necessity any confessor is obliged to hear the confessions of the faithful, and in danger of death any priest. (Can. 986)

There must be regularly scheduled times for the celebration
of the sacrament in each parish. It is not sufficient simply to allow
penitents to come whenever they wish, or by appointment.

The proper place for hearing sacramental confession is a church or
oratory. Confessions should not be heard outside the confessional

except for a just cause. (Can. 964, §§ 1, 3)

The episcopal conference should establish norms governing the confessional, but ensuring that the confessionals, which the faithful who so desire may freely use, are always located in an accessible place and have a fixed grille between the penitent and the confessor. (Can. 964, §2)

> *In the United States,* a reconciliation chapel or room is permitted, which must allow the option for the penitent's kneeling at a fixed grille. (See NCCB, decree, *BCL Newsletter* 10 (1974) 450. See also *Environment and Art in Catholic Worship* (Washington: NCCB, 1978), n. 81.)

t w o
Roles and Ministries

The whole Church, as a priestly people, acts in different ways in the work of reconciliation that has been entrusted to it by the Lord. Not only does the Church call sinners to repentance by preaching the word of God, but it also intercedes for them and helps penitents with a maternal care and solicitude to acknowledge and confess their sins and to obtain the mercy of God, who alone can forgive sins. (See RPen, 8.)

Only a priest is the minister of the sacrament of penance. (Can. 965) For the valid absolution of sin it is required that the minister, besides having the power of order, also have the faculty to exercise the power on behalf of the faithful to whom he gives absolution (Can. 966, §1)

Those who attempt to impart sacramental absolution or hear a sacramental confession when they are unable validly to do so automatically incur an interdict if a lay person or a suspension if a cleric. (Can. 1378, §2, 2°)

A. Faculty by Law

The following possess the faculty to hear confessions in virtue of the law itself:

1) The pope and cardinals for anywhere in the world (See can. 967, §1.)

2) All bishops anywhere in the world, unless a local Ordinary has denied this in a particular case. (See can. 967, §2.)

3) In virtue of their office, within the limits of their jurisdiction, local Ordinaries, canons penitentiary, pastors, and those who take the place of pastors unless a local Ordinary denies it in a particular case. (See cans. 968, §1 and 967, §2.)

The one who takes the place of the pastor is the administrator or the parochial vicar when the parish is vacant or the pastor is impeded. (See cans. 540-41.)

If a local Ordinary denies an outside priest the faculty in a particular case, that priest may not validly absolve in that territory except in danger of death.

4)   In virtue of their office, superiors of religious institutes or societies of apostolic life—if they are clerical and of pontifical right, and if the superiors have executive power of governance according to the Constitutions—for their own subjects and others who live in the house day and night; they use this faculty licitly unless a major superior denies this in a particular case for his own subjects. (See cans. 968, §2 and 967, §3.)

Superiors include local superiors, provided they have executive power of governance according to the Constitutions. Ordinarily the Constitutions will not explicitly state this power is possessed by the local superior, but it is implicit in virtue of the kinds of acts that the local superior can perform, e.g., dispensing members in certain cases. If even implicit indications are lacking, but there are no contrary indications that the local superior does not possess this power, the superior may safely hear the confessions of his subjects and others who live in the house in virtue of the faculty supplied in the case of a doubt of law. (See can. 144.)

A major superior can deny a local superior, or another major superior subject to him, permission to hear the confessions of his subjects and those who live in the house, but this affects liceity only.

5)   All priests, even if they lack the faculty, for those in danger of death, absolving from all sins and censures, even if an approved priest may be present. (See cans. 976; 1357, §1.)

B.   Delegated Faculty

The faculty to hear confessions should not be granted except to presbyters whose suitability has been demonstrated by examination or by some other means. (Can. 970)

The faculty may be granted for a determinate or indeterminate period. (See can. 972.) The faculty for hearing confessions habitually should be granted in writing. (Can. 973)

A habitual faculty granted verbally would be valid but illicit. (Cf. can. 10.)

From the local Ordinary. Only the local Ordinary is competent to grant to any presbyter at all the faculty for hearing confessions of any of the faithful. Presbyters who are members of religious institutes are not to use the faculty without at least the presumed permission of their superior. (Can. 969, §1) The local Ordinary should not grant the faculty for hearing confessions habitually to a presbyter, even one having domicile or quasi-domicile in his jurisdiction, unless he has first consulted that presbyter's Ordinary insofar as possible. (Can. 971)

> The presumed permission of the superior means that a religious priest may hear confessions with a faculty granted by a local Ordinary unless the superior forbids it. If the superior forbids it, the priest hears confessions validly but illicitly.

From the superior. The superior of a religious institute or society of apostolic life who enjoys executive power of governance according to the Constitutions is competent to grant to any presbyter at all the faculty for hearing confessions of the superior's subjects or others who reside day and night in the house. (Can. 969, §2)

> Even a local superior who has executive power of governance is competent to grant any priest—even one not of the institute—the faculty for hearing the confessions of his subjects and those who live in the house. However, the local superior must be a priest because the concession of the faculty rests on the principle that the faculty depends upon a power residing in the grantor over those to whom or for whom the priest ministers the sacrament. (See CLSA Comm., 685.) One cannot delegate power that one does not have.

Presbyters who have this faculty use it licitly unless some major superior denies it in a particular case for his own subjects. (See can. 967, §3.)

> For example, the provincial of province X grants the faculty to a member, but the provincial of province Y refuses to allow that priest to hear the confessions of the members of province Y. Such a prohibition affects liceity only. Only one's own major superior (general or provincial) can revoke the faculty. (See can. 974, §4.)

Outside the diocese. The faculty of hearing confessions habitually, whether in virtue or office or by delegation, can be exercised wherever the priest travels, unless a local Ordinary denies it in a particular case. (See can. 967, §2.)

C. Supplied Faculty

Inadvertence. An act of delegated power, which is exercised only in the internal forum and which is placed through inadvertence after the elapse of the time for it, is valid. (Can. 142, §2)

> For example, a priest is given the faculty for confession during the time of the parish mission he is giving. On the morning after the mission has closed and his faculty has expired because the time for which it was granted has run out, a woman approaches him for the sacrament of penance. Inadvertently, he hears her confession and absolves her, not recalling that his faculty has expired. The absolution is valid, even if during the course of the celebration of the sacrament he should remember that the faculty had ceased.

Common error. In common error of fact or law, the Church supplies executive power of governance for both the external and the internal forum. This norm also applies to the faculty for confessions. (See can. 144.)

> The error here envisioned concerns the existence of the faculty; it is based upon a factual situation which gives rise to the belief that a priest has the faculty to hear confessions, whereas he does not. Common error, as opposed to merely private error, affects some sort of community and is, in some manner, common to the people of a diocese, parish, religious community, etc. However, in order for common error to exist, it is not at all required that the majority of the persons in a place actually elicit a false judgment concerning the existence of a public fact which normally is capable of leading people into error. Rather, there exists a public circumstance from which all reasonable persons, without any error of law, would naturally conclude that the faculty exists. It is not necessary that a number of persons actually err concerning the existence of the faculty, provided that the circumstances are such that they would err.
>
> Furthermore, the Church only supplies the faculty when the common good is at stake, not when merely the private good of one or several persons is in question. For example, a priest without the faculty is sitting in the confessional, or other place where the sacrament of penance is ordinarily celebrated. By this very set of circumstances, the community would erroneously conclude that the priest has the faculty, or else he would not be there. The Church supplies the faculty because the common good is at stake, namely, the potential invalidity of many absolutions. Even if only one per-

son approaches that priest, the Church still supplies the faculty because the potential is there for harm to the common good.

In practice, the mere fact that a priest is actually in the confessional, or other place where penance is ordinarily celebrated, is sufficient to constitute the foundation for common error; people would commonly judge that any priest hearing confessions there has the faculty.

On the other hand, if a priest is hearing confession outside a place where penance is ordinarily celebrated, the Church would not supply the faculty because there would be no basis for the community to believe that such a priest should have the faculty. For example, a priest is approached by a passenger at the airport who asks to confess before boarding the plane. The Church would not supply the faculty on the basis of common error in such a case.

In positive and probable doubt of law or of fact, the Church supplies the executive power of governance both for the internal and the external forum. (See can. 144.)

A doubt is positive and probable when there is a good and serious reason to conclude that one has the power of governance, although there is also good reason to say that one has not. The mind, therefore, is unable to reach a certain judgment concerning the fact of possessing the power. A doubt of law regards the existence, the extent, or the meaning of the law. It must be an objective doubt, i.e., the law is interpreted variously even by the experts; the law itself is not clear. On the other hand, the Church does not supply power of governance for merely subjective doubt, which is ignorance. An example of a doubt of law would be a doubt whether the Constitutions of a religious institute grant local superiors executive power of governance.

A doubt of fact regards the existence of some circumstances which the law certainly requires in order that an act be included within its ambit; e.g., I doubt whether this particular person is really in danger of death, whether a given case meets all the requirements for an automatic censure, whether my one year faculty has elapsed, whether the faculties from my new diocese have been granted while I am in transit, etc. Again, the doubt must be positive and probable; there must be some objective basis for the doubt, not just ignorance of the facts. Note that in the last analysis, the doubt always comes back to this question: Do I have the power in this case? Once the situation of positive and probable doubt is verified, the Church supplies the power of governance to cover the case in question.

D. Loss of Faculty

In addition to revocation, the faculty for hearing confessions habitually in virtue of one's office ceases by the loss of that office; the faculty for hearing confessions habitually in virtue of delegation by the local Ordinary or the Ordinary of incardination ceases by excardination or by loss of domicile. (See can. 975.)

> Once one loses the habitual faculty by loss of office, excardination, or loss of domicile, it is lost everywhere until a new one is granted. The only exception is when a local Ordinary prohibits a priest in a particular case from hearing confessions only in his territory.

Revocation. The local Ordinary, and also the competent superior, should not revoke a faculty for hearing confessions habitually except for a serious reason. If the faculty is revoked by the local Ordinary of incardination or domicile who granted it, the presbyter loses the faculty everywhere; but if it is revoked by some other local Ordinary, he loses it only in the territory of the one who revoked it. (See can. 974, §§ 1, 2.)

> Serious reasons for revoking the faculty would include evidence of incompetence as a confessor, violation of the seal or related indiscretions which jeopardize the seal, and other abuses mentioned in the canons.

Any local Ordinary who has revoked the faculty of some presbyter shall notify the Ordinary proper to him by reason of incardination or, if it is a question of a member of a religious institute, of his competent superior. If the faculty is revoked by one's own major superior, the presbyter loses it for members of the institute everywhere; but if the faculty is revoked by some other competent superior he loses it only for those subjects under that superior's jurisdiction. (Can. 974, §§ 3, 4)

> The principle behind the law is this: the one who grants the faculty is able to revoke it. Hence, if one's own Ordinary grants the faculty and then revokes it, it is lost everywhere. If another Ordinary grants it for his own jurisdiction and then revokes it, it is lost only in that jurisdiction. For example, the bishop of a diocese grants the habitual faculty to a religious priest. The faculty is good everywhere in the world as long as the priest retains domicile in that diocese. The priest also has the faculty from his major superior to hear confessions of members of the institute. The bishop revokes the faculty, but the major superior does not. The priest

may continue hearing the confessions of members of the institute and those who live in its houses, but not of any others.

The faculty is also revoked by the censure of excommunication or interdict or another penalty which specifies the loss of the faculty. This applies both to the faculty obtained by law and that obtained by delegation. (See cans. 1331-33.)

Any priest, even one who has been excommunicated, interdicted, suspended, laicized, or in any other way has lost the faculty, may hear confessions in danger of death. If a priest has incurred an automatic censure but it has not been declared, he may hear the confession of any of the faithful who requests it for any just cause. (See can. 1335.)

E. Seal of Confession

The sacramental seal is inviolable. Therefore it is absolutely forbidden for the confessor to betray the penitent either by words or by any other means for any reason whatsoever. Also bound to the observance of secrecy are the interpreter, if there is one, and all others who have gained knowledge in any way of a sinner's confession. (Can. 983)

The confessor who directly violates the sacramental seal incurs the penalty of automatic excommunication reserved to the Apostolic See. If he violates it only indirectly, he is to be punished in accordance with the gravity of the offense. An interpreter or any others who violate the secret are to be punished with a just penalty, not excluding excommunication. (See can. 1388.)

The sacramental seal is the obligation to keep secret all those things known through sacramental confession, the revelation of which would betray both the sin and the sinner.

A *direct violation* of the seal consists in revealing both the person of the penitent and the sin of the penitent. A direct violation can occur not only by stating the penitent's name and the sin, but also by revealing circumstances by which this could be known.

An *indirect violation* occurs when, from the things the confessor says or does, there arises a danger that others will come to know a sin confessed and the identity of the penitent. (See Mathis/Bonner, 130.)

Both direct and indirect violations of the seal are forbidden by canon 983, but only the direct violation by a confessor results in the automatic penalty of excommunication reserved to the Apostolic See.

The confessor is totally prohibited from using knowledge acquired in confession to the detriment of the penitent, even when there is no danger of revelation. Anyone who has a position of authority may not in any way use for external governance knowledge of sins which he has gained at any time in confession. (Can. 984)

> Any knowledge gained in the sacrament of penance, even if not of sins, may not be used by the confessor to the detriment of the penitent. For example, a confessor has reason to believe that a certain penitent, who is going to be ordained to the permanent diaconate, is psychologically unstable. He may not use this knowledge against the penitent if it was gained primarily from what the penitent said in confession.
>
> Also, any knowledge of sins cannot be used by anyone in a position of authority for external governance, even if it could benefit the penitent, or even if there is no danger that the sin will be revealed. For example, a confessor knows that a certain person is a compulsive thief. The confessor is later appointed pastor of a parish where that person is on the parish finance council. The pastor may not remove the person solely on the basis of the knowledge gained from the confession.

The master of novices and his assistant and the rector of the seminary or other educational institution should not hear the sacramental confessions of their students who are living in the same house unless the students in particular cases spontaneously request it. (Can. 985)

F. Rules for Confessors

The priest should remember in hearing confessions that he acts as judge as well as healer, and that he has been constituted by God as a minister of divine justice as well as mercy, so that he may have regard for divine honor and the salvation of souls. As a minister of the Church, the confessor, in administering the sacrament, should faithfully observe the teachings of the magisterium and the norms of competent authority. (Can. 978)

The priest, in asking questions, should proceed with prudence and discretion, attentive to the condition and age of the penitent, and he should refrain from inquiring about the name of an accomplice. (Can. 979)

In order that the faithful might receive the healing remedy of the sacrament of penance, they must be so disposed that they are converted to God by repudiating the sins which they committed and having the intention of reforming their lives. (Can. 987) If the confessor does not doubt the disposition of the penitent who seeks absolution, he should not deny or defer the absolution. (Can. 980)

The confessor should impose salutary and appropriate penances according to the kind and number of sins, keeping in mind the penitent's condition. The penitent is obliged personally to perform the penance. (Can. 981)

> The refusal of the penitent to perform the penance would be sufficient reason for the confessor not to absolve in the case of serious sin. The penance may be in the form of prayer, self-denial, and especially service to neighbor and works of mercy, and it should correspond to the gravity and nature of the sins. (See RPen 18.)

Except in danger of death, the absolution of an accomplice in a sin against the sixth commandment is invalid. (Can. 977) A priest who acts contrary to this prescription incurs automatic excommunication reserved to the Apostolic See. (See can. 1378, §1.)

> An accomplice is one who participates immediately with the priest in the same act of impurity which is a grave sin. It does not suffice that one cooperate, even proximately, in the sin of another, e.g., by advising one to commit sin, procuring the occasion, etc. Both must take part in the same action. It is required that the sin, on the part of both persons, be certain, external, and grave. If there is a doubt whether the sin was committed, or whether it was external and grave, the censure is not incurred. (See Mathis/Bonner, 131-35.)

A priest who in the act or on the occasion or under the pretext of confession solicits a penitent to commit a sin against the sixth commandment is to be punished, in accord with the gravity of the offense, by suspension, prohibitions, privations and, in more serious cases, is to be dismissed from the clerical state. (Can. 1387)

If anyone confesses that he or she had falsely denounced to ecclesiastical authority a confessor innocent of the crime of solicitation to a sin against the sixth commandment, that person should not be absolved unless he or she first formally retracts the false denunciation and is prepared to make amends for damages, if there are any. (Can. 982) Anyone who before an ecclesiastical superior falsely denounces a confessor of committing the crime of solicitation incurs automatically the penalty of interdict and, if he is a cleric, also suspension. (Can. 1390)

G. Confessors for Religious

Superiors should recognize the proper freedom of members concerning the sacrament of penance and the direction of conscience, without prejudice to the discipline of the institute. In accordance with their proper law, superiors should be solicitous to have available worthy confessors for their members so that they may confess frequently. In monasteries of nuns, in houses of formation, and in the larger houses of lay religious there should be ordinary confessors approved by the local Ordinary, chosen in consultation with the community, but with no obligation on anyone's part of approaching them. Superiors should not hear the confessions of their subjects unless the members themselves spontaneously request it. (Can. 630, §§ 1-4)

The master of novices likewise may not hear the confessions of the novices or others living in the novitiate unless they ask him on their own initiative. (See can. 985.)

Members of religious institutes should approach their superiors with trust, and they may freely and spontaneously be open with them. However, superiors are forbidden from inducing them in any way to make a manifestation of their conscience to them. (Can. 630, §5)

> Under a manifestation of conscience comes all matters of the internal forum, matters such as sins, thoughts, feelings, etc., namely, matters treated in the sacrament of penance, in spiritual direction, and in counselling. These are privileged matters that the member is free to reveal or not reveal to superiors, but superiors are prohibited from using their authority to exact such matters from a subject.
>
> Can. 630 also applies to societies of apostolic life. (See can. 734.)

H. Obligation to Confess

The faithful are bound by obligation to confess in kind and number all serious sins committed after baptism which have not yet been directly remitted by the keys of the Church and admitted in individual confession. They are to confess those serious sins of which they are conscious after a diligent examination of conscience. It is recommended that the faithful also confess their venial sins. (Can. 988) All the faithful, after they have reached the age of discretion, are obliged to confess faithfully their serious sins at least once a year. (Can. 989)

Seminarians are to be accustomed to approach the sacrament of penance frequently. (See can. 246, §4.) *Clerics* are to be solicitous in going to the sacrament of penance frequently. (See can. 276, §2, 5°.) *Members of religious and secular institutes* are to frequently approach the sacrament of penance. (See cans. 664 and 719, §3.)

One who is conscious of a serious sin may not celebrate Mass or receive the body of the Lord without previous sacramental confession unless there is a grave reason and there is no opportunity for confessing. In such a case the person should be mindful of the obligation to elicit an act of perfect contrition, which includes the intention of confessing as soon as possible. (Can. 916)

J. Choice of Confessors

All the faithful are free to confess their sins to a lawfully approved confessor of their own choice, even to one of another rite. (Can. 991)

In seminaries, besides the ordinary confessors, other confessors should regularly come to the seminary. Without prejudice to the discipline of the seminary, it is always the right of a student to go to any confessor either in or outside the seminary. (See can. 240, §1.)

K. Reception into Full Communion

If the profession of faith and reception take place within Mass, the candidates, according to their own conscience, should confess their sins beforehand. They should first inform the confessor that they are about to be received into full communion. Any confessor who is lawfully approved may hear such a confession. (*Rite of Receiving Baptized Christians into the Full Communion of the Catholic Church,* 9; RCIA, US, 482)

> *U.S. law.* The celebration of the sacrament of reconciliation with candidates for confirmation and Eucharist is to be carried out at a time prior to and distinct from the celebration of confirmation and the Eucharist. As part of the formation of such candidates, they should be encouraged in the frequent celebration of this sacrament. (NSC, 27)

three

Remission of Censures by the Confessor

It is rare that a confessor encounters a penitent with an inflicted or declared penalty, neither of which may be remitted in the sacrament of penance by the typical confessor, except in danger of death. Thus, the treatment of penal law here will focus mainly on automatic (*latae sententiae*) penalties. There are three kinds of censures: excommunication, interdict, and suspension. A suspension affects clerics only.

A. Automatic Excommunication

The penalty of excommunication is incurred automatically upon commission of any of the following crimes:

1)   apostasy, heresy, schism (can. 1364, §1);
2)   violation of the consecrated species (can. 1367);
3)   physical attack on the pope (can. 1370, §1);
4)   absolution of an accomplice in a sin against the sixth commandment (can. 1378, §1);
5)   unauthorized ordination of a bishop, incurred by the ordaining bishop and the bishop who is ordained (can. 1382);
6)   direct violation by a confessor of the seal of confession (can. 1388);
7)   procuring an abortion (can. 1398);
8)   by means of a technical instrument recording or divulging in the communications media what was said by a confessor or a penitent in a sacramental confession, whether performed by oneself or another. (CDF, decree *Urbis et Orbis*, Sept. 23, 1988, AAS 80 (1988) 1367)

Concerning the excommunication for abortion, the Pontifical Commission for the Authentic Interpretation of the

Code of Canon Law decreed that an abortion is to be understood not only as the ejection of an immature fetus but also as the killing of a fetus procured in any manner and at any time from the moment of conception. (See interpretation, May 23, 1988, AAS 80 (1988) 1818-19.)

The eighth penalty was promulgated in 1988. It refers to the use of a tape recorder in the confessional or similar device that can record the voice of penitent or confessor and then be divulged to the media.

N.B. The remission of the crimes in nn. 2-6 is reserved to the Apostolic See.

The excommunicate is prohibited from: (1) having any ministerial participation in the celebration of the Eucharist or any other ceremonies of worship; (2) celebrating the sacraments or sacramentals and receiving the sacraments; (3) exercising any ecclesiastical offices, ministries, or functions, or placing acts of governance. (Can. 1331, §1)

B. Automatic Interdict

Commission of any of the following crimes results in the penalty of automatic interdict:

1)   physical attack on a bishop (can. 1370, §2);

2)   pretended celebration of the Eucharist by a non-priest (can. 1378, §2, 1°);

3)   attempt to impart sacramental absolution or hear confession by one who cannot do so validly (can. 1378, §2, 2°);

4)   false accusation of the crime of solicitation in the confessional (can. 1390, §1);

5)   attempted marriage, even civil, by a lay religious in perpetual vows (can. 1394, §2).

The crimes mentioned in nn. 2 and 3 result in automatic suspension, rather than interdict, if the offender is a cleric. The crimes in nn. 1 and 4 result in both automatic interdict and suspension if the offender is a cleric.

The interdicted is prohibited from: (1) having any ministerial participation in the celebration of the Eucharist or any other ceremonies of worship; and (2) celebrating the sacraments or sacramentals and receiving the sacraments (See can. 1332.)

C. Automatic Suspension

In addition to those who commit the crimes mentioned in nn. 1-4 above under interdict, the following also incur automatic suspension:

(1) a cleric who attempts marriage, even civil (can. 1394, §1); (2) a cleric who is ordained by a bishop who does not have legitimate dimissorial letters. The suspension affects only the order received illicitly, not a prior order received lawfully. (See can. 1383.)

Suspension, which affects only clerics, prohibits: (1) all acts of the power of order; (2) all acts of the power of governance; (3) the exercise of all rights or functions connected with an office. (See can. 1334, §2; 1333, §1.)

A cleric who is automatically suspended as a result of illicit ordination by a bishop lacking legitimate dimissorial letters is prohibited only from exercising that order, not a lower order licitly received. (See can. 1383.)

D. Exceptions to Observance of Censures

If a censure prohibits the celebration of sacraments or sacramentals or placing an act of governance, the prohibition is suspended whenever it is necessary to provide for the faithful who are in danger of death. If it is an automatic censure which has not been declared, the prohibition is moreover suspended whenever the faithful request a sacrament or sacramental or an act of governance. They may make this request for any just reason at all. (Can. 1335)

If the penalty forbids the reception of the sacraments or sacramentals, the prohibition is suspended as long as the person in question is in danger of death. The obligation of observing an automatic penalty, which has not been declared and is not notorious in the place where the offender is living, is suspended totally or partially insofar as the offender is unable to observe it without the danger of grave scandal or infamy. (Can. 1352)

E. Those Subject to Penalties

In general, those subject to the law are subject to a penalty if they break the law, with the exceptions noted below. A penalty binds personally, not territorially, and therefore remains in effect wherever one goes until it is remitted. (See cans. 11-13.)

A penalty cannot be incurred or inflicted unless the delict be perfectly executed according to the strict letter of the law. Laws which establish a penalty are subject to strict interpretation. (See can. 18.)

Whoever does or omits anything in attempting to commit a crime but, contrary to his or her desire, has not completed the crime, is not bound to the penalty attached by law to the completed crime, unless a law or precept should state otherwise. (Can. 1328, §1; see also can. 1328, §2.)

No one is punished unless the external violation of the law or precept committed by that person is gravely imputable to him or her by reason of malice or culpability. One is bound to the penalty established by a law or precept if that person deliberately violates the law or precept. If the violation occurs as a result of a lack of due diligence the person is not punished, unless the law or precept states otherwise. If the violation is external, imputability is presumed, unless it should appear otherwise. (Can. 1321)

Those who habitually lack the use of reason, even if they seem to have been of sound mind when they violated a law or precept, are considered incapable of committing a crime. (Can. 1322)

If a law has changed after a crime is committed, that law is to be applied, whether the earlier or later, which is the more favorable to the offender. If the later law abolishes the earlier one, or at least the penalty connected with it, the penalty ceases immediately. (Can. 1313)

Accomplices who are not named in a law or precept incur an automatic penalty connected with an offense if the offense would not have been committed without their efforts and the penalty is of such a nature that it is able to affect them. Otherwise they can be punished by inflicted penalties. (Can. 1329, §2)

F. Those Exempt from All Penalties

1)   Anyone under 16.

2)   Anyone inculpably ignorant of the law; also inadvertence to or error of the law.

3)   One who acts under physical force or in virtue of a mere accident which either could not be foreseen or could not be prevented.

4)   One who violates the law out of grave fear, even if only relatively grave, or out of necessity or serious inconvenience, unless the offense is intrinsically evil or brings harm to souls.

5)   One who acts with due moderation in legitimate self-defense or defense of another against an unjust aggressor.

6)   One lacking the use of reason.

7)   A person who without fault thought that any of the circumstances in nn. 4 or 5 were present. (Can. 1323)

G. Those Exempt from Automatic Penalties

1)   A person having only the imperfect use of reason.

2)   One lacking the use of reason due to drunkenness or another similar mental disturbance which was culpable.

3)   Someone in the serious heat of passion, which nevertheless did not precede or impede all deliberation of the mind and consent of the will, provided the passion was not voluntarily excited or fostered.

4)   Minors (under 18).

5)   Anyone who was forced, out of serious fear, even though only relatively serious, or out of necessity or serious inconvenience, if the offense was intrinsically evil or tends to be harmful to souls.

6)   One who for the sake of the legitimate protection of oneself or another acted against an unjust aggressor but did not observe due moderation.

7)   One who acted against another who gravely or unjustly provoked it.

8)   One who through error or culpability thought that any of the circumstances in can. 1323, nn. 4 or 5 were present.

9)   One who without fault did not know that there was a penalty attached to the law or precept.

10)   One who acted without full imputability, provided it remained serious. (Can. 1324, §1)

Crass, supine, or affected ignorance can never be considered in applying the prescriptions of canons 1323 and 1324. Likewise not exempting are drunkenness or other disturbances of the mind, if they are deliberately induced to perpetrate the crime or excuse it, or passion which is willfully excited or fostered. (Can. 1325)

H. Remission of Automatic Penalties Not Reserved

Automatic penalties not reserved to the Apostolic See, including abortion, can be remitted by any of the following persons, provided the penalties have not been declared, i.e., the competent ecclesiastical authority has not made any public declaration that the offender has incurred a penalty automatically upon the commission of some delict:

1)   All Ordinaries for their subjects; and all local Ordinaries for their subjects and those in their territory or those who committed an offense there. (See can. 1355, §2.)

2)   All bishops in the act of sacramental confession. (See can. 1355, §2.)

3)   Canons penitentiary (or their equivalent) in the sacramental forum. (See can. 508.)

4)   Chaplains in hospitals, prisons, and on ships on voyages. (See can. 566, §2.)

5)   Any confessor in the internal sacramental forum if it would be hard on the penitent to remain in a state of serious sin for the duration necessary for the competent superior to provide the remission. This applies only to automatic excommunications and interdicts, but not suspensions. In granting the remission the confessor should enjoin the penitent with the burden of having recourse within one month to, and obeying the mandates of, any of the authorities in nn. 1-3 above, under pain of reincidence of the penalty. Meanwhile he should impose

an appropriate penance and, to the extent indicated, should impose the repair of scandal and harm. However, recourse can also be taken by the confessor without mentioning any names. (Can. 1357, §§ 1, 2)

> The confessor may presume that anyone who comes to confession is finding it hard to remain in serious sin. According to the traditional commentators, even if the penitent finds it hard to remain in serious sin for one day, the above provisions may be used by the confessor. (See CLSA Comm., 917.)

6) Any priest, even one without the faculty to hear confessions, may absolve from all penalties if the penitent is in danger of death, even if an approved priest is present. (Can. 976) Should the penitent recover, recourse is not necessary unless the censure is reserved to the Apostolic See. (See can. 1357, §3.)

> In the case of the automatic censure of excommunication for the crime of abortion, confessors of the mendicant religious orders and certain other institutes enjoy the privilege of absolving the censure if it has not been declared. (See Apostolic Penitentiary, instruction *Legislator canonicus*, private, June 29, 1990.)

J. Automatic Penalties Reserved to Apostolic See

The following can remit automatic penalties reserved to the Apostolic See:

1) The Apostolic See. Recourse is had by the penitent or the confessor, without mentioning any names, to the Apostolic Penitentiary.

2) Any confessor in the internal sacramental forum if it would be hard on the penitent to remain in a state of serious sin during the time necessary to receive a remission from the Apostolic See. The conditions of canon 1357 are to be observed as described above at H, 5 with the Apostolic See being the competent authority to which recourse is made. (See can. 1357, §§ 1, 2.)

3) Any priest, even one without the faculty to hear confessions, may absolve from all penalties if the person is in danger of death. If the person recovers, recourse must be made to the Apostolic See. (See cans. 976, 1357, §3.)

K. Formula of Remission

When a priest, in accord with the norm of law, remits an automatic censure in the sacramental forum, the formula of absolution is not to be changed. It suffices that he intend to remit the censure as well as absolve the sins. Nevertheless, the confessor can remit the censure before he absolves the sins by using the formula given below for use outside the sacrament of penance. (See RPen, Appendix I, n. 1.)

When a priest, according to the norm of law, remits a censure outside the sacrament of penance, the following formula is used: "By the power granted to me, I absolve you from the bond of excommunication (suspension, interdict). In the name of the Father, and of the Son, + and of the Holy Spirit." (See ibid., n. 2.)

> The remission of a penalty is a separate act from the absolution of sin. However, it suffices that a confessor who has the power to remit the penalty intend to do so at the same time he absolves from sin. With this intention, by reciting the formula of absolution the confessor simultaneously remits the penalty and absolves from the sins. A second option would be to remit the censure using the special formula above before giving absolution.

L. Eastern Canon Law

It is reserved to the Apostolic See to absolve from the following sins: (1) a direct violation of the sacramental seal; and (2) absolution of an accomplice in a sin against chastity. It is reserved to the eparchial bishop to absolve from the sin of procuring a completed abortion. (CCEC, can. 728)

Any reservation of the absolution from the sin lacks all force: (1) if a sick person cannot leave the house or if a spouse made the confession for the purpose of celebrating marriage; (2) if in the prudent judgment of the confessor the faculty of absolving cannot be sought from the competent authority without serious inconvenience to the penitent or without danger of violating the sacramental seal; (3) outside the boundaries of the territory in which the authority who has reserved the sin exercises his power. (CCEC, can. 792)

> The Eastern canon law is considerably different from and simpler than the Latin law on the issue of reserved penalties. There are no automatic penalties in the Eastern code, so the above reserved sins (two reserved to the Apostolic See and one to the eparchial bishop) would concern the confessor more than the various penalties which must be imposed and remitted by a competent ecclesiastical authority. Among the crimes in the Eastern code, only one is reserved to the Apostolic See. The crime of using physical force against the pope or causing him some other grave injury is to be punished with a major excommunication whose remission is reserved to the pope himself. (See CCEC, can. 1445, §1.)

four
Remission of Penalty for Abortion

Abortion, which results in automatic excommunication, is likely the crime most often encountered in the sacrament of penance, and so it is a practical example to demonstrate how a confessor should handle automatic censures. In this discussion the typical case will be assumed, i.e., not the danger of death situation and not a priest who has power to remit censures as discussed above (bishops, Ordinaries, canons penitentiary, mendicant religious, chaplains in hospitals, prisons, and on sea journeys). When the priest hears the sin of abortion confessed, he must determine whether a crime was truly committed by ascertaining certain facts from the penitent. If the answer is yes to any of the following questions, then the crime was not committed and the sin can be handled as usual.

1) Was it only an attempted abortion that did not succeed, or was it indirect?

> An example of an indirect abortion would be a hysterectomy when the intention was not to abort the fetus but only to remove a diseased uterus.

2) If the penitent was an accomplice to the abortion, would the crime have been committed without the accomplice's action or advice?

> For example, the doctor who directly procures the abortion might well incur the penalty; on the other hand, the assistance rendered by a nurse may not be so direct and decisive as to incur

148

the penalty. Or a parent who advises the abortion may have incurred the penalty if the daughter would not have acted without such advice.

3)   Was the penitent ignorant, through no fault of his or her own, that a penalty was attached to the law forbidding abortion?

It is not enough to know that abortion is a mortal sin. One must also know that a penalty is incurred, although precise knowledge about the nature of the penalty is not required to incur it.

4)   Was the penitent under 18 at the time the crime was committed?

5)   Was there inadvertence to or error of the law?

Had the penitent acted without recalling that this was an offense which resulted in a penalty? Did the penitent make a mistake about the law, e.g., thinking it applied only to the person having the abortion and not accomplices?

6)   Was it accidental and not intentional?

If the mother, e.g., intended to get an abortion, but accidentally had a fall which resulted in an abortion, she would not have incurred the penalty. It must be intentional with the result that an inviable fetus is aborted.

7)   Did the penitent have an imperfect use of reason?

For example, borderline mentally retarded, psychological disturbance, etc.

8)   Had the penitent acted out of serious fear, even if only relatively serious, or through necessity or serious inconvenience?

Was there, e.g., a serious fear about parental or societal reaction to a pregnancy? Was it a necessity, e.g., a doctor who performs an abortion to save the life of the mother?

9)   Did the penitent erroneously believe that one of the circumstances in n. 8 above was verified?

For example, did she think that having a child was a serious enough inconvenience in her circumstances to warrant an abortion when objectively it is not?

10) Did the penitent erroneously believe that the abortion was done in self-defense and therefore was justifiable?

> For example, if her life was in danger, did she think an abortion was an acceptable alternative?

11) Did the person procure the abortion while lacking the use of reason due to drunkenness or another mental disturbance which was culpable but not deliberately induced to commit or excuse the offense?

12) Was the abortion induced by a person in the serious heat of passion which was not voluntarily excited or fostered?

If the answer is yes to any one of these questions, the automatic censure of excommunication was not incurred. If the answer is no to ALL of the above questions, then the person has likely incurred an automatic excommunication. If that is the case, a bishop, an Ordinary, or a canon penitentiary (or his equivalent) can absolve the censure. However, if it would be hard on the penitent to remain in a state of serious sin during the time necessary for the competent superior to provide a remission, any confessor can remit the censure.

A good way to proceed is for the confessor to arrange for the penitent to return to him at an agreed upon time within the next month, notifying the penitent of the reason for this, namely, that he has the power only to absolve the censure temporarily but he must have recourse to someone who has the power for definitive remission. (The penitent can return either in confession or outside of it, although if he or she confesses behind the grille it should be presumed that anonymity is desired.) Before the penitent returns the confessor should request a remission from the local Ordinary, and if the confessor knows the penitent's identity, it should not be mentioned. When the penitent returns, the confessor informs the penitent of the remission.

> In some dioceses all confessors have the delegated faculty to remit the censure of abortion without recourse.

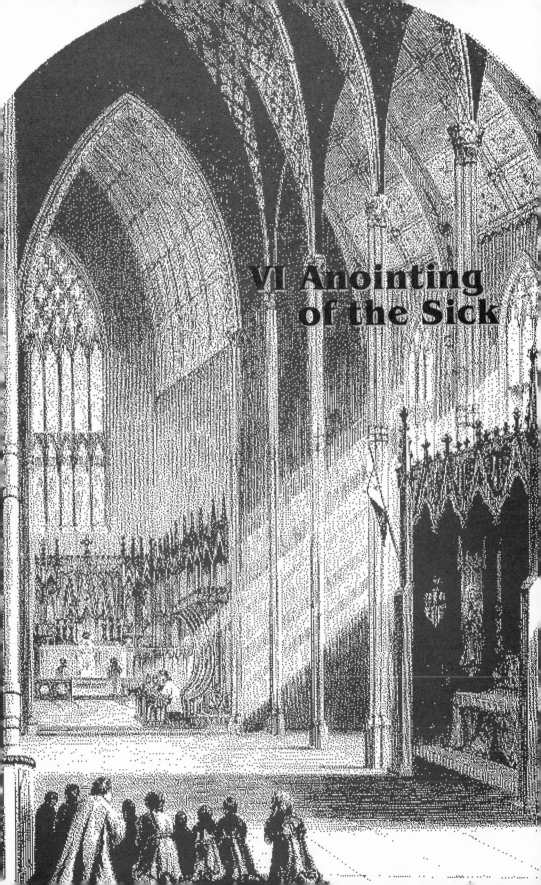

VI Anointing of the Sick

one
Celebration
of the Sacrament

A. The Liturgical Books

The anointing of the sick is conferred on seriously ill persons by anointing them with oil using the words prescribed in the liturgical books. (See can. 998.)

The liturgy for the sacrament is the 1972 *Rite of Anointing of the Sick*. In the dioceses of the United States, the approved rites are found in *Pastoral Care of the Sick; Rites of Anointing and Viaticum* of 1983 (PSC).

B. Matter and Form

The celebration of this sacrament consists especially in the laying on of hands by the priests of the Church, the offering of the prayer of faith, and the anointing of the sick with oil made holy by God's blessing. (See RA, 5)

The sacramental form for the anointing of the sick in the Latin church is: "Through this holy anointing may the Lord in his love and mercy help you with the grace of the Holy Spirit. May the Lord who frees you from sin save you and raise you up." (See RA, 25.)

The sick person is anointed on the forehead and on the hands. It is appropriate to divide the sacramental form so that the first part is said while the forehead is anointed, the latter part while the hands are anointed. (See RA, 23.)

The matter. The minister must use olive oil or some other plant oil which has been recently blessed by the bishop; he may not use old oil except in necessity. The pastor should obtain the sacred oils from his own bishop and keep them in a suitable place. (See can. 847.) Priests should make sure that the oil remains fit for use and should replenish it from time to time, either yearly when the bishop blesses the oil on Holy Thursday or more frequently if necessary. (See RA, 22.) Every priest may carry blessed oil with him so that, in case of necessity, he may administer the sacrament of anointing. (Can. 1003, §3)

> The remote matter is the blessed oil; the proximate matter is the anointing with the oil. According to the more common opinion, the blessing of the oil is necessary for the validity of the sacrament. (See Chiappetta, n. 3404.) The oil used for the anointing is the oil of the sick *(oleum infirmorum)*. For the lawful administration of the sacrament it is required that it be *recently* blessed, i.e., at the Chrism Mass most recently celebrated. However, if the new oils are not at hand, it is licit to use the old oils. After obtaining the new oils each year, the old oils are to be absorbed in cotton and burned. In necessity, the volume of blessed oil may be increased by adding new oil in lesser quantity, but this may not be done routinely for the sake of convenience. (See Congregation for Divine Worship and the Discipline of the Sacraments, reply, Apr. 18, 1994; *BCL Newsletter* 30 (1994) 32.)

C. Blessing of Oil

The oil of the sick ordinarily is blessed by the bishop at the Chrism Mass on Holy Thursday. Besides a bishop, those who can bless the oil to be used in the anointing of the sick are: (1) those who are equated in law with the diocesan bishop; and (2) any presbyter in case of necessity provided it is blessed during the celebration of the sacrament itself. (See can. 999; RA, 21.)

> A case of necessity for a presbyter to bless the oil would be, e.g., whenever a presbyter is celebrating the sacrament and oil blessed by the bishop is not at hand.

D. The Anointings

The anointings are to be carefully administered in accord with the words, order, and manner prescribed in the liturgical books. The sick person is anointed on the forehead and on the hands. It is appropriate to divide the sacramental form so that the first part is said while the forehead is anointed, the latter part while the hands are anointed. In case of necessity, it suffices that there be one anointing on the forehead or even on some other part of the body, while the entire sacramental form is said. (See can. 1000, §1; RA, 23.)

> A case of necessity would mainly involve the fear of conta-

gion from the hands or forehead; or it may be lack of time due to the large number of persons to be anointed, in which case a single anointing on the forehead would suffice.

Depending upon the culture and traditions of the place, as well as the condition of different peoples, the number of anointings and the place of anointing may be changed or increased. Provision for this should be made in the preparation of particular rituals. (RA, 24)

> *In the United States,* the priest may also anoint additional parts of the body, for example, the area of pain or injury. He does not repeat the sacramental form. (See PCS, 124.) If the anointing is to be an effective sacramental symbol, there should be a generous use of oil so that it will be seen and felt by the sick person as a sign of the Spirit's healing and strengthening presence. For the same reason, it is not desirable to wipe off the oil after the anointing. (See PCS, 107.)

The minister performs the anointings with his own hand, but for a serious reason he may use an instrument. (Can. 1000, §2)

> The anointings are made with the thumb in the form of a cross. In case of danger of contagion, extreme repugnance, or some other serious reason, the minister may use some instrument such as a ball of cotton attached to a small stick.

When two or more priests are present for the anointing of a sick person, one of them may say the prayers and carry out the anointings, saying the sacramental form. The others may take the remaining parts, such as the introductory rites, readings, invocations, or instructions. Each priest may lay hands on the sick person. (RA, 19; see also PCS, 108-10.)

E. Communal Celebrations

The communal celebration of anointing for a number of the sick at the same time may be held in accord with the prescriptions of the diocesan bishop. Those to be anointed must be suitably prepared and rightly disposed. (Can. 1002)

> The practice of indiscriminately anointing numbers of people on these occasions simply because they are ill or have reached an advanced age is to be avoided. Only those whose health is seriously impaired by sickness or old age are proper subjects for the sacrament. (See PCS, 108.)

F.   Place of Celebration

When the state of the sick person permits it, and especially when he or she is going to receive holy Communion, the anointing may be conferred within Mass, either in church or even, with the consent of the Ordinary, in some suitable place in the home of the sick person or in the hospital. (RA, 80)

> In light of can. 932, §1 which states that in necessity the Eucharist may be celebrated outside a sacred place, the permission of the Ordinary usually would not be necessary in this case. If the seriously sick person is unable to come to church for Mass, this in itself constitutes a case of necessity which would allow Mass to be celebrated outside a sacred place without further permission.
>
> Ordinarily the anointing of the sick is celebrated in church, at home, or in a hospital or other institution. In necessity it can be celebrated in any fitting place. The *Rite of Anointing* has three rites: the ordinary rite, the rite of anointing during Mass, and the celebration of anointing in a large crowd. In the United States the three rites have been adapted and are called anointing outside Mass, anointing within Mass, and anointing in a hospital or institution.

two
Roles and Ministries

A. The Community

It is especially fitting that all baptized Christians share in this ministry of mutual charity within the Body of Christ by doing all that they can to help the sick return to health, by showing love for the sick, and by celebrating the sacraments with them. Like the other sacraments, these too have a community aspect, which should be brought out as much as possible when they are celebrated. (RA, 33)

> Because of its very nature as a sign, the sacrament of the anointing of the sick should be celebrated with members of the family and other representatives of the Christian community whenever this is possible. (See PCS, 99.)

B. Family and Friends

The family and friends of the sick and those who take care of them in any way have a special share in this ministry of comfort. If the sickness grows worse, the family and friends of the sick and those who take care of them have the responsibility of informing the pastor and by their kind words of prudently disposing the sick for the reception of the sacraments at the proper time. (See RA, 34; can. 1001.)

C. The Minister

Any priest, and only a priest, validly administers the anointing of the sick. All priests who are entrusted with the care of souls have the duty and right to administer the anointing of the sick to the faithful committed to their pastoral office. This duty is ordinarily exercised by bishops, pastors and parochial vicars, chaplains, seminary rectors, and superiors in clerical institutes. For a reasonable cause, any other priest can administer this sacrament with at least the presumed consent of the proper priest mentioned above. Every priest may carry blessed oil with him so that, in case of necessity, he may administer the sacrament of the anointing of the sick. (See cans. 1003; 262; 530, 3°; 566; RA 16.)

> The priest should ensure that the abuse of delaying the reception of the sacrament does not occur, and that the celebration takes place while the sick person is capable of active participation. (See PCS, 99.)

Eastern law. In churches in which it is the custom to administer the sacrament of anointing of the sick by several priests at the same time, care should be taken, as far as possible, to preserve this custom. (CCEC, can. 737, §2)

> In some Eastern churches the sacrament, from ancient tradition, can be administered by more than one priest simultaneously as, for instance, in the Byzantine rite, by three, five, or seven priests. (See Pospishil, 315.)

three
Recipient of Anointing

A. Eligibility for Reception

The anointing of the sick may be administered to the faithful who have the use of reason and begin to fall into danger as a result of illness or old age. Great care and concern should be taken to see that those of the faithful whose health is seriously impaired by sickness or old age receive this sacrament. (See can. 1004, §1; RA, 8.)

Among those who may be anointed, the ritual mentions in particular: those undergoing surgery whenever a serious illness is the reason for the surgery; elderly people if they have become notably weakened even though no serious illness is present; sick children if they have sufficient use of reason to be strengthened by this sacrament. (See RA, 10-12.)

A prudent or reasonably sure judgment, without scruple, is sufficient for deciding on the seriousness of an illness; if necessary a doctor may be consulted. (See RA, 8.)

> The serious condition for the anointing could be due to a disease, wound, accident, notable weakness of old age, etc. One who is in danger of death due to some external cause cannot be anointed, e.g., a soldier before battle, a criminal awaiting execution. (See Mathis/Bonner, 174.)

In public and private catechesis, the faithful should be educated to ask for the sacrament of anointing and, as soon as the right time comes, to receive it with full faith and devotion. They should not follow the wrongful practice of delaying the reception of the sacrament. All who care for the sick should be taught the meaning and purpose of the sacrament. (RA, 13)

It is a serious mistake to wait too long, perhaps until the advanced stages of a disease, to anoint a sick person. As soon as the sick person *begins* to be in danger is the fitting time for the anointing.

The anointing may be administered to sick persons who at least implicitly asked for it when they were in control of their faculties. (Can. 1006)

Implicit requests for anointing include the cases of those who ask that a priest be summoned, or declare that they wish to die as a Christian, or give some other sign of repentance. They very likely would have asked for the sacrament, if in life they had faithfully fulfilled the duties of a Christian, or even if they had not always been faithful in these duties, they did not altogether neglect them. In practice, the intention of receiving the sacrament of anointing of the sick is presupposed in all Catholics until the contrary is proven. (See Genicot 2, n. 427.)

On the other hand, those who have neglected their religion entirely and have refused the ministration of the priest, if they gave no sign of repentance before becoming unconscious, cannot be anointed because they lack the intention which is requisite for the validity of the sacrament.

The anointing of the sick should not be administered to those who obstinately persist in manifest serious sin. (Can. 1007)

A manifest sin is one that is publicly known, even if only by a few. Obstinate persistence implies that the person neglects to heed the teachings of the Church or the warnings of ecclesiastical authority. The clearest case of such obstinate persistence in manifest serious sin is the person with an imposed or declared censure who refuses reconciliation by having the censure remitted. If such persons are unconscious and have given no previous sign of repentance, they may not be anointed. If they are conscious and ask for the sacrament, they may not be anointed unless the censure is remitted. In danger of death, all censures may be remitted by means of the sacrament of penance. (See can. 976.)

Another case is a notorious criminal or other public sinner who refuses reconciliation and gives no sign of repentance. Such persons may not be anointed.

One reason for the requirement of this law is the necessity of the recipient having the proper disposition for the sacrament. Ordinarily one should not presume that a person who is divorced and remarried does not have the proper disposition or had given no sign of repentance. Often the divorced and remarried may have repented of past sins but are unable to quit the second invalid union due to moral obligations to spouse and children. Perhaps they are making use of the approved form of the internal forum solution. Thus, in doubt about their disposition, they may and should be anointed.

B. Doubt about Eligibility

If there is doubt whether the sick person has the use of reason, is seriously ill, or is dead, the sacrament may be administered. (Can. 1005)

> There is no longer a provision for conditional anointing; the sacrament is to be administered with the usual form. The 1972 *Rite of Anointing,* n. 15 spoke of conditional anointing (also in the 1983 U.S. version). However, this was changed after the code was promulgated. (See *Notitiae* 20 (1983) 552.)
> A person who once had the use of reason but lost it due to sickness, old age, or other reason may always be anointed, even if there is no doubt that they lack the use of reason. The requirement of the use of reason applies only to infants and others who have never had the use of reason. (See CLSA Comm., 710.)

When a priest has been called to attend a person who is already dead, he should pray for the dead person, asking that God forgive his or her sins and graciously receive him/her into his kingdom. The priest is not to administer the sacrament of anointing. (See RA, 15.)

> Conditional anointing of certainly dead persons is forbidden. Instead the priest or other minister should say the prayers for the dead found in the ritual.

C. Repetition of the Sacrament

The anointing of the sick may be repeated if the sick person has become better and again falls into a serious illness or, if during the same illness, a more serious crisis develops. (Can. 1004, §2)

> A person may be anointed again whenever there is a new serious illness after recovery from a previous serious illness, or if during a protracted illness the patient's condition appreciably worsens. If there is any doubt whether this worsening of condition constitutes a more serious crisis, the sacrament may be celebrated. The law excludes frequent anointings during the same illness even if the patient's condition is gradually deteriorating. Traditional canonical opinion holds that in such cases the person should not be anointed again unless a notable time has elapsed.

(See Noldin 3, n. 448.) In view of this canon, however, this does not mean that the sacrament should be administered on some regular basis, such as monthly, to the ill person, without any reference to the progress of the illness. (See CLSA Comm., 710.)

VII Holy Orders

one
Candidates for Ordination

A. Requirements for Ordination

Capability. Only a baptized male validly receives sacred ordination. (Can. 1024).

Free choice. For anyone to be ordained, he must have due freedom; it is absolutely wrong in any way or for any cause to force someone to receive orders, or to prevent someone from receiving it who is canonically suitable. (Can. 1026)

Prerequisites. Candidates for the diaconate and presbyterate are to be formed by careful preparation in accord with the norm of law. (Can. 1027) Candidates for the presbyterate may be promoted to the diaconate only after the completion of a five year curriculum of philosophy and theology. (Can. 1032, §1) Candidates are to have an integral faith, be motivated by the proper intention, endowed with the requisite knowledge, enjoy a good reputation, have moral probity and proven virtues, and other physical and psychic qualities appropriate to the order to be received. (See can. 1029.)

Only those who have received the sacrament of confirmation may licitly be promoted to orders. (Can. 1033) Before diaconate can be received, a member of a religious institute must have made perpetual profession; a member of a society of apostolic life must have been definitively incorporated in the society. (See cans. 266, §2 and 1052, §2.)

Each nation is to prepare its own plan for priestly formation in accord with the *Ratio Fundamentalis Institutionis Sacerdotalis* of 1970 and the *Code of Canon Law,* canons 232-64. The particular law in the United States is the *Program of Priestly Formation,* 4th ed. (Washington: USCC, 1993).

Age. Those to be ordained transitional deacons, that is, deacons who are preparing for the presbyterate, must be at least 23 years of age. A permanent deacon who is celibate must be at least 25; a married deacon must be at least 35 and have the consent of his wife. A candidate for the presbyterate must be at least 25. The episcopal conference can establish a higher age for the presbyterate and permanent diaconate. Age requirements can be dispensed by the Holy See, or by the diocesan bishop if the candidate is no more than one year younger than the requisite age in the universal law. (See can. 1031.)

> *Eastern law.* A deacon may be ordained at 23; a presbyter may be ordained at age 24, unless the particular law of the church *sui iuris* requires an older age. In cases where a candidate for ordination is more than a year younger than the required age, the patriarch may dispense if the candidate resides within the territory of the patriarchal church; otherwise the Apostolic See may dispense. (See CCEC, can. 759.)
>
> *In the United States,* the minimal age for both celibate and married deacons is 35. (See NCCB, *Permanent Deacons in the United States: Guidelines on Their Formation and Ministry,* 3rd ed., n. 66b (Washington: USCC, 1985.)

Ministries and intervals. Those who are preparing for orders must first be inscribed as a candidate by means of the liturgical rite of admission to candidacy. Members of religious institutes are exempt from this requirement. (See can. 1034.) Candidates are also to receive the ministries of lector and acolyte and exercise them for a suitable period of time. Between the conferral of acolyte and diaconate there should be an interval of at least six months. (See can. 1035.) A transitional deacon is to exercise his diaconal order for a suitable period of time as determined by the bishop or competent major superior. (See can. 1032, §2.) This interval is to be at least six months in duration. (See can. 1031, §1.)

> Although the ministry of lector is usually conferred before acolyte, it is not contrary to law to reverse the order. The diocesan bishop is competent to dispense from the requirements of the intervals. *In the United States* there is also a six month interval between the institution of lector and that of acolyte in order for the reader or acolyte to exercise the ministry received; either the bishop or the major superior may dispense from this interval in accord with the requirements of the NCCB. (See NCCB requirements, Nov., 1972; CLD 8:630.)
>
> *Eastern law.* Each church *sui iuris* may have its own law con-

cerning minor clerics below the rank of deacon. (See CCEC, can. 327.) The Byzantine tradition and some of the other churches *sui iuris* have retained the minor orders of lector-cantor and subdeacon. (See Pospishil, 205.)

Petition and retreat. In order that a candidate may be promoted to the order of deacon or presbyter, he is to make a declaration to his own bishop or major superior, written and signed in his own handwriting, that testifies that he is to receive the sacred order on his own accord and with freedom and that he will devote himself perpetually to the ecclesiastical ministry, and likewise requesting that he be admitted to the order. (Can. 1036) All those who are to be promoted to any order are to make a retreat for at least five days in a place and in the manner determined by the Ordinary. (See can. 1039.)

> The petition is required of all candidates for the orders of deacon and presbyter (including permanent deacons). The retreat requirement also includes those to be ordained bishops.

Promise of celibacy. Those to be promoted to the permanent diaconate who are not married and likewise those to be promoted to the presbyterate are not to be admitted to the order of deacon unless they shall have publicly assumed the obligation of celibacy before God and the Church by the prescribed rite. (See can. 1037.) Those who have professed a vow of perpetual chastity in a religious institute are also bound to make this public manifestation of celibacy. (*De Ordinatione Episcopi, Presbyterorum et Diaconorum* (1990), n. 177; hereafter RO for Rite of Ordination.)

> The promise of celibacy is part of the rite of ordination to the diaconate (n. 200 in the Latin version). The 1990 revised rite of ordination derogated from canon 1037 of the code which had exempted religious in perpetual vows from making this public promise of celibacy.

B. Simple Impediments and Irregularities

They are prohibited from receiving orders who are affected by any impediment whether it is perpetual, which comes under the name of an irregularity, or it is simple. However, no impediment is contracted unless it is contained in the code. (See can. 1040.)

> An impediment is some fact or quality about a person that prevents him from being licitly ordained. There are two kinds: (1) An irregularity is an impediment that is perpetual in nature, due

either to a defect or a delict. (2) A simple impediment is one that can cease, e.g., a man whose wife dies is no longer impeded from presbyteral orders.

Irregularities. The following persons incur an irregularity preventing their ordination:

1) one who has any kind of insanity or other psychic infirmity which, after consulting experts, is judged to incapacitate him from properly functioning in the ministry;

2) one who has committed the delict of apostasy, heresy, or schism;

3) one who attempted marriage, even if only a civil marriage, either while he was impeded from entering marriage due to a pre-existent matrimonial bond or by reason of sacred ordination or a public, perpetual vow of chastity, or if he attempted marriage with a woman who was already in a valid marriage or who herself was restricted by a perpetual vow of chastity;

4) one who committed intentional homicide or who has effectively procured an abortion as well as all who cooperated positively in an abortion;

5) one who has gravely and maliciously mutilated himself or another person, or who has attempted to take his own life;

6) one who has performed an act of orders reserved to those who are in the order of the episcopacy or presbyterate while he either lacked that order or had been prohibited its exercise by some declared or inflicted canonical penalty. (See can. 1041.)

There are also canonical penalties which can be incurred or imposed for the commission of the delicts mentioned in nn. 2, 4, 5 and 6. See canons 1364; 1397; 1398; 1378, §2; and 1384.

Simple impediments. The following are simply impeded from receiving orders:

1) a man having a wife, unless he is going to be ordained to the permanent diaconate;

2) one who has an office or administrative position which is forbidden to clerics by canons 285 and 286 for which he must render an account; the impediment binds until he is has become freed of the position by resigning from it and rendering an account of it;

3) a neophyte unless, in the judgment of the Ordinary, he is sufficiently proven. (See can. 1042.)

A man who obtains an annulment or dissolution of marriage no longer is bound by the impediment mentioned in n. 1. Canons

285 and 286 are given in the section below on the obligations and rights of clergy. *In the Eastern Catholic churches,* marriage is not an impediment to orders.

A neophyte is an adult who recently received the sacraments of initiation, but for purposes of this canon it should also include anyone already baptized who has recently been received into full communion with the Catholic Church. (See CLSA Comm., 731.)

The faithful are obliged before ordination to reveal to the Ordinary or pastor any knowledge they may have of impediments to holy orders. (Can. 1043) *In the Eastern Catholic churches* it is required that the names of candidates for sacred ordination be made known publicly in the parish church of each candidate. (See CCEC, can. 771, §1.)

Irregularities to the exercise of an order. The following clerics are irregular as to the exercise of orders already received:

1) one who unlawfully received orders while he was affected by an irregularity to receiving orders;

2) one who committed the delict of apostasy, heresy, or schism, if the delict was public;

3) one who committed the delicts in canon 1041, nn. 3, 4, 5, and 6. (Can. 1041, §1)

Impediments to the exercise of an order. The following are impeded from the exercise of an order already received:

1) one who unlawfully receives orders when he was prevented by an impediment to the reception of orders;

2) one who is afflicted with insanity or another psychic infirmity, as stated in canon 1041, n. 1, until the Ordinary, having consulted an expert, permits the exercise of the order. (Can. 1044, §2)

Ignorance of irregularities and impediments does not exempt from them. (Can. 1045)

Dispensations. The Ordinary may dispense from irregularities and impediments which are not reserved to the Holy See. (Can. 1047, §4)

In cases not reserved to the Holy See, the Ordinary who may dispense is the proper Ordinary of the cleric or candidate, namely, the major superior for members of clerical religious institutes or societies of apostolic life of pontifical right, and the local Ordinary for all others. The Ordinary in question should also take note of canons 1046, 1048, and 1049.

A dispensation from all irregularities is reserved to the Apostolic

See alone if the fact on which they are based has been brought to the judicial forum. A dispensation from irregularities and impediments to receiving orders is also reserved to the Holy See as follows:

1) from the irregularities arising from the public delicts mentioned in canon 1041, nn. 2 and 3;

2) from the irregularity arising from the delict, whether public or occult, mentioned in canon 1041, n. 4;

3) from the impediment mentioned in canon 1042, n. 1.

Also reserved to the Apostolic See is the dispensation from the irregularities to the exercise of orders received which is mentioned in canon 1041, n. 3, but only in public cases, and in the same canon, n. 4, even in occult cases. (Can. 1047, §§ 1-3)

> Dispensation from an irregularity which has been brought before a judicial forum is reserved to the Apostolic See. The judicial forum could be either secular or ecclesiastical. It would seem that the case must be accepted by the judge for trial before one could say that the case has been brought before the judicial forum. If the judge does not accept the petition, there is no judicial case. (See cans. 1505 and 1506.)

C. Documents and Inquiry

Before a bishop may proceed to an ordination which he is doing in his own right, he himself must be certain that the documents mentioned in canon 1050 have been furnished and that, following the inquiry prescribed by law, the suitability of the candidate has been proved through positive arguments. (Can. 1052, §1)

> Canon 1050 requires that the following be documented before a person is promoted to sacred orders: (1) that the studies required by law were successfully completed; (2) that the candidate for the priesthood has been first ordained a deacon; (3) in the case of ordination to the diaconate, that baptism and confirmation have been received and the ministries of lector and acolyte have been received; (4) that the declaration and petition of the candidate have been completed as required in canon 1036; (5) in the case of a married man being ordained a deacon, that his marriage was celebrated and that his wife consents to his ordination.
>
> Canon 1051 deals with the inquiry into the qualities of the ordinand as required by law. It says the rector of the seminary or house of formation is to supply certification of the qualities required for receiving the order, namely, sound doctrine, genuine piety, good morals, aptitude for exercising the ministry and, after the proper investigation, the state of his physical and psychological health.

When a bishop is going to ordain some other Ordinary's subjects, it is sufficient that the dimissorial letters refer to the fact that the necessary documentation is all in order, and that the inquiry has been made in accord with the law and the candidate has been found worthy. If the ordinand is a member of a religious institute or a society of apostolic life, the dimissorial letters must also testify that he has professed perpetual vows in the institute or has been definitively incorporated in the society, and also that he is a subject of the superior who is providing the dimissorials. (See can. 1052, §2.)

A dimissorial is a letter written by one's Ordinary to the ordaining bishop attesting that all the requirements for ordination have been met. The ordaining bishop himself does not have to see all the necessary documentation, provided the Ordinary assures him that everything is in order as required above. He can then proceed to the ordination unless he has certain reasons for doubting the suitability of the candidate. (See can. 1052, §3.) For further rules regarding the dimissorial letter, see canons 1018-23.

two
Celebration of Ordination

A. Matter and Form

The matter necessary for the validity of ordination is the imposition of hands by a validly ordained bishop on the head of the candidate. The form necessary for validity is a part of the consecratory prayer as prescribed for the ordinations of bishops, presbyters, and deacons in the rites of ordination. (See can. 1009, §2; see also RO, 6-7.)

> The essential form for the ordination of deacons are the words: "Lord, send forth upon them the Holy Spirit, that they may be strengthened by the gift of your sevenfold grace to carry out faithfully the work of the ministry."
>
> For presbyters, the form is: "Almighty Father, grant to these servants of yours the dignity of the priesthood. Renew within them the Spirit of holiness. As co-workers with the order of bishops may they be faithful to the ministry that they receive from you, Lord God, and be to others a model of right conduct."
>
> For bishops: "So now pour out upon this chosen one that power which is from you, the governing Spirit whom you gave to your beloved Son, Jesus Christ, the Spirit given by him to the holy apostles, who founded the Church in every place to be your temple for the unceasing glory and praise of your name." (See Paul VI, apostolic constitution *Pontificalis Romani recognitio,* June 18, 1968, AAS 60 (1968) 369-73; DOL 2609-11; see also RO, 187, 112, 25.)

B. Time and Place

An ordination is to be celebrated during a solemn Mass on a Sunday or holy day, but for pastoral reasons it can be done also on other days, not excluding ferial days. (Can. 1010; RO, 9) Excluded days are the paschal triduum, Ash Wednesday, all of Holy Week, and All Souls Day. (See RO, 109; 184.)

> If an ordination is held on a solemnity or on a Sunday in Advent, Lent, or the Easter season, or during Easter week, the Mass texts are taken from these days, and the vestments' color is proper to the season. On other days the ritual Mass for ordination may be used, and the vestments' color is white. (See RO, 110, 185; 117, 192.) If the ordination is celebrated on a Sunday or during the Easter season, all present except the prostrated ordinands stand during the singing of the litany of the saints; otherwise they kneel.

Ordinarily an ordination is celebrated in the cathedral church; however, for pastoral reasons it can be celebrated in another church or oratory. The clergy and other members of the faithful are to be invited to the ordination so that the greatest number can participate. (Can. 1011) The ordination of deacons and presbyters may also be held in the churches of those communities from which one or several of the candidates came, or in some other church of significance. If those to be ordained are from a religious community of any kind, the ordination can be held in a church of their community in which they will exercise their ministry. (RO, 108-09; 182)

> The words "religious community of any kind" indicate that the law is not speaking only about religious institutes in the strict sense, but also of societies of apostolic life, personal prelatures, and other clerical societies that have the right of incardinating clergy.

C. Registration and Certificate

After the ordination the names of each of the ordained, the name of the ordaining minister, and the place and date of the ordination are to be recorded in a special book diligently kept in the curia of the place of ordination. All documents of each ordination are to be carefully preserved. The ordaining bishop should give to the newly ordained an authentic certificate of ordination. If they have been promoted through dimissorial letters by a bishop other than their own, they are to show the certificate to their own Ordinary for the purpose of recording the ordination in a special book kept in the archives. (Can. 1053)

The local Ordinary, in the case of secular clergy, or the competent major superior, in the case of his own subjects, should send notice of each ordination celebrated to the pastor of the place of baptism of the newly ordained; the pastor is to record it in the baptismal register in accord with canon 535, §2.

three
Incardination
and Excardination

A. Incardination

Every cleric must be incardinated in some particular church, personal prelature, institute of consecrated life, or society that has the faculty to incardinate; acephalous or transient clerics are in no way acceptable. (Can. 265)

> Incardination is the word for the act by which a legal bond involving mutual rights and obligations is established between a cleric and some diocese or other particular church, religious institute, or other group of clergy. Clerics cannot be "free agents" in the Catholic Church. They will only be ordained if some juridic person, as above, sponsors them and permits their ordination to the diaconate. Once ordained, they must always remain connected with that juridic person, or become incardinated elsewhere, in order to remain clerics in good standing. "Acephalous" means "headless;" all clerics must have some "head," some Ordinary to whom they are responsible. Nor may clergy be transient, independently wandering from place to place looking for work in the ministry without sponsorship.
>
> The commentary that follows will use "diocese" in place of the less familiar "particular church," but it should be understood as including the other particular churches mentioned in canon 368.
>
> *The Eastern code* uses the term "enrollment" *(ascriptio)* instead of incardination, but juridically they are equivalent terms. (See CCEC, cans. 357-66.)

Through ordination to the diaconate one becomes a cleric and is incardinated in a particular church or a personal prelature for whose service he is ordained. A perpetually professed member of a religious institute and a definitively incorporated member of a clerical society of apostolic life is incardinated by diaconal ordination as a cleric in that institute or society, unless, in the case of a society, the constitutions provide otherwise. A member of a secular institute is incardinated by diaconal ordination in a particular church for whose service he is ordained, unless he be incardinated in the institute itself by virtue of a concession of the Apostolic See. (Can. 266)

These rules are variations on the same theme: a man becomes a cleric when he is ordained a deacon, and he is incardinated when he is ordained a deacon. Note that members of secular institutes generally are incardinated in a diocese, not in the institutes unless they have been granted this favor by the Apostolic See.

B. Excardination

In order for an already incardinated cleric to become validly incardinated in another particular church, he must obtain a letter of excardination signed by his diocesan bishop; likewise, he must obtain a letter of incardination from the diocesan bishop in whose particular church he desires to be incardinated. Excardination thus granted does not take effect unless incardination is obtained in another particular church. (Can. 267)

Excardination is the act of dissolving the legal bond between a cleric and his diocese or other clerical society. Excardination occurs only upon incardination elsewhere, or by the loss of the clerical state. Thus the firm rule against acephalous clergy is safeguarded in law. Ordinarily, incardination in the new diocese only occurs after a period of probation, which may not exceed five years. This law also applies to personal prelatures.

Excardination is granted only for just reasons, but may be denied only for serious causes. (See can. 270.) Just causes may be the good of the Church or for the cleric's own good. John E. Lynch, C.S.P. gives some examples of just causes: The cleric's "talents may be better utilized in another diocese because either greater opportunities are offered or because his ministry has become inefficacious through loss of reputation. Health reasons warranting a more favorable climate, for example, would certainly be legitimate. It may even happen that an animosity between the cleric and his bishop suggests a change. Long years of service spent in the host diocese has also been recognized as sufficient... Examples of unjust or unworthy reasons would be ambition or avarice. In cases of restlessness or instability, counselling is to be recommended; a transfer will simply postpone facing the problem." (CLSA Comm., 196.)

C. From One Diocese to Another

A cleric who has lawfully moved from his own particular church to another one is incardinated by the law itself in this particular church after five years there; this occurs provided the cleric has manifested in writing his desire to excardinate both to the diocesan bishop where he now is and to his own diocesan bishop, and neither of them has opposed it in writing within four months of having received the cleric's letter. (Can. 268, § 1)

> This canon addresses the case of a cleric who moves from his own diocese to some other diocese with the intention of incardinating there. (It also applies to personal prelatures.) If the cleric has written to the bishop of his former diocese and to the bishop where he has moved, and if neither one opposes in writing his move, then he is incardinated in the new diocese by the law itself after he has been there for five years. The letter can be written at any time: at the beginning of or any time during the five year period. It is not necessary that the cleric be given a ministerial assignment, but only that he legitimately resides in the new diocese for five years. (See Apostolic Signatura, sentence, June 27, 1978, *Communicationes* 10 (1978) 152-58; CLD 9:52-60.)

D. From a Diocese to an Institute or Society

By perpetual or definitive admission in an institute of consecrated life or in a society of apostolic life a cleric who, in accord with the norm of canon 266, §2, is incardinated in that institute or society, is excardinated from his own particular church. (Can. 268, § 2)

> This rule addresses the case of a secular cleric who becomes a member of an institute of consecrated life or a society of apostolic life. In the case of religious, the cleric becomes incardinated in the religious institute by the profession of perpetual vows. For societies of apostolic life, the secular cleric becomes incardinated by definitive incorporation in the society. A secular cleric who joins a secular institute remains incardinated in his own diocese, unless the Holy See has granted the secular institute the faculty of incardinating clergy. For further rules on incardination and excardination, see canons 269-72.

E. From an Institute or Society

If a clerical member of an institute of consecrated life or society of apostolic life requests an indult of departure from the institute or society, the indult is not granted before he finds a bishop who will incardinate him into the diocese or at least receive him for a probationary period. If he is received on probation, he is incardinated in the diocese by the law itself after five years, unless the bishop has refused him. (See cans. 693, 727, and 743.)

These rules address the case of a member of a religious or secular institute or a society of apostolic life who wishes to incardinate in a diocese or other particular church. If he is a perpetually professed religious, a perpetually or definitively incorporated member of a secular institute that has the faculty of incardinating, or a definitively incorporated member of a society of apostolic life, he must obtain the necessary permissions before he can seek incardination in a diocese. (See cans. 691-92, 727-28, and 742-43.) He is excardinated from the institute or society at the time of his acceptance by the bishop, or after five years by the law itself unless the bishop has refused him within those five years.

A member of an institute of consecrated life or society of apostolic life may also transfer to another institute of consecrated life or society of apostolic life. If the member is a cleric, incardination in the new institute or society occurs when the member is perpetually professed in the religious institute or perpetually or definitively incorporated in the secular institute or definitively incorporated in the society of apostolic life. The laws on transfer are found in canons 684-85, 730, and 744.

four
Obligations and Rights of Clergy

The obligations and rights of clerics are given in canons 273-89. The obligations are listed below in categories according to their degree of binding force. The obligations listed in the first category are the strongest because the verbs used in the canons are strongly preceptive. The second category are negative subjunctive commands that prohibit specific activities by clerics. The third category are exhortations; these are positive subjunctive commands that speak about ideal, generalized patterns of behavior that clerics should strive to emulate. The fourth category consists of recommendations.

A. Strongest Obligations

1) *Obedience.* Clerics are bound by a special obligation to show reverence and obedience to the Supreme Pontiff and to their own Ordinary. (Can. 273)

2) *Fidelity to duties.* Unless they are excused by a legitimate impediment, they are bound to undertake and faithfully fulfill a duty (*munus*) that has been entrusted to them by their Ordinary. (Can. 274, §2)

3) *Sanctification.* Clerics are especially bound to pursue holiness in leading their lives because they are consecrated to God in orders by a new title as stewards of the mysteries of God in the service of his people. (Can. 276, §1)

4) *Divine office.* Priests as well as deacons preparing for the priesthood are bound by obligation to celebrate daily the liturgy of the hours in accord with the proper and approved liturgical books. (Can. 276, §2, 3°)

5) *Retreat.* Likewise they are bound to make a retreat as prescribed by particular law. (Can. 276, §2, 4°)

6) *Celibacy.* Clerics are bound by obligation to observe perfect and perpetual continence for the sake of the kingdom of heaven, and therefore to observe celibacy, which is a special gift of God, by which sacred ministers can more easily remain close to Christ with an undivided heart and can more freely dedicate themselves to the service of God and humanity. (Can. 277, §1)

Violations of celibacy can be penalized. See canons 1394, §1 and 1395.

B. Prohibited Acts and Activities

1) *Certain associations.* Clerics are to refrain from establishing or participating in associations whose purposes or activity cannot be reconciled with the obligations proper to the clerical state or which could hinder the diligent fulfillment of their duty committed to them by the competent ecclesiastical authority. (Can. 278, §3)

On this issue, the Congregation for the Clergy declared: "It is the right and duty of the competent ecclesiastical authority to see to it that clerics refrain from establishing or joining associations or unions of any kind whatever which are not compatible with the priestly state.... As a matter of fact, whoever acts against the legitimate prohibitive prescription of the said competent authority, can be punished with a just penalty, not excluding censures, but with the requirements of the law observed. (See declaration, n. V, Mar. 8, 1982, AAS 84 (1982) 642; CLD 9:17.)

2) *Unlawful absence.* Even if they do not have a residential office, nevertheless clerics are not to leave their diocese for a notable time, as determined by particular law, without at least the presumed permission of their Ordinary. (Can. 283, §1)

Examples of offices requiring residence are pastor and parochial vicar.

3) *Anything unbecoming.* Clerics are to refrain completely from everything that is unbecoming to their state, in accord with the prescripts of particular law. (Can. 285, §1)

4) *Anything alien.* Clerics are to avoid whatever is alien to their state, even if it is not unbecoming to it. (Can. 285, §2)

5) *Civil offices.* Clerics are prohibited from assuming public

offices which entail participation in the exercise of civil power. (Can. 285, §3)

6) *Secular financial obligations.* Without the permission of their Ordinary, clerics are not to become agents for goods belonging to laypersons nor to assume secular offices which entail the obligation to render an account. They are prohibited from acting as surety, even on behalf of their own goods, without consulting their own Ordinary. Likewise, they are to refrain from signing promissory notes whereby they undertake the obligation to pay an amount of money with no determined reason. (Can. 285, §4)

> On this norm John Lynch comments that its purpose is "to safeguard clerical decorum and to prevent distractions that would detract from ministerial performance. [Clerics] are not to manage the money or property of lay men. They need permission, therefore, to be guardians of children, executors of wills, or trustees of funds. They would, of course, be permitted to do so in case of relatives for whom they are responsible. They must also have authorization to hold secular offices for which they are accountable, such as in a savings bank, a cooperative, or a charitable association." (See CLSA Comm., 225.)

7) *Business and trade.* Whether by themselves or through others, whether for their own benefit or another's, clerics are prohibited from engaging in business or trade without the permission of the legitimate ecclesiastical authority. (Can. 286)

> Clerics who violate this canon can be punished with a canonical penalty whose gravity is in keeping with the gravity of the offense. (See can. 1392.) In doubt whether something constitutes prohibited business or trade, the cleric should consult his own Ordinary to see whether the cleric needs permission.

8) *Political parties and labor unions.* Clerics are not to take part actively in political parties and in the direction of labor unions unless, in the judgment of the competent ecclesiastical authority, it is required to protect the rights of the Church or to promote the common good. (Can. 287, §2)

9) *Military service.* Clerics and also candidates for holy orders are not to volunteer for the military without the permission of their Ordinary, since military service is not compatible with the clerical state. (Can. 289, §1)

> Service as a chaplain in the armed forces is compatible with

the clerical state, but other military roles are not. Permission of one's Ordinary is, nevertheless, needed to be a military chaplain.

Permanent deacons are not bound by nn. 5, 6, 7, and 8 above unless particular law determines otherwise. (See can. 288.)

C. Exhortations

1)   *Fraternity.* Clerics are to be united among themselves by the bond of fraternity and prayer, since they all work toward the same purpose, the building up of the body of Christ; they are to strive for cooperation among themselves in accord with the prescripts of particular law. (Can. 275, §1)

2)   *Mission of laity.* Clerics are to acknowledge and promote the mission which the laity exercise in their own way in the Church and in the world. (Can. 275, §2)

3)   *Pastoral ministry.* They are faithfully and untiringly to fulfill the duties of the pastoral ministry. (Can. 276, §2, 1°)

4)   *Spiritual nourishment.* They are to nourish their spiritual life from the twofold table of sacred scripture and the Eucharist. (Can. 276, §2, 2°)

5)   *Permanent deacons* are to celebrate that part of the liturgy of the hours as determined by the episcopal conference. (See can. 276, §2, 3°.)

> *In the United States,* "permanent deacons should not hold themselves lightly excused from the obligation they have to recite morning and evening prayer." (See NCCB, *Permanent Deacons in the United States: Guidelines on Their Formation and Ministry,* 3rd ed., n. 97 (Washington: USCC, 1985). Thus, permanent deacons in the U.S. have a binding obligation to say morning and evening prayer.

6)   *Spiritual practices.* Clerics are to be conscientious in devoting time regularly for meditation, going frequently to the sacrament of penance, cultivating a special veneration to the Virgin Mother of God, and using other ordinary and special means of sanctification. (Can. 276, §2, 5°)

7)   *Prudence.* Clerics are to conduct themselves with due prudence in associating with persons whose company could be a danger to their obligation to observe continence or could cause scandal to the faithful. (Can. 277, §2)

8)   *Continuing education.* Clerics are to continue to pursue sacred studies, even after ordination to the priesthood; they are to adhere to

that solid teaching rooted in sacred scripture, which has been handed down by their predecessors and commonly received by the Church, as determined especially in the documents of the councils and popes; and they are to avoid profane novelties of expression and false science. In accord with the prescripts of particular law, priests are to attend pastoral lectures after ordination to the priesthood; and, at times required by particular law, to attend other lectures and theological meetings or conferences which afford the occasion to acquire a fuller knowledge of the sacred sciences and of pastoral methods. They are also to seek a knowledge of the other sciences, especially those which are connected with the sacred sciences, particularly insofar as they benefit the exercise of the pastoral ministry. (Can. 279)

9)   *Lifestyle.* Clerics are to cultivate a simple style of life and to refrain from anything which smacks of vanity. (Can. 282, §1)

10)   *Attire.* Clerics are to wear appropriate ecclesiastical dress in accord with the norms of the conference of bishops and legitimate local customs. (Can. 284)

> *Permanent deacons* are not bound by this norm unless particular law determines otherwise. (See can. 288.)

11)   *Peace and justice.* Clerics are always to foster as much as possible among people the observance of peace and harmony based on justice. (Can. 287, §1)

12)   *Civil exemptions.* Clerics are to make use of those exemptions from exercising duties and public civil offices alien to the clerical state which laws and agreements or customs grant in their favor, unless in particular cases their own Ordinary has decreed otherwise. (Can. 289, §2)

D. Recommendations

1)   *Daily Eucharist.* Priests are earnestly invited to offer daily the Eucharistic sacrifice and deacons to participate daily in that same oblation. (See can. 276, §2, 2°.)

> Canon 904 says daily celebration or concelebration of the Eucharist by priests is "earnestly recommended" *(enixe commendatur).*

2)   *Associations of secular clergy.* The secular clergy are to hold in high esteem those associations in particular which, having statutes recognized by competent authority and which, by a suitable and appropriately approved rule of life and by fraternal support, they fos-

ter holiness in the exercise of the ministry and promote the unity of the clergy with one another and with their bishop. (Can. 278, §2.)

Although this norm is literally an exhortation, it only asks that the secular clergy hold priestly associations in high esteem. It is placed in this category because there is an implied recommendation or suggestion that secular clerics consider joining such an association.

3)   *Communal life.* Some kind of communal life is highly recommended to clerics; wherever it exists it is to be maintained as far as possible. (Can. 280.)

4)   *Surplus income.* They should want to use for the good of the Church and for works of charity those goods which they receive on the occasion of exercising an ecclesiastical office and which are in excess of what is needed for their decent support and the fulfillment of all the duties of their state. (Can. 282, §2.)

This, too, is an exhortation, but so attenuated ("they should want to use") that its force has more the character of a recommendation.

The Eastern code has a number of differences from the Latin code in respect to clerical obligations, but the similarities between the two are greater. (See CCEC, cans. 367-93.) Three differences will be mentioned by way of example: (1) Since celibacy is not an obligation, one canon speaks of a special obligation of married clergy: "In leading family life and raising their children, married clerics should provide an outstanding example to other members of the faithful." (CCEC, can. 375) (2) Another canon exhorts clerics to avoid controversies of any kind, but if they do arise, they should be referred to the forum of the Church. (See CCEC, can. 389.) (3) Canon 393 exhorts clerics to care for all the churches and to serve wherever there is great necessity, showing willingness to volunteer for the missions or regions with a shortage of clergy.

E. **Rights of Clergy**

1)   *Ecclesiastical offices.* Only clerics are able to obtain offices for whose exercise is required the power of orders or the power of ecclesiastical governance. (Can. 274, §1)

Some examples of offices that can only be held by priests include episcopal vicar, judicial vicar, vicar general, pastor, and parochial vicar. Qualified priests and deacons can be judges in church tribunals. A lay person can serve as judge as part of a judicial college with two other judges who are clerics. (See can. 1421, §2; see also cans. 129 and 145.)

2)   *Association.* It is the right of secular clerics to associate with others to pursue purposes befitting their clerical status. (Can. 278, §1)

3)   *Salary, insurance, pension.* When clerics dedicate themselves to the ecclesiastical ministry, they deserve the remuneration that befits their condition, in accord with the nature of their duties and with the conditions of time and place; it should provide for the necessities of their life and for the equitable remuneration of those whose services they need. Likewise, provision is to be made for them to have that social assistance by which their necessities are provided for if they suffer from illness, incapacity, or old age. (Can. 281) Married deacons who devote themselves full time to the ecclesiastical ministry deserve a remuneration which can provide for their sustenance and that of their family. (See can. 281, §3.)

> Married deacons who receive a salary from a secular job are not entitled to remuneration for their service to the Church. (See can. 281, §3.)

4.   *Vacation.* Clerics are entitled to a due and sufficient annual vacation, as determined by universal or particular law. (Can. 283, §2)

Loss of the Clerical State

Sacred ordination, once validly received, never becomes invalid. Nevertheless, a cleric loses the clerical state: (1) by a judicial sentence or administrative decree which declares the invalidity of sacred ordination; (2) by the penalty of dismissal lawfully imposed; (3) by rescript of the Apostolic See, which is granted by the Apostolic See only for serious reasons in the case of deacons and very serious reasons in the case of presbyters. (Can. 290)

Holy orders, like baptism and confirmation, confers an indelible character. (See can. 845.) A man validly ordained cannot cease to be a cleric, but he can lose the clerical state. The first way mentioned in the canon that he can lose the clerical state is by a judicial sentence or administrative decree which declares that his ordination was invalid in the first place, that he never truly was ordained. (See cans. 1708-12.)

The second way is penal dismissal. Crimes for which a cleric can be dismissed from the clerical state are given in canons 1364, §2; 1367; 1370, §1; 1387; 1394, §1; and 1395, §§ 1, 2. The penalty can only be imposed after a judicial trial before a collegiate tribunal of three judges. (See cans. 1336, §1, 5° and 1425, §1, 2°_.)

The third way that the clerical state is lost is by rescript of the Apostolic See. Known as laicization, this is a favor that may or may not be granted by the Apostolic See, depending on the cleric's condition, age, and reasons for requesting laicization.

Except for the case in canon 290, n. 1, the loss of the clerical state does not bring with it a dispensation from the obligation of celibacy, which is granted only by the Roman Pontiff. (Can. 291)

If a man's ordination has been declared invalid, he is free to marry in the Church. However, the other two ways of losing the clerical state—by penal dismissal or by laicization—do not in themselves dispense from the obligation of celibacy. That requires a dispensation specially reserved to the pope. Even in danger of death or other emergencies, this dispensation is restricted by law to the pope. (See can. 87, §2.)

A cleric who loses the clerical state in accord with the norm of law loses along with it the rights proper to the clerical state, and he is no longer bound to the obligations of the clerical state, except for celibacy. He is prohibited from exercising the power of order, without prejudice to canon 976. By the very fact of the loss of the clerical state he is deprived of all offices, functions and any delegated power. (See can. 292.)

One who loses the clerical state can no longer function as a cleric; he loses his rights as a cleric, and is no longer bound to clerical obligations except celibacy, unless he receives a dispensation from the pope. However, the law itself supplies him the faculty to hear the confession of a person in danger of death. (See can. 976.)

A cleric who has lost the clerical state is unable again to be enrolled among the clergy except by rescript of the Apostolic See. (Can. 293)

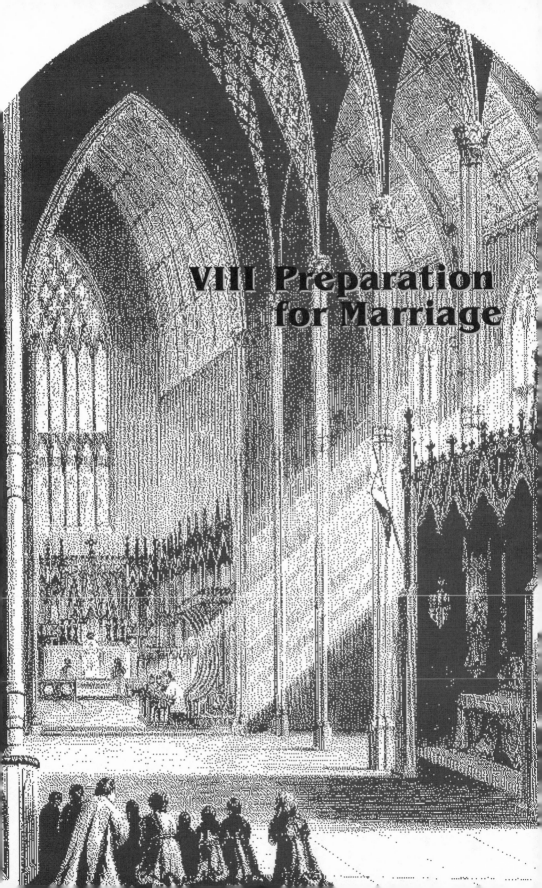

VIII Preparation for Marriage

Jurisdiction Over Marriage

A revised rite of marriage was promulgated by the Holy See
in 1990. It is this Latin version that will be cited whenever reference is made to the *Rite of Marriage* (RM).

A. Marriage of One or Two Catholic Parties

The marriage of Catholics, even if only one party is Catholic, is regulated not only by divine law, but also by canon law, without prejudice to the competence of the civil authority concerning the merely
civil effects of the marriage. (Can. 1059)

> The Church claims authority over the marriage of a Catholic
> and a non-Catholic, even a non-sacramental marriage involving a
> non-baptized spouse. Thus, whenever at least one party is Catholic,
> the Catholic canon law must be followed. To be sacramental, or
> ratified, both parties must be baptized, whether Catholic or non-
> Catholic. Canon law accepts the jurisdiction of the state regarding
> the civil effects of marriage, e.g., the requirement of a marriage
> license, although the lack of a license would not affect the validi-
> ty of a Catholic marriage as far as the Church is concerned. *In the
> United States*, it is usually sufficient for the civil validity of a mar-
> riage if the couple obtain a marriage license before the church
> wedding; some states, however, have special rules about who can
> perform the marriage ceremony.
>
> *Inter-ecclesial (inter-ritual) Marriages.* Inter-ecclesial mar-
> riages involving two Catholics of different ritual churches (e.g., a
> Latin Catholic and a Ukrainian Catholic) are governed by the laws
> of both churches. Both parties must be free of all diriment impedi-
> ments (whether relative or absolute) as specified by the law of

both churches *sui iuris* before the parties can marry validly. Dispensations, if needed, are obtained from the local Ordinary of the parish which the couple approached for marriage, unless the dispensation only affects one party, e.g. age, in which case the dispensation is obtained from that party's Ordinary. (See Pospishil, 374.)

B. Marriage of a Catholic and a Baptized Non-Catholic

Without prejudice to the divine law, the marriage between a Catholic party and a baptized non-Catholic party is also regulated by: (1) the law proper to the church or ecclesial community to which the non-Catholic party belongs, if this community has its own marriage law; and (2) the law which binds the non-Catholic party if the ecclesial community to which he or she belongs does not have its own marriage law. (CCEC, can. 780, §2)

> Although this law is found in the Eastern and not in the Latin code, it should be seen as suppletory law for the Latin church because it establishes a fundamental principle of law as established by the common supreme legislator of all the Catholic churches, the pope. This rule reflects ecumenical sensitivity, but is also necessary for legal clarity. A baptized non-Catholic who marries a Catholic is also subject to the marriage law of his or her church or ecclesial community, if it has a marriage law. If it does not have its own marriage law, then the church or ecclesial community is subject to the laws of the state. For example, Eastern non-Catholic churches consider marriage a sacrament, and have their own marriage law. In case of conflict between the two laws, the law of the church prevails in which the couple marries. For example, if a Latin Catholic woman marries an Eastern Orthodox man in his church, the blessing of the priest is needed for validity. But if that same marriage took place in the Latin Church, it could be validly performed by a deacon who has the faculty to assist at marriages.
>
> On the other hand, Protestants generally do not consider marriage a sacrament and usually do not have their own marriage law. When two Protestants marry, canon law recognizes that they marry validly if they observe the divine law and the laws of the state, provided any such laws are not contrary to the divine law, such as the divine law of indissolubility, the necessity of giving true consent to marriage, the impediment of impotence, et al. (See can. 22.)
>
> *The marriage of the unbaptized.* When two unbaptized persons marry, the Church claims no jurisdiction and the parties are

bound by the laws of the state, or by their own religion if the state recognizes the force of that religion's marriage law (e.g. Islamic law in many countries), provided these laws are not contrary to the divine law. However, Church law does come into play when a divorced, unbaptized person now wants to marry a Catholic. The unbaptized party has the right to present a petition for annulment or dissolution of his or her previous marriage, to be judged by application of the divine law as it is understood by the Catholic Church. (Cf. cans. 1143, 1476.)

To sum up: (1) Canon law binds whenever there is a marriage involving at least one Catholic party. (2) If there are two Catholic parties, but from separate churches *sui iuris* (e.g. Latin and Ruthenian), the canon law of both churches is applicable. (3) The marriage of non-Catholic Christians is governed by the laws of their own church or ecclesial community or, if they do not have such laws, by the laws of the state. (4) The marriage of the unbaptized are regulated by the laws of the state, including laws of a religion that may be recognized by the state. (5) All marriages are subject to the divine law as it is understood by the Catholic Church; all marriages, even between two non-Catholics, must be free of divine law impediments and the marriage consent must be freely and validly given.

t w o
Catechetical
and Spiritual Preparation

A. Duties of Ministers and Catechists

Pastors of souls are bound to see to it that their own ecclesial community offers assistance to the faithful by which the married state is preserved in its Christian spirit and progresses toward perfection. This assistance should be offered especially by:

1) preaching and catechesis adapted to minors, young people, and adults, and also by the use of other means of communication, so that the faithful are instructed on the meaning of Christian marriage and on the duty of spouses and Christian parents;

2) personal preparation for entering marriage by which the couple is disposed for the holiness and duties of their new state;

3) a fruitful liturgical celebration of marriage, which brings out the fact that the spouses signify and participate in the mystery of unity and fruitful love between Christ and the Church;

4) help offered to married persons, that by faithfully observing and protecting the conjugal covenant, they may grow day by day toward a holier and fuller family life. (Can. 1063; see also RM, 14.)

This canon addresses three stages of formation for marriage. The first is remote preparation, a regular program of instruction on Christian marriage given to students and adults as part of their catechetical program. The second stage, addressed in nn. 2 and 3, treats the immediate preparation of the engaged couple and the liturgical celebration of marriage, which itself discloses the nature of marriage in the Church. The third stage is ongoing assistance to married couples so that their marital life may truly reflect the love between Christ and his Church.

192

The preparation for and celebration of marriage, which especially concerns the future spouses themselves and their families, pertains by reason of pastoral care and the liturgy to the bishop, to the pastor and his vicars, and, at least in some fashion, to the whole church community. (RM, 12)

Pastoral ministers (*pastores*), guided by the love of Christ, should first of all strengthen and nourish the faith of those about to be married, for the sacrament of marriage presupposes and demands faith. (RM, 16)

The engaged couple should be given a review of the fundamentals of Christian doctrine. This should include catechesis both on the doctrine concerning marriage and the family, and on the sacrament and its rites, prayers, and readings, so that they may be able to celebrate it consciously and fruitfully. (RM, 17)

On the preparation for marriage, Pope John Paul II wrote: "The immediate preparation for the celebration of the sacrament of matrimony should take place in the months and weeks immediately preceding the wedding so as to give a new meaning, content, and form to the so-called premarital inquiry required by canon law. This preparation is not only necessary in every case, but is also more urgently needed for engaged couples who still manifest shortcomings or difficulties in Christian doctrine and practice....

"Although one must not underestimate the necessity and obligation of the immediate preparation for marriage—which would happen if dispensations from it were easily given—nevertheless such preparation must always be set forth and put into practice in such a way that omitting it is not an impediment to the celebration for marriage." (See apostolic exhortation on the family, *Familiaris consortio,* n. 66, Dec. 15, 1981, AAS 74 (1982) 165; translation in *On the Family* (Washington: USCC, 1982, pp. 65–66.)

The pope makes it clear that immediate preparation of the engaged couple for marriage is highly desirable, and pastoral ministers are obliged to offer such preparation to help the couple grow in faith and celebrate the sacrament with the proper disposition. However, he equally makes it clear that the omission of this catechesis is not a reason for denying a Catholic the right to a wedding in the Church. There may be good reasons for omitting or modifying the catechesis depending on the circumstances of the couple, e.g., a couple who are entering a second marriage after the death of a spouse or after an annulment; a couple who live at a great distance from each other while attending college or serving in the military; a couple whose work schedules make it difficult or impossible for one or both to attend the regular catechetical program; etc. On the other hand, the pastoral minister must be cautious if the reason for omitting preparation is due to the couple's hostility to the Church from causes such as atheism, agnosticism, bias, or an obnoxious personality. Such hostility could be a sign that one or both parties might lack the necessary disposition to consent validly to Christian marriage.

Faith and disposition. If, in spite of all efforts, engaged couples show that they reject openly and expressly what the Church intends when it celebrates the marriage of the baptized, pastors of souls are not permitted to admit them to the celebration. Although he might find it disagreeable, the minister must take note of the situation and tell those concerned that in these circumstances it is not the Church that is trying to prevent the celebration but rather it is they themselves. (RM, 21)

Because a Catholic has a right to a wedding in the Catholic Church, the above law must be interpreted strictly. (See can. 18.) That means all the terms of the law must be applicable before a couple could be denied the right to marry. They must *openly* and *expressly* reject some essential doctrine of marriage, e.g., that a marriage between the baptized is a sacrament, that it is indissoluble, that it requires fidelity to each other, etc. Such erroneous beliefs and intentions can be uncovered in the course of marital preparation, especially by means of the pre-nuptial investigation. If, after instruction and admonition, either party continues to reject the Church's teaching with such vehemence that they will not consent to a marriage as the Church intends it to be, then they should be told that their marriage will be deferred until they have acquired the proper disposition.

Since Christian worship, in which the common priesthood of the faithful is exercised, is a work that proceeds from faith and is rooted in faith, sacred ministers should zealously strive to arouse and enlighten faith, especially by the ministry of the word, through which faith is born and is nourished. (Can. 836)

The ministry of the word includes preaching and catechesis as well as other forms of evangelization. (See can. 761.) The period of preparation for marriage has as an important goal the growth of the engaged couple's faith, so that their marriage liturgy will be more fruitful and their living out of the sacrament of marriage will be grace filled, rooted in the love that Christ has for his Church.

The obligation of the law is placed on the minister to arouse and enlighten faith; not on the parties to demonstrate the sufficiency of their faith. A Catholic may not be denied a church wedding merely because one or both parties do not regularly attend Mass. They should be exhorted to be faithful to their Christian responsibilities, but their failure to live up to these duties does not cancel their right to a marriage in church. On this point, Pope John Paul II has taught: "In fact, the faith of the person asking the Church for marriage can exist in different degrees, and it is the primary duty of pastors to bring about a rediscovery of this faith and to nourish it and bring it to maturity. But pastors must also understand the reasons that lead the Church to admit to the celebration of marriage those who are imperfectly disposed.... It must not be forgotten that these engaged couples by virtue of their baptism are already really sharers in Christ's marriage covenant with the Church, and that, by their right intention, they have accepted God's plan regarding marriage and therefore, at least implicitly, consent to what the Church intends to do when she celebrates marriage." (*Familiaris consortio,* 68.)

B. Reception of Confirmation, Penance, Eucharist

Catholics who have not yet received the sacrament of confirmation should receive it before being admitted to marriage, if it can be done without serious inconvenience. (Can. 1065, §1; see also RM, 18.)

> In the Latin church, a presbyter must receive the faculty from the diocesan bishop to confirm an adult who was baptized as an infant. (See can. 884, §1.) If an unconfirmed Latin Catholic is marrying an Eastern Catholic, the Eastern Catholic priest may validly confirm the Latin Catholic. (Pospishil, 394)

If it is foreseen that the conditions for a fruitful reception of confirmation cannot be satisfied, the local Ordinary will judge whether it is better to defer confirmation until after marriage. (RConf, 12)

In order for the sacrament of marriage to be received fruitfully, it is highly recommended that the parties receive the sacraments of penance and the holy Eucharist. (Can. 1065, §2; see also RM, 18.)

> The engaged couple cannot be compelled to receive the sacraments before marriage, but they should be encouraged. They should be reminded that they are obliged to confess any serious sins they may have before receiving the sacraments of Eucharist and marriage. The pastoral experience of many priests suggest that the wedding rehearsal is not a suitable time to schedule the sacrament of penance for the wedding party due to the various other pressures and concerns the bridal party has at that time. They could be told to approach the sacrament of penance the week before their wedding when they would be able to celebrate it with greater reflection and devotion.

three
Pre-marital Investigation

A. General Principles

All persons are able to contract marriage unless they are prohibited by law. (Can. 1058) Ordained ministers may not refuse the sacraments to those who ask for them under suitable circumstances, who are properly disposed, and who are not prohibited by law from receiving them. (Can. 843, §1)

> In virtue of these canons, as well as the general right of the faithful to receive the sacraments (can. 213), ministers should not deny a Catholic marriage celebration to a couple unless they have some legal basis for doing so, whether that basis exists in universal or particular law.

Before a marriage is celebrated, it must be evident that nothing prevents its valid or licit celebration. (Can. 1066) The one who assists at marriage acts illicitly unless he has established according to the norm of law the free status of the parties. (See can. 1114.)

> The pastoral minister can best be assured of the validity and liceity of marriage celebrations by carefully following the premarital preparation programs and policies of their particular church as well as by observing the norms of universal law. The principal proof of a party's freedom to marry is a baptismal certificate issued within six months of the date of marriage because the baptismal certificate will have notations regarding enrollment in a church *sui iuris*, confirmation, possible prior marriage, an annulment, religious profession, or ordination. If a previous

marriage was annulled, the pastoral minister should check with the local Ordinary or tribunal to determine whether a prohibition was attached to a future marriage in the Church. If it was, the marriage may not licitly be celebrated until the prohibition has been lifted by the local Ordinary.

The faithful. Before the celebration of a marriage, all the faithful who know of any impediments are bound to reveal them to the pastor or local Ordinary. (Can. 1069)

If knowledge of an impediment comes from hearing or overhearing a sacramental confession, the impediment cannot be revealed. (See cans. 983-84.) However, the confessor should admonish the party that he or she cannot marry validly unless that impediment ceases or is dispensed.

The one who assists. If someone other than the pastor is to assist at the marriage and conducts the investigation, that person as soon as possible should notify the pastor of the results by means of an authentic document. (Can. 1070)

The pastor is ultimately responsible for seeing that the premarital investigation is conducted even if he does not do it personally. When someone outside the parish handles the investigation or, for that matter, any other aspects of the preparation for marriage, the proper pastor should be notified by means of an authentic document, i.e., one that is signed, dated, and sealed if possible.

The pastor of the Catholic party is responsible for the premarital catechesis and investigation. If both parties are Catholic, the pastors of both are competent. Usually that pastor who is first approached by the parties for the wedding must undertake this responsibility.

The episcopal conference may establish regulations for the examination of the parties as well as for the marriage banns or other suitable means for carrying out the investigation which is necessary before marriage. After these regulations have been diligently followed, the pastor [or other official witness] may proceed to assist at the marriage. (Can. 1067)

The universal law does not require marriage banns, but leaves such regulations to the episcopal conference. *In the United States,* the National Conference of Catholic Bishops has left it to each diocese to make its own regulations governing marriage banns and the pre-marital investigations and preparation. (Plenary session, Nov., 1984) Hence, particular law must be followed in all of these matters.

In danger of death, if other proofs are unavailable, it suffices, unless there are contrary indications, that the parties affirm, even under oath if the case calls for it, that they are baptized and are not prevented by an impediment. (Can. 1068)

> In danger of death of one or both parties, the usual pre-marital preparation is not required. The danger of death refers to probable danger from either extrinsic causes (e.g., war, natural disasters, execution) or intrinsic causes (e.g. serious illness, wounds, etc.) on the part of either or both parties. (See CLSA Comm., 752.) This exception regarding danger of death may apply in other cases, e.g., political refugees who are unable to obtain the requisite proofs regarding their freedom to marry due to circumstances beyond their control. (See Pospishil, 390.)

B. Cases Requiring the Local Ordinary's Permission

In addition to the permission needed for mixed marriages, canon 1071, §1 requires the permission of the local Ordinary to assist at a marriage involving the following persons:

1)   *Transients* (*vagi*), i.e., those who have no domicile or quasi-domicile. (Can. 1071, §1, 1°) If the parties have a month-long residence in the parish, it is not necessary to get the local Ordinary's permission. (See can. 1115.)

> Particular law in many places requires a specified period of preparation longer than one month. In such cases the permission of the local Ordinary will be needed to dispense from the obligation of the particular law in question.

2)   Those whose marriage cannot be recognized or celebrated according to the civil law. (Can. 1071, §1, 2°)

> Among the impediments of many civil law jurisdictions are prior marriage, lack of minimum age, blood relationship within specified degrees, severe mental disorder, adoptive relationship, and venereal disease. Ordinarily, such civilly prohibited marriages should not be celebrated by the Church until the impediment ceases or the marriage is allowed by court order. (See CLSA Comm., 753-54.) In any case, the local Ordinary's permission is always required for such marriages except in necessity.

3)   Those bound by natural obligations towards another party or towards children from a previous union. (Can. 1071, §1, 3°)

Natural obligations toward a former spouse would include a serious illness or financial need that may impose some moral obligation to assist the former spouse. There also may be legal obligations such as the payment of alimony and child support. The minister conducting the pre-marital investigation should inquire about this matter whenever the party's prior marriage had been invalid or was dissolved and the former spouse is still living or the children of the previous union are still minors.

4)   A person who has notoriously rejected the Catholic faith. (Can. 1071, §1, 4°) The local Ordinary should not grant permission to assist at the marriage of one who has notoriously rejected the Catholic faith unless the regulations of canon 1125 are observed, making appropriate adaptations. (See can. 1071, §2.)

For a rejection of the Catholic faith to be notorious, it is not enough that it is be the private, occult act of the person, but it must be known publicly. (See Chiappetta, n. 1017.) Notorious rejection of the faith means public rejection, namely, the case either of a person who has formally joined another religion, or when the person no longer considers him or herself a Catholic, and this is known by family, friends, etc. Such a person may be hostile to the Catholic faith and could pose a danger to the spouse who is a practicing Catholic. Thus, this marriage is treated like a mixed marriage. The declaration and promise on the part of the (practicing) Catholic party and the other requirements of canon 1125 are to be observed as given below. N.B. Permission of the local Ordinary is not necessary in the case of a person who has not practiced the Catholic faith without notoriously rejecting it; however, special pastoral attention, such as additional catechesis, may be necessary for such persons.

5)   A person who is bound by a censure. (Can. 1071, §1, 5°)

Those bound by the censures of excommunication and interdict are prohibited from celebrating or receiving the sacraments and sacramentals. (See cans. 1331, §1, 2° and 1332.) Therefore, in the case of a sacramental marriage involving two baptized persons, the local Ordinary could not give permission for such a marriage until the censure is remitted. Even in the case of a non-sacramental marriage between a non-baptized person and a Catholic who has a declared or inflicted censure, it seems highly inappropriate for the local Ordinary to grant permission for such a marriage until the censure has been remitted. The requirement of the local Ordinary's permission is best seen as a provision of the law to ensure that the necessary steps are taken to have the censure remitted before the celebration of the marriage.

In the case of a person who has notoriously abandoned the Catholic faith, he or she might have incurred the penalty of automatic excommunication due to the crime of apostasy, heresy, or schism. (See can. 1364, §1.) The excommunication is not incurred, however, if the person was unaware that a penalty was attached to the crime. (See can. 1324, §1, 9° and 1324, §3.) Therefore, if a baptized Catholic has joined another religion, intending to leave the Catholic Church but unaware of the censure, now wants to marry a Catholic in the Church, it can be permitted by the local Ordinary. However, if the censure was knowingly incurred, marriage should not be permitted until the excommunicated party goes to confession and returns to the practice of the Catholic faith.

6)   A minor [under 18], when the parents are unaware of the marriage or when they are reasonably opposed to it. (Can. 1071, §1, 1°) Pastoral ministers should see to it that young people are prevented from marrying before the age which is customary in the region. (Can. 1072)

A boy under 16 or a girl under 14 may not marry validly. However, even those older than these ages should be dissuaded from marrying if they are younger than the usual age in the region. The civil law should also be consulted, for many civil jurisdictions require the permission of the parents for the marriage of minors. Particular law should also be observed since episcopal conferences can establish a higher age for liceity. (See can. 1083, §2.)

Except in necessity, no minister without the permission of the local Ordinary may perform the marriage ceremony of a person under 18 whose parents are unaware of it or opposed to it. Even if only one party is a minor, such a case must be referred to the local Ordinary. The pastor or other minister should interview the parents of the minor party when they are opposed to the marriage to determine what their reasons are, and should make a recommendation to the local Ordinary who determines whether the marriage can proceed or should be delayed. Although not required by universal law, it is wise to seek the judgment of the local Ordinary in all marriages where the minister doubts the maturity of one or both parties, even when the parents do not oppose the marriage. Many particular churches have marriage preparation programs that detect such immaturity, and have policies that should be followed, including counselling and the possible delay of marriage.

7)   A proxy as provided in canon 1105. (Can. 1071, §1, 1°)

A proxy marriage is one in which one or both parties are represented by someone else who has been mandated in accord with canon 1105. Since proxies should only be allowed in extraordinary circumstances, the permission of the local Ordinary for such marriages is necessary except in necessity such as danger of death.

The above seven cases indicate special problems when the local Ordinary's intervention is required by law. However, there may be other circumstances, not mentioned in the law, when it would be appropriate to consult the local Ordinary before proceeding with a marriage, e.g., an immature couple who appears to want to get married solely because of a pre-marital pregnancy, a couple who seems seriously deficient in their communication with each other, a couple who appears to want to marry in church solely to please a parent, etc.

In a case of necessity, it is not necessary to get the local Ordinary's permission before proceeding to assist at the marriage of any of the above. (See can. 1071.)

A case of necessity would include danger of death or some other serious necessity according to the circumstances. Extra-marital pregnancy does not constitute a sufficient reason to proceed without the local Ordinary's permission, but rather is a circumstance calling for even greater preparation for marriage to ensure readiness for a lifetime commitment. The necessity for proceeding without permission must clearly outweigh the dangers that may arise in each case. (See CLSA Comm., 755-56.)

four
Mixed Marriages

In the strict sense of the term, a mixed marriage is one between a Catholic and a baptized non-Catholic. In the broad sense, it includes marriages between a Catholic and a non-baptized. The former require permission of the competent authority for the liceity of the celebration. The latter require a dispensation from the impediment of disparity of cult for the validity of the marriage. The following rules also apply in the case of a Catholic who wishes to marry a Catholic who has notoriously abandoned the faith. (See can. 1071, §2.)

A. Permission Needed to Marry a Baptized Non-Catholic

Without the express permission of the competent authority, marriage is prohibited between two baptized persons, one who was baptized in the Catholic Church or was received into it after baptism and who has not left it by a formal act, and the other who belongs to a church or ecclesial community which does not have full communion with the Catholic Church. (Can. 1124)

The local Ordinary is the competent authority to grant permission. It may be the local Ordinary of the Catholic party or of the place where the marriage is being celebrated. It could even be the local Ordinary of the place where the Catholic party is staying temporarily. The local Ordinary may also delegate others, even habitually, to grant this permission. Some dioceses, as part of the diocesan faculties, routinely allow the pastor or the priest or deacon who assists at marriage to grant this permission.

B. Declaration and Promise of Catholic Party

The local Ordinary can grant permission for a mixed marriage if there is a just and reasonable cause. (See can. 1125.)

> A just and reasonable cause includes negative reasons, such as the danger of a civil marriage or defection from the faith, and also positive reasons such as the couple's awareness of the responsibilities of a sacramental marriage, their commitment to their respective churches, their maturity and other strengths. (See CLSA Comm., 802.) Particular churches often provide convenient forms so that the minister need only check the appropriate reason or reasons. Despite the routine granting of such permission, the minister should see to it that the engaged couple has considered the implications for their marriage of their different faiths, and should take account of any disagreements or conflicts. If such disagreements are serious and cannot be resolved, the minister should not proceed with the marriage, or he may recommend that the permission of the local Ordinary not be granted.

The local Ordinary should not grant permission for a mixed marriage, or grant a dispensation from a disparity of cult marriage (cf. can. 1086, §2), unless the following conditions are fulfilled:

1) The Catholic party declares that he or she is prepared to remove dangers of falling away from the faith and makes a sincere promise to do all in his or her power to have all the children baptized and brought up in the Catholic Church. (Can. 1125, 1°) The episcopal conference may establish regulations governing the manner in which these declarations and promises, which are always required, are to be made, and it may define the way in which they are to be proven in the external forum and made known to the non-Catholic party. (Can. 1126)

> Broad interpretation of this requirement is necessary because the permission for a mixed marriage should be considered as a favor which protects the natural right to marry the person of one's choosing. Hence, it may be necessary, as when the Catholic is reluctant to make the promise, to explain to the parties the broad meaning of the phrase, "to do all in one's power." In fact, there may be times when the Catholic party is not able to have the children baptized and raised Catholic. Perhaps the faith of the non-Catholic is stronger; or perhaps the insistence that all the children be baptized and raised Catholic will be disruptive to the marriage. In such cases one is required to do only what is in one's power to do, even if the children in the end may not be baptized and raised Catholic.
> The 1993 Directory for Ecumenism is instructive on this point:

"In carrying out this duty of transmitting the Catholic faith to the children, the Catholic parent will do so with respect for the religious freedom and conscience of the other parent and with due regard for the unity and permanence of the marriage and for the maintenance of the communion of the family. If, notwithstanding the Catholic's best efforts, the children are not baptized and brought up in the Catholic Church, the Catholic parent does not fall subject to the censure of canon law. [See can. 1366.] At the same time, his or her obligation to share the Catholic faith with the children does not cease. It continues to make demands, which could be met, for example, by playing an active part in contributing to the Christian atmosphere of the home; doing all that is possible by word and example to enable the other members of the family to appreciate the specific values of the Catholic tradition; taking whatever steps are necessary to be well informed about his or her own faith so as to be able to explain and discuss it with them; praying with the family for the grace of Christian unity as the Lord wills it." (See DE, 151; see also n. 150.)

In the United States. The declaration and promise are made in the presence of a priest or deacon either orally or in writing as the Catholic prefers. The promise must be sincerely made. If the priest or deacon has reason to doubt the sincerity of the promise made by the Catholic, he may not recommend the request for the permission or dispensation and should submit the matter to the local Ordinary. (See NCCB, Statement on the Implementation of the Apostolic Letter on Mixed Marriages, Nov. 16, 1970; CLD 7:730–40.)

2)   The other party is to be informed at a suitable time of the Catholic party's promises so that it is clear that the non-Catholic is truly conscious of the promise and obligation of the Catholic party. (Can. 1125, 2°)

The suitable time for informing the non-Catholic party of the Catholic's promise is to be determined by the circumstances, but it should be done before the marriage so that any problems it may cause can be discussed and resolved ahead of time. Frequently it is best to discuss the requirements of canon 1125 and the implications of a mixed marriage with both parties together so that an attitude of openness and dialogue on the important subject of religion are there from the beginning.

In the United States. At an opportune time before marriage, and preferably as part of the usual pre-marital instructions, the non-Catholic must be informed of the promises and of the responsibility of the Catholic. No precise manner or occasion of informing the non-Catholic is prescribed. It may be done by the priest, deacon, or the Catholic party. No formal statement of the non-Catholic is required. But the mutual understanding of this question beforehand should prevent possible disharmony that might otherwise arise during married life. (NCCB Statement, loc. cit., n. 8)

3)   Both parties are to be instructed on the ends and essential properties of marriage which are not to be excluded by either party. (Can. 1125, 3˚)

This requirement can be satisfied for the most part by observing the preparation program of the particular church. It is important to note that the non-Catholic party does not have to believe in the Church's doctrine on the ends and essential properties of marriage, but may not exclude them by a positive act of the will. For example, a non-Catholic groom may believe that divorce and remarriage are acceptable, but he must intend to enter this marriage with this Catholic woman for life.

IX Impediments to Marriage

Impediments in General

A. Division

A diriment impediment renders a person incapable of contracting marriage validly. (Can. 1073) Only the supreme authority of the Church can declare authentically when the divine law prohibits or invalidates marriage. It is also the right of the supreme authority alone to establish other impediments for the baptized. (Can. 1075) A custom which introduces a new impediment or which is contrary to existing impediments is reprobated. (Can. 1076)

Impediments are of *divine law or of ecclesiastical law*. Prior bond, impotence, and consanguinity in the first degree of the direct line (marriage between a parent and child) are considered with certainty as impediments of the divine law; consanguinity in other degrees of the direct line and in the second degree of the collateral line (brother and sister) is at least treated as if it were of the divine law because it too is never dispensed. Divine law impediments bind everyone and cannot be dispensed; ecclesiastical impediments bind only Catholic marriages, even marriages involving only one Catholic. Canon law also recognizes the binding force for the marriage of non-Catholics of civil law impediments. N.B. Before November 27, 1983, when the revised code took effect, even baptized non-Catholics were bound to canon law, and thus subject to ecclesiastical impediments. Marriages which were contracted before this date are subject to the former law.

Canon 1075, §2 states that the supreme authority may establish ecclesiastical impediments for the baptized. While the Church therefore has the power to establish impediments for all the baptized, in keeping with the principle of canon 11 which states that merely ecclesiastical laws bind only Catholics, the "baptized" here should be understood as referring in practice to baptized Catholics.

Eastern law. The particular law of an Eastern Catholic church *sui iuris* may establish diriment impediments in addition to those in the Eastern code; however, it may do so only for a serious reason and after consulting eparchial bishops of other churches *sui iuris* who may have an interest in it and also consulting the Apostolic See. (See CCEC, can. 792.)

A *public* impediment is one that can be proved in the external forum; otherwise it is an *occult* impediment. (Can. 1074)

Possibility of proof in the external forum exists when the impediment can be proved by an authentic document or by two witnesses giving concordant testimony of things of which they have personal knowledge, or by the testimony of an official in reference to matters pertaining to his office, e.g., a pastor asserting he assisted at a certain marriage; also by the testimony of experts or by the confession of the party made in court. Note however that proof in the external forum must be not only theoretically possible but also practically, i.e., in the concrete case the impediment can be proved. (See Vermeersch/Creusen, 2:297.)

A case is to be considered occult if the impediment is by nature public but is in fact occult. (See CodCom, Dec. 28, 1927; AAS 20 (1928) 61; CLD 1:503.) Thus an impediment which is public by nature (because it arises from a fact which is in itself public), e.g., consanguinity, age, holy orders, affinity, etc., can be occult in fact because it is not known and not likely to become known. A public case is one in which the impediment is known or very likely will become known. In the granting of dispensations a local Ordinary may accept this distinction of public and occult or the distinction given in canon 1074. (See Gasparri, 1, n. 210.)

B. Prohibitions

The local Ordinary can prohibit marriage in a particular case but only temporarily for a serious reason and only while that reason exists. He may do this for his own subjects anywhere they are staying and for anyone actually in his territory. Only the supreme authority of the Church may add an invalidating clause to the prohibition. (Can. 1077)

The local Ordinary therefore can forbid a marriage for a time and because of a serious reason, but his prohibition affects only the liceity and not the validity of the marriage. Some serious reasons for such a prohibition may be: grave immaturity, a hasty

engagement due to an unexpected pregnancy, psychological problems and, in general, any serious doubt whether either party, for
whatever reason, is able or intends to consent validly to marriage.
It is common for a prohibition to be placed on a party after an
annulment; the prohibition can be lifted once the party undergoes
counselling or whatever else may be required in the wording of
the prohibition.

C. Dispensations

Competent authority. The local Ordinary may dispense from all
impediments of ecclesiastical law except those whose dispensation is
reserved to the Apostolic See. He may dispense his own subjects everywhere they are staying and everyone actually in his territory. (Can.
1078, §1)

The local Ordinary may not dispense from the impediments
of prior bond, impotence, consanguinity in the direct line and second degree collateral line, and from impediments which are
reserved to the Apostolic See. The dispensation may be given by
the Ordinary of the place where the marriage is celebrated or the
Ordinary of the place where either party, if Catholic, or the
Catholic party in a mixed marriage, has domicile or quasi-domicile.

Eastern Catholics. The Latin local Ordinary may also dispense
Eastern Catholics subject to him, but not Eastern Catholics who
have their own Ordinary unless one of the parties to the marriage
is from the Latin Church. At the present time the following Eastern
Catholics have their own Ordinaries in the United States and
Canada: Ukrainians, Ruthenians, Maronites, Melkites, Armenians,
Slovaks, Chaldeans, and Romanians.

A dispensation is given in the external forum if the impediment is public; in the internal forum if the impediment is occult. If
both a public and occult impediment occur in the same case, the
dispensations may be asked for separately: that from the public
impediment from the diocesan chancery or, if the impediment is
reserved, from the Apostolic See, without mentioning the other
impediment; the dispensation from the occult impediment should
be obtained from the chancery (or from the Apostolic
Penitentiary if the impediment is reserved) without endangering
the sacramental seal.

Whenever the impediment is public, a dispensation should be
obtained in the external forum. If the case is *de facto* occult, even
if the impediment is public by nature and even though it is public
according to the definition given in canon 1074, one may still petition for the dispensation in the internal forum.

Necessity of reason for dispensation. No dispensation from an ecclesiastical law can be granted without a just and reasonable cause proportionate to the gravity of the law from which a dispensation is given; otherwise the dispensation from a universal law given by the local Ordinary is invaliḍ. (See can. 91, §1.) Therefore the one applying for the dispensation must give a reason which is true. If the cause is false the dispensation will ordinarily be invalid.

When there is doubt about the sufficiency of the reason, the dispensation may be licitly asked for and licitly and validly granted. (See can. 90, §2.) According to the common opinion, the same rule applies when there is doubt as to the very existence of the reason; and if after the dispensation is granted it should become evident that the reason for the dispensation was not sufficient or was non-existent, it is probable that the dispensation is still valid, provided that all concerned acted in good faith. (See Coronata, 1, n. 115.)

Reserved impediments. A dispensation from the following impediments is reserved to the Apostolic See: (1) the impediment arising from holy orders or from a public perpetual vow of chastity in a religious institute of pontifical right; (2) the impediment of crime treated in canon 1090. (See can. 1078, §2.)

Clerics in any grade of holy orders may not marry without a dispensation from the pope. (See can. 291.) This includes married permanent deacons who may not remarry (when their wife dies or their marriage is annulled or dissolved) without this dispensation. A dispensation from the impediment of a public perpetual vow of chastity in a religious institute is ordinarily not dispensed. Rather, the vow itself can be dispensed, either by the Apostolic See in the case of a religious in an institute of pontifical right, or by the diocesan bishop in the case of a religious in an institute of diocesan right.

The impediment of crime, rarely encountered in pastoral ministry, will typically be occult. The competent tribunal to grant the dispensation is the Apostolic Penitentiary. If the impediment was revealed in the sacrament of penance, the confessor should write to the Apostolic Penitentiary for the dispensation, describing the case without mentioning the name of the penitent or otherwise violating or endangering the sacramental seal.

Impediments never dispensed. Besides the impediments of prior bond and impotence, a dispensation is never given from the impediment of consanguinity in the direct line or in the second degree of the collateral line. (See can. 1078, §3.)

The practice of the Holy See has also been never to dispense from the order of episcopate and from the impediment of crime when it is public; it rarely dispenses from affinity in the first degree of the direct line after the marriage from which affinity arose has been consummated, or from the presbyterate. Regarding the latter, the general practice is to obtain a dispensation from the obligations of celibacy rather than a dispensation from the impediment of holy orders. Once the dispensation from celibacy has been obtained from the pope, the impediment to marriage ceases.

D. Dispensation In Danger of Death

Powers of the local Ordinary. In danger of death, the local Ordinary may dispense from the form to be observed in celebrating marriage and from each and every impediment of ecclesiastical law whether public or occult, except for the impediment arising from the order of the presbyterate. He may dispense his own subjects wherever they are staying and everyone actually in his territory. (Can. 1079, §1)

The local Ordinary's power is ordinary power and hence may be delegated to others, even habitually; it may be used even if recourse to the Holy See is possible; it may be used on behalf of one's subjects everywhere and on behalf of non-subjects when they are in the local Ordinary's territory; it extends to all impediments that are certainly of ecclesiastical law only, with the exception of the impediment arising from the order of the presbyterate; it extends to impediments from which the Holy See only rarely dispenses, e.g., crime; it does not extend to impediments which are certainly or most probably of divine law, i.e., consanguinity in the direct line and in the second degree collateral line, previous bond, certain impotence; it extends to the form of marriage, but not to the renewal of consent. (See Vermeersch/Creusen, 2, n. 307.)

For the valid use of the power to dispense in danger of death, it is necessary that the danger probably exists; it need not be *articulum mortis,* i.e., the last moment, but the "danger" of death suffices, provided that the danger is certain or seriously probable. The danger may affect only one of the parties, the party directly dispensed or the other party, the Catholic or the non-Catholic party. The danger may arise from intrinsic causes (e.g., sickness) or extrinsic causes (e.g., floods, impending serious surgery, war, proximate execution, etc.).

There must be some reason for the dispensation, such as the quieting of conscience or the legitimation of the children.

Powers of the pastor, assisting minister, confessor. In the same circumstances mentioned in canon 1079, §1, but only for cases in which the local Ordinary cannot be reached, the same power to dispense in danger of death is enjoyed by the pastor, the ordained minister who is properly delegated to assist at marriage, and the priest or deacon who assists at a marriage celebrated according to the norm of canon 1116, §2. The local Ordinary is not considered as being able to be reached if this can be done only by means of the telegraph or telephone. The pastor or priest or deacon should immediately notify the local Ordinary of a dispensation granted for the external forum, and it should be recorded in the marriage register. In danger of death the confessor enjoys the power to dispense from occult impediments for the internal forum whether within or outside the sacrament of penance. (See cans. 1079, §§ 2–4; 1081.)

> In danger of death, for the purpose of peace of conscience or of legitimation of children or some other reason, the above-mentioned ordained ministers may dispense from the form (but not from renewal of consent) and from impediments of ecclesiastical law as above. The local Ordinary is also considered out of reach if he cannot be approached without danger of violating the sacramental seal or a secret.

E. Dispensation in Urgent Cases

Powers of the local Ordinary. The local Ordinary may dispense from all impediments of ecclesiastical law, public as well as occult, except the impediments arising from holy orders or from a public perpetual vow of chastity in a religious institute of pontifical right, whenever an impediment is discovered and everything is already prepared for the wedding and the wedding cannot, without probable danger of grave harm, be deferred until a dispensation is obtained from the Holy See. This power also holds for the convalidation of a marriage already contracted, if there is the same danger in delay and there is not sufficient time for recourse to the Apostolic See. (See can. 1080.)

> They may dispense their own subjects wherever they may be staying, and all others actually staying in their territory. For the use of this power it is required that there be probable danger of grave harm in delay. Examples are scandal, danger of a merely civil marriage, notable financial loss. (See Matthis/Bonner, 245.)

The possible loss of money already invested in the wedding preparations or the fear of temporary embarrassment are not sufficient reasons to dispense from an impediment if it appears that the relationship is not secure and will be imperiled. (See CLSA Comm., 763–64.)

The time required for obtaining a dispensation from the Apostolic See can be taken as from six to eight weeks. Means such as telegraph or telephone need not be used, since these are considered extraordinary in law.

It is required that preparations have already been made for the marriage. The fact that the invitations have not been issued does not necessarily exclude the use of the power. The condition is verified when the wedding is so imminent that it must be celebrated within a shorter time than that which, under the circumstances, is required to obtain the dispensation from the Holy See. (See Roman Rota, sentence, May 25, 1925; CLD 2:278.)

The existence of the impediment is discovered only after preparations have been made and it is too late to defer the marriage; that is, it is only then that the impediment is discovered by the minister or the local Ordinary, even though the parties may have known it beforehand, so that to avoid grave harm the wedding must be celebrated within a shorter time than that which is required to obtain a dispensation from the Apostolic See. (See CodCom, interpretation, Mar. 1, 1921, AAS 13 (1921) 177; CLD 1:502.)

When the local Ordinary uses canon 1080 to convalidate a marriage already contracted, it is not necessary that the impediment be just now discovered. Danger in delay exists if the parties cannot be separated without grave harm (e.g., because all think them to be husband and wife, because there are children to care for, etc.).

By virtue of canon 87, §2 the Ordinary can dispense from the above mentioned impediments if recourse is difficult and there is a danger of grave harm even if all the preparations for the wedding have not been made, provided it is a dispensation which the Holy See is accustomed to grant, namely, the impediment of crime in occult cases.

Powers of the Pastor, Assisting Minister, Confessor. In the same circumstances of canon 1080, §1 given as above for the local Ordinary, but only for occult cases, the same power to dispense when everything is prepared for the wedding is enjoyed by the pastor, the properly delegated ordained minister, or the priest or deacon who assists at marriage in accord with canon 1116, §2, and the confessor (but the latter only for the internal forum whether within or outside the sacrament of penance). (See can. 1080, §1.)

This power can be used only for occult cases when the local Ordinary cannot be reached or when he cannot be reached without the danger of the violation of a secret. Hence, this power can be used only:

1) if preparations have been made for the marriage and there is probable danger of grave harm in delay (as above);

2) if the local Ordinary or Apostolic See (in the case of crime) cannot be reached by the ordinary means of the mail in time to avoid the danger of grave harm, or cannot be reached without the danger of the violation of a secret, including any professional secret as well as the secret of the seal of confession;

3) to dispense from all impediments of ecclesiastical law, with the exceptions noted above;

4) for occult cases, i.e., not only impediments which are occult by nature but also those occult in fact, namely, that are not publicly known.

If there is danger of harm in delaying until a dispensation can be obtained from the competent authority, the power may be used also for the convalidation of an invalid marriage. (See can. 1080, §2.)

If the dispensation was granted in the external forum, the pastor or priest or deacon should immediately notify the local Ordinary and the dispensation should be recorded in the marriage register. (See can. 1081.)

Unless a rescript from the Apostolic Penitentiary stipulates otherwise, a dispensation in the internal nonsacramental forum for an occult impediment should be recorded in a book reserved in the secret archives of the diocesan curia. Another dispensation for the external forum is unnecessary should the occult impediment later become public. (Can. 1082)

Impediments in Particular

The treatment of each impediment will cover the Latin rite law from the 1983 code and, where significant, the Eastern canon law, the civil law, and the law from the 1917 code. The Eastern law and the Latin law must both be observed in marriages involving a Latin Catholic and an Eastern Catholic. The Eastern law is given only when it is at variance with the Latin law.

The civil law is recognized by canon law as applicable to the marriages of non-Catholics, and therefore if a marriage contracted between two non-Catholics is invalid in the civil law, it is also invalid according to canon law. The former law from the 1917 code can also be important for annulment cases, because the marriages of the baptized contracted before November 27, 1983 were subject to the laws of the former code.

Unless noted otherwise, dispensations from any impediment can be given by the local Ordinary, or by the others mentioned in canons 1079 and 1080 in danger of death and urgent cases.

A. Age

For validity. A man before he has completed his sixteenth year and a woman before the completion of her fourteenth year are not able to marry validly. (Can. 1083, §1)

For liceity. The episcopal conference may establish a higher age for the licit celebration of marriage. (Can. 1083) Pastoral ministers should see to it that young people are dissuaded from marrying before the customary age of the region. (Can. 1072) Except in a case of necessity, no one without the permission of the local Ordinary may assist at the marriage of a minor child [under 18] whose parents are unaware of it or reasonably opposed to it. (Can. 1071, §1, 6°)

The impediment is that marriage under the age of 16 for males and under the age of 14 for females is invalid. Any higher age specified in particular law is for liceity only. Note that the day of birth is not computed in the age and hence one completes the sixteenth or fourteenth year at the close of the day on which the birthday is celebrated. (Can. 203) Furthermore, a marriage contracted invalidly by reason of lack of age is not convalidated by the mere running of time, but the consent must be renewed. (See cans. 1156-58.) The law states the canonical age irrespective of actual puberty; hence the marriage is presumably valid even if the parties are not yet physically adolescent and capable of the marriage act. (See Genicot, 2, n. 548.)

Civil law in the United States. Practically all the states of the union have the impediment of nonage; however, there is variation as to its effect. One must consult the laws of the state in which the marriage takes place, for the impediment may or may not be civilly invalidating. In some states the marriage may be validated upon the cessation of the impediment by mere cohabitation freely accepted and granted. In some states the judge or other public official is authorized to grant a dispensation from the impediment especially in cases of pregnancy. Practically all the states have, besides the age at which the impediment of nonage is established, another and higher age under which parental consent is required. This latter form of impediment, however, is usually only a conditional prohibition in reference to the issuance of the marriage license and does not affect the validity of the marriage. (See Abbo/Hannan, 2, n. 1067.)

Knowledge of the impediments of civil law is important for the minister who is faced with the necessity of investigating the validity of marriages contracted by two non-Catholics.

B. Impotence

Antecedent and perpetual impotence for intercourse, whether on the part of the man or the woman, whether absolute or relative, by its very nature renders marriage invalid. (Can. 1084, §1)

Impotence is an impediment of the divine natural law and therefore binds everyone, Catholic and non-Catholic, and cannot be dispensed. By the law of nature, marriage is ordered, in part, to the generation and upbringing of children. (See can. 1055.) Marriage is also a community of the whole life of the partners, involving intimacy, sharing, love and mutual support, all of which are enhanced by conjugal intercourse. Marriage, by the law of nature, involves the mutual exchange of the right to sexual intercourse. Someone who is impotent is incapable of exchanging this right and of performing the human act necessary for God's gift of children.

Impotence is the incapacity for intercourse which is in itself suitable for generation. Impotence is the impossibility of having normal sexual intercourse. Impotence in the male is verified if he fails to achieve erection, penetration of the vagina, and ejaculation, though the ejaculation need not be true semen capable of conception. In the case of a man with a double vasectomy, marriage is not to be impeded or declared null. (See CDF, decree, May 13, 1977, AAS 69 (1977) 426; CLD 8:676.) For the female to be impotent means that she is incapable of receiving the erect penis of the husband.

Impotence may be organic or functional. In either case it constitutes the impediment. Organic impotence is due to some physical cause. In the male it may be the lack of a penis or an abnormally sized penis which prohibits vaginal insertion. Female organic impotence occurs when a woman lacks a vagina, either natural or artificial, of sufficient length and width to receive the erect penis. Functional impotence can result from physical or psychic causes. Paraplegia can cause functional organic impotence. It is a paralysis of the lower extremities of the body resulting from disease or injury to the central nervous system. About 10% of paraplegics are capable of ejaculation but 70% are capable of erection.

There are three kinds of male psychic impotence: (1) the inability to attain or sustain an erection; (2) an excessive excitability resulting in premature ejaculation; (3) ejaculatory incompetence, namely, the inability to ejaculate during intercourse. A female can be functionally impotent when she suffers from vaginismus. Vaginismus is the painful spasm of all the muscles surrounding and supporting the vagina which happens when intercourse is attempted or even when the area is merely touched and which renders intercourse impossible. Not all forms of vaginismus, however, constitute impotence. (See Wrenn, 7-18.)

Impotence can be either absolute or relative. Absolute impotence prevents marital intercourse with all persons; relative impotence prevents it with a certain person or persons. Relative impotence is an impediment only in regard to the persons with whom the person affected cannot have intercourse.

To be invalidating the impotence must be both antecedent (before the marriage is celebrated) and perpetual, i.e., incapable of being cured by ordinary means. Extraordinary means include a miracle, illicit means, danger to one's life, serious harm to health, or doubtfully successful means.

If the impediment of impotence is doubtful, whether it be a doubt of law or of fact, marriage is not to be impeded nor, while the doubt persists, declared null. (Can. 1084, §2)

> The reason for this rule is the extreme difficulty of directly solving doubts of law or fact regarding this impediment. To settle the consciences of the faithful in these cases, the Church declares that in all probable and prudent doubts, the natural right to marry prevails, even though the impediment is of the divine natural law.
>
> If the doubt exists before marriage, the marriage cannot be licitly celebrated until there is an investigation of the facts that create the doubt. If the doubt remains after the investigation, marriage may be celebrated provided the other party is informed. If the impotence is detected after the marriage the presumption of canon 1060 in favor of the validity of the marriage holds until the contrary is proven before an ecclesiastical tribunal.
>
> A doubt of law occurs when it is not certain that the law on impotence can be applied to a specific case. A doubt of fact occurs when some fact about a case is dubious, e.g., a medical fact that would establish impotency.

Sterility neither prohibits nor invalidates marriage, without prejudice to canon 1098. (Can. 1084, §3)

> Sterility is the incapacity for generation. People who are sterile are capable of having intercourse (*capaces coeundi*) but are not capable of propagating offspring. Thus, the sterile include young people before they attain puberty, old people, women after they have reached menopause and ovulation ceases, women who have no ovaries, or no uterus, etc. Sterility does not affect the validity or the liceity of a marriage because the couple does not exchange the right to have children but they exchange the right to acts which are per se apt for the generation of children. (See can. 1061, §1.) Whatever hinders the human act of generation (intercourse) constitutes impotence; whatever hinders the natural process of generation constitutes sterility.
>
> Canon 1098 refers to one who fraudulently marries another. Although sterility itself does not prohibit marriage, the fraudulent concealment of one's sterility in order to obtain the consent of the other party might be invalidating.

C. Prior Bond

Anyone who is held by a prior bond of marriage, even if not consummated, invalidly attempts marriage. (Can. 1085, §1)

> This is an impediment of the divine positive law and also

binds non-Catholics. The prior marriages of non-Catholics as well as Catholics must be annulled by a competent tribunal or dissolved by the competent ecclesiastical authority before a new marriage with a Catholic can be celebrated.

Even though a former marriage be invalid or dissolved for any reason whatever, it is not therefore allowed to contract another marriage until the nullity or dissolution of the former shall have been legally and certainly established. (Can. 1085, §2)

> *Death of a former spouse* can be proved from an authentic document, either ecclesiastical or civil, stating the fact of this person's death. If the death can be proved by an authentic document, the minister may allow the living spouse to enter a new marriage. If such a document is not available, there must be a declaration of presumed death of the spouse made by the diocesan bishop in accord with canon 1707 before a new marriage can be celebrated.
>
> *A lack of form case,* in which a Catholic marries without observing the canonical form or being dispensed from it, does not require an annulment from the tribunal. Such a person can remarry in the Church provided it is certain that the canonical form was not observed in the prior marriage. However, canon 1071, §1, n. 3 requires the permission of the local Ordinary for a marriage when either party has natural obligations to a former spouse or the children of a previous marriage. In some dioceses the priests have been delegated by the local Ordinary to grant this permission.
>
> Proof of the lack of form requires the following: a baptismal certificate or certificate of reception into full communion of the Catholic Church or other proof of being Catholic (see can. 876); a civil marriage record (obtained from the county clerk); a civil divorce record (obtained from the clerk of the circuit court); a sworn statement that the marriage has never been celebrated in the form prescribed by the Church, and that the party had not left the Catholic Church by a formal act prior to the celebration of the previous marriage.
>
> *Other cases* require an annulment of the previous marriage by the competent tribunal or its dissolution by the competent ecclesiastical authority.

D. Disparity of Cult

A marriage between two persons, one of whom was baptized in the Catholic Church or received into it and who has not left it by a formal act and the other of whom is not baptized, is invalid. (Can. 1086, §1)

> This impediment serves to forewarn pastoral ministers and

the faithful, especially the engaged couple, about difficulties that may arise in an interfaith marriage when a Catholic spouse has a non-believing partner. Such cases require special attention to the issue of religion during the preparations for marriage. The impediment also recognizes the Church's high esteem for sacramental marriage, which is impossible when a Catholic marries an unbaptized person because both parties must be baptized for there to be a sacrament. (See can. 1055, §2.)

The marriage of a Catholic and a nonbaptized is invalid without a dispensation from the impediment. Considered to be Catholics by baptism are:

1) adults (seven and older with the use of reason) who are baptized in the Catholic Church or who are received into it;

2) all infants (under seven or lacking the use of reason) whose parents or guardians had them baptized with the intention of aggregating them to the Catholic Church;

3) all infants or adults who were unconscious when baptized by a Catholic minister in danger of death, provided, in the case of the adult, that she or he wanted to be baptized;

4) infants baptized by a Catholic minister in the case where the parents do not wish or are not able to exercise parental rights over the child.

Reception into the Catholic Church occurs when a baptized non-Catholic makes a profession of faith and is received into full communion according to the *Rite of Reception of Baptized Christians into Full Communion with the Catholic Church.*

Those not bound by the impediment of disparity of cult are:

1) all adults baptized in a non-Catholic church;

2) infants whose non-Catholic parents or guardians have them baptized with the intention of aggregating them to their own church or ecclesial community;

3) infants who are baptized by a non-Catholic minister with the intention of aggregating them to his church or ecclesial community, the parents not objecting when it is possible for them to do so. (See Vermeersch/Creusen 2, n. 344.)

Also not bound to the impediment are Catholics who have left the Church by a formal act, e.g., by joining another religion, or publicly declaring or signing a document attesting that they are no longer Catholic. Regular attendance at the worship services and other participation in the activities of that church, together with non-practice of the Catholic faith, could also indicate an intention to leave the Catholic Church.

Mere non-practice of the faith does not constitute leaving the Church by a formal act. Even one baptized a Catholic in infancy, but who has never been brought up in the faith, is still bound by the impediment unless there was some formal act taken to leave the Church.

Not bound to the impediment are children of non-Catholic parents who were baptized in infancy by a Catholic minister when there was not a founded hope that they would be brought up in the Catholic religion. On the other hand, anyone baptized in infancy in danger of death by a Catholic minister is bound by the impediment. (See CLSA Comm., 768.)

The impediment of disparity of cult should not be dispensed unless the conditions mentioned in canons 1125 and 1126 are fulfilled. (Can. 1086, §2)

These canons were treated above in chapter eight. A dispensation granted without the fulfillment of these conditions would be invalid. (See can. 39.)

If a party, at the time the marriage was celebrated, was commonly held to be baptized or his or her baptism was doubtful, the validity of the marriage, in accord with canon 1060, is to be presumed, unless it is proven with certainty that one party was baptized and the other was not. (Can. 1086, §3)

Canon 1060 says that when there is a doubt about the validity of a marriage, it is to be presumed valid unless the contrary is proven. If doubt arises about the fact or validity of baptism before the marriage is celebrated, the case should be handled according to the norm of canon 869. (See the commentary in chapter two on conditional baptism and in chapter fifteen on doubtful baptism, pp. 41, 340.) If the doubt arises after the marriage, the presumption of the law is in favor of the validity of the marriage. If it can be proved with moral certainty that one person was baptized and the baptism of the other was invalid, the presumption falls and the marriage is held as invalid if no dispensation from the impediment of disparity of cult had been obtained.

Eastern law. The Eastern code does not excuse from the impediment those Catholics who left the Church by means of a formal act. Therefore, if such an "ex-Catholic" marries a non-baptized person outside the Church, the marriage is valid if the Catholic belonged to the Latin church but invalid if he or she belonged to an Eastern Catholic church. (See CCEC, can. 803; Pospishil, 419–20.)

E. Holy Orders

One who has received holy orders invalidly attempts marriage. (Can. 1087)

> Three conditions must be fulfilled before the impediment is incurred: (1) the cleric must be validly ordained; (2) he must be ordained with full knowledge of the obligations assumed; and (3) he must be ordained freely without grave force or fear being inflicted upon him. (See Cappello, 5:437, 420; CLSA Comm., 769.)
>
> The impediment binds deacons, including permanent deacons, presbyters, and bishops. A permanent deacon may not marry after ordination, even if his wife should die, although a dispensation from celibacy is sometimes given by the pope in such cases. In order for a cleric to marry validly, he must receive a dispensation from the obligation of celibacy which is granted by the pope alone. (See can. 291.) Bishops are never dispensed from celibacy.
>
> A cleric who attempts marriage, even if only civil marriage, is *ipso facto* removed from any ecclesiastical office. (See can. 194, §1, 3°.) Moreover, he incurs an automatic suspension; and if he has been warned and has not reformed and continues to give scandal, he can be further punished with deprivations and even dismissal from the clerical state. (See can. 1394, §1.)

> In danger of death, deacons can be dispensed in accord with canon 1079. Priests, however, may only be dispensed by the Apostolic See even in danger of death. No cleric may be dispensed by the local Ordinary in urgent cases when everything is prepared for the wedding. (See can. 1080.)
>
> The order of subdeacon, abolished in 1972, was also an impediment to marriage. Those who were ordained subdeacons are still bound to the impediment and must be dispensed from celibacy before they can marry validly, except for the dispensation given in danger of death.

F. Public Perpetual Vow of Chastity in a Religious Institute

Those who are bound by a public perpetual vow of chastity in a religious institute invalidly attempt marriage. (Canon 1088)

> The impediment binds perpetually professed members of either clerical or lay institutes, whether they are of pontifical or diocesan right. The perpetual vow may be either solemn or simple. Not bound by the impediment are religious in temporary vows, or members of secular institutes or societies of apostolic life.

A member of a religious institute who contracts marriage or attempts it, even only civilly, is *ipso facto* dismissed from the institute. (See can. 694, §1, 2°.) Moreover, a religious in perpetual vows who is not a cleric incurs an automatic interdict. (See can. 1394, §2.) A religious who is a cleric incurs the penalties as noted above under the impediment of holy orders.

In danger of death, the local Ordinary, pastor, other priest or deacon, or confessor, in accord with canon 1079, may dispense from the impediment. However, for a dispensation in an urgent case when everything is prepared for the wedding, only those in an institute of diocesan right may be dispensed by the local Ordinary.

In the law of the 1917 code, the diriment impediment applied only to attempted marriages by persons in solemn vows. The only exception was for members of the Society of Jesus whose simple vows also invalidated the contracting of marriage.

G. Abduction

There can be no marriage between a man and a woman who was abducted or at least detained for the purpose of marrying, unless the woman later has been separated from her abductor and while in a safe and free place willingly chooses marriage. (Can. 1089)

The impediment applies only to the abduction or detention of a woman by a man, and not vice-versa. However, if a woman abducted a man and compelled him to marry, it could be invalid on the grounds of force or fear. (See can. 1103.)

Eastern law. The impediment also applies in the case of a woman who abducts a man. (See CCEC, can. 806.)

H. Crime

One invalidly attempts marriage who, in view of marrying a certain person, has brought about the death of the person's spouse or one's own spouse. They also marry each other invalidly who have brought about the death of the spouse of either of them through physical or moral cooperation. (Can. 1090)

There are two degrees of crime which create the impediment: (1) a person who, with a view to marrying another, kills his or her own spouse or the spouse of the other; and (2) when two persons conspire and bring about the death of the spouse of either even without an intention of marrying each other. In either case the murder must be actually committed for the impediment to be incurred, whether it be committed by the man or woman or both, or by someone else acting in the service of either or both, such as a hired killer.

The dispensation from the impediment is reserved to the Apostolic See. It is not given in public cases. A dispensation for the internal forum is sought from the Apostolic Penitentiary without mentioning any names if it is for the internal sacramental forum, i.e., if the crime was revealed in the sacrament of penance. It may be dispensed in danger of death and urgent cases in accord with canons 1079-82.

A third species of crime existed in the 1917 code and in the previous Eastern law. This was the crime of adultery by which a Catholic in a valid marriage committed adultery and exchanged with the adulterous partner a promise of contracting marriage or actually attempted marriage itself.

J. Consanguinity

In the direct line of consanguinity marriage is invalid between all ancestors and descendants both legitimate and natural. In the collateral line it is invalid up to the fourth degree inclusive. (Can. 1091, §§ 1, 2)

> Direct line consanguinity is the blood relationship between direct ancestors and descendants, e.g., grandfather, mother, son, granddaughter, etc. Collateral consanguinity is the blood relationship when two persons have a common ancestor, but neither is the direct ancestor of the other, e.g., brother and sister, uncle and niece, first cousins, second cousins, etc. The impediment invalidates any marriages between persons related in the direct line and, on the collateral line, between brothers and sisters (second degree), aunt and nephew or uncle and niece (third degree), first cousins (fourth degree), and great aunt and grandnephew or great uncle and grandniece (fourth degree). On the computation of degrees of consanguinity, see chapter one, page 16.
>
> Since carnal generation is the basis of consanguinity, the relationship arises from both legitimate and illegitimate generation.

Marriage is never permitted if there is any doubt whether the parties are related by blood in any degree of the direct line or in the second degree of the collateral line. (Can. 1091, §4)

> In the direct line, consanguinity is an impediment of the divine law certainly in the first degree, more probably in the other degrees. In the collateral line it is more probably an impediment of divine law in the second degree, although some authors

doubt it. In all other degrees of the collateral line it is certainly an impediment of ecclesiastical law only.

Non-Catholics are not bound by the impediment in the degrees in which it is certainly of ecclesiastical law only. If the impediment exists in a degree in which it is not certainly an impediment by divine law, the marriage is to be considered valid. However, the unbaptized are bound by the impediment of consanguinity established by the civil law and hence the validity of the marriage must be judged according to the civil laws under which the marriage was contracted. (See Mathis/ Bonner, 232-33.)

A dispensation is never given from the impediment of consanguinity in the direct line or in the second degree of the collateral line. (Can. 1078, §3)

Third and fourth degree collateral consanguinity can be dispensed by the local Ordinary. The practice of the Holy See in the past has been to dispense third degree consanguinity very rarely and only for extraordinarily grave reasons, and to dispense fourth degree rarely and only for grave reasons. (See CLSA Comm., 772.)

Civil law. In almost all of the states the impediment of consanguinity is an invalidating one and it extends to all degrees of the direct line and to the third degree of the collateral line. In over half the states the impediment extends to first cousins; in a few states it extends to the fifth degree; in Oklahoma, to second cousins (sixth degree). (See Alford, nn. 135-45.)

The following states permit marriages of first cousins: Alabama, California, Connecticut, District of Columbia, Florida, Georgia, Kentucky, Maine, Maryland, Massachusetts, New Jersey, New York, Rhode Island, South Carolina, Texas, Vermont, Virginia. (See CLSA Comm., 772.)

In the law of the 1917 code, besides the direct line, the impediment extended to what formerly was called the third degree of the collateral line. Second cousins could not validly marry under the former law without a dispensation. The impediment could also be multiplied as often as the common ancestor was multiplied. (See CIC, can. 1076.)

K. Affinity

Affinity in the direct line in any degree at all invalidates marriage. (Can. 1092)

Affinity arises from valid marriage, even if not consummated. It exists between the husband and the blood relatives of the wife, and between the wife and the blood relatives of the husband. For further discussion, see chapter one, page 17.

Affinity arises from any valid marriage, and affinity contracted when one is a non-Catholic becomes an impediment when one is baptized a Catholic or received into the Church. (See Congregation of the Holy Office, response, Jan. 31, 1957, AAS 49 (1957) 77; CLD 4:89.)

Civil law. In more than half the states of the union the impediment of affinity does not exist in the civil law. In states where the impediment exists one must study the laws of the respective state to ascertain whether it is a diriment (invalidating) impediment or an impediment which is not invalidating. In some states the impediment ceases upon the death of one's spouse. Only in a few states does it extend to the collateral line, for usually the impediment is restricted to the direct line and extends to the mother and father-in-law, the daughter and son-in-law, the stepmother or stepfather, the stepson or stepdaughter. (See Alford, nn. 151–60 for details.)

Eastern canon law. Affinity invalidates marriage in any degree of the direct line and in the second degree of the collateral line. (CCEC, can. 809, §1)

Unlike the Latin law, an Eastern Catholic would not be free to marry a sister-in-law or brother-in-law upon the death of the spouse without getting a dispensation from the impediment.

In the law of the 1917 code, the impediment invalidated marriage in all degrees of the direct line and up to what was formerly called the second degree of the collateral line (first cousins). The impediment was multiplied as often as the impediment of consanguinity on which it is based was multiplied, or through a subsequent marriage with a blood relative of one's deceased spouse. (See CIC, can. 1077.)

L. Public Propriety

The impediment of public propriety arises from an invalid marriage after common life has been established or from notorious or public concubinage; it invalidates marriage in the first degree of the direct line between the man and the blood relatives of the woman, and vice-versa. (Can. 1093)

An invalid marriage is one which has at least the appearance of marriage but is invalid for some reason. The impediment only exists once the couple begins to live together in the invalid union.

Concubinage is when two persons live as husband and wife for the purpose of habitually having sexual intercourse, but the union does not have even the appearance of marriage. For the impediment to arise it is necessary that the concubinage be notorious or public, i.e., well known to the community.

The impediment prohibits valid marriage between a man and his lover's mother or daughter, and likewise prohibits valid marriage between a woman and her lover's father or son. There is no blood relationship prohibiting this marriage, since the lovers' children came from another relationship, but such a marriage would still be unseemly and likely scandalous.

The impediment is of itself perpetual. Even if the invalid marriage or concubinage has been dissolved, the impediment still exists and must be dispensed. It is doubtful whether or not the impediment remains or is rather absorbed by the impediment of affinity in case the invalid marriage is validated or those living in concubinage contract marriage; a dispensation should be obtained *ad cautelam.*

The Eastern code specifies that the impediment also applies to those who established common life after attempting civil marriage or before a non-Catholic minister when they were bound to a required form for the celebration of marriage. (See CCEC, can. 810, §1, 3°.) This case is implicit in the Latin law.

In the law of the 1917 code, the impediment also included the second degree of the direct line.

M. Legal Relationship

They are unable validly to contract marriage between themselves who are related in the direct line or in the second degree of the collateral line by the legal relationship arising from adoption. (Can. 1094)

Canon law relies on the civil law to determine what constitutes legal adoption. The impediment arises only if the adoption is legal in accord with the civil law.

In the law of the 1917 code, those who are disqualified for marriage by the civil law because of legal relationship arising from adoption cannot validly marry under canon law either. (See CIC, can. 1080.)

U.S. civil law. An invalidating impediment because of adoption exists in Puerto Rico. Massachusetts prohibits marriages between adoptive parents and children. Mississippi prohibits marriages between a father and his adoptive daughter. (See CLSA Comm., 774.) Persons who come to the United States from other countries, if they intend to stay here only temporarily, still remain subject to the laws of their own country.

According to a general principle of law, a contract is governed by the laws of the place where the contract is made; however, some exceptions may be made to this principle for the matrimonial contract. Some states demand that the stranger be qualified to marry by the laws of his own country or of his own state, and likewise that residents of the state intending to remain residents may not marry in another state if their marriage would be illegal in the home state. Other states recognize the general principle of contracts, i.e., if the contract is valid in the place where it was made, it is valid everywhere, and if invalid in the place where made, it is invalid everywhere. (See Woywod, n. 1038.)

N. Spiritual Relationship

From baptism arises a spiritual relationship that invalidates marriage between the godparent and the baptized and between the godparent and the parents. If baptism is repeated conditionally, the spiritual relationship does not arise, unless the godparent is once again the same. (CCEC, can. 811)

This impediment binds only the members of Eastern Catholic churches.

In the law of the 1917 code, invalidating spiritual relationship exists between the one baptizing and the person baptized as well as between the godparents and the person baptized. (See CIC, cans. 1079; 768.)

X Matrimonial Consent

$$o\,n\,e$$

Nature of
Matrimonial Consent

A. Definition and Effect

Marriage comes about by the parties' consent legitimately manifested between persons who are legally capable, and no human power can substitute for this consent. Matrimonial consent is an act of the will by which a man and a woman mutually give and accept each other in an irrevocable covenant for the purpose of establishing marriage (Can. 1057)

The Church teaches that, by the divine natural law, the essence of marriage is the free consent of the parties. The parties must be capable of giving consent and must actually give their consent to marriage in the way the Church understands it. If consent is lacking or canonically defective, whether on the part of one or both parties, the marriage is invalid. The vast majority of marriage annulments are given on some ground of defective consent. Church tribunals can annul not only Catholic marriages, but also the marriages of baptized and unbaptized non-Catholics. Since true consent to marriage is necessary by divine law and since everyone is bound to the divine law, a competent ecclesiastical tribunal can judge cases of marriage nullity of all who assert their marriage was invalid.

No "human power" can replace the consent of the parties. This means that only the parties themselves can consent to marry each other. Parents, families, rulers, etc. cannot do this. "Arranged" marriages, in societies where this still exist, are valid only insofar as the man and woman freely accept each other and freely consent to the marriage, even though the marriage may have been arranged by negotiation between the families rather than directly by the man and woman themselves.

Matrimonial consent is an act of the will. The canon law of marriage presupposes a distinction between the human faculties of intellect and will. The will judges, intends, decides, chooses, obeys, etc. The intellect thinks, believes, reasons, opines, deliberates, understands, etc. There is not an absolute distinction between will and intellect, since the two functions of the human mind do not work independently of each other. Indeed, an act of the will presupposes an act of the intellect. In order to consent to marriage, one must know what marriage is, what it entails, who the partner is, and so forth. Some of the grounds for defect of consent are due to a defect of the intellect, notably lack of sufficient reason, ignorance, error and fraud. If one lacks basic knowledge about the nature of marriage or the partner one is marrying, one cannot consent validly because it is not possible to make an informed choice about marriage.

Since consent makes the marriage, all marriage annulment cases on some ground of defective consent must prove that the consent was lacking or defective at the time consent was given. For example, a woman married to a man who has been seriously injured in the head and loses the use of reason cannot obtain an annulment on the grounds of lack of sufficient reason, because this condition came about after consent was given. However, some disorders and conditions of a person may exist but be latent at the time of consent, and only are manifested during the marriage. If the condition that prevents valid consent is shown to have existed at the time of consent, even though it was latent, an annulment can be granted.

The knowledge or belief that the marriage is null does not necessarily exclude matrimonial consent. (Can. 1100)

The reason for this is that together with the knowledge or the opinion of nullity there can exist a will to enter marriage insofar as one can; true matrimonial consent can easily exist even though the marriage itself is invalid. For example, a couple can truly consent to marry each other, even though they know the marriage is invalid due to a prior bond. Or one may think the marriage is null when it is not, e.g., a Catholic woman marrying a non-baptized man who thinks she does not have a dispensation when in fact she does. In either case, the consent is valid. Whether the marriage is valid depends on whether the impediment or dispensation exists or not.

B. Perseverance

Even though a marriage was entered invalidly because of an

impediment or lack of form, the consent which has been given is presumed to persevere until its revocation shall have been proved. (Can. 1107)

A marriage can be invalid for any of three general reasons: the presence of an impediment, lack of required form, or defective consent. Each of these are separate realities. There may be an impediment that makes a marriage invalid, or it may be invalid due to lack of form or defective form, but the consent might still be valid. Although the marriage is invalid, the consent is not necessarily invalid. For example, a priest who does not have the faculty to assist at marriages does so anyway. The couple gives their consent validly because they truly choose to marry each other, but the marriage is invalid because the priest was not authorized to perform the marriage ceremony.

The most important application of the presumption stated in this canon takes place in a radical sanation where an invalid marriage is convalidated without the renewal of consent. Consent must exist at the time when the sanation takes place, but the presumption of this canon is sufficient to show that the consent once given still exists, unless it can be proved that it was revoked.

two
Defective Consent

A. Lack of Sufficient Use of Reason

They are incapable of contracting marriage who lack sufficient use of reason. (Can. 1095, 1°)

> The use of reason required for marriage is not the simple use of reason that the law presumes is attained by age seven, but "sufficient" use of reason to understand that marriage is a community of conjugal life for the good of the spouses and the generation and education of children. (Can. 1055, §1) Such use of reason could be lacking by reason of a transitory disturbance such as alcoholic intoxication or an epileptic ictal twilight state, or it could be lacking by a habitual disorder such as schizophrenia or profound mental retardation. Such persons cannot give consent, and it is consent which makes the marriage. (See Wrenn, 19-21.)

B. Lack of Due Discretion

They are incapable of contracting marriage who suffer from some serious defect of discretion of judgment concerning the essential matrimonial rights and duties which must be mutually given and accepted. (Can. 1095, 2°)

> This differs from lack of sufficient reason because lack of due discretion involves the will and not just the intellect. Due discretion for marriage requires that the intellect make a mature judgment and that the will consent freely. One's decision to marry should be rational and informed. Moreover, parties to marriage "must be able to make at least a rudimentary assessment of the

236

capacities of themselves and their spouse, and to decide freely that they wish to establish a perpetual and exclusive community of life with this person, a community that will involve a lifetime of fundamentally faithful caring and sharing." (Wrenn, 23) Sufficient discretion for marriage involves the ability to evaluate critically the decision to marry in light of consequent obligations and responsibilities, one's own motivation for marriage, one's strengths and weaknesses as well as those of the other party, and one's abilities to live up to the demands of marriage. (See CLSA Comm., 776.)

To have sufficient discretion for marriage, it is necessary not only to have some general appreciation of the fact that marriage is a permanent, heterosexual partnership, but that marriage involves obligations to another person, including being truthful and self-revelatory with the spouse, understanding and appreciating the spouse as a separate person, and caring for the spouse's welfare.

Those lacking in due discretion are frequently young and/or immature, or they may have an identity disorder or personality disorder of at least moderate degree. At times there are certain extrinsic factors connected with lack of due discretion including: premarital pregnancy or abortion; unhappy, burdensome life with the parents with a desire to escape; a brief courtship; belated reluctance to marry together with family pressure or fear of embarrassment. (See Wrenn, 24.)

C. Lack of Due Competence

They are incapable of contracting marriage who, for reasons of a psychic nature, are not able to assume essential marital obligations. (Can. 1095, 3°)

> With lack of due discretion, one is incapable of consenting to marriage because one does not fully understand and appreciate the responsibilities that marriage entails, and therefore one cannot make a correct judgment about what one is undertaking and freely choose it. With lack of due competence, one may well understand and appreciate what marriage entails, but still not validly consent because one is incapable of assuming and fulfilling those obligations. The consent is defective because the person is not able to undertake that which is being consented to, namely, the essential obligations of marriage.
>
> One of the essential obligations of marriage is the mutual exchange of the right to sexual intercourse open to the procreation of children. When someone is incapable of sexual intercourse a marriage is invalid due to the impediment of impotence. The other essential obligations involve "personalist" aspects of marriage, arising from the definition of the marriage covenant as a

"partnership of the whole of life which by its nature is ordered toward the good of the spouses and the procreation and education of children." (See can. 1055, §1.) In particular, these obligations include self-revelation, understanding, and caring, both regarding the spouse and the children. Self-revelation is the ability to see oneself as a fairly consistent person, have a reasonable degree of respect for the spouse, and convey a knowledge of oneself to the spouse. Understanding is the ability to see the spouse as a separate person, and appreciate the spouse's way of thinking without distorting it excessively. Caring is the ability to pledge oneself with reasonable maturity to a lifelong communion with the spouse not out of a need to possess the other but out of a desire to share one's life with the other in mutual respect and affection. (See Wrenn, 40–42.)

In short, this personalist dimension of marriage involves the capacity for an interpersonal relationship. The spouses must be able to give and accept each other as distinct persons, relating to each other in a way that is distinct to marriage. They must be "other-oriented." More than just a physical reality, a covenant marriage involves "a true intertwining of the personalities," which presupposes the development of an adult personality. (See CLSA Comm., 777.)

The "psychic reasons" behind lack of due competence are many. It is a broad term that may include personality disorders, anxiety disorders, schizophrenia, mood disorders, alcohol dependence, homosexuality, and other causes of a psychic nature. Lack of due competence can also arise from "emotional immaturity," not the normal chronological immaturity of youth, but a permanent psychological condition which affects the ability to make judgments, control one's actions, and relate to others.

Note that homosexuality is not classified as a psychological disorder, but it not infrequently gives rise to an inability to establish the heterosexual "partnership of the whole of life" that is an essential element of marriage.

The psychic reason for lack of due competence must be severe, not just a mild disturbance. It also must be antecedent, i.e., at the time consent was given. For example, alcoholism which develops a number of years after the marriage and cannot be proved to have existed before marriage is not grounds for nullity. The psychic cause in question can be either absolute and affect any marriage, or relative, affecting only this marriage or marriages with certain kinds of people. (See Wrenn, 43–45.)

D. Ignorance

In order for matrimonial consent to be possible, it is necessary that the parties at least not be ignorant of the fact that marriage is a permanent partnership between a man and a woman for the procreation of children by means of some sexual cooperation. This ignorance is not presumed after puberty. (Can. 1096)

> For a valid matrimonial consent the parties must know at least two things. First, they must know that marriage is a partnership of the whole of life. Thus, there must be some realization of the personalist element in marriage, including the knowledge of some mutual cooperation, support, and companionship. If a man, e.g., regarded marriage as simply a convenience to enable him to have a housekeeper or secretary, or a servant for his children, he would be ignorant of the personalist dimension of marriage. (See CLSA Comm., 779; Wrenn, 83.)
>
> Second, the parties to marriage must know that marriage involves some sexual cooperation for the purpose of procreation. The person does not have to know precisely how the sexual organs of both sexes function, provided there is knowledge that the marital act involves some physical coming together of the sex organs for the purpose of generation.
>
> Ignorance can arise as a result of societal and cultural values that conflict with the Catholic understanding of marriage, and people can come to adulthood and still be lacking an understanding of marriage as a permanent commitment ordered to the good of the spouse and the children. The principal difference between ignorance and the grounds for defective consent in canon 1095 is that ignorance does not necessarily involve a person who has subnormal intelligence, or is immature, or has some psychological problem or other condition rendering it impossible to assume minimal obligations. Rather, the person could be completely normal, but simply lacks basic knowledge about what marriage minimally entails.

E. Error of Person or Quality of Person

Error regarding the person renders a marriage invalid. (Can. 1097, §1)

> Such error would be mistaken identity. One believes one is consenting to marry a certain person, but in reality is marrying someone else. There is little or no practical application of this rule. It comes from the day when marriages were arranged between families before the couple met each other. If a spouse other than the one agreed upon is substituted at the wedding, the marriage is invalid due to error of person.

Error regarding a quality of a person, even if it is the cause of the contract, does not render a marriage invalid, unless this quality was directly and principally intended. (Can. 1097, §2)

A quality of a person may be determined as "some aspect of the person that contributes to the shaping of the overall personality." (See CLSA Comm., 780.) It could be moral, physical, social, religious, or legal in nature, e.g., honesty, good health, wealth, occupation, marital status, education, religious convictions, etc. If one makes a mistake about some quality, it has no effect on the validity of the consent unless that quality was directly and principally intended. That quality, and not the person for better or worse, must be the primary reason for marrying.

For example, a woman always wanted to marry only a rich man, and thought her fiance was rich because he had expensive clothes and a nice car, charged gifts and dinners on his credit cards, etc. After marriage she discovers he is deeply in debt, and this revelation leads to the breakup of the marriage. In this example, the woman directly and principally intended to marry only a man with the quality of wealth, and did not give consent to a poor man. On the other hand, if she thought she were marrying a wealthy man and she later discovered he was poor but accepted him anyway, the error would not be invalidating because the quality was not directly and principally intended.

In tribunal cases nullity has been decided on the fact that the quality, whether or not it was common to many, was truly significant, discovered after the marriage, and when discovered resulted in a serious disruption of marital life. (See CLSA Comm., 780.)

F. Fraud

One invalidly contracts marriage when one enters it deceived by fraud, perpetrated to obtain consent, concerning some quality of the other party which of its very nature can seriously disturb the partnership of the conjugal life. (Can. 1098)

This ground for nullity is related to error regarding a quality of a person, in that the person contracting invalidly makes a mistake about some significant quality of the other party which can seriously disturb the marriage. The difference is that here the mistaken spouse was deceived in order to obtain consent to marry. Note that the deceiver does not have to be the other spouse, although that is the usual case.

For example, a woman wishes to marry only a doctor. Her fiance is aware of this desire and, after failing his medical exams, tells her he passed so that she will marry him. When the fraud is later discovered, the marriage breaks up.

Fraud, also called deceit, is "a deliberate act of deception by which one person hides a significant fact from another to achieve a given end." (CLSA Comm., 781.) Certain essential elements must be proved in nullity cases on the grounds of fraud: (1) the fraud is deliberately perpetrated in order to obtain consent; (2) the quality is real, grave, and present (or absent) at the time of consent; (3) the quality must be unknown to the other party; and (4) the discovery of the absence or presence of the quality must precipitate the end of the marriage. (Ibid.)

Examples of such qualities that might be grave enough to nullify marriage when concealed are: homosexuality, alcoholism, drug addiction, sexual dysfunction, previous marriage, prior criminal record, mental illness, sterility, a serious or contagious disease. Qualities might also be subjectively grave as, e.g., a woman who always said she would never marry a man who smoked cigarettes, and her fiance concealed his addiction to tobacco in order to obtain her consent. Smoking is not an objectively grave quality, but for this particular woman it is grave enough to vitiate her consent to marry a man who smokes.

G. Error Regarding Essential Properties

Error concerning the unity or indissolubility or sacramental dignity of marriage, provided it does not determine the will, does not vitiate matrimonial consent. (Can. 1099)

Error concerning the unity of marriage would be to regard polygamy or marital infidelity as legitimate options. Error concerning indissolubility would be the belief that civil divorce can end a marriage or that there is no permanent marital bond which exists even after the spouses have separated and even after they remarried. Error concerning the sacramental dignity of marriage is the belief that marriage between two baptized is not *ipso facto* a sacrament (see can. 1055, §2), or that the marriage of the baptized is purely a secular affair. As long as this error does not affect the will, it does not invalidate marital consent.

Error is called "simple" if it remains in the mind without passing over to the will. It exists when error in the mind remains speculative and is not actually incorporated in the choice made by the will. Despite this error concerning indissolubility, unity, or sacramental dignity of the marriage, the will wishes to contract a marriage that is valid, a marriage as it has been instituted by the law of nature. The fact that one would not have chosen marriage in the absence of the error is a hypothetical fact; the actual fact is that the will has chosen marriage, without making any explicit modification or reservation.

For example, a person may erroneously believe that divorce and remarriage are possible, or that there is no sacrament of marriage. But if this error is only in the mind, it does not affect the consent which is an act of the will. On the other hand, if the person were to marry while reserving the right to divorce if things do not work out, or deliberately refusing to accept the sacramentality of marriage but embracing only a civil union, then the error passes over to the will and the marriage is invalid. Likewise, if someone were to marry with the belief that infidelity is not contrary to the nature of marriage, and was even theoretically open to the possibility of an occasional extra-marital affair, the consent would be valid because these erroneous notions remain only in the mind. However, if that person were to marry actually intending to have an affair with one or more other persons, then that mistaken belief has passed over to the will and the consent is invalid.

If the error modifies the act of the will, so that the consent is explicitly directed to a dissoluble marriage, or a non-sacramental marriage, or a polygamous or adulterous marriage, it is no longer simple error. It is then an error explicitly incorporated as a condition or reservation in the contract and hence the matrimonial consent is vitiated. (See Vlaming/Bender, 385.) It is one thing, e.g., to contract a marriage which one thinks is dissoluble, or even to contract because one thinks it is dissoluble, but it is another thing not to intend to contract unless it is dissoluble. Thus, if one wishes to contract a trial marriage the consent is invalid because indissolubility is positively excluded.

H. Simulation

The internal consent of the mind is presumed to be in conformity with the words or signs used in the marriage celebration. But if either party or both parties by a positive act of the will should exclude marriage itself, or some essential element of marriage, or some essential property, they contract invalidly. (Can. 1101)

The essential elements of marriage are the personalist (the partnership of the whole of life for the good of the spouses) and the procreational. (See can. 1055, §1.) The essential properties are unity and indissolubility. (See can. 1056.) Total simulation is the exclusion of the marriage itself, or the exclusion of the personalist element. Partial simulation is the exclusion of the procreational element (intention against children), or the property of unity (intention against fidelity), or the property of indissolubility (intention against perpetuity). (See Wrenn, 89-90.)

A positive act of the will can be either explicit or implicit, i.e., one can consciously exclude marriage or some essential element or property, or this exclusion can be implicitly revealed by the circumstances. In either case, the exclusion is an act of the will, something chosen by the party at the time the marriage was outwardly consented to, and not the result of extraneous or later events.

1. Total simulation

Total simulation occurs when one does not have the intention to contract marriage even though he or she goes through the formalities, i.e., where the person does not intend any union at all with the other, or does not intend to enter a partnership of the whole of life for the good of the spouse. This simulation invalidates marriage since matrimonial consent is lacking. There is no intention to contract a marriage, as marriage is understood by the law of nature. (See can. 1055, §1.) However, simulation must be proved, since "the internal consent of the mind is presumed to be in conformity with the words or signs used in the marriage celebration." (Can. 1101, §1)

The exclusion of marital consent in total simulation does not have to be explicit to be invalidating. There are three principal ways in which the partnership of the whole of life may be implicitly excluded: (1) by permanently excluding the right to cohabitation; (2) by going through a marriage ceremony solely for an extraneous reason, e.g., a man who marries a foreigner so that he can legally emigrate to another country; (3) by substituting for true marriage one's own idea of marriage, e.g., a man who thinks a wife is only a housekeeper and a governess but not an equal partner (See can. 1135; Wrenn, 92-93.)

2. Partial simulation

There are three kinds of partial simulation: intention against children *(contra bonum prolis)*, intention against fidelity *(contra bonum fidei)*, and intention against perpetuity *(contra bonum sacramenti)*. Each of them vitiates marital consent. In cases of partial simulation one must be careful to distinguish the intention not to grant the right or not to assume the obligation from the intention merely of not fulfilling the obligations imposed by the marriage covenant. Thus, if a person enters a marriage by a consent which excludes the right to or obligation of normal intercourse, perpetuity of the bond, or fidelity, the marriage is invalid. On the other hand, if one acknowledges the rights in question but merely desires to abuse the right, consent is valid. For example, a couple enters marriage planning to practice birth control, but they do not deny each other the right to have children when one of them wishes. That would not be an intention against children.

Intention against children. When a person enters marriage excluding the right to acts which are per se apt for the generation of children, the consent is invalid. Hence, it is not the exclusion of children that is invalidating, but the exclusion of sexual intercourse which is open to procreation. The actual procreation of children is not a requirement of marriage, as evidenced in canon 1084, §3 which permits marriage by those who are sterile. Likewise, it is not the absence of sexual intercourse that invalidates, but the intention to deny the right of the other party to the conjugal act.

Thus, e.g., if a man and a woman agree to practice birth control for five years before having children, the marriage is not invalid. They are simply agreeing not to use their right to have sexual intercourse which is per se apt for generation. On the other hand, if after two years the wife decided it was time to have children, and the husband adamantly refused, this could be an indication that he had intended from the beginning not to acknowledge his wife's right to have intercourse that is open to procreation. The intention to deny the right to the procreative act, even for a limited time, is invalidating. On the other hand, the premarital, mutual agreement not to exercise the right is not invalidating.

Intention against fidelity. One essential property of marriage is unity. (See can. 1056.) Unity means there can be but one partner in marriage, i.e., no polygamy. Although fidelity is different from unity in the strict sense, it is related. Fidelity means that the married person can have only one's spouse as a sex partner, that there can be no adultery. This is also indicated in canon 1134 which states that the marriage bond is "exclusive," excluding other partners whether heterosexual or homosexual. If either or both parties to marriage exclude fidelity by a positive act of the will, the marriage is null. (See can. 1101, §2.) A marriage would not be invalid merely because one has engaged in adultery, but only if one had intended to be unfaithful at the time when consent to marriage was given. It must be proven that this intention existed from the moment the marriage was contracted.

Wrenn explains this intention *contra bonum fidei* as follows: "In order to result in invalidity, fidelity must be excluded as part of the marriage covenant. It may happen, for example, that in entering marriage a man foresees and even intends that he will have an extramarital affair should he have the opportunity. If, however, this remains casual and incidental, his intention does not invade, and therefore does not vitiate, the covenant. If, on the other hand, his intention is so intense and important to him that it actually becomes part of his central agreement or exchange of rights, with the result that he would regard his wife's demands that he be hers alone as an undue extension of the agreement he entered, then such a man excludes the very right to fidelity." (Wrenn, 103)

Intention against perpetuity. A second essential property of marriage is indissolubility. (See can. 1056.) A "perpetual bond" arises from a valid marriage. (See can. 1134.) If, at the time consent is given, indissolubility is excluded by a positive act of the will, the marriage is invalid. (See can. 1101, §2.) Perpetuity is an essential property of marriage by the law of nature, and therefore one consenting to anything less than a perpetual marriage is not consenting to marriage at all.

Canon 1099 states in part that error concerning the indissolubility of marriage does not vitiate marital consent provided it does not determine the will. Thus, one can erroneously believe that a marriage can end by civil divorce, yet still marry validly. A person may believe that divorce, in general, is a viable option, yet still choose to marry perpetually this person. On the other hand, if the error concerning indissolubility affects the will such that one intends to enter a union that can be dissolved, then the consent is invalid.

The intention *contra bonum sacramenti* is often placed hypothetically, as, e.g., "I marry you till death do us part as long as everything works out all right." Nor does the intention against perpetuity have to be explicit. It can be implicit when "the circumstances are so unusual and compelling that the only reasonable conclusion that can be drawn from them is that indissolubility was excluded." (Wrenn, 107) For example, a person who believes in the possibility of divorce marries someone he does not love, divorces soon after the marriage, and attempts marriage with another. The person had not made a conscious and explicit decision against perpetuity, but the intention was there implicitly as demonstrated by subsequent circumstances.

J.   Conditional Consent

Future condition. A marriage cannot be validly contracted on the basis of a condition regarding the future. (Can. 1102, §1)

A condition is a circumstance attached to a legal agreement on which the validity of the agreement depends. A future condition suspends the validity of the marriage until it is fulfilled. For example, "I marry you on the condition that I will find happiness with you." Such a marriage is invalid, because marriage is made by consent given in the present; it cannot be suspended until some future circumstance is realized. (Future licit conditions were possible under the 1917 code, can. 1092, 3°; such marriages became valid only when the condition was fulfilled.)

A true future condition that invalidates marriage is one whose fulfillment is regarded as being more important than the marriage itself. Some examples: I marry you provided you make me happy; provided I am happy and fulfilled; provided you do not want to have children. For a circumstance to be a true condition, ordinarily it must have real and objective importance and be related to the marital relationship. (See CLSA Comm., 787.) On the other hand, a condition can sometimes be so important subjectively that there is no consent unless that condition is fulfilled. A woman, e.g., who was raised by alcoholic parents, insists she will never marry a heavy drinker; five years after marriage her husband begins drinking heavily and the marriage breaks up. If her consent was truly based on the future condition that her husband never become a heavy drinker, it was invalid.

Conditions are usually not explicitly placed and, even when implicit, future conditions invalidate consent. In the example above, the woman who would never marry a heavy drinker would not have to place this condition explicitly and consciously. It can be demonstrated to exist implicitly by the circumstances: her childhood experience, her aversion to people who drink heavily, the disruption of the marriage and her departure caused directly by the heavy drinking, etc.

Past and present conditions. A marriage, entered into on the basis of a condition regarding the past or the present, is valid or not depending on whether the basis for the condition exists or not. Such a condition may not be placed licitly without the written permission of the local Ordinary. (Can. 1102, §§ 2, 3)

A past condition is based on a circumstance that occurred or existed before consent was given, e.g., "I marry you provided you have not had sexual intercourse with another." A present condition is based on a circumstance that occurs or exists at the time consent is given, e.g., "I marry you provided you do not have venereal disease." If the condition is not met, the marriage is invalid; if the condition is met, the marriage is valid. The general remarks on condition under "future condition" above are also applicable to past and present conditions.

For liceity, the written permission of the local Ordinary is required to place a past or present condition. This has little practical importance because conditions are usually placed implicitly and, even if explicit, most Catholics are unaware of this requirement.

K. Force or Fear

A marriage is invalid when entered into by force or grave fear from without, even if not inflicted intentionally, such that, in order to be freed from it, the person is forced to choose marriage. (Can. 1103)

Force is a physical or moral coercion from outside the person which the person cannot resist. Any legal act is invalid when it is placed as a result of extrinsic force brought to bear on a person who is not able to resist it. (See can. 125, §1.) Since marriage is made by the free consent of the parties, a marriage that is forced against one's will is invalid.

Fear comes from within the person. In order to be invalidating it must be grave, inflicted from without, and causative of the marriage in order to be freed from the fear. Grave fear can be objectively serious and imminent, e.g., fear of loss of life or physical harm; or it can be subjectively grave, being perceived by one person as serious and imminent but not so by others. For example, an immature and impressionable nineteen year old girl, who has strict parents, may experience grave fear when she discovers an unwanted pregnancy and feel compelled to choose marriage so as not to displease her parents. On the other hand, a thirty year old woman who becomes pregnant may not have the same reaction.

The fear must also be inspired from without, that is, by another person. Reverential fear may be internal to oneself and not at all inspired by one's parents, for it may arise from one's imagination rather than from the action of the parents. However, the fear can even result from a person who did not intend to cause it. For example, the parents may have given past warnings about disowning their daughter if she ever became pregnant out of wedlock, but they would not actually do so in the real situation.

The fear must force one to choose marriage in order to be free of it. The person feels no other choice but to enter the marriage in order to be free of the fear. Fear is the cause of the marriage which would not take place without it.

three
Manifestation of Consent

A. Presence

In order that marriage be contracted validly, it is necessary that the contracting parties be present either in person or by proxy. (Can. 1104, §1)

> In virtue of this requirement, marriage is not contracted validly if the parties are only morally present, i.e., by telephone, radio, letter, etc. (See Vlaming/Bender, 377.) This prescription is of ecclesiastical law only and does not bind marriages between non-Catholics.

The parties must express matrimonial consent in words; but if they are unable to speak, in equivalent signs. (Can. 1104, §2)

> The use of speech by those who can speak, as well as the use of the precise words of the *Roman Ritual,* concern the liceity and not the validity of the marriage consent.

B. Marriage by Proxy

In order for a marriage to be validly contracted by proxy it is required that there be a special mandate to contract with a certain person, that the proxy be designated by the person giving the mandate, and that the proxy exercise this function in person. (Can. 1105, §1)

> For validity, the mandate must be signed by the one giving the mandate and also by the pastor or Ordinary of the place

where the mandate is given, or by a priest delegated by either of them, or at least by two witnesses; or it must be drawn up by an authentic document in accordance with civil law. If the one mandating cannot write, this is to be noted in the mandate itself and another witness should be added who also is to sign it, or else the mandate is invalid. (Can. 1105, §§ 2, 3)

A special mandate is required, i.e., a written document for contracting marriage; it is not sufficient that one give a general mandate for the placing of all legal acts in one's name. The mandate must be to contract marriage with a specific person; hence, one cannot give a mandate which would allow the proxy to choose a spouse and marry her in the name of the one giving the mandate. The proxy must be designated by the one giving the mandate and this designation may not be committed to others. (See CodCom, interpretation, May 31, 1948, AAS 40 (1948) 302; CLD 3:448.)

For liceity, the permission of the local Ordinary is necessary to allow a marriage to be celebrated with a proxy. (See can. 1071, §1, 7°.) N.B. Many states do not allow proxy marriages. (See CLSA Comm., 791.)

If the one mandating, before the proxy contracts marriage in that person's name, shall revoke the mandate or become insane, the marriage is invalid, even if the proxy or other contracting party does not know of this. (Can. 1105, §4)

Eastern law. Marriage cannot validly be celebrated by a proxy unless the particular law proper to a church *sui iuris* establishes otherwise, in which case there must be provided the conditions under which such a marriage can be celebrated. (CCEC, can. 837, §2)

C. Marriage Through an Interpreter

Marriage can be contracted through an interpreter. Nevertheless, the pastor should not assist at such a marriage unless he is convinced of the trustworthiness of the interpreter. (Can. 1106)

XI The Celebration of Marriage

The Canonical Form

o n e

A. The Minister and Two Witnesses

Only those marriages are valid which are contracted in the presence of the local Ordinary, the pastor, or the priest or deacon delegated by either of them, and in the presence of two witnesses, in accord with the regulations expressed in the canons which follow, and without prejudice to the exceptions in canons 144; 1112, §1, 1116; and 1127, §§ 1 and 2. (Can. 1108, §1)

> Assistance at marriage is not an act of governance nor an act of the power of order. It is very similar, however, to governance, for the right and power to assist at marriages is had by reason of one's office, or it can be delegated, and the act of assistance is requisite for the validity of the marriage. The exceptions to the canonical form are discussed below.

The one who assists at marriage is understood to be only the person who is present and asks for the manifestation of the consent of the parties and receives it in the name of the Church. (Can. 1108, §2)

> The minister who assists must do so actively. He must ask for and receive the consent of both parties, not only of one. (See CDF, reply, Nov. 28, 1975, CLD 8:820-22.) Mere passive assistance is invalid, e.g., when the minister allows the couple to give their consent without his asking for and receiving it. The words for this assistance are found in the *Rite of Marriage*, nn. 61 and 64 (1990 revised edition). These precise words are necessary for liceity, but not for validity as long as the minister asks for the consent of the parties and receives it in the name of the Church.

The two witnesses who must assist at the marriage with the minister must be present physically, and indeed simultaneously with the minister. They must be present morally so that they can testify to what is taking place. They must be used as witnesses, but for validity it seems sufficient that they be implicitly designated by the parties, as they are whenever the parties in any way at all wish to contract before persons present for the celebration of the marriage. (See Genicot 2, n. 627.) Anyone capable of being a witness by natural law acts as a valid witness in a Catholic marriage, whether the witness be a minor, a non-baptized person, an excommunicated person, etc. Therefore, the witness must have the use of reason and be capable of understanding what is happening by the exchange of consent. The law presumes the use of reason is attained at age seven.

Eastern canon law. The form of marriage is different from the Latin code. For validity, in addition to at least two witnesses, the marriage must be celebrated with a sacred rite, i.e., with the assistance and blessing by a priest. Deacons are not permitted to bless marriages in the Eastern churches. (See CCEC, can. 828.) The active request by the priest for the exchange of consent and its acceptance by him in the name of the Church is not essential, although Eastern Catholic marriage rituals contain explicit questions by the priest and responses by the partners. (See Pospishil, 472, 480.)

Since the blessing of the priest is required in the Eastern churches, what of the validity of a marriage of an Eastern Catholic celebrated in the Latin church before a deacon or a lay officiant? Similarly, what of the case of an Eastern Catholic subject to a Latin priest when the Eastern Catholic marries a non-baptized and the Latin priest does not impart a blessing? Such marriages should be considered valid on the basis of the principle, *locus regit actum* (the place determines the act). (See Pospishil/Faris, 32-33.)

B. Those Bound to the Form

The above mentioned form must be observed if at least one of the parties to the marriage was baptized in the Catholic Church or was received into it and has not left it by a formal act, without prejudice to canon 1127, §2. (Can. 1117)

In short, any marriage involving at least one Catholic requires the canonical form for validity in ordinary circumstances. All exceptions to this general rule are given below. For a discussion of what it means to leave the Church by a formal act, see chapter 9, page 222.

C. Faculty in Virtue of Office

The local Ordinary and the pastor, unless they have been excommunicated or interdicted or suspended from office by a sentence or decree, or have been declared to be such, by virtue of their office and within their territory, validly assist at marriages not only of their subjects but also of non-subjects, provided at least one of them is of the Latin rite. (Can. 1109)

> The pastor or local Ordinary cannot validly assist at marriages even of his own subjects outside of his territory; but within his territory he may validly assist at the marriages of people who are not his subjects, provided at least one of them is of the Latin church *sui iuris.* The territory of a parish is that within the parish boundaries, not simply the church property.
>
> *Eastern canon law.* At least one party must be of the same Eastern church *sui iuris* as the pastor or local hierarch who assists within his territory. A patriarch, however, may bless a marriage of a member of his church anywhere in the world. (See CCEC, can. 829.) The Latin code permits marriage in the church of either party, but the Eastern code prefers that the marriage be in the church of the groom: "A marriage shall be celebrated before the pastor of the groom, unless particular law or a just cause excuses." (CCEC, can. 831, §2) Nevertheless, in the case of an inter-ecclesial marriage between a Latin and an Eastern Catholic, the marriage can be celebrated in the church of either party.

Personal Ordinaries and pastors, in virtue of their office and within the limits of their jurisdiction, validly assist only at those marriages in which at least one party is their subject. (Can. 1110)

> A personal Ordinary or pastor is one whose jurisdiction is not based on territory, but on a certain class of persons, e.g., members of a certain nationality, language, profession, etc. It would include military chaplains, migrant chaplains, and others who may assist at marriages of special groups.

D. Delegated Faculty for Marriage

The local Ordinary and the pastor, as long as they validly hold office, can delegate the faculty, even a general one, to assist at marriage within their territory to priests and deacons. In order for the delegation of the faculty to assist at marriage to be valid, it must be expressly given to specified persons; if it is a question of special delegation, it must be given for a specific marriage; but if it is a question of general delegation, it must be granted in writing. (Can. 1111)

A pastor may validly delegate any priest or deacon to assist at marriages in his parish. General delegation must be given in writing—for the validity of the delegation. The following conditions also must be met for validity:

1) *A definite priest or deacon must be delegated;* the minister must be determined by name, or by office, etc. The priest or deacon is not sufficiently designated when the pastor notifies the superior of a monastery that he delegates as the priest to assist at a marriage whatever priest the superior shall select to send to the parish. (See CodCom, reply, May 20, 1923, AAS 16 (1924) 115; CLD 1:540-41.) However, several ministers may be delegated for one and the same marriage, provided that each is determined by name, or office, etc., i.e., is specifically designated. (See Sipos/Galos, §134.)

2) *The marriage must be determinate;* the marriage is specified by the names of the contracting parties, or by the hour and place of marriage, etc. However delegation can be given to one priest or deacon for several determinate marriages, provided each marriage is specifically designated. (See Capello 5, n. 674.) This requirement applies only in the case of special delegation, not general delegation.

3) *The delegation must be express,* i.e., given explicitly by words or in writing, or implicitly by signs or other actions. A tacit or presumed delegation is invalid. The mere silence of the pastor who knows another priest is assisting at a marriage in his parish is only tacit delegation and not sufficient; it is invalid.

4) *The marriage must take place in the territory of the delegating pastor.* A personal pastor cannot delegate another priest or deacon to witness a marriage in his church if neither of the parties is subject to him. (See CLSA Comm., 795.)

Subdelegation

One who has received general delegation for marriages can subdelegate another priest or deacon in individual cases. (See can. 137, §3.)

A parochial vicar or deacon, who has received general delegation to assist at marriages from the pastor or local Ordinary, can subdelegate another priest or deacon to assist at a definite marriage. (See CodCom, reply, Dec. 28, 1927, AAS 20 (1928) 61; CLD 1:541.)

One who has received a special delegation for a determinate marriage or marriages can subdelegate another priest or deacon to assist at the marriage only if this power of subdelegating is expressly conceded to him by the one delegating. (See can. 137, §3.)

A pastor or local Ordinary can delegate a certain priest or deacon to assist at a certain marriage and can also give him power to subdelegate another priest or deacon to assist at that marriage. No subdelegated power can be subdelegated again unless it is expressly permitted by the one delegating. (See can. 137, §4.) A parochial vicar who receives general delegation cannot grant his subdelegate the power to subdelegate again, unless this power was expressly granted to him by the pastor or Ordinary who delegated him.

Before special delegation is granted, everything must be done which the law requires to prove the freedom of the parties to marry. (Can. 1113)

The one who grants the special delegation, not the one who receives it, is responsible for seeing that the pre-marital investigation is conducted and all other marriage preparation requirements of universal or particular law are observed.

E. Some Conditions for Licit Assistance

The one who assists at marriage acts illicitly unless he has first established the freedom of the parties to marry in accord with the law and, if possible, has the permission of the pastor whenever he assists in virtue of general delegation. (Can. 1114)

The one who assists can be assured of the parties' freedom to marry if he ascertains that all the marriage preparation requirements of universal and particular law have been fulfilled. The permission of the pastor by one who has general delegation can often be presumed. Since the assistance at marriages and the nuptial blessing are functions especially committed to the pastor by canon 530, n. 4, the pastor may reserve any or all weddings in the parish to himself.

F. Marriage to an Eastern non-Catholic

The canonical form stated in canon 1108 is to be observed in mixed marriages; if, however, a Catholic contracts marriage with an Eastern non-Catholic party, the canonical form must be observed only for the liceity of the celebration; for validity, however, the blessing of the priest is required, observing the other requirements of the law. (See can. 1127, §1; CCEC, can. 834, §2.)

If a Catholic wishes to marry an Eastern non-Catholic in the Eastern non-Catholic church, the dispensation from the observance of the canonical form is required for liceity only. For validity, the marriage must take place before the Eastern non-Catholic priest, because the blessing of the priest is required for the validity of the marriage in the Eastern churches.

It is forbidden, either before or after the celebration of the marriage in the Eastern non-Catholic church, to have another religious celebration of the same marriage to give or renew marital consent. It is likewise forbidden to have any religious celebration in which a Catholic assistant and non-Catholic minister together, following their own rite, ask for the consent of the parties. (See can. 1127, §3.)

> Not forbidden by this law is a second ceremony, following the Catholic form, in which the Eastern non-Catholic priest imparts a marriage blessing without a renewal of consent. (See CDF, reply, June 16, 1966, CLD 6:22-23.)

G. Dispensation from Form in Mixed Marriages

If serious difficulties prevent the observance of the canonical form, the local Ordinary of the Catholic party has the right to dispense from it in individual cases, after consulting the Ordinary of the place where the marriage is celebrated. For validity, there must be some public form of celebrating the marriage. The episcopal conference may enact norms by which the above stated dispensation can be granted uniformly. (Can. 1127, §2)

> In any mixed marriage other than one with an Eastern non-Catholic, the canonical form is required for validity. Therefore a dispensation is necessary for the validity of such a marriage if the canonical form is not going to be observed.
>
> A requirement for the dispensation is the presence of serious difficulties. Any dispensation requires a just and reasonable cause (can. 90), so the serious difficulties mentioned here must be something more than that. According to the statement on mixed marriages of the NCCB, the following are types of reasons which qualify for granting the dispensation: to achieve family harmony or to avoid family alienation, to obtain parental agreement to the marriage, to recognize the significant claims of relationship or special friendship with a non-Catholic minister, to permit the marriage in a church that has particular importance to the non-Catholic. (See NCCB, statement, Nov. 16, 1970, CLD 7:737.)
>
> For validity, there must be some public form of a marriage celebrated with a dispensation from form. This can be in the non-Catholic church, before a justice of the peace, in the reception hall,

etc., so long as it is a public celebration with witnesses present.

Although a common law marriage is valid in some civil jurisdictions, it would not be valid in canon law in this case because it
lacks a public form of celebration. (On the other hand, if two non-
Catholics contract a common law marriage, it is recognized as
valid by canon law provided the civil law recognizes its validity.)

A dispensation from form for marriages involving two Catholics
can be given only by the Holy See, except in danger of death. (See can.
1079; Pontifical Commission for the Authentic Interpretation of the
Code of Canon Law, interpretation, AAS 77 (1985) 771; CLD 11:14.)

Eastern law. Dispensation from the form prescribed by law for the
celebration of marriage is reserved to the Apostolic See or the patriarch,
nor should they grant it except for a most serious reason. (CCEC, can.
835)

H. Supplied Faculty

In common error, whether of fact or of law, and also in positive
and probable doubt, whether of law or fact, the Church supplies executive power of governance both for the external and internal forum.
This also applies to the faculty for marriage. (See can. 144.)

> The use of canon 144 to supply the faculty for assisting at mar-
> riage in the case of common error can be done only in very limited
> circumstances. It is not sufficient for the community mistakenly
> to believe the minister has the faculty when in fact he does not.
> Rather, the circumstances must be such that the community errs
> concerning the *status* of the priest or deacon, e.g., believing the
> priest to be the pastor or the parochial vicar with general delega-
> tion, or the deacon as being assigned to the parish with general del-
> egation for marriages. This can happen, e.g., when a priest is merely
> in residence in the rectory, and is not assigned as parochial vicar,
> such that the community would think he has a general delegation
> for marriages when in fact he does not; or when a priest is
> involved on a regular basis with the pastoral care of a parish, even
> if not in residence. Thus, there must be some public fact as the basis
> for the error.
> The Church supplies the faculty here for the common good,
> because the community errs in thinking that this priest can be
> approached for any weddings in that parish. On the other hand, a
> visiting priest or deacon, who lacks special delegation for one or a
> few marriages, is not supplied with the faculty in virtue of canon
> 144. The reason is that the Church supplies the faculty for cases that
> affect the common good, and in the case of a lack of special delega-

tion, the good of the community is not at stake because it is only one or several determinate marriages in question.

A 1972 decision of the Rota summarizes well the question of supplied jurisdiction for marriage in the case of common error:

a)   In the practical order, common error exists whenever there is publicly placed a fact from which, if it were known by the community in question (e.g., a parish), all or nearly all would prudently think that power to assist at marriage belongs to a specified priest or deacon who as a matter of fact lacks it.

b)   The sole and adequate reason for which the Church supplies a lack of power is the necessity of promoting the common good or of avoiding a common evil. But not for a merely private good....

Consequently, it is not probable that the Church supplies power in cases where, even though common error exists, no danger of public harm is had, because ... there is no probable danger that many other members of the community would, as a matter of fact, approach the priest and celebrate invalid marriages. Therefore, there would be question of a purely speculative, not a really practical common error. In such a situation the Church would not supply jurisdiction ... because it is not to be believed that the supreme authority wishes to repair violation of a law ... for the sake of a purely private good which can be met by the convalidation of the marriage, even by granting a radical sanation for it.

From what has been said, it is clear that power is supplied when common error is verified relative to a priest to whom the parishioners can freely have recourse to celebrate marriages.... It is not applied, however, when the common error concerns a priest who is thought to have been delegated to assist at a specified marriage. (See Roman Rota, sentence, Dec. 11, 1972, CLD 8:172-73; see also Roman Rota, sentence, June 25, 1977, CLD 9:660-76.)

The above interpretation of supplied jurisdiction, as it applies to marriage, has not been changed with the revised Code. (See *Handbuch,* 785-86; Roman Rota, sentence, Apr. 29, 1983, *Monitor Ecclesiasticus* 109 (1984) 308-26.)

J.   Lay Officiant

Where priests and deacons are lacking, the diocesan bishop, with the previous favorable vote of the episcopal conference and permission obtained from the Holy See, can delegate lay persons to assist at marriages. A worthy lay person is to be chosen who is capable of giving instructions to the couples to be married and who can properly perform the marriage rite. (Can. 1112)

> *In the United States,* the NCCB "recommends to the Holy See that it favorably entertain the requests of those individual diocesan bishops who, in view of the severe shortage of ordained ministers in certain vast territories of the United States, seek the faculty to delegate lay persons to assist at marriages." (General meeting, Nov., 1989; see *The Jurist* 53 (1993) 406.)

K. The Extraordinary Form

If a person who is competent to assist at marriages in accord with the law cannot be present or cannot be approached without grave inconvenience, a couple who intends to enter a true marriage can validly and licitly contract before witnesses alone: (1) in danger of death; (2) outside the danger of death, provided it is prudently foreseen that this state of affairs will last for one month. In both cases, if another priest or deacon is available and can be present, he must be called upon for the celebration of the marriage together with the witnesses, without prejudice to the validity of the marriage before witnesses alone. (Can. 1116)

1. In danger of death

To contract marriage before witnesses only, it must be a case of true danger of death, either from an intrinsic cause (sickness) or an extrinsic cause (war, flood, etc.). The *articulum mortis* is not required, i.e., death need not be imminent.

It is also necessary that it be either absolutely or morally impossible for an authorized witness to be present or approached. It is absolutely impossible when there is no time to approach the official witness or to obtain from him delegation to assist at the marriage. It is morally impossible when this cannot be done without grave inconvenience, e.g., a dangerous journey during time of war, persecution, floods, etc.

It is also morally impossible for the official witness to be present or approached when he, although materially present in the place, is unable by reason of grave inconvenience to assist at the marriage asking and receiving the consent of the contracting parties. (See CodCom, interpretation, July 25, 1931, AAS 23 (1931) 388; CLD 1:542.) For example, if the pastor is forbidden by civil law to assist at the marriage of certain parties under penalties to be inflicted either on the pastor or on the parties, the pastor can be considered absent and unavailable in the sense of canon 1116. (See CSacr, reply, Apr. 24, 1935, CLD 2:336.) Note that the grave inconvenience mentioned in the canon is not only one which threatens the official witness, but also one which threatens both parties or either party to the marriage. (See CodCom, interpretation, May 3, 1945, AAS 37 (1945) 149; CLD 3:454.)

2.   Outside the danger of death

To contract marriage before witnesses only, it is required that it be either absolutely or morally impossible for an authorized witness (priest or deacon with the faculty) to be present or approached. It is also necessary that it be prudently foreseen that this situation is to last for a month.

The impossibility of an authorized witness being present or approached has been explained above. This is the case especially in mission countries and remote areas, and also in other places during time of war and persecution.

It must be foreseen that this situation will last for a month. A past month's absence does not suffice, but it is required that one prudently judge that the situation will last for a month yet. For the valid and licit use of canon 1116 the mere fact of the official witness's absence does not suffice, but it is required that there exist moral certainty, based either on common knowledge or on inquiry, that for one month the pastor, delegated priest or deacon (or lay officiant where applicable) will be neither available nor accessible without grave inconvenience. (See CodCom, interpretation, Nov. 10, 1925, AAS 17 (1925) 583; CLD 1:542.) The marriage would not, however, be invalid if the assistance of a competent minister became possible before the month elapsed, provided that at the time of the marriage there was little hope of this. (See Sipos/Galos, §134.)

3.   The priest or deacon of canon 1116, §2

If there is another priest or deacon at hand, he is to be called to the wedding to assist together with the witnesses. The priest or deacon of canon 1116, §2 is one who lacks the faculty to assist at marriages as the official witness. However, he is given ample faculties to dispense from matrimonial impediments and from the form of marriage according to the norms of canons 1079-1081. This priest or deacon is to be called both in danger of death and also outside the danger of death for marriages legally celebrated before two witnesses alone.

Canon 1116 speaks of a priest or deacon who is available; if there is none available, one need not be sought out. (See Vermeersch/Creusen 2, n. 406.) Even if he is available, the marriage is celebrated validly without him, provided two witnesses are used. Another opinion holds that in extreme circumstances a marriage would be valid before one witness or even no witnesses. (See CLSA Comm., 797.)

L. Common Law Marriage

Common law marriage, i.e., one in which a man and a woman contract marriage by the expression of true matrimonial consent but without any ceremony, i.e., without the intervention of a civil or religious official or of witnesses, is considered valid in some states of the union. In most states it is required by law that marriage be celebrated before a qualified civil or religious official, and common law marriages are considered invalid.

Since the laws of the states change in this matter, no attempt is made to enumerate the states in which common law marriages are considered valid. In marriage cases involving common law marriages, the following information must be ascertained: the date of the marriage, the domicile of the parties, the place of the marriage, and the law of the states involved as the law existed at the time the marriage was celebrated. Investigations may also be necessary to ascertain the competence of the civil or religious official who assisted at a marriage in states which do not recognize common law marriages. As is evident, a civil lawyer should be consulted in these matters.

Common law marriage between two non-Catholics is valid only in the manner recognized by the civil law to which the parties are bound. If the civil law recognizes the validity of such a marriage, the marriage is valid; if the civil law does not recognize the validity of common law marriage, such a union is invalid, even though the parties give a consent that by the law of nature would suffice.

1917 Code. For marriages contracted before November 27, 1983, the following rule applies: Common law marriage between two baptized non-Catholics or between a baptized non-Catholic and an unbaptized person was valid, even in states which did not recognize common law marriage, provided there was no impediment or defective consent. The reason for this is that marriages involving the baptized were not subject to the civil authority under the former law. (See Mathis/Bonner, 274-75.)

t w o
Liturgical Celebration and Recording

A. The Marriage Rites

Except for a case of necessity, the rites contained in the liturgical books approved by the Church, or those received by legitimate customs, are to be observed in the celebration of marriage. (Can. 1119)

There are four different rites of marriage in the 1990 *Ordo celebrandi matrimonium* (abbreviated RM for *Rite of Marriage*). The appropriate rite must be followed except in a case of necessity, such as danger of death, when the exchange of consent suffices.

It is fitting that the same presbyter who prepares the couple should, in the celebration of the sacrament, give the homily, ask and receive their consent, and celebrate the Mass. (RM, 23)

If a marriage is celebrated on a day that has a penitential character, especially during the season of Lent, the pastor should advise the couple to take into consideration the special nature of that day. The celebration of marriage is prohibited on Good Friday and Holy Saturday. (RM, 32)

B. Rite of Marriage During Mass

Whenever marriage is celebrated at Mass, the ritual Mass for weddings is used, with white vestments or some other festive color. On the days given in nn. 1-4 of the table of liturgical days, the Mass of the day is used with its readings, retaining the nuptial blessing and, if opportune, the proper formula for the final blessing. But if the wedding is celebrated at a parish Mass during the Christmas season or on a Sunday throughout the year, the Mass of the day is used. (See RM, 34.)

Ordinarily, the ritual Mass for marriage is used. However, on certain days the readings and other Mass texts must come from the day itself, retaining the nuptial blessing and, if opportune, the proper formula for the final blessing. These days are: Holy Week; the Easter octave; Christmas, Epiphany, Ascension, and Pentecost; the Sundays of Advent, Lent, and Easter; Ash Wednesday; solemnities of the Lord, of the Blessed Virgin Mary, and of the saints in the general calendar; All Souls' day; the solemnity of the principal patron of the place, city, or state; the solemnity of the dedication and anniversary of the dedication of a particular church; the solemnity of the titular saint of a particular church; the solemnity of the titular saint, founder, or principal patron of an order or congregation. Also, during the Christmas season and on Sundays throughout the year, the Mass texts proper to the day must be used if marriage is celebrated at a parish Mass.

The celebration of the sacrament must be carefully prepared together with the couple as much as can be done. By custom, marriage is celebrated within Mass. Nevertheless, the pastor should determine whether it would be better to suggest the celebration of marriage within Mass or outside of it, after he has considered both the need for pastoral care and the mode of ecclesial life of the participants, whether of the couple or the guests. (See RM, 29.)

Marriage of two Catholics

The Rite for Celebrating Marriage Within Mass should normally be used for the marriages of two Catholics. Some of the reasons for not using the rite when two Catholics marry are: (1) when a deacon or lay officiant is presiding; (2) when the priest has already binated on a weekday or trinated on a Sunday or holy day; (3) when one or both of the parties and perhaps also one or both families are not practicing Catholics.

Mixed marriage

With the permission of the local Ordinary, the marriage rite during Mass may also be used in mixed marriages between a Catholic and a baptized non-Catholic, if the situation warrants it. (See RM, 36.) Members of the non-Catholic Eastern churches may be invited to holy Communion. A Protestant may not receive holy Communion without the permission of the diocesan bishop. (See DE, 159; can. 844, §§ 3, 4.) According to the 1993 Directory for

Ecumenism, "the decision as to whether the non-Catholic party of the marriage may be admitted to Eucharistic Communion is to be made in keeping with the general norms existing in the matter both for Eastern Christians and for other Christians, taking into account the particular situation of the reception of the sacrament of Christian marriage by two baptized Christians." (See DE, 159.)

In most places where mixed marriages are commonplace, the local Ordinary's permission for a marriage celebration during Mass can often be presumed. The non-Catholic must be validly baptized. N.B. A wedding Mass is forbidden in non-sacramental marriages involving a Catholic and a non-baptized person.

It is forbidden to have any religious celebration in which a Catholic assistant and non-Catholic minister together, following their own rite, ask for the consent of the parties. (See can. 1127, §3.)

Not forbidden by this law is a second ceremony, after the Catholic form, in which the non-Catholic minister imparts a blessing or has a ceremony without the exchange or renewal of consent.

In the United States. With the permission of the local Ordinary and the consent of the appropriate authority of the other church or community, a non-Catholic minister may be invited to participate in the Catholic marriage service by giving additional prayers, blessings, or words of greeting or exhortation. (See NCCB statement, n. 15, CLD 7:738.)

C. Rites of Marriage Outside Mass

1. Rite of Marriage Without a Mass

This second rite of marriage is used at a mixed marriage between a Catholic and a baptized non-Catholic, and also between two Catholics for reasons such as those noted above.

Upon the request of the couple, the local Ordinary may permit the Catholic priest to invite the minister of the non-Catholic party to participate in the celebration of marriage, to read from the scriptures, give a brief exhortation, and bless the couple. (See DE, 158.)

Holy Communion should not be given at a mixed marriage outside of Mass, not only because the law prefers that Communion be given during Mass (cf. can. 918), but also because it is ecumenically sensitive not to give Communion when only the Catholic party and guests are permitted by law to receive. The

Catholic party who wants to receive Communion on his or her wedding day should be encouraged to attend Mass earlier that day.

2 *Rite of Marriage before a Lay Officiant*

A lay person who has the faculty from the diocesan bishop to assist at the celebration of marriage should be solicitous regarding both the catechetical formation of the couple and their spiritual preparation. He or she is to arrange everything that is required by law and whatever pertains to the rites, prayers, readings, and participation of the community so that the rite of the sacrament of marriage is correctly, consciously and fruitfully celebrated. The lay officiant has the duty not only of receiving the consent of the parties but should preside over the whole celebration of marriage. (RM, 119)

> This rite may only be used in those places that have been given approval to allow lay ministers to assist at marriages. (See can. 1112.)

3 *Rite of Marriage between a Catholic and a Catechumen or non-Christian*

This rite is used when a Catholic contracts marriage with a catechumen or a non-Christian, when two catechumens marry, or when a catechumen marries a non-Christian. The celebration may take place in the church or in some other convenient place. (See RM, 152.)

> There may be no Mass or Communion with this rite of marriage.

D. **Place of Celebration**

1. *Sacramental marriages*

A marriage between two Catholics or between a Catholic party and a baptized non-Catholic is to be celebrated in the parish church; with the permission of the local Ordinary or the pastor, it may be celebrated in some other church or oratory. (Can. 1118, §1; see also RM, 27.)

> The parish church of the Catholic party, whether of the bride or the groom, is the typical place for the marriage celebration. The Catholic pastor of the bride or the groom could give permission for it to be celebrated in another Catholic church or oratory only; the local Ordinary's permission would be needed for some non-Catholic place. Also necessary is the permission of the rector or competent superior of the church or oratory where the wedding is to be held.

In the Eastern Catholic churches, as noted above, the law requires that marriage be celebrated in the church of the groom unless particular law determines otherwise or a just cause excuses. (See can. 831, §2.)

An oratory is a place for divine worship for the benefit of some community or assembly of the faithful to which other members of the faithful may go with permission of the competent superior. (See can. 1223.) Oratories would include the places of worship in a religious house, seminary, Catholic school, etc. A church is a place of worship to which the faithful have a right to go, such as a parish church or cathedral. (See can. 1214.)

The local Ordinary may permit marriages to be celebrated in some suitable place besides a church or oratory. (See can. 1118, §2.)

This permission is needed only for sacramental marriages. For non-sacramental marriages, see below. A suitable place would include a non-denominational chapel, or a place of worship of another Christian church or ecclesial community when there is good reason for having it there, such as a mixed marriage. The local Ordinary is free to determine what constitutes a suitable place, and thus he may exclude certain kinds of places, such as garden weddings, reception hall weddings, etc. since the ecclesial significance of a sacramental marriage is not well signified in such places.

N.B. This permission does not constitute a dispensation from form; it presumes the Catholic minister will assist at the wedding. On the other hand, when a dispensation from form is obtained, this permission is unnecessary.

2.   Non-sacramental marriages

A marriage between a Catholic party and a non-baptized party can be celebrated in a church or in some other suitable place. (Can. 1118, §3)

Permission of the local Ordinary is not necessary to have a non-sacramental marriage outside a church or other sacred place. However, it would be within the diocesan bishop's authority to establish guidelines for what constitutes "suitable" places even for nonsacramental marriages.

E.   The Secret Celebration of Marriage

The local Ordinary can permit a marriage to be celebrated in secret for a serious and urgent reason. (Can. 1130)

Some examples of a serious and urgent reason for a secret marriage are: marriages contrary to civil law if the prohibition is contrary to natural or ecclesiastical law, such as interracial marriages; marriages in countries where the church is persecuted and religious marriages are forbidden; marriages of those living in concubinage when they are believed by the community to be married. (See CLSA Comm., 807.)

The permission to celebrate a marriage in secret also requires: (1) that the investigations which must precede marriage be conducted in secret; and (2) that secrecy concerning the marriage be observed by the local Ordinary, the one who assists at the marriage, the witnesses, and the spouses. (Can. 1131) This obligation to observe the secret on the part of the local Ordinary ceases if there arises from the observance of the secret either serious scandal or serious harm to the sanctity of marriage. This fact is to be made known to the parties before the marriage celebration. (Can. 1132)

For the law on the recording of a secret marriage, see below.

F.   Recording of Marriages

After a marriage has been celebrated the pastor of the place of celebration, or the one who takes his place, even if neither has assisted at the marriage, should record in the marriage register as soon as possible the names of the spouses, the minister who assisted, and the witnesses, and the place and date of celebration, in accord with the manner prescribed by the episcopal conference or by the diocesan bishop. (Can. 1121, §1)

Marriages are also to be recorded in the baptismal register of the place in which the baptism of the spouses has been recorded. If a spouse has contracted marriage in a place other than the parish of baptism, the pastor of the place of celebration should send as soon as possible notification of the marriage to the pastor of the place where baptism was conferred. (Can. 1122)

Marriages with a dispensation from form. The local Ordinary who granted the dispensation is responsible for recording the dispensation and the celebration of the marriage. (See can. 1121, §3.)

The extraordinary form. When a marriage is celebrated according to canon 1116 without a competent minister assisting either in danger of death or a month's absence of the minister, the priest or deacon, if present at the celebration, is obliged to inform the pastor or local Ordinary;

if there was no priest or deacon present, the witnesses have this obligation. (See can. 1121, §2.)

A marriage celebrated in secret is recorded only in the special register kept in the secret archives of the curia. (Can. 1133)

Convalidations, annulments, dissolutions. Whenever a marriage is convalidated in the external forum, or is declared null, or is legitimately dissolved except for death, the pastor of the place of the celebration of marriage must be notified so that a notation may be duly made in the marriage and baptismal registers. (Can. 1123)

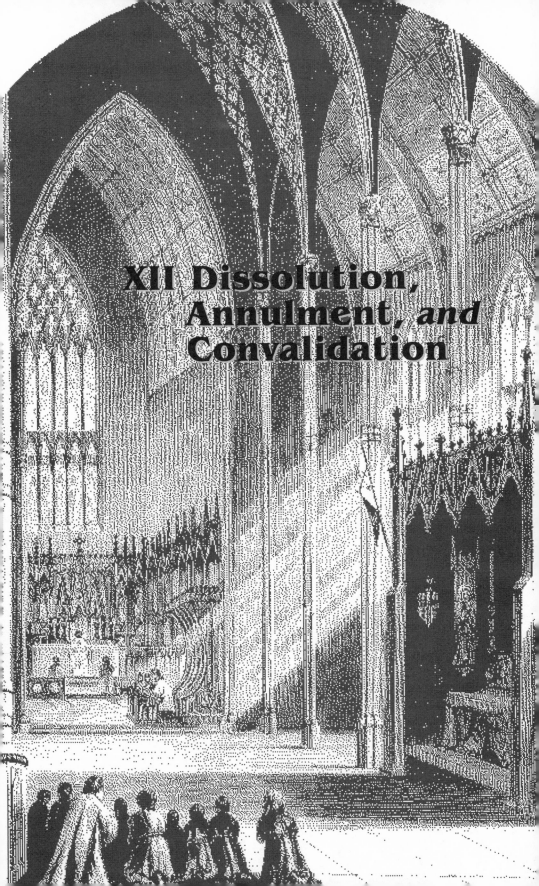

XII Dissolution, Annulment, and Convalidation

o n e

Dissolution of the Bond

A. The Bond of Marriage

From a valid marriage there arises between the spouses a bond which by nature is perpetual and exclusive. In Christian marriage, additionally, the spouses are strengthened and, as it were, consecrated by a special sacrament for the duties and dignity of their state. (Can. 1134)

> The bond of marriage arises from a valid marriage when true consent is given. This bond is exclusive and perpetual. Even when the two parties divorce, the bond persists and remarriage is considered invalid and adulterous. Therefore, it is necessary for prior marriages to be annulled or dissolved before a subsequent marriage is permitted in the Catholic Church.

A ratified marriage (*matrimonium ratum*) is a valid marriage between baptized persons; a ratified and consummated marriage (*matrimonium ratum et consummatum*) is a valid marriage between baptized persons after there occurs the conjugal act in a human manner which is per se apt for the generation of children, to which marriage is ordained by its very nature and by which the spouses become one flesh. After marriage has been celebrated and the spouses have lived together, consummation is presumed unless the contrary is proven. (See can. 1061, §§ 1, 2.) A ratified and consummated marriage cannot be dissolved by any human power or by any other cause except death. (Can. 1141)

> For consummation to occur, there must be an act of sexual intercourse after the marriage is validly contracted, and it must be

done in a "human manner," i.e., not with force, fear, or induced by drugs or other means against one's will. Rape is not consummation.

The principle enunciated in canon 1141 applies to the marriage of all the baptized, even of non-Catholics, provided both parties are validly baptized. No authority, civil or ecclesiastical, can dissolve sacramental (ratified) marriages after they have been consummated. The civil authority has no power to dissolve any kind of valid marriage, even the marriage of the unbaptized.

B. Non-Consummated Marriages

A non-consummated marriage between baptized persons or between a baptized party and a non-baptized party can be dissolved by the Roman Pontiff for a just cause, either by both parties requesting it, or by one of them, even if the other party is opposed. (Can. 1142)

> The procedure to be followed in non-consummation cases is found in Book VII of the code, canons 1697-1706. The dissolution is granted only by the pope, but the petition for the dissolution is handled by the diocese of the petitioner and then forwarded to the Apostolic See for adjudication. There must be proof of the fact of non-consummation, or that it did not take place in a human manner, as, e.g., in the case of forced sexual intercourse. There must also be proof of the existence of a just cause for granting the dispensation. (See cans. 1698-99.)
>
> Just causes for granting the dispensation include: subsequent impotence; possible existence of antecedent impotence; irreconcilable discord; contagious disease contracted or discovered after the marriage; desertion; partial proof that the marriage was invalid for want of consent. Often in impotence cases the impediment cannot be proved with certainty, but it can be proved that the marriage was not consummated so dispensation from a non-consummated marriage is sought. (See Mathis/Bonner, 282.)
>
> The papal power spoken of in canon 1142 extends to the following marriages: (1) ratified non-consummated marriage (between two baptized persons); (2) non-consummated marriage between a baptized and non-baptized person; (3) a legitimate consummated marriage which becomes a ratified non-consummated marriage, i.e., the marriage is contracted between two unbaptized persons and consummated by them, then both are baptized but the marriage is not consummated again after the baptism; (4) the same as in n. 3 if only one party receives baptism and the marriage is not again consummated after baptism.
>
> Non-consummated marriages between two unbaptized persons are not dissolved in virtue of canon 1142. Non-consummated

marriages can no longer be dissolved by solemn religious profession as was possible under the 1917 code.

C. Introduction to the Privilege of the Faith

The privilege of the faith may be defined as the right to act in a way that is favorable to the acquiring or preserving of the faith. In reference to marriage the term is used to designate the Pauline privilege, the Petrine privilege, and the special cases provided for in canons 1148 and 1149.

1) The Pauline privilege is based on I Cor 7:12-15. It applies to the marriage of two unbaptized persons, even if consummated, when one of the spouses later is baptized.

2) The Petrine privilege is the dissolution of a legitimate marriage of a baptized party with an unbaptized person granted by the pope in favor of the faith.

3) Canons 1148 and 1149 are based on missionary faculties granted by Paul III (Constitution, *Altitudo*, June 1, 1537), Pius V (Constitution, *Romani Pontificis*, Aug. 2, 1571), and Gregory XIII (Constitution, *Populis*, Jan. 25, 1585). They deal with cases of converts who had been in polygamous marriages and converts separated from their first spouse by reason of captivity or persecution.

Presumption in favor of faith. In a doubtful matter the privilege of the faith enjoys the favor of the law. (Can. 1150)

> According to this principle, doubtful matters in privilege of the faith cases are resolved in favor of the convert or baptized party to marry again. A matter is doubtful when every effort has been made to ascertain the truth but the doubt remains insoluble, i.e., certitude cannot be obtained either by evidence or by presumptions. The doubt may concern the validity of the former marriage, the identity of the first spouse, the sincerity of the answers of the party requesting the privilege, the baptism of one party, etc. N.B. If the doubt concerns the baptism of both parties the privilege of the faith is not given because it may be a *ratum et consummatum* marriage from which the pope does not dispense. (See Congregation of the Holy Office, decree, June 10, 1937, AAS 29 (1937) 305; CLD 2:343.)

D. The Pauline Privilege

1. *The privilege*

A marriage of two unbaptized persons can be dissolved by the Pauline privilege in favor of the faith of the party who received baptism by the very fact that a new marriage is contracted by that party, provided the unbaptized party departs. The unbaptized party is considered to have departed if he or she does not wish to cohabit with the baptized party or to cohabit peacefully without contumely toward the Creator, unless the baptized party after baptism has given just cause for the unbaptized party's departing. (Can. 1143)

> The privilege can be used in the following cases: (1) a Catholic who wishes to marry a convert to Catholicism, who was previously non-baptized and had been married to another non-baptized; (2) a Catholic who wishes to marry a validly baptized non-Catholic, who was previously non-baptized and married to another non-baptized; (3) a convert to Catholicism who was formerly non-baptized and married to a non-baptized person who now wishes to marry a baptized or non-baptized person. (See CLSA Comm., 814.) In short, the Pauline privilege only applies to marriages where both parties were unbaptized, and then one of them receives baptism. If both of them receive baptism, the marriage could be handled as a non-consummation case provided there was no sexual intercourse in a human manner after the baptism of both, since that would make the marriage *ratum et consummatum.*
>
> Two further conditions are necessary for the privilege: (1) that one of the parties is baptized before the second marriage; and (2) that the non-baptized departs. The departure of the non-baptized party is usually indicated by the civil divorce of the parties who were married as unbaptized persons. If the parties are not separated at the time of the baptism of one of them, the Pauline privilege can be used only in two circumstances: (1) if the non-baptized is the cause of the later separation; or (2) if the non-baptized, though not separating or divorcing, will not live in peace with the baptized party without contumely toward the Creator. The phrase, "without contumely toward the Creator" refers to the case of a non-baptized spouse who does not depart but makes it difficult for the baptized party to fulfill the obligations of the Christian life or to live peacefully. (See CLSA Comm., 814-15.)
>
> The privilege may not be used if the fault for the departure of the unbaptized spouse was that of the baptized spouse, after the latter had received baptism. A just cause for the departure of the non-baptized would be adultery or some other offense, provided it is not condoned by the unbaptized spouse. Adultery on the part of the convert would not be the cause of the departure if the unbaptized had also been guilty of adultery, or had condoned it, or was unaware of it so that it had no influence on the breakdown of the marriage. If there is a doubt about the cause of departure, the judgment is to be given in favor of the faith according to

the presumption of canon 1150. If the party who caused the unbaptized party's departure is baptized only after this departure occurred, the privilege may still be used.

The dissolution of the marriage of the parties who had married when unbaptized occurs at the moment when the party now baptized marries again. Such a new marriage can be permitted only after the interpellation has been conducted by the local Ordinary according to canons 1144-1146.

2   The interpellation

In order for the baptized party validly to contract a new marriage, the non-baptized party must be asked whether: (1) he or she also wishes to receive baptism; (2) he or she at least is willing to cohabit peacefully with the baptized party without contumely toward the Creator. (Can. 1144, §1)

> Asking the unbaptized party these two questions is called the interpellation or interrogation. Both questions must be asked of the non-baptized party for the validity of the new marriage, unless the interpellation is dispensed.

The interpellation is ordinarily conducted under the authority of the local Ordinary of the converted party. The local Ordinary must grant the unbaptized party, if he or she requests it, a period of grace before responding, warning the said party, however, that if this period of grace elapses without reply, the person's silence will be considered a negative response. (See can. 1145, §1.)

> The reason for this rule is to give the unbaptized person sufficient time to consider his or her reply without creating undue delays, whether deliberate or unintentional.

An interpellation made privately by the converted party is also valid and, if the form prescribed above cannot be observed, it is also licit. (Can. 1145, §2)

> It is licit for the party to make the interpellation on his or her own authority only when it cannot be made on the authority of the local Ordinary. In this case the party should see to it that several witnesses can testify to the answers given by the non-baptized party, or to the fact that letters have been sent to that party and a negative answer or no answer has been received. In the absence of witnesses, a letter signed by the unbaptized party or the sworn testimony of a knowledgeable witness would be sufficient proof. (See Vermeersch/Creusen 2, n. 432.)

In either case, the fact of the interpellation and its outcome must be legitimately established in the external forum. (Can. 1145, §3)

> There must be some external forum proof that the interpellation took place and the responses to the two questions must be stated.

Dispensation from the interpellation. The interpellation must be done after the baptism; but the local Ordinary, for a serious reason, can permit the interpellation to be conducted before the baptism; or he can even dispense from the interpellation, whether before or after baptism, provided it is established by means of at least a summary and extra-judicial process that the interpellation could not be done or would be useless. (Can. 1144, §2)

> A decree of the civil divorce of the marriage originally contracted between the unbaptized parties is sufficient reason for dispensing from the interpellation, unless there is contrary evidence that the non-baptized party still desires to be married to the baptized party and would answer affirmatively to either of the questions asked in the interpellation. Other reasons for a dispensation should be established by some process, either judicial or extra-judicial, depending on the nature of the evidence.

3. The new marriage

The baptized party has the right to contract a new marriage with a Catholic party: (1) if the other party has responded negatively to the questions, or if the interpellation has been legitimately omitted; (2) if the unbaptized party, whether already interpellated or not, first persevered in peaceful cohabitation without contumely toward the Creator, but afterward departed without a just cause, with due regard for canons 1144 and 1145. (Can. 1146)

> Even though the baptized party may have continued the marriage after baptism, he or she does not lose the right to contract a new marriage with a Catholic party, and therefore can use this right if the unbaptized party later has a change of mind and departs without just cause or ceases to cohabit peacefully without contumely toward the Creator. Thus, the possibility for using the Pauline privilege lasts as long as the other party remains unbaptized.
>
> A negative response would also include long delays on the part of the unbaptized party, or obstinate silence, or subterfuges to impede the serving of the interpellation, etc., if from these acts

moral certitude exists that he or she does not wish to convert or at least to cohabit peacefully without contumely toward the Creator.

The local Ordinary, for a serious reason, can permit the baptized party using the Pauline privilege to contract a marriage with a non-Catholic or another unbaptized party, observing the canons on mixed marriages. (Can. 1147)

> A serious reason for permitting the Catholic convert to remarry a non-Catholic would be evidence that this would strengthen the baptized party's faith rather than endanger it. In case of doubt, the local Ordinary may grant permission for a marriage with a baptized non-Catholic, or a dispensation from disparity of cult for a marriage with another non-baptized.

E. The Petrine Privilege

> For a just cause, the pope can dissolve any marriage that is not both ratified and consummated, provided at least one of the parties is baptized at the time the dissolution is given. Whereas the Pauline privilege is used in cases where two unbaptized persons marry and one converts, the Petrine privilege may be used in a non-sacramental marriage contracted by one baptized and one unbaptized, even if consummated.

1) In order that a dissolution may be validly granted, three conditions are absolutely required:

a) lack of baptism of one of the two spouses during the whole time of their married life;

b) nonuse of the marriage [no consummation] after the baptism perchance received by the party who was not baptized;

c) that the person who is not baptized or baptized outside the Catholic Church yields freedom and ability to the Catholic party to profess his or her own religion and baptize and educate the children as Catholics: this condition must be safeguarded in the form of a promise (*cautio*). (CDF, instruction and norms, Dec. 6, 1973, CLD 8:1177)

> The person in question who is unbaptized or baptized outside the Catholic Church is the party who wishes to marry the Catholic after the dissolution of the first marriage. Such a person must promise that the Catholic will be able to practice the Catholic faith and raise the children in the faith. This promise is required to ensure that the privilege will truly be granted "in favor of the faith" of the Catholic party.

2)   It is further required:

a) that there is no possibility of restoring married life because of persistent radical and irremediable discord;

b) that from the grant of the favor no danger of public scandal or serious wonderment be had;

c) that the petitioner is not the culpable cause of the breakdown of the valid, non-sacramental marriage and the Catholic party with whom the new marriage is to be contracted or convalidated did not provoke separation of the spouses by reason of fault on his or her part;

d) that the other party of the previous marriage be interpellated if possible, and does not offer reasonable opposition;

e) that the party seeking the dissolution take care that children who may have been born of the previous marriage be brought up in a religious manner;

f) that equitable provisions be made according to the laws of justice for the abandoned spouse and for the children who may have been born;

g) that the Catholic party with whom a new marriage is to be entered live in accord with his or her baptismal promises and take care of the new family;

h) that when there is question of a catechumen with whom marriage is to be contracted, moral certitude be had regarding the baptism to be received shortly, if the baptism itself cannot be waited for (which is to be encouraged). (Ibid., 1178)

These conditions are all for liceity.

3)   Dissolution is more readily granted if on some other ground there is serious doubt about the validity of the marriage itself.

4)   A marriage between a Catholic party and a party not baptized entered into with a dispensation from disparity of cult can also be dissolved provided that the conditions set down in nn. 2 and 3 are verified and provided it is established that the Catholic party, because of the particular circumstances of the region, especially because of the very small number of Catholics in the region, could not have avoided marriage and lead a life consonant with the Catholic religion in that marriage. Moreover, the Congregation for the Doctrine of the Faith must be instructed about the publicity of the marriage celebrated.

5)   Dissolution of a valid, non-sacramental marriage entered into with a dispensation from the impediment of disparity of cult is not granted to a Catholic party who petitions to enter a new marriage with a non-baptized person who is not a catechumen.

6) Dissolution of a valid, non-sacramental marriage is not granted if it was contracted or convalidated after a dissolution had been obtained from a previous, valid, non-sacramental marriage. (Ibid., 1178-79)

> Petrine privilege cases are prepared under the jurisdiction of the local Ordinary who is competent to handle marriage annulment cases.

F. Polygamous Converts

A non-baptized man who simultaneously has several unbaptized wives, after he receives baptism in the Catholic Church, can keep one of them and dismiss the others if it is hard on him to remain with the first wife. The same is applicable to a non-baptized woman who simultaneously has several unbaptized husbands. In these cases the marriage, after the reception of baptism, must be contracted in the legitimate form, also observing, if necessary, the norms on mixed marriage and any other requirements of the law. The local Ordinary, bearing in mind the moral, social, and economic condition of the area and of the persons, should see to it that adequate provision is made for the needs of the first wife and the other wives dismissed, observing principles of justice, Christian charity, and natural equity. (Can. 1148)

G. Separation Due to Captivity or Persecution

A non-baptized person who, after receiving baptism in the Catholic Church, is unable to restore cohabitation by reason of captivity or persecution, may contract another marriage even if the other party has meanwhile received baptism, with due regard for canon 1141. (Can. 1149)

> Canon 1141 states that a ratified and consummated marriage cannot be dissolved by any human power or for any reason except death. Therefore, this privilege can be used only in cases where there has been no consummation of a marriage after both parties were baptized.

t w o
Annulments

An annulment is a declaration by a competent tribunal of the Church that what had the appearance of marriage was in fact invalid according to canon law. Annulments are granted as a result of some impediment or on various grounds related to defective consent or lack of form. The most frequent ground for marriage nullity is defective consent, especially lack of due discretion and lack of due competence, canon 1095, nn. 2 and 3.

A. Presumption in Favor of Marriage

Marriage enjoys the favor of law; therefore, when there is a doubt, the validity of a marriage is to be upheld until the contrary is proven. (Can. 1060)

> When there is doubt concerning the validity of a marriage that was certainly celebrated, the marriage is considered valid until the contrary is proved with moral certainty. The presumption presupposes an "appearance of marriage," i.e., some wedding ceremony according to the canonical form for Catholics or some publicly recognized exchange of consent for non-Catholics. (See CLSA Comm., 744.) If the very fact of the celebration of the marriage is doubtful, but it is favored by the fact that the parties are in possession of a decent public reputation as husband and wife, the marriage is likewise considered as valid until the opposite is proved. (See Mathis/Bonner, 197.)
>
> The presumption of canon 1060 holds not only for the marriages of Catholics but also of non-Catholics.

When there is a positive and insolvable doubt concerning the validity of a first marriage, a second marriage is to be declared invalid in virtue of canon 1060. The case is, however, to be handled according to the norms of law, i.e., not merely in a summary and administrative manner. (See CodCom, reply, June 26, 1947, AAS 39 (1947) 374; CLD 3:404.)

> A second marriage is to be declared invalid if it was celebrated at the time a former marriage existed that was doubtfully valid.

B. Who May Petition For an Annulment

Anyone, whether baptized or not, who was a party to a marriage involving at least one baptized person, whether Catholic or not, may petition a competent tribunal for an annulment. (See can. 1671.) Moreover, even an unbaptized person who was married to another unbaptized and now wants to marry a Catholic in the Church may petition for an annulment. (See cans. 1476 and 1674, 1°.)

> The party who petitions the tribunal for an annulment is called the petitioner. The other party who is asked to respond to the petition for a declaration of nullity is called the respondent. Annulment cases are handled as contentious processes, even if both parties wish to obtain the annulment.

C. The Competent Tribunal

In matrimonial cases which are not reserved to the Apostolic See, the following are competent:
1) the tribunal of the place where the marriage was celebrated;
2) the tribunal of the place where the respondent has a domicile or quasi-domicile;
3) the tribunal of the place where the petitioner has a domicile, provided that both parties live in the territory of the same episcopal conference and that the judicial vicar of the respondent's domicile, having heard the respondent, gives his consent;
4) the tribunal of the place where *de facto* most of the proofs are to be collected, provided the judicial vicar of the respondent's domicile gives consent and, before doing so, asks the respondent whether he or she has any objection. (Can. 1673)

> The following cases are reserved to the Apostolic See: heads of state, including governors (can. 1405, §1, 1°); non-consummation cases (can. 1698); and Petrine privilege cases.

three
Simple Convalidation
of Marriage

Convalidation is a legal remedy by which a couple's original marriage consent, which was invalid, is subsequently made valid. The consent may have been invalid for reasons of a diriment impediment, defective consent, or a defect of form. While the consent was invalid, the marital relationship still exists. The marriage is generally recognized as valid in the civil law, and the couple considers themselves to be married. Thus, convalidation is a means for granting Church recognition to a marriage that had been considered invalid according to canon law. Convalidations can only be given when there is an appearance of marriage; concubinage cannot be convalidated. (See *Handbuch*, 809.)

There are two categories of convalidation: simple convalidation which takes place by a private renewal of consent or according to the canonical form; and radical sanation (*sanatio in radice*) which involves no action on the part of the couple themselves but is a "healing to the roots" of the marriage by the intervention of competent ecclesiastical authority.

Pastoral ministers should not agree to a convalidation if they have serious doubts concerning the stability of the marriage, as, e.g., an immature couple, a hastily arranged civil marriage with a pregnancy involved, etc. It is better to wait for a suitable period, several years if necessary, to determine the stability of the marriage. If such a couple or the parents insist on a convalidation, the case should be referred to the local Ordinary. Such cases should be handled with extreme sensitivity so that the couple are not lost to the faith.

A. Convalidation Because of an Impediment

To convalidate a marriage that is invalid because of a diriment impediment, it is required that the impediment cease or it be dispensed, and that at least the party who knows of the impediment renew consent. This renewal of consent is required by ecclesiastical law for the validity of the convalidation, even if both parties gave consent in the beginning and have not since revoked it. (Can. 1156)

The impediment may cease in three ways: (1) automatically (e.g., prior bond, by the death of the former spouse; disparity of cult, by the conversion of the unbaptized; age, by mere lapse of time); (2) by dispensation; or (3) by a change in law (e.g., the former impediments of spiritual relationship and adultery with a promise to marry or with an attempted marriage). In danger of death or in urgent cases when everything is prepared for the wedding, canons 1079-1081 may be used to dispense.

The renewal of consent is required by ecclesiastical law only. It is not required by the natural law, for after the removal of the impediment, the consent given in the beginning and not since revoked would now take effect and bring about the validation of the marriage. Hence an invalid marriage of two non-Catholics would be validated upon the cessation of the impediment by mere continuation of conjugal life. This rule is generally recognized also in civil law, especially when the impediment was nonage or defective consent. However, in some states limitations are placed, so that marriages invalid because of certain types of impediments are not convalidated by mere marital cohabitation upon the cessation of the impediment. Hence, marriages involving two non-Catholics call for special investigation in individual cases. (See Mathis/Bonner, 298.)

In the former law, all the baptized, including non-Catholics, were bound to renew consent.

If a confessor discovers an impediment and the marriage cannot be convalidated, he should ordinarily leave the parties in good faith if they are inculpably ignorant of the invalidity of their marriage, especially if he foresees that they cannot be induced to separate, or that grave harm would come to them or their children by a separation. (See Sipos/Galos, 1142; Genicot 2, nn. 703, 706.)

The renewal of consent must be a new act of the will directed to a marriage which the renewing party knows or thinks was invalid from the beginning. (Can. 1157)

Knowledge or belief of the invalidity of the marriage must be had before the renewal of consent will effect the convalidation of the marriage. This is also a requirement of ecclesiastical law, so if only the non-Catholic party is aware of the impediment, a renewal of consent is not necessary. If the non-Catholic party, however, accepts the force of canon law and believes the original consent to have been invalid, then he or she also must renew consent by a new act of the will in accord with canon 1158. (See CLSA Comm., 824.)

If the impediment is public, consent must be renewed by both parties by the canonical form, without prejudice to canon 1127, §2. (Can. 1158, §1)

The impediment is public when it can be proved in the external forum (e.g., consanguinity, age, prior bond); otherwise it is occult. (See can. 1074.) Note, however, that the possibility of proof must be practical, i.e., one can find witnesses who are able and willing to testify; documents are available to prove the existence of the impediment, etc. Theoretical possibility of proof does not suffice, e.g., when the impediment is of its nature public and therefore should be able to be proved. (See Vermeersch/Creusen 2, n. 297.) For example, if the parties are related by blood but the fact cannot be proved, the impediment is occult.

The form required by law is the presence of the local Ordinary or pastor (or delegated priest or deacon) and two witnesses. However, if the impediment is by law public but in fact occult, the form can be observed quietly and secretly; if the impediment is also factually public, the form is to be observed publicly and openly. (See Sipos/Galos, §142.) Under the former law, baptized non-Catholics, when marrying other non-Catholics, were not bound to the form, but they were bound to the law to renew consent in a convalidation by means of some external act, provided they were conscious of the invalidity of the marriage. (See Mathis/Bonner, 299.)

The consent must be renewed by both parties. If the impediment is public by law but nevertheless unknown to one of the parties, he or she should be told and the marriage consent renewed with the observance of the canonical form. If this cannot be done, a *sanatio in radice* should be requested. (See Genicot 2, n. 707.)

Since a non-Catholic marrying a Catholic is bound to observe the canonical form for the validity of the marriage, in the case of public impediments, the renewal of consent by the non-Catholic according to the canonical form is also necessary for the validity of the convalidation. However, the canonical form may be dispensed from in mixed marriages in accord with canon 1127, §2 when there are serious difficulties that prevent the observance of the form. For example, the non-Catholic might refuse to renew consent before a priest or deacon, because he or she believes that the marriage was valid from the beginning. In such a case, a dispensation from the canonical form for the convalidation of a mixed marriage could be given, provided the non-Catholic gives assurances that the original consent still exists.

A dispensation from canonical form requires some public form of celebration for validity, and therefore a convalidation with a dispensation from form would require some public renewal of consent at least before witnesses, with the Catholic party renewing consent and the non-Catholic at least affirming that his or her original consent still exists. (See CLSA Comm., 824.) A better pastoral solution in such a case would be to request a *sanatio in radice.*

Whenever the case is public, the convalidation should be recorded in the marriage register. No record is made of a convalidation when the impediment cannot be proved.

If the impediment cannot be proved to exist, it suffices that consent be renewed privately and in secret, either by the party aware of the impediment, provided that the other's consent perseveres, or by both parties if the impediment is known to both of them. (Can. 1158, §2)

In occult cases the canonical form need not be observed and the consent is renewed without the intervention of the minister and witnesses. If, however, the marriage is also invalid because the canonical form was not observed in the first place, it is now necessary to renew consent in the presence of the authorized priest or deacon and two witnesses. If only one party knows of the impediment, it suffices that consent be renewed internally. If both know of the impediment, they should renew consent by some appropriate words or signs, such as sexual intercourse with affection as a sign of giving oneself in marriage. (See Gasparri 2, n. 1200.)

If both parties are Catholic, and both know of the occult impediment, both must renew consent. If one party is Catholic and the other non-Catholic, only the Catholic party must renew the consent, and the non-Catholic may do so. However, the non-Catholic party must affirm that the original consent still exists. If the non-Catholic party accepts the force of canon law and holds the original consent to be invalid, then he or she must renew consent. (See CLSA Comm., 824.) If only the non-Catholic party knows of the impediment, no renewal of consent is necessary unless the non-Catholic accepts the force of canon law and believes the marriage to be invalid.

B. Convalidation Because of Defective Consent

A marriage that is invalid because of defective consent is convalidated if the party who did not consent, now consents, provided that the consent given by the other party perseveres. (Can. 1159, §1)

> For the convalidation of a marriage where the original consent was defective for some reason or other (cans. 1095–1105), it is necessary that a new and valid consent be given. According to the norm of canon 1157, this renewal of consent must be a new act of the will directed to a marriage which is known or thought to be invalid from the beginning. Hence, if the party was unaware of the invalidity of the marriage, subsequent consent or the granting of marital rights would not convalidate the marriage. (See Roman Rota, case, July, 29, 1926, AAS 18 (1926); CLD 1:523.)
>
> Since true consent is necessary for the validity of any marriage, the necessity of a renewal of consent where it is defective is necessary for the validity of the convalidation of the marriages of Catholics and non-Catholics alike.

If the defect of consent cannot be proved, it is sufficient that the party who had not consented gives consent privately and in secret. If the defect of consent can be proved, it is necessary that the consent be given according to the canonical form. (Can. 1159, §§ 2, 3)

> The defect cannot be proved in the external forum if, e.g., witnesses refuse to testify, there are no witnesses, the witnesses can prove nothing (as is often the case with intentions contrary to the substance of marriage). In such cases, the party or parties who are aware of the defect need only consent internally. If the defect can be proved in the external forum, the canonical form is required for the convalidation. A dispensation from the form in mixed marriages can be given as explained above under canon 1158.
>
> Non-Catholics can convalidate a marriage that was invalid due to a defect of consent only if they are aware that the marriage was invalid from the beginning, and then, through a new act of the will, consent to the marriage.

C. Convalidation for Want of Form

In order that a marriage which is invalid because of a defect of form be made valid, it must be contracted anew according to the canonical form, without prejudice to canon 1127, §2. (Can. 1160)

There are two kinds of defect of form: total lack of form when there was no appearance of a marriage according to the form, as when a couple marries outside the Catholic Church without a dispensation; and lack of substantial form when there was an appearance of the form but the form was invalid due to an absence of an essential element, namely, lack of the faculty to assist on the part of the minister, lack of witnesses or only one witness, omission of the exchange of consent, or omission of the asking for and receiving the consent by the minister who assists. (See CLSA Comm., 826.)

If the nullity is occult, the marriage may be contracted secretly before the minister and two witnesses. If the nullity is publicly known, the form should be observed publicly.

If the non-Catholic party in a mixed marriage refuses to renew consent before a priest or deacon, or does not acknowledge the invalidity of the original consent, a dispensation from canonical form can be obtained as explained above under canon 1158, or a *sanatio in radice* can be requested.

four
Radical Sanation

A. Nature and Effects of Radical Sanction

The radical sanation (*sanatio in radice*) of an invalid marriage is its convalidation, without renewal of consent, granted by competent authority, that includes a dispensation from an impediment, if there is one, and from the canonical form, if it had not been observed, as well as the retroactivity to the past of the effects of the marriage. The convalidation occurs from the moment the favor is granted; however, it is understood as being retroactive to the moment of the celebration of the marriage, unless something else is expressly stated. A radical sanation should not be granted unless it is probable that the parties wish to persevere in their conjugal life. (Can. 1161)

The principal feature of a radical sanation, as opposed to a simple convalidation, is that no renewal of consent is necessary for the convalidation of the marriage. Once the impediment or lack of form has been dispensed by the sanation, the consent previously given, which was naturally valid but juridically invalid, becomes efficacious and produces its effect, namely, a valid marriage. Therefore, a radical sanation is not to be given unless it is likely that the original consent still exists.

A sanation can be granted validly even if one party or both parties do not know about it, but this cannot be done without a serious reason. (Can. 1164)

Sanations made without the knowledge of either of the parties are sometimes granted in *globo*, e.g., sanations of marriages invalidly contracted due to lack of authorization of the minister officiating. (See CSacr, rescript, July, 21, 1919, CLD 3:451.) They are also given in cases where the invalidity of the marriage is the fault of an ecclesiastical personage. The Holy Office sanated a marriage contracted by an erroneous application of the Pauline privilege. (See Congregation of the Holy Office, June 19, 1947, CLD 3:482.)

Before granting a radical sanation without the knowledge of both parties, there should be discreet inquiries into the stability of the marriage in question. If there are any somewhat serious problems in the marriage, a sanation should not be granted. It can also happen, especially in a mixed marriage, that one party desires the sanation and the other is opposed, believing the marriage to have been valid from the beginning. In such a case a sanation can be granted even with the other party not knowing of it provided there is no reason to think that his or her consent no longer exists.

B. Conditions For Radical Sanation

If the consent is wanting in both parties or in one party, the marriage cannot be radically sanated, whether the consent was lacking from the beginning or was originally given but later revoked. But if consent was lacking in the beginning but is later given, the sanation can be granted from the moment when the consent was given. (Can. 1162)

> Since consent makes the marriage, a sanation given where consent is lacking would be invalid.

A marriage that is invalid due to an impediment or a defect of legitimate form can be sanated provided the consent of both parties perseveres. (Can. 1163, §1)

> The consent must be naturally valid, i.e., not defective by reason of intentions contrary to the essential elements or properties of marriage, nor by error or fraud, or lack of due competence or lack of due discretion, etc. Note, however, that the knowledge or belief that a marriage is null does not necessarily exclude a valid matrimonial consent, for, together with the knowledge or the opinion of nullity there can exist a will to enter marriage insofar as one can. True matrimonial consent can certainly exist even though the marriage itself is known to be invalid by reason of some diriment impediment. (See can. 1100.)

Even though a marriage has been contracted invalidly because of an impediment or lack of form, the consent which has been given is presumed to persevere until its revocation has been proven. (Can. 1107)

In a sanation, the consent must exist at the time the marriage is convalidated. However, if the consent was once given, it is presumed that it still exists unless one can prove that it was revoked.

Marriages sanated for reason of an impediment or lack of form include a dispensation from observing the canonical form.

A marriage which is invalid on account of an impediment of the natural law or the divine positive law can be sanated only after the impediment has ceased. (Can. 1163, §2)

Impotence is an impediment of the natural law which is by definition perpetual and therefore does not cease to exist. Even if impotence had ceased by some extraordinary means such as a miracle, doubtfully successful or illicit means, or surgery involving probable danger to one's life or serious harm to one's health, a sanation would not be necessary due to the presumption of canon 1060.

Likewise the impediments of consanguinity in the direct line and in the second degree collateral cannot cease. Even if they were impediments of ecclesiastical law, they could not be sanated since they are never dispensed. (See can. 1078, §3.)

A marriage which is invalid due to the divine positive law impediment of prior bond can be sanated by the Apostolic See after the death of the first spouse.

C. Competent Authorities

The Apostolic See can grant radical sanations for any possible case. Only the Apostolic See can grant sanations of marriages invalid by reason of the impediments of holy orders, a public perpetual vow of chastity in a religious institute of pontifical right, crime, or the impediments of the natural law and divine positive law which have ceased to exist. (See can. 1165.)

The diocesan bishop, in individual cases, even if there are several grounds for nullity in the same marriage, can grant a radical sanation for all cases other than those which can be given only by the Apostolic See; in the sanation of a mixed marriage the conditions of canon 1125 are to be fulfilled. (See can. 1165, §2.)

The diocesan bishop can grant radical sanations only in individual cases, i.e., not to whole groups of people.

The diocesan bishop can grant a sanation in a mixed marriage only if the conditions of canon 1125 have been fulfilled. The Catholic party must declare that he or she is prepared to remove dangers of falling away from the faith and make a since promise to do all in his or her power to have all the children baptized and raised in the Catholic Church; the non-Catholic is to be informed of this declaration and promise and both parties must be instructed on the essential ends and properties of marriage. It suffices that these conditions were fulfilled when the marriage was originally attempted invalidly. If they were not fulfilled then and cannot now be fulfilled, the case should be referred to the Apostolic See.

postscript
The Internal Forum Solution

Canon law does not speak about the internal forum solution, because canon law, of its very nature, deals with matters of the external forum. In truth, this is a matter best reserved for moral theology. However, since it is related to a canonical issue, namely, the public reception of the sacraments, it is appropriate that this topic also be treated by canonists.

It is sometimes necessary for pastoral ministers and catechists to clarify a not infrequent misconception that Catholics who divorce civilly are barred from the sacraments. That is not true. They remain in good standing with the Church and can receive the sacraments, provided they do not remarry. If they remarry without first obtaining an annulment or dissolution of the previous marriage, they are still obliged to Church law, including the precept to attend Mass on Sundays and holy days, but they lose the right to receive the sacraments. This applies also to a person who, although never married, has married a divorced person who has not obtained an annulment or dissolution of the previous marriage.

Persons in an irregular marriage may not receive holy Communion because, as Pope John Paul II affirmed, "their state and condition of life objectively contradict that union of love between Christ and the Church which is signified and effected by the Eucharist." The sacrament of penance can be received only if they "are sincerely ready to undertake a way of life that is no longer in contradiction to the indissolubility of marriage." This means that they "take on themselves the duty to live in complete continence, that is, by abstinence from the acts proper to married couples." (John Paul II, apostolic exhortation *Familiaris consortio*, 84e, Dec. 15, 1981, AAS 74 (1982) 165; *On the Family* (Washington: USCC, 1982), pp. 83-83; see also CDF, letter, Oct. 14, 1994; *Origins* 24 (1994) 337-40.)

A solution to an irregular marriage in the "external forum" is always preferable, namely, an annulment or a dissolution of the previous marriage and the convalidation of the new marriage. However, in some circumstances an external forum solution is not possible, e.g, when a non-Catholic spouse refuses to petition for an annulment; when witnesses for a case are lacking or they do not cooperate; when there is no local tribunal that can process a case expeditiously; when a tribunal has given a negative judgment on the nullity of the previous marriage. In such situations, persons in irregular unions may receive the sacraments if they abstain from sexual relations and their reception of the sacraments does not cause scandal.

This is called the "internal forum" solution because it is not handled or recorded in a public way; it is strictly a matter of personal conscience. The person may come to this solution on his or her own, or upon the advice of a confessor or pastoral minister. Due to the possibility of this solution, it is not proper for ministers of the Eucharist to invoke canon 915 to deny holy Communion to persons in irregular marriages, unless they are certain that such persons are acting in defiance of Church teaching, or unless there is genuine scandal by the faithful.

XIII Other Acts of Divine Worship

$\underline{o\,n\,e}$
Sacramentals

A. Common Norms

Sacramentals are sacred signs by which, similar to sacraments, spiritual effects in particular are signified and are obtained by the intercession of the Church. (Can. 1166) Only the Apostolic See can establish new sacramentals or interpret authentically those already accepted, or abolish or change any of them. In confecting or administering the sacramentals the rites and formulas approved by authority of the Church are to be accurately observed. (Can. 1167)

While a sacrament is of divine origin (instituted by Christ), a sacramental is ecclesiastical in origin (instituted by the Church). Sacramentals may be either actions or material things. The *Code of Canon Law* treats four kinds of sacramentals that are actions: consecrations, dedications, blessings, and exorcisms. These sacramentals are transitory, i.e., they exist only during the course of the action. Sacramentals which are things are sacramentals intended for repeated use, such as holy oils, holy water, blessed ashes, blessed palms, the paschal candle, the wearing of scapulars, etc. (See CCLA, 732-33.)

Ministers. The minister of sacramentals is a cleric endowed with the necessary power. Some sacramentals, in accord with the norm of the liturgical books and the judgment of the local Ordinary, can also be administered by lay persons who are endowed with the appropriate qualities. (Can. 1168)

This norm refers principally to transitory sacramentals, the actions treated in the code. Deacons and lay persons, as will be seen below, are permitted to give certain blessings. To a lesser extent this norm also refers to the public application of certain sacramentals that are things, e.g., the distribution of ashes on Ash Wednesday. It does not refer to the private use of sacramentals, e.g., holy water, scapulars, etc.

B. Consecrations and Dedications

Consecrations and dedications may validly be performed by those who possess the episcopal character as well as by presbyters to whom it is permitted by the law or by a lawful deputation. (Can. 1169, §1)

> Dedications pertain to places, namely, churches and altars. *The law of the Eastern Catholic churches sui iuris* speaks of the "consecration" instead of the dedication of churches. (See CCEC, can. 869.) In the Latin church, the word "consecration" is used in reference to the consecration of virgins and the consecration of the sacred chrism. The postconciliar *Rite of Ordination* does not speak of the consecration of bishops but of their "ordination," although the 1983 code in many places anachronistically refers to episcopal consecration. A consecration or dedication implies that the dedicated or consecrated person, place, or object is destined in a permanent manner for divine worship or the service of the Lord.

C. Blessings

Blessings are given in the first place to Catholics, although they may also be given to catechumens and even to non-Catholics unless a prohibition of the Church prevents it. (Can. 1170) Sacred things which are destined for divine worship by a dedication or blessing are to be treated reverently and may not be used for a profane or improper purpose, even if they belong to private persons. (Can. 1171)

> A blessing is a less solemn rite than a consecration or dedication. There are two general kinds of blessings. (1) A *constitutive blessing* which, like a dedication, renders a place sacred, e.g., an oratory, a private chapel, a cemetery; or it makes sacred an *object* to be used only for sacred purposes, e.g., a chalice and paten, oil of catechumens, oil of the sick. (2) An *invocative blessing* invokes the favor and protection of God on persons, places, objects, animals, etc. Invocative blessings do not change the profane character of the person, place, or thing that is blessed. (See Chiappetta, 3896.)
>
> The typical celebration of blessings consists of two principal

parts: the first is the proclamation of God's word, and the second is the praise of God's goodness and intercession for heavenly aid. (See *Rite of Blessings* (RB), 20.) The principal signs used in blessings are: extending, elevating, or folding of the hands; the imposition of hands; the sign of the cross; sprinkling with blessed water; and incensation. A minister who is a priest or deacon says the prayer of blessing with hands outstretched over those being blessed; a lay minister says the prayer with hands joined. (See RB, 57.) To ensure active participation of the faithful in the celebration of blessings and to guard against superstition, it is ordinarily not permissible to impart the blessing of any article or place merely through a sign of blessing without either the word of God or any sort of prayer being said. (See RB, 26, 27.)

D. Ministers of Blessings

Bishops and presbyters. It belongs to the ministry of the *bishop* to preside at celebrations that involve the entire diocesan community and that are carried out with special solemnity and with a large attendance of the faithful. The bishop, accordingly, may reserve certain celebrations to himself, particularly those celebrated with special solemnity. It belongs to the ministry of a *presbyter* to preside at those blessings especially that involve the community he is appointed to serve. Presbyters may preside at the celebration of all blessings in the *Rite of Blessings,* unless a bishop is present as presider. (See RB, 18, a, b; see also can. 1169, §2).

> *In the United States,* the approved rite that must be used is called the *Book of Blessings,* promulgated in 1989.

Deacons. A deacon can give only those blessings which are expressly permitted him by law. (Can. 1169, §3) Whenever a priest is present, it is more fitting that the function of presiding be assigned to him and that the deacon assist by performing his proper functions. (See RB, 18c.)

> In addition to the many blessings that a deacon can give in the *Rite of Blessings,* he may also give the blessings that are part of other liturgical rites at which he may preside, including marriage, baptism, holy Communion and Viaticum outside Mass, the blessing at the conclusion of morning and evening prayer from the liturgy of the hours, and non-sacramental penance services.

Lay persons. Lay persons, in virtue of their universal priesthood, a dignity they possess because of their baptism and confirmation, may celebrate certain blessings as indicated in the *Rite of Blessings.* They exercise this ministry either in virtue of their office (for example, parents on behalf of their children) or by reason of some special liturgical ministry or in fulfillment of a particular responsibility when appointed by the local Ordinary. But whenever a priest or deacon is present, the office of presiding should be left to him. (See RB, 18d.)

> *In the United States,* the blessing of throats on the feast of St. Blase can be given by deacons and lay ministers as well as priests. A lay minister says the same formula as the cleric but without making the sign of the cross over the recipient. (See *Book of Blessings,* 1626, 1634.) The blessing of ashes is reserved to a priest or deacon, but the *administration of ashes on Ash Wednesday* may be done by lay ministers as well as clergy. (See ibid., 1659.)

Vestments of ministers. The presbyter or deacon, when he presides over blessings in a communal form, especially in a church or with special solemnity, should wear an alb and stole. In more solemn celebrations a cope may be used. The color of the stole or cope should be white or the color of the liturgical season or feast. Lay ministers should dress appropriately as prescribed by the conference of bishops or the local Ordinary. (See RB, 36–38.)

E. Exorcisms

Minister. No one may lawfully perform exorcisms on the possessed unless he has obtained the special and express permission of the local Ordinary. This permission is to be granted by the local Ordinary only to a presbyter endowed with piety, wisdom, prudence, and integrity of life. (Can. 1172)

> This canon refers to the solemn exorcism using the approved rite of the Church on behalf of a person believed to be possessed by the devil. It does not refer to simple exorcisms that are part of another rite, as during the catechumenate and at infant baptism. Nor does it refer to prayers said over a possessed person that do not constitute the official rite. The official rite may not be used, however, unless the priest has been expressly so authorized by the local Ordinary. This permission is necessary on a case by case basis, unless the episcopal conference of a nation has received approval from the Apostolic See to establish the office of exorcist. (See CCLA, 736; Paul VI, *motu proprio Ministeria quaedam,* Aug. 15, 1972, AAS 64 (1972) 529–34; CLD 7:692. On certain abuses regarding exorcisms, see CDF, letter, Sept. 29, 1985, AAS 77 (1985) 1169–70; CLD 11:276–77.)

Place. If it can be done conveniently the possessed person should be led to church or to some other sacred and worthy place, where the exorcism will be held, away from the crowd. But if the person is ill, or for any valid reason, the exorcism may take place in a private home. (*Rite for Exorcism,* general rules, 13.)

At the time of this writing there is no postconciliar revised rite of exorcism, so the old one from the *Roman Ritual* must be used. For an English translation, see *The Roman Ritual: Complete Edition,* ed. Philip T. Weller (Milwaukee: Bruce, 1964).)

t w o
The Liturgy of the Hours

A. Communal Celebration with the Laity

The Church, fulfilling Christ's priestly function, celebrates the liturgy of the hours in which, hearing God speaking to his people and remembering the mystery of salvation, it praises God without interruption in song and prayer and intercedes for the salvation of the whole world. (Can. 1173)

Celebration in common shows more clearly the ecclesial nature of the liturgy of the hours. It fosters the active participation of all, according to each person's condition, through acclamations, dialogues, alternating psalmody and the like. Communal celebration is to be preferred to individual and quasi-private celebration. (See GILH, 33.)

Whenever possible, groups of the faithful should celebrate the liturgy of the hours communally in church. This especially applies to parishes—the cells of the diocese, established under their pastors, taking the place of the bishop. (See GILH, 21.) Inasmuch as it is an action of the Church, lay members of the faithful should earnestly be invited to participate in the liturgy of the hours in accord with the circumstances. (See can. 1174, §2.)

Those in holy orders or who have a special canonical mission have the responsibility of initiating and directing the prayer of the community. They must therefore see to it that the people are invited, and prepared by suitable instruction, to celebrate the principal hours in common, especially on Sundays and holydays. (See GILH, 23.) Morning and evening prayer are to be accorded the highest importance as the prayer of the Christian community. Indeed, the recitation of these hours should be recommended also to individual members of the faithful unable to take part in a celebration in common. (See GILH, 40.)

Lay groups gathering for prayer, apostolic work, or any other reason are encouraged to fulfill the Church's duty by celebrating part of the liturgy of the hours. The laity must learn above all how in the liturgy they are adoring God the Father in spirit and in truth; they should bear in mind that through public worship and prayer they reach all humanity and can contribute significantly to the salvation of the whole world. Finally, it is of great advantage for the family, the domestic sanctuary of the Church, not only to pray together to God but also to celebrate some parts of the liturgy of the hours as occasion offers, in order to enter more deeply into the life of the Church. (GILH, 27)

Pastoral suggestions. For communal celebration to succeed in parishes it will often be necessary to adapt the liturgy of the hours to a simple, standard format. (See GILH, 246-52.) Not everyone present needs to have the breviary. It would be sufficient for them to have a book of the psalms and canticles, or a pamphlet containing several exemplars of morning and/or evening prayer that could be used over and over. A number of Catholic publishers have books and pamphlets with settings for the liturgy of the hours suitable for parish celebration. The hymn could be taken from the parish hymnal. Only the presider and other available ministers, such as reader and cantor, would need books for the proper parts.

When a cleric participates in a celebration adapted for the laity, he need not repeat the hour to fulfill his obligation. (See GILH, 242.) The value of celebrating the hours communally is greater than that of praying the texts exactly as they appear in the breviary.

Eastern law. The Eastern code does not treat the liturgy of the hours most likely because of the differences among the various churches *sui iuris.* In the Eastern churches parts of the divine office are celebrated in many churches every Sunday; and they are obligatory on some holy days, such as during Holy Week. (See Pospishil, 530.)

B. Time of Celebration

In celebrating the liturgy of the hours, the true time of each hour is to be observed as much as possible. (Can. 1175) The purpose of the liturgy of the hours is to sanctify the day and the whole range of human activity. Therefore its structure has been revised in such a way as to make each hour once more correspond as nearly as possible to natural time and to take account of the circumstances of life today. (GILH, 11)

> Morning and evening prayer are the two most important hours. Morning prayer is celebrated upon rising or at some convenient hour in the morning. Evening prayer is celebrated any time in the evening, that is, after about 4:00 in the afternoon. Mid-morning prayer is celebrated at 9:00 or anytime after morning prayer and before mid-day prayer. Mid-day prayer is prayed at noon or before or after the mid-day meal. Mid-afternoon prayer is prayed at 3:00 or it may be prayed any time in the afternoon until late afternoon.

The office of readings may be recited at any hour of the day, even during the night hours of the previous day, after evening prayer has been said. (See GILH, 59.) Some religious are obliged by their proper law and others may commendably wish to retain the character of this office as a night office of praise (either by saying it at night or very early in the morning and before morning prayer). (See GILH, 58.)

Night prayer is the last prayer of the day, said before retiring, even if that is after midnight. (GILH, 84)

> If a community has no opportunity to gather for evening prayer but is able to pray before retiring, it is preferable to pray evening prayer at this time. Evening prayer is the more important liturgical celebration, and ideally should be prayed in common, whereas night prayer readily lends itself to individual celebration immediately before retiring.

C. Clerical Obligation

Sacred ministers have the liturgy of the hours entrusted to them in such a particular way that even when the faithful are not present they are to pray it themselves with the adaptations necessary under these circumstances. The Church deputes them to celebrate the liturgy of the hours so as to ensure at least in their persons the regular carrying out of the duty of the whole community and the unceasing continuance of Christ's prayer in the Church. (GILH, 28, §1) Even when they have no obligation to celebrate in common, all clerics who live together or who are meeting together should arrange to say at least some part of the liturgy of the hours in common, especially morning and evening prayer. (See GILH, 25.)

Permanent deacons are to celebrate the liturgy of the hours as specified for them by the episcopal conference. (See can. 276, §2, 3°.)

In the United States, "permanent deacons should not hold themselves lightly excused from the obligation they have to recite morning and evening prayer." (See NCCB, *Permanent Deacons in the United States: Guidelines on Their Formation and Ministry,* 3rd ed., n. 97 (Washington: USCC, 1985). Thus, permanent deacons in the U.S. have a binding obligation to say morning and evening prayer.

Bishops, presbyters, and deacons aspiring to the priesthood have received a mandate from the Church to celebrate the liturgy of the hours; they should recite the full sequence of the hours each day, as far as possible at the appropriate times. They should, first and foremost, attach due importance to those hours that are, so to speak, the two hinges of the liturgy of the hours, that is, morning prayer and evening prayer, which should not be omitted except for a serious reason. They should faithfully pray the office of readings, which is above all a liturgical celebration of the word of God. In this way they fulfill daily a duty that is especially their own, that is, of receiving the word of God into their lives, so that they may become more perfect as disciples of the Lord and experience more deeply the unfathomable riches of Christ. In order to sanctify the whole day more completely, they will also treasure the recitation of daytime and night prayer, to round off the whole *Opus Dei* and to commend themselves to God before retiring. (See GILH, 29; see also cans. 276, §2, 3° and 1174, §1.)

Outside choir, without prejudice to particular law, it is permitted to choose from the three daytime hours the one most appropriate to the time of day, so that the tradition of prayer in the course of the day's work may be maintained. (GILH, 77)

> The obligation to celebrate daily the liturgy of the hours is a personal obligation binding all clergy except permanent deacons. It includes the religious clergy who may also be held to communal celebration in virtue of their proper law. The obligation begins with ordination to the diaconate.
>
> The liturgical law establishes a "hierarchy" of hours. The severity of the cleric's obligation to pray the hours varies with the importance of the hour. The two most important hours are morning and evening prayer, called the "hinges" of the divine office. They may not be omitted except for a serious reason, e.g., illness, an emergency, or the like.
>
> The Bishops' Committee on the Liturgy in the United States says the omission of morning and evening prayer by a cleric should be exceptional. However, it says the law "leaves to the ordained ministers the discretion to judge the seriousness of the

cause which may allow the omission of one or both of the chief parts of the daily liturgy of the hours." (See "A Call to Prayer: The Liturgy of the Hours," BCL *Newsletter* 13 (1977) 88.)

There is also an obligation to celebrate the office of readings. Since this office does not have to be done at any particular time during the day, it should not be difficult ordinarily to fulfill this obligation. However, it can be omitted in a particular case for a less serious reason than is required for the omission of morning or evening prayer.

The law itself permits the cleric to choose one of the three daytime hours and omit the other two. Night prayer ranks with these daytime hours as the least important of the hours. These hours can be omitted for a just cause, even on a regular basis when the reasons apply, e.g., the demands of the apostolate, travel, fatigue, etc.

> *In the Eastern churches sui iuris,* clerics are obliged to celebrate the liturgy of the hours as required by the particular laws of their own church *sui iuris.* (See CCEC, can. 377.)

D. Institutes of Consecrated Life and Societies of Apostolic Life

In accord with the prescripts of their proper law, members of institutes of consecrated life and societies of apostolic life should worthily celebrate the liturgy of the hours. (See cans. 663, §3; 1174, §1.)

Religious communities bound to the recitation of the liturgy of the hours and their individual members should celebrate the hours in keeping with their own particular law. Communities bound to choir should celebrate the whole sequence of the hours daily in choir; when absent from choir their members should recite the hours in keeping with their own particular law. (See GILH, 31b.) The liturgical practice of saying the three daytime hours is to be retained, without prejudice to particular law, by those who live the contemplative life. (See GILH, 76.)

Other religious communities and their individual members are advised to celebrate some parts of the liturgy of the hours, in accord with their own situation, for it is the prayer of the Church and makes the whole Church, scattered throughout the world, one in heart and mind. (GILH, 32)

> The references to "particular law" should be understood as "proper law," namely, the constitutions and other sources of law proper to the institutes themselves.

Priests and deacons who belong to an institute of consecrated life or a society of apostolic life, even if not bound to the communal celebration of the liturgy of the hours by their proper law, are held to the universal law obligations to pray the liturgy of the hours that are binding on all the clergy. Lay members of institutes and societies, even if not bound by law, are strongly encouraged to pray at least some of the liturgy of the hours, especially in a communal celebration.

three
Funeral Rites

The principal source of law for funeral rites is the 1969 *Rite of Funerals* (RF). The adapted version used in the United States is the *Order of Christian Funerals* (OCF) of 1989. The latter is binding in the United States. Also noteworthy are the 1975 guidelines from the National Catholic Cemetery Conference (NCCC) of the United States.

A. Prohibited Days for Funeral Mass

The funeral Mass has first place among the Masses for the dead and may be celebrated on any day except solemnities that are days of obligation, Holy Thursday, the Easter triduum, and the Sundays of Advent, Lent, and the Easter season. (GIRM, 336)

> "Funeral rites" refer to all the rites: the vigil, the funeral Mass or liturgy of the word, and the committal rite. "Funeral liturgy" applies more specifically to the funeral Mass or, when there is no Mass, to the liturgy of the word. The funeral rites consist of three principal parts, called stations. These are: (a) the service in the home of the deceased person, the funeral parlor, a chapel or other place where the body of the deceased has been placed during the period before the funeral rite; (b) the Eucharistic celebration in the church or the liturgy of the word; and (c) the rite of burial.
>
> If the funeral liturgy is to take place on a day when Mass is prohibited, there should be a liturgy of the word with a rite of committal as provided in the *Rite of Funerals*. (See RF, 6; US, 178.) Readings should be selected according to their appropriateness to the liturgical season. Whereas singing is permitted during the celebration, the distribution of Communion is not. (See *Notitiae* 11

(1975) 288; *BCL Newsletter* 12 (1976) 8.) A memorial Mass for the deceased may then be celebrated later at the convenience of the family and the rector of the church.

B. Place of Celebration

1. The church

Generally the funeral rites of any deceased member of the faithful must be celebrated in one's own parish church. However, each of the faithful is allowed to choose another church for the funeral with the consent of the rector of that church. One's pastor should be notified of this arrangement. One may personally choose the other church, or it may be done by the person who is in charge of the funeral arrangements. If death occurs outside one's parish and the body was not returned to it, and another church was not legitimately chosen for the funeral, the funeral rites should be celebrated in the parish church within whose boundaries the death occurred, unless particular law has specified another church. (Can. 1177)

> Ordinarily funeral rites are celebrated in one's parish church. However, the faithful have a right to choose some other church with the consent of its rector, notifying the proper pastor. Since the canon speaks only of some other church, it seems that the possibility of choosing an oratory or other sacred place is not included. A dispensation from the diocesan bishop would be necessary to hold funeral rites in, e.g., the oratory of a religious house, unless legitimate custom, acquired rights, or a privilege is in force.

Ordinarily the funeral rites of religious or members of a society of apostolic life are celebrated in their own church or oratory by the superior, if the institute or society is clerical, or by the chaplain if not. (Can. 1179)

2. The cemetery

If the parish has its own cemetery, the faithful departed are to be buried in it unless another cemetery was legitimately chosen by the deceased or by those who have charge of the burial. However, all may choose their own cemetery, unless they are prohibited by law. (Can. 1180)

Parishes and religious institutes may have their own cemetery. Also, other juridic persons or families may have a special cemetery or burial place to be blessed in accord with the judgment of the local Ordinary. (Can. 1241) Corpses are not to be buried in churches, unless it is a question of the Roman Pontiff or cardinals or diocesan bishops, even retired, being buried in their own church. (Can. 1242)

The Church is to have its own cemeteries, where possible, or at least space in secular cemeteries destined for the faithful departed. If this cannot be done, individual graves are to be properly blessed as often as necessary. (Can. 1240)

> In those situations in which a Catholic is to be interred in a non-Catholic cemetery, the priest or deacon, after the liturgy in church, may conduct the committal service at the graveside. He should bless the individual grave and then follow the usual ritual for the burial of a Catholic. (See RF, 53; US, 321.)
>
> *United States.* On those occasions when a non-Catholic is to be buried in a Catholic cemetery, the ordained minister of the church in which he shared belief or communion may conduct the committal service. (NCCC Guidelines, The Burial Rite, A, B; CLD 9:687.)

C. Cremation

The Church earnestly recommends that the pious custom of burying the bodies of the dead be observed. However, cremation is not prohibited unless it is chosen for reasons contrary to Christian doctrine. (Can. 1176, §3)

> An example of a reason for choosing cremation contrary to Christian doctrine would be the denial of the resurrection of the body.

The funeral is to be celebrated according to the model in use in the region. It should be carried out in a way, however, that clearly expresses the Church's preference for the custom of burying the dead, after the example of Christ's own will to be buried, and that forestalls any danger of scandalizing or shocking the faithful. The rites usually held in the cemetery chapel or at the grave may in this case take place within the confines of the crematorium and, for want of any other suitable place, even in the crematorium room. Every precaution is to be taken against the danger of scandal or religious indifferentism. (See RF, 15.)

> *United States.* When cremation has been chosen, the various elements of the funeral rite will be conducted in the usual way, and normally, with the body present, if practical. The remains of the deceased after cremation must always be treated with respect and placed in consecrated ground. (NCCC Guidelines, C, F, CLD 9:698)

Although the rite of final commendation at the catafalque or pall is excluded, it is permitted to celebrate the funeral service, including the commendation, in those cases where it is physically or morally impossible for the body of the deceased person to be present. (*BCL Newsletter* 7 (1971) 274)

D. Offices and Ministries

The faithful. In the celebration of a funeral all the members of the people of God must remember that to each one a role and an office is entrusted: to relatives and friends, funeral directors, the Christian community as such, and finally the priest, who as the teacher of faith and the minister of comfort presides at the liturgical rites and celebrates the Eucharist. (RF, 16)

The community's principal involvement in the ministry of consolation is expressed in its active participation in the celebration of the funeral rites, particularly the vigil for the deceased, the funeral liturgy, and the rite of committal. For this reason these rites should be scheduled at times that permit as many of the community as possible to be present. The assembly's participation can be assisted by the preparation of booklets that contain an outline of the rite, the texts and songs belonging to the people, and directions for posture, gesture, and movement. (OCF, 11)

Priests, as teachers of faith and ministers of comfort, preside at the funeral rites, especially the Mass; the celebration of the funeral liturgy is especially entrusted to pastors and associate pastors. (See OCF 14.)

Deacons and lay ministers. Except for the Mass, a deacon may conduct all the funeral rites. As pastoral needs require, the conference of bishops, with the Apostolic See's permission, may even depute a lay person for this. (See RF, 19.)

The law in the United States is less generous than the universal law, specifying that a deacon may lead funeral rites "when no priest is available." Unavailability includes sickness, travel, work or other commitments that prevent or make it difficult for the priest to preside. When no priest or deacon is available, a lay minister may preside at the vigil and related rites or the rite of committal. (See OCF, 14.) For a lay minister to lead the liturgy of the word, a dispensation from the diocesan bishop would be necessary, since the NCCB has not formally approved this as a general practice.

Whenever possible, ministers should involve the family in planning the funeral rites: in the choice of texts and rites provided in the ritual, in the selection of music for the rites, and in the designation of liturgical ministers. (See OCF, 17.)

E. Non-Catholics who are Granted Funeral Rites

1) Catechumens are equated with the faithful in matters pertaining to funeral rites. (Can. 1183, §1)

2) The local Ordinary can permit ecclesiastical funeral rites for children who died before baptism if their parents had intended to have them baptized. (Can. 1183, §2)

> The *Roman Missal* contains a funeral Mass for a child who died before baptism. The U.S. *Order of Christian Funerals* has an entire section on funerals for children. In the case of an infant, the vigil and funeral liturgy might not be appropriate; only the rite of committal and perhaps prayer with the family may be desirable. (See OCF, 48.)

3) In the prudent judgment of the local Ordinary, ecclesiastical funeral rites can be granted to baptized persons belonging to some non-Catholic church or ecclesial community, provided they are unable to have their own minister. This cannot be done if it is against their wishes. (Can. 1183, §3)

> The judgment of the local Ordinary in nn. 2 and 3 must be made on a case by case basis unless he has given general delegation to pastors and/or priests and deacons to make these decisions.
> The inability to have the proper non-Catholic minister may result from moral as well as physical unavailability. Physical unavailability would be, e.g., when there is no minister of the non-Catholic deceased in the area. Moral unavailability would be, e.g., when there is a minister of the non-Catholic deceased in the area, but the non-Catholic has not practiced his or her faith, and the practicing Catholic spouse or other next of kin would like to have the funeral in the Catholic church. N.B. This favor cannot be granted to those who were unbaptized or baptized invalidly.
> In the case of non-Catholics who had been practicing their religion during life, it should be presumed that they would have wanted to have the funeral in their own church, and therefore it would be contrary to their wishes to have it in a Catholic church. To presume otherwise would be ecumenically insensitive.

F. Catholics who are Denied Funeral Rites

Unless before death there was some indication of repentance, ecclesiastical funeral rites are denied to:

1) Notorious apostates, heretics, and schismatics.

This restriction applies only to those who had been baptized Catholic or had been received into full communion with the Catholic Church. Heresy is the obstinate post-baptismal denial of some truth which must be believed by divine and Catholic faith, or the obstinate doubt about the same; apostasy is the total repudiation of the Christian faith; schism is the refusal of subjection to the Supreme Pontiff or of communion with the members of the Church subject to him. (Can. 751) Unlike the former code (can. 2197), the revised code makes no distinction between a crime that is notorious in law or notorious in fact. Hence, notoriety should be understood in the normal sense of the word, namely, anything that is "publicly known." It is often difficult in practice to determine who are notorious apostates, heretics, or schismatics unless they have been declared excommunicate. Thus it is prudent in all such cases to consult the local Ordinary. Note that the mere nonpractice of the faith does not exclude the right of a Catholic to a Church funeral.

2)   Those who have chosen cremation of their bodies for reasons contrary to the Christian faith.

The faithful who choose cremation are presumed to have the proper motives and good intentions, unless the contrary is clear. When a doubt persists as to the proper motivations of the person who has chosen cremation, the matter should be referred to the local Ordinary. (Cf. NCCC Guidelines, Cremation, G-J, CLD 9:698.)

3)   Other manifest sinners for whom ecclesiastical funeral rites cannot be conducted without public scandal to the faithful. (Can. 1184, §1)

A manifest sin is one for which there are eyewitnesses who can give testimony about it. (See CLSA Comm., 840.) Excluded from funeral rites are only those who are both manifest sinners and whose funeral will cause public scandal, such as gangsters who have given no signs of repentance. A sign of repentance would include summoning a priest at the time of death, entering a confessional shortly before death, making an act of perfect contrition, stating a desire to die in the state of grace, or making some other evident attempt to be reconciled with God and the Church.

Also included as public sinners are those under an imposed or declared penalty of excommunication or interdict, but even such manifest sinners are not to be deprived of funeral rites unless there is public scandal to the faithful. Ordinarily, those who are in invalid marriages may have a church funeral if they had preserved their attachment to the Church and there is no scandal. (See CDF, letter, May 29, 1973, CLD 8:862-63.) Indeed, in many localities it would be a greater scandal to the faithful if an invalidly married deceased person were to be denied ecclesiastical funeral rites.

Persons committing suicide should not as a rule be deprived of full burial rites in the Church. (See NCCC Guidelines, CLD 9:694.) The U.S. *Order of Christian Funerals* provides two special prayers for persons who committed suicide. (See OCF, 398, prayers 44 and 45.)

The continued neglect of Mass and sacraments, even though the neglect of the delinquent Catholic is generally known, is not sufficient cause for the denial of funeral rites.

If any doubt occurs in this matter, one should consult the local Ordinary whose decision is to be followed. (Can. 1184, §2)

Because Christian burial is not to lead the faithful away from the Church, but to draw them closer to God, the priest confronted with a case of denial of Church burial should lean to leniency and mercy. (NCCC Guidelines, CLD 9:694)

Any funeral Mass whatsoever is also to be denied to someone who is excluded from ecclesiastical funeral rites. (Can. 1185)

Not excluded is a priest offering Mass for the intention of such a person, provided the Mass is not a funeral Mass, even a funeral Mass without the body present. (See can. 901.)

G. Adaptations for the United States

Liturgical colors. The liturgical color chosen for funerals should express Christian hope but should not be offensive to human grief or sorrow. In the United States, white, violet, or black vestments may be worn at the funeral rites and at other Masses for the dead. (OCF, 39)

Special symbols. Besides the Easter candle, if it is the custom, other candles may also be placed near the coffin as a sign of reverence and solemnity. (See OCF, 35.)

If it is the custom in the local community, a pall may be placed over the coffin when it is received at the church. A reminder of the baptismal garment of the deceased, the pall is a sign of the Christian dignity of the person. The use of the pall also signifies that all are equal in the eyes of God (see James 2:1-9). A book of the Gospels or a Bible may be placed on the coffin as a sign that Christians live by the word of God and that fidelity to that word leads to eternal life. A cross may be placed on the coffin as a reminder that the Christian is marked by the cross of baptism and through Jesus' suffering on the cross is brought to the victory of his resurrection. Fresh flowers, used in moderation, can enhance the setting of funeral rites. Only Christian symbols may rest on or be placed near the coffin during the funeral liturgy. Any other symbols, for example, national flags, or flags or insignia of associations, have no place in the funeral liturgy. (OCF, 38)

Any national flags or the flags or insignia of associations to which the deceased belonged are to be removed from the coffin at the entrance of the church. They may be replaced after the coffin has been taken from the church. (OCF, 132)

If a symbol of the Christian life is to be placed on the coffin, it is carried in the entrance procession and is placed on the coffin by a family member, friend, or the minister at the conclusion of the procession. (See OCF, 134.)

Funeral liturgy outside Mass. This rite may be used on days when a funeral Mass is prohibited, when no priest is available or, when for pastoral reasons, the pastor and the family judge that the funeral liturgy outside Mass is a more suitable form of celebration. (See OCF, 178.)

> According to the circumstances, it would be appropriate to have a funeral liturgy outside Mass if the deceased is a baptized non-Catholic and his or relatives are mostly non-Catholic.

Rite of committal. Whenever possible, the rite of committal is to be celebrated at the site of committal, that is, beside the open grave or place of internment, rather than at a cemetery chapel. It may be celebrated at the grave, tomb, or crematorium and may be used for burial at sea. (See OCF, 204.)

The rite of committal may be celebrated in circumstances in which the final disposition of the body will not take place for some time, for example, when winter delays burial or when ashes are to be interred at some time after cremation. The rite of committal may then be repeated on the later occasion when the actual burial or interment takes place. In the case of a body donated to science, the rite of committal may be celebrated whenever internment takes place. (See OCF, 212.)

In the absence of a parish minister, a friend or member of the family should lead those present in the rite of committal. The minister should vest according to local custom. (OCF, 215)

Office for the dead. The vigil for the deceased may be celebrated in the form of some part of the office for the dead. (See OCF, 348.) The office for the dead may be celebrated in the funeral home, parlor, chapel of rest, in the church, or the home of the deceased. (See OCF, 369-70.) A priest or deacon should preside or, in their absence, a lay person. Whenever possible, ministers should involve the family of the deceased in the planning of the hour and in the designation of ministers. The minister vests according to local custom. If morning prayer or evening prayer is celebrated in the church, a priest or deacon who presides wears an alb or surplice with stole (a cope may also be worn). (See OCF, 371.)

H. Special Questions

The following norms are from the guidelines of the National Catholic Cemetery Conference of the United States (CLD 9:700-02).

1. Burial of stillborns and fetuses

The Church urges that stillborns and fetuses of Catholic parents be interred in a Catholic cemetery, or another cemetery of the parents' choosing. [See cans. 1180 and 1183, §2.] The decision and procedure for the internment will be left to the parents and their pastor.

2. Disposal of amputated limbs

It is recommended that amputated limbs be buried in a blessed place. However, hospital personnel may dispose of portions of bodies in a manner they deem most suitable and hygienic. Cremation is not excluded but the preference of the person and his family are not to be disregarded.

3. Organ transplants and donation of body for science

Because of the achievements of science and medicine, particularly in the matter of organ transplants, occasionally requests are made to donate organs or to donate one's body to science. Such requests are legitimate and not contrary to Christian principles. However, in keeping with Christian respect for the body, when it is possible and practicable, there should be reasonable assurance that the remains be disposed of in a proper, reverent, and dignified manner upon completion of the scientific research. In these donations, when the body is not embalmed, a wake or a Funeral Mass is usually impossible. The family should be urged to schedule the celebration of a Memorial Mass as soon after death as is practical. The Mass texts would be those of the Funeral Mass.

4. *Removal of a body*

While internment is *per se* permanent, removal of a body from its place of burial may at times become necessary or appropriate. Other than legal necessities such as the exercise of eminent domain, examples would be where scattered family members may wish to be joined together in a common lot, where preferred burial facilities not previously available become available (including the establishment of a Catholic cemetery where none existed), and where relocation of a family may suggest the possibility of removal. For whatever reason, in addition to obtaining the required permission of the civil authorities, the permission of the Chancery Office or Cemetery Office must be obtained to disinter a body from a Catholic cemetery.

If the funeral rites at the grave site were observed in the first burial, none are prescribed in the second. However, they may be held, especially if the body is being returned to the deceased's domicile as, e.g., in the case of someone killed in the military and buried in a foreign country. (See Congregation for the Council, reply, Jan. 12, 1924, AAS 16 (1924) 188; CLD 1:571.)

XIV Sacred Places and Sacred Times

one
Sacred Places

A. General Principles

Sacred places are those which have been designated for divine worship or the burial of the faithful by means of a dedication or blessing which the liturgical books prescribe for this. (Can. 1205)

> The law requires two things to have a sacred place: (1) that a place be designated for divine worship or the burial of the faithful; and (2) that the place be dedicated or blessed according to the proper liturgical rite. Sacred places in canon law are churches, oratories, private chapels, shrines, altars, and cemeteries. The principal liturgical book in question is the *Rite of Dedication of a Church and an Altar* (RDCA) from the *Roman Pontifical.*

> *Dedications and blessings.* The dedication of any place is the competency of the diocesan bishop and those who are equivalent to him in law; these may entrust to any bishop or, in exceptional cases, to a presbyter the task of dedication in their own territory. (Can. 1206) Sacred places are blessed by an Ordinary; however the blessing of churches is reserved to the diocesan bishop; but either of these can delegate another priest to do it. (Can. 1207)

> Churches and altars that are to be set aside permanently for sacred use should be dedicated, such as a cathedral, a parish church, or a fixed altar. A church should be merely blessed when it is foreseen that it may later be converted to profane use, e.g. a temporary space used for parish worship prior to the building of a proper church. Dedications are the special competency of the diocesan bishop. Oratories and private chapels are blessed, not dedicated,

even if it is not foreseen that they may be converted later to profane use. (See RDCA, chapter V.) Likewise, cemeteries are blessed, not dedicated. (See *Rite of Blessings*, chapter 35; US, chapter 43.)

Exclusion of profane uses. In a sacred place only those things are to be admitted which serve the exercise or promotion of worship, piety, or religion; and anything not consonant with the holiness of the place is forbidden. The Ordinary, however, can permit in individual instances other uses provided they are not contrary to the holiness of the place. (Can. 1210)

> Concerts of sacred or religious music may take place in a church or other sacred place since they are consonant with the sacred character of the place. A concert of secular music, however, may be admitted only in individual instances by permission of the Ordinary (local or personal). (See Congregation for Divine Worship, circular letter, Nov. 5, 1987, *Notitiae* 24 (1988) 3-10; *Origins* 17 (1987-1988) 468-70.)

Desecration. Sacred places are violated by gravely injurious actions done there with scandal to the faithful which, in the judgment of the local Ordinary, are so grave and contrary to the holiness of the place that it is not permitted to celebrate worship in them until the harm is alleviated through a penitential rite according to the norm of the liturgical books. (Can. 1211)

> An example of a gravely injurious action would be a homicide in a church. If the desecrated place was dedicated, the rite in the Pontifical is to be used; if it was blessed, the rite in the Ritual is used. At the time of this writing, a revised liturgical rite for this purpose has not yet been published. The revised rite will provide two penitential services; one within Mass and one that takes place within a celebration of the word. For further regulations on this matter, see the *Ceremonial of Bishops*, 1070-1092.

Loss of dedication or blessing. Sacred places lose their dedication or blessing if the greater part of them has been destroyed or if they have been permanently reduced to profane uses either by decree of the competent Ordinary or in fact. (Can. 1212) If a *church* cannot in any way be used for divine worship and there is no possibility of repairing it, the diocesan bishop may reduce it to profane but not sordid use. Where other serious reasons suggest that a certain church no longer be used for divine worship, the diocesan bishop, after hearing the presbyteral council, may reduce it to profane but not sordid use, provided no harm should come to the good of souls; he must also have the consent of those who lawfully might claim rights regarding the church. (Can. 1222) Altars, whether fixed or moveable, do not lose their dedication or blessing through the reduction of a church or other sacred place to profane uses. (Can. 1238, §2)

B. Churches

By the word "church" is understood a sacred building destined for divine worship to which the faithful have the right to go for divine worship, especially when it publicly celebrated. (Can. 1214) All acts of divine worship may be performed in a church that has been lawfully dedicated or blessed, without prejudice to parochial rights. (Can. 1219) Entrance to a church at the time of sacred celebrations should be free and gratuitous. (Can. 1221)

> Examples of churches are cathedrals, parish churches, abbey churches, shrine churches. Certain rites are generally restricted to parish churches, notably the sacraments of initiation and marriage; these rites could not be performed elsewhere without authorization from the competent authority.
>
> *In the law of the Eastern Catholic churches sui iuris,* the definition of a church does not include mention of the right of the faithful to go there. It merely states that "a church is a building dedicated exclusively for divine worship by consecration or blessing." (CCEC, can. 869) The Eastern code uses the word "consecration" instead of "dedication."

No church may be built without the express consent of the diocesan bishop given in writing. The diocesan bishop should not give consent unless, having heard the presbyteral council and the rectors of neighboring churches, he judges that a new church is able to serve the good of souls, and that the means necessary for building the church and for divine worship are not lacking. Religious institutes, although they may have obtained the consent of the diocesan bishop to erect a new house in the diocese or the city, nevertheless must also obtain his permission before they build a church in a certain and determined place. (Can. 1215)

> For clerical religious institutes, consent to erect a new religious house brings with it the right to have a church. (See can. 611, 3°.) Nevertheless, permission to build a church is still required in addition to the permission to erect a house. Since the faithful have a right to go to a church for divine worship, and since the diocesan bishop regulates the public exercise of divine worship, it is possi-

ble for a serious reason for the bishop to deny clerical religious the right to establish a church connected with their religious house. (See can. 678, §1.) They could not be prevented, however, from building an oratory for their own use.

In the building and repair of churches experts are to be consulted and the principles and norms of liturgy and sacred art are to be observed. (Can. 1216)

> A noteworthy text on liturgical and aesthetical principles for church art and architecture is that of the Bishops' Committee on the Liturgy, *Environment and Art in Catholic Worship* (Washington: USCC, 1978).

Dedication and title. After the construction is properly completed, a new church should as soon as possible be dedicated or at least blessed, observing the laws of the sacred liturgy. Churches, especially cathedrals and parish churches, are to be dedicated with a solemn rite. (Can. 1216; see RDCA, 28-85.) Each church should have its own title which, after the church is dedicated, may not be changed. (Can. 1218) The title may be the Blessed Trinity, our Lord Jesus Christ invoked according to a mystery of his life or a title already accepted in the liturgy, the Holy Spirit, the blessed Virgin Mary invoked according to some title already accepted in the liturgy, one of the angels, or a saint inscribed in the Roman Martyrology or in a duly approved Appendix. A blessed may not be the titular without an indult of the Apostolic See. (See RDCA, chapter II, 4.)

Dedication of a church in use. One of the following conditions must be met to dedicate a church already in use: (1) that the altar has not already been dedicated, since it is rightly forbidden both by custom and by liturgical law to dedicate a church without dedicating the altar, for the dedication of the altar is the principal part of the whole rite; (2) that there be something new or notably altered about the edifice, relative either to its structure, e.g., a total restoration, or its status in law, e.g., the church's being ranked as a parish church. (See RDCA, chapter III, 1.)

C. Oratories and Private Chapels

By the word *oratory* is understood a place for divine worship designated by permission of the Ordinary for the convenience of some community or group of the faithful who assemble there, to which other members of the faithful may also go with the consent of the competent superior. (Can. 1223)

Examples of oratories include the worship spaces of religious communities, hospitals, seminaries, schools and universities, and other institutions. The competent superior who can admit outsiders to liturgical celebrations in an oratory is the one who is in charge of the house or institution, e.g., the local superior of a religious community, the rector of a seminary, etc.

The Ordinary should not grant the required permission for erecting an oratory unless he personally or through another first has visited the place which will become the oratory and has found that it is suitably constructed. After the permission is given, the oratory may not be converted to profane uses without authorization of the same Ordinary. (Can. 1224)

An oratory should not be erected merely for the purpose of adoration of the Blessed Sacrament. If the Blessed Sacrament is to be reserved, there must also be provision made for the celebration of Mass there, ordinarily at least twice a month, and the space must be suitable for liturgical celebration. (See can. 934, §2.) This is not only for the practical reason of the renewal of the consecrated hosts, but more importantly for the theological value of maintaining the connection between the Eucharist celebrated and reserved. Note that a Blessed Sacrament chapel is not an oratory or a private chapel but is considered a part of a church or oratory, even though physically separated from the body of the church. It is not necessary to have an altar or the celebration of the Eucharist in a Blessed Sacrament chapel that is part of a church or oratory.

In lawfully established oratories all sacred celebrations may be carried out unless they are excluded by law or by prescript of the local Ordinary, or they are forbidden by liturgical laws. (Can. 1225)

The law especially entrusts to pastors of parishes certain liturgical functions: the celebration of baptism, confirmation of those who are in danger of death, Viaticum and anointing of the sick; the imparting of the apostolic blessing; assistance at marriages and the imparting of the nuptial blessing; funerals; the blessing of the baptismal font during the Easter season; leading processions outside the church and imparting solemn blessings outside the church; the more solemn celebration of the Eucharist on Sundays and holy days. (See can. 530; see also cans. 857; 1011, §1; 1118, §1; 1177.) These functions are ordinarily celebrated in parish churches unless the competent authority or legitimate custom permits their celebration in an oratory.

The term *private chapel* means a place designated for divine worship, with the permission of the local Ordinary, for the advantage of one or several physical persons. (Can. 1226) Except in the case of a bishop's chapel, the permission of the local Ordinary is needed to have liturgical celebrations in a private chapel. (See can. 1228.)

> All the restrictions mentioned above on liturgical celebrations in oratories apply all the more in the case of private chapels. Since the liturgy is an ecclesial act, ordinarily it should not be celebrated in a place erected for the convenience of one person or a few persons, but should be done in the sacred place of a community or group of the faithful. Note that permission to erect a private chapel does not bring with it permission to reserve the Blessed Sacrament. This requires a separate permission from the local Ordinary who should ensure that Mass is celebrated there ordinarily at least twice a month. (See can. 934.)

It is fitting that oratories and private chapels be blessed according to the rite prescribed in the liturgical books. They must be reserved exclusively for divine worship and kept free from all domestic uses.

> It is not strictly required to bless oratories and private chapels, but they are not truly sacred places without the blessing. The appropriate rite is that of chapter five of the *Rite of Dedication of a Church and an Altar.*
>
> A multi-purpose space that is used for worship and other activities is not blessed according to this rite; it is not a sacred place because it is not reserved exclusively for religious and cultic purposes. It may, however, be blessed with an appropriate blessing as may other buildings. (See the US version of the *Rite of Blessings,* chapter 16.)

D. Shrines

By the term "shrine" is understood a church or other sacred place to which, for a special reason of piety, the faithful who frequent it make pilgrimage with the approval of the local Ordinary. (Can. 1230) For a shrine to be called national, it is necessary to have the approval of the episcopal conference; to be called international, the approval of the Holy See is required. (Can. 1231) The local Ordinary is competent to approve the statutes of a diocesan shrine; for statutes of a national shrine, the episcopal conference; for statutes of an international shrine, the Holy See. These statutes are to determine especially the purpose of the shrine, the authority of its rector, and the ownership and administration of goods. (Can. 1232)

Pilgrimages to shrines were placed under the supervision of local Ordinaries by a February 11, 1936 decree of the Sacred Congregation of the Council, AAS 28:167; CLD 2:573–75. All pilgrimages to shrines must be promoted or at least approved by the local Ordinary. The rules for naming a shrine "national" or "international" and for the approval of shrine statutes are new to the 1983 code. They are not retroactive and are not binding with respect to shrines already in existence before November 27, 1983.

E. Altars

An altar is a table on which the Eucharistic sacrifice is celebrated; it is called *fixed* if it is so constructed that it is attached to the floor and cannot be moved; it is called *moveable* if it can be removed. It is fitting that in every church there should be a fixed altar; but in other places designated for divine worship the altar may be fixed or moveable. (Can. 1235) In new churches there should be no more than one altar, although a second altar is permitted in a separate Blessed Sacrament chapel for the placement of the tabernacle. (See RDCA, chapter IV, n. 7.) Fixed altars must be dedicated; moveable altars must be dedicated or blessed, according to the rites prescribed in the liturgical books. (Can. 1237, §1) The Eucharist is to be celebrated on a dedicated or blessed altar. When Mass is celebrated outside a sacred place, a suitable table can be used. (See can. 932, §2.)

The ancient tradition of conserving the relics of martyrs and other saints under a fixed altar is to be preserved in accord with the norms given in the liturgical books. (Can. 1237, §2) Both a fixed and moveable altar must be reserved for divine worship alone and completely excluded from any profane use. No corpse may be buried under an altar; otherwise Mass may not be celebrated on it. (Can. 1239)

Further norms governing altars are found in the *Rite of Dedication of a Church and an Altar,* chapter IV; the *General Instruction of the Roman Missal,* 259-267; and the *Ceremonial of Bishops,* 972-983.

Eastern law. There is no provision in the Eastern code for oratories, private chapels, shrines, or altars. These matters, if applicable, are regulated in the particular law of each church. (See Pospishil, 532-33.)

F. Cemeteries

Where possible the Church should have its own cemeteries or at least spaces in civil cemeteries designated for the faithful departed and properly blessed. But if this cannot be done, individual graves should be duly blessed as often as needed. (Can. 1240)

There is no blessing of the grave in a Catholic cemetery, since the entire cemetery has already been blessed and made thereby a sacred place. In a non-Catholic cemetery the grave is blessed by the priest or deacon at the committal service. (See *Rite of Funerals,* 53; US, 218.)

$$t\ w\ o$$

Sacred Times

A. Sundays and Holy Days

Sunday is the day on which the paschal mystery is celebrated from apostolic tradition; it is to be observed in the universal Church as the primordial holy day of obligation. Also to be observed as days of precept are the Nativity of Our Lord Jesus Christ, Epiphany, Ascension, the Feast of the Body and Blood of Christ, Mary Mother of God, the Immaculate Conception, Assumption, Saint Joseph, the apostles Saints Peter and Paul, and All Saints. With the prior approval of the Apostolic See, the episcopal conference may, however, abolish some of the holy days of obligation or transfer them to a Sunday. (Can. 1246)

> The holy days that are common to the *Eastern churches sui iuris* are: Christmas, Epiphany, the Ascension, the Dormition of Holy Mary Mother of God, and the Holy Apostles Peter and Paul. (See CCEC, can. 880, §3.) Families in which the parents belong to different Catholic churches *sui iuris* may observe the norms of one or the other church in regard to the obligation of Sundays and holy days. (See CCEC, can. 883, §2.)

Mass obligation. On Sunday and other holy days of obligation the faithful are obliged to participate in the Mass. (See can. 1247.) The precept of participating at Mass is satisfied by one who attends Mass wherever it is celebrated in a Catholic rite either on the feast day itself or on the evening of the preceding day. (Can. 1248, §1)

> The obligation binds Catholics who are at least seven years old and have the use of reason. Participating at Mass minimally

331

means one's physical presence at Mass. An evening Mass on the day before Sunday or a holy day should not begin before 4:00 in the afternoon. (See Pius XII, apostolic constitution *Christus Dominus,* Jan. 6, 1953, AAS 45 (1953) 14–24, n. VI; CLD 4:275–76.) It is no longer possible to fulfill one's Sunday obligation at the Divine Liturgy of an Eastern non-Catholic church. (See *Directory for Ecumenism,* 115.)

In the United States the feasts of Epiphany and the Body and Blood of Christ are transferred to Sundays; the solemnities of Saint Joseph and Saints Peter and Paul are not observed as days of precept. Whenever the Solemnity of Mary Mother of God (January 1), Assumption (August 15), or All Saints (November 1) falls on a Saturday or on a Monday, the precept to attend Mass is abrogated. (See *BCL Newsletter* 28 (1992) 47.)

Eastern law. On Sundays and holy days the faithful are obliged to participate in the divine liturgy or, in accord with the prescripts or legitimate custom of their own church, in the celebration of the liturgy of the hours. (See CCEC, can. 881, §1.)

Sunday rest. On Sundays and holy days the faithful also are to abstain from those works and business concerns which would impede the worship to be rendered to God, the joy proper to the Lord's day, or the proper relaxation of mind and body. (Can. 1247)

According to moral theologian Bernard Häring, work which interferes with the performance of one's religious duties would more easily fall under the ban than work which can be performed without making any inroad on time to be spent worshiping God. (See Häring, 2:335–36; Matthis/Bonner, 338.) Although the liturgical celebration of feast days begins on the evening before the feast, the precept of rest binds only on the day itself from midnight to midnight. (See *Communicationes* 12 (1980) 359.)

If an ordained minister is lacking or for some other serious reason it is impossible to participate in the Eucharistic celebration, it is highly recommended that the faithful take part in a liturgy of the word, if it is celebrated in a parish church or some other sacred place in accord with the norms of the diocesan bishop, or by praying for a suitable time either personally, as a family or, as occasion may offer, in groups of families. (Can. 1248, §2)

Note that this law is a recommendation. When there is no Mass on a Sunday or holy day, the obligation to attend no longer binds. If a service of the word is held, the faithful are strongly encouraged but not bound by precept to attend.

Sunday celebrations in the absence of a priest. After hearing the presbyteral council, the diocesan bishop is competent to decide whether Sunday assemblies without the celebration of the Eucharist may be held on a regular basis in his diocese. After considering the place and persons involved, the bishop is also competent to set out both general and particular norms for such celebrations. These assemblies are to be conducted only in virtue of their convocation by the bishop and only under the pastoral ministry of the pastor. (Congregation for Divine Worship, *Directory for Sunday Celebrations in the Absence of a Priest,* June 2, 1988, *Notitiae* 24 (1988) 366-78, n. 24; *Origins* 18 (1988) 301-07).

The *Directory for Sunday Celebrations in the Absence of a Priest* lists several conditions for holding such celebrations, among which are the following: (1) It is preferable for the faithful, if possible, to go to the Eucharist on Sunday at a neighboring parish rather than to attend a celebration at their own parish without the Eucharist. (2) The celebration should include the scriptural readings of the Sunday; it may be a celebration of the word, the liturgy of the hours, or in certain circumstances it may be combined with the celebration of one or more of the sacraments or especially the sacramentals. (3) Such a celebration may never be held on a Sunday in places where Mass has already been celebrated that day or the preceding evening, or where it will be celebrated later on Sunday. Nor may there be more than one assembly of this kind on any given Sunday. (4) The faithful must be taught the difference between this kind of celebration and the Eucharist. (5) The pastor should see that holy Communion is given when Mass cannot be celebrated and that the Eucharist is celebrated in due time. (6) The ministers of these celebrations are, in the first place, deacons, followed by instituted acolytes and readers if there are any, or by other lay persons who are chosen by the pastor and given the necessary formation. (See nn. 18-34.)

> *In the United States* this matter is governed by two documents: *Sunday Celebrations in the Absence of a Priest: Leader's Edition* (New York: Catholic Book Publishing Company, 1994), and *Gathered in Steadfast Faith: Statement of the Bishops' Committee on the Liturgy on Sunday Worship in the Absence of a Priest* (Washington: USCC, 1991).

B. Days of Penance

The penitential days and times in the universal Church are every Friday and the season of Lent. (Can. 1250) Abstinence from eating meat or from another food prescribed by the episcopal conference is to be observed on each Friday of the year, unless it is a solemnity; abstinence and fast are to be observed on Ash Wednesday and Good Friday. (Can. 1251) The conference of bishops may determine more precisely the observance of fast and abstinence and may substitute other forms of penance for fast and abstinence, either in whole or in part, especially works of charity and pious exercises. (Can. 1253)

The law of fast prescribes that only one full meal a day be taken. Two lighter meals are permitted to maintain strength according to each one's needs. Eating between meals is not permitted, but liquids, including milk and fruit juices, are allowed. The law of abstinence forbids the eating of meat, but eggs, milk products, and condiments made from meat may be eaten. Fish and all cold blooded animals may be eaten, e.g., frogs, clams, turtles, etc. (See Paul VI, apostolic constitution *Paenitemini,* Feb. 17, 1966, AAS 58 (1966), n. III; CLD 6:676-78.)

In the United States, Catholics who are obliged to abstain from eating meat must do so on Ash Wednesday and all Fridays during the season of Lent. Those obliged to fast must do so on Ash Wednesday and Good Friday. (See NCCB, pastoral statement, Nov. 18, 1966, CLD 6:679-84.) Self-imposed observance of fasting on all weekdays of Lent is strongly recommended. Abstinence from meat on other Fridays of the year is recommended, but not required. Also recommended on all Fridays of the year is prayer, penance (especially by eating less food), and almsgiving for the sake of world peace. (See NCCB, *The Challenge of Peace: God's Promise and Our Response,* May 3, 1983, n. 298.)

The law of abstinence binds those who have completed their fourteenth year; the law of fast binds all from the age of majority up to the beginning of their sixtieth year. Pastors of souls and parents should see to it that even those who, due to their young age, are not bound to the law of fast or abstinence, are nevertheless educated in a genuine sense of penance. (Can. 1252)

Those bound to abstain are those fourteen and older; those bound to fast are those between the ages of 18 and 59, exclusive. One is not bound on the fourteenth or eighteenth birthdays respectively, but begins to abstain or fast at midnight at the close of the birthday. One is still bound to fast on the 59th birthday; the obligation ceases the next day. (See can. 203.)

Eastern law. Days of penance are regulated by the particular law of each church *sui iuris.* The faithful who are outside the territorial boundaries of their own church may adopt the feast days and days of penance which are in force where they are staying.

This means, e.g., that in the United States Eastern Catholics can follow the law of the Latin church which permits the eating of meat on Fridays except during Lent. In families in which the parents belong to different churches *sui iuris,* they may observe the laws of either church pertaining to feast days and days of penance. (See CCEC, cans. 882-83; Pospishil, 541.)

C. Dispensations and Commutations

The pastor, for a just cause and in accord with the norms of the diocesan bishop, in individual cases can grant a dispensation from the obligation of observing a feast day [Sunday or holy day] or a day of penance, or he can commute them to other pious works. (See can. 1245.)

> The dispensations in question refer to the precepts to attend Mass and to rest from labor on feast days, and the laws of fast and abstinence on days of penance. The pastor cannot grant a general dispensation for the whole parish. He may, however, by one and the same act dispense several individuals or several families to whom the same reason for dispensation is applicable, e.g., a number of families taking part in a wedding celebration, as well as the various individuals invited to the celebration. He may dispense his own parishioners anywhere as well as others in his parish territory.
>
> Since this faculty of the pastor is ordinary power, it may be delegated to others, even habitually. Parochial vicars, deacons, and confessors have no power to dispense from the observance of feast days and days of penance unless it is delegated to them. The diocesan pagella may grant this faculty.
>
> Latin pastors and Ordinaries may dispense individuals and families subject to them from regulations of an Eastern church *sui iuris* concerning feasts and fasts.

Clerical superiors. The superior of a religious institute or a society of apostolic life, if they are clerical institutes or societies of pontifical right, for a just cause and in accord with the norms of the diocesan bishop, in individual cases, and on behalf of his own subjects and others staying day and night in the house, can grant a dispensation from the observance of a feast day or day of penance or he can commute the obligations to other pious works. (See can. 1245.)

> The superior in question can grant a dispensation or commutation of the obligation of feast days and days of penance to individual members or groups of those subject to him. Since this faculty of superiors is placed on a par with that of pastors, it seems that the

local superior, per se, cannot use it to dispense his entire community as such, nor a provincial superior his entire province. However,
by one and the same act, a local superior may dispense several
individual members to whom the same reason for the dispensation applies, e.g., a celebration of a community feast day, even
though in fact the dispensation is granted to every single member
of the community. (Note that if the feast day is a solemnity, even
in proper law, abstinence is not required in any case.) The same
applies to a provincial superior who, for a reason applicable to
each of them, dispenses every individual community in the entire
province. The dispensing power of superiors is ordinary power of
governance, and can be delegated to others, even habitually.
Besides members, those who stay day and night in the house
might include employees and pupils who stay regularly, and
guests or patients who stay overnight for one or more days.

Dispensations by law. In virtue of special privileges, the following
are dispensed from the laws of fast and abstinence: seamen, airport personnel, anyone aboard a ship or airplane for the duration of the trip,
circus people, merchants, and nomads. However, it is recommended
that those who enjoy this dispensation compensate the law by a befitting work of piety and, insofar as possible, observe the law at least on
Good Friday. (See Pontifical Commission for the Spiritual Care of
Migrants and Travellers, decree, Mar. 19, 1982, AAS 74 (1982) 742, n. II, 1-3;
CLD 10:36-37.)

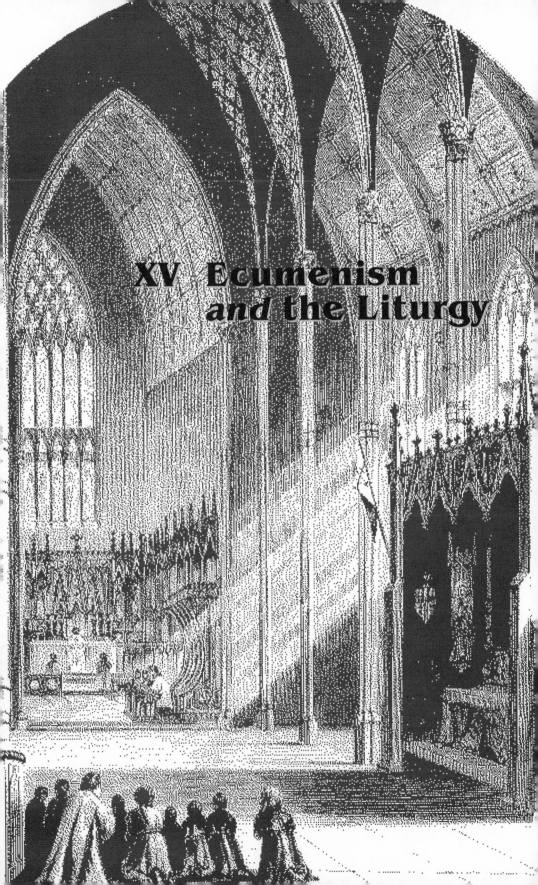

XV Ecumenism and the Liturgy

Baptism and Confirmation

one

A. Joint Celebration

While by baptism a person is incorporated into Christ and his Church, this is only done in practice in a given church or ecclesial community. Baptism, therefore, may not be conferred jointly by two ministers belonging to different churches or ecclesial communities. Moreover, according to Catholic liturgical and theological tradition, baptism is celebrated by just one celebrant. For pastoral reasons, in particular circumstances, the local Ordinary may sometimes permit, however, that a minister of another church or ecclesial community take part in the celebration by reading a lesson, offering a prayer, etc. Reciprocity is possible only if a baptism celebrated in another community does not conflict with Catholic principles or discipline. (*Directory for the Application of Principles and Norms on Ecumenism* (DE), 97)

> For a Catholic minister to participate in a non-Catholic baptismal celebration, the baptism must be valid in that church or ecclesial community. A church is one that has preserved "the substance of the Eucharistic teaching, the sacrament of orders, and apostolic succession," notably the separated Eastern churches. (See Secretariat for Promoting Christian Unity, communication, Oct. 17, 1973, AAS 65 (1973) 616; CLD 8:471, n. 9.) An ecclesial community is the generic term in canon law for what is commonly known as a Protestant denomination.

B. Godparents and Witnesses

Eastern non-Catholics. Because of the close communion between the Catholic Church and the separated Eastern churches, it is permissible for a just cause that a member of a separated Eastern church act as godparent together with a Catholic godparent at the baptism of a Catholic infant or adult, so long as there is provision for the Catholic education of the person being baptized, and it is clear that the godparent is a suitable one. A Catholic is not forbidden to stand as godparent in a separated Eastern church if he or she is invited. In this case the duty of providing for the Christian education of the baptized person binds in the first place the godparent who belongs to the church in which the child is baptized. (DE, 98b)

Other Christians. A baptized person who belongs to a non-Catholic ecclesial community may be admitted only as a witness to baptism together with a Catholic godparent. (Can. 874, §2) It is not permissible for a member of a separated community to act as godparent in the liturgical and canonical sense at baptism or confirmation. Nor may a Catholic be permitted to fulfill this function for a member of a separated community. However, because of ties of blood or friendship, a Christian of another communion, since he or she has faith in Christ, can be admitted with a Catholic godparent as a Christian witness of the baptism. In comparable circumstances, a Catholic can do the same for a member of a separated community. (See DE, 98, 98a.)

> When a person is admitted as Christian witness of baptism in another communion, the responsibility for the Christian education of the baptized belongs to the godparent who is a member of the church in which the person is baptized. Pastoral ministers should carefully explain to the faithful the evangelical and ecumenical reasons for this regulation, so that all misunderstanding of it may be prevented.
>
> The reason for these rules is that the godparents are not merely assuming responsibility for the Christian education of the person receiving baptism or confirmation; they are also representatives of the community of faith, standing as guarantees for the faith of the candidate and desire for ecclesial communion. (See DE, 98.)

Recording of names. The name of a non-Catholic godparent or witness is to be recorded together with the name of the Catholic godparent in the baptismal register. (See can. 877, §1.)

C. Doubts Regarding Validity

Eastern non-Catholics. There can be no doubt cast upon the validity of baptism as conferred among separated Eastern Christians. It suffices, therefore, to establish the fact that baptism was administered.

Since in the Eastern churches the sacrament of confirmation is always lawfully administered by the priest at the same time as baptism, it often happens that no mention is made of the confirmation in the canonical testimony of baptism. This does not give grounds for doubting that the sacrament was conferred. (DE, 99a)

Other Christians. Baptism is conferred with water and with a formula which clearly indicates that baptism is done in the name of the Father, Son and Holy Spirit. It is therefore of the utmost importance for all the disciples of Christ that baptism be administered in this manner by all and that the various churches and ecclesial communities arrive as closely as possible at an agreement about its significance and valid celebration. (DE, 93)

> In some places there are agreements between Catholic and non-Catholic churches on the mutual recognition of baptism, as recommended by the *Directory for Ecumenism,* 94. However, even the absence of such a formal agreement should not automatically lead to a doubt about the validity of the non-Catholic baptism. (See DE, 99b.) A true doubt should not be confused with ignorance. Ignorance is mere lack of knowledge. A doubt means that one has some reason for questioning the validity of baptism in another denomination. A doubt may arise about any of the following: the matter, the form, the intention of an adult baptized or the intention of the minister.

Concerning the matter and form. Water baptism by immersion or pouring, together with the Trinitarian formula, is of itself valid. Therefore, if the rituals, liturgical books or established customs of a church or ecclesial community prescribe either of these ways of baptism, the sacrament is to be considered valid unless there are serious reasons for doubting that the minister has observed the regulations of his or her own community or church. (DE, 95a)

> Baptism by sprinkling, although illicit in the Latin church, is valid provided the water makes physical contact with the candidate while the Trinitarian formula is being said by the minister.

Wherever doubts arise about whether or how water was used, respect for the sacrament and deference toward these ecclesial communities require that a serious investigation of the practice of the community concerned be made before any judgment is passed on the validity of its baptism. (DE, 95c)

Concerning faith and intention. Insufficient faith on the part of the minister never, of itself, makes baptism invalid. Sufficient intention in the baptizing minister is to be presumed, unless there is serious ground for doubting that the minister intended to do what the Church does. (DE, 95b)

Likewise, the intention to receive baptism in the adult who was baptized is to be presumed unless there is a serious reason for doubting it. An adult for purposes of baptism is anyone seven and older with the use of reason. The intention of the minister, whether explicit or implicit, is to do what the Church does when it baptizes.

The following are some non-Catholic churches which have valid baptism: all Eastern non-Catholics, Adventists, African Methodist Episcopal, Amish, Anglican, Assembly of God, Baptists, the Christian and Missionary Alliance, Church of the Brethren, Church of God, Congregational Church, Disciples of Christ, Episcopalians, Evangelical Churches, Evangelical United Brethren, Liberal Catholic Church, Lutherans, Methodists, Church of the Nazzerine, Old Catholics, Old Roman Catholics, Polish National Church, Presbyterian Church, Reformed Churches, United Church of Christ.

The validity of baptism in the Church of Jesus Christ of Latter-day Saints (Mormons) is doubtful. The Holy See has ruled that there are insufficient grounds to declare it invalid, but nevertheless it permits conditional baptism of Mormons who desire to become Catholics. In respect to marriage cases, Mormon baptism is to be presumed valid. (See CDF, private reply, Mar. 16, 1991, *Roman Replies and CLSA Advisory Opinions* (Washington: CLSA, 1991) 14-15.)

Some churches without valid baptism are: Apostolic Church, Bohemian Free Thinkers, Christadelphians, Christian Community (Rudolf Steiner), Christian Scientists, Church of Divine Science, Jehovah's Witnesses, Masons (no baptism at all), the New Church of Mr. Emmanuel Swedenborg (called the Church of the New Jerusalem in the U.S.), Pentecostal churches, Peoples Church of Chicago, Quakers, Salvation Army, Unitarians.

Conditional baptism. If there is a doubt whether someone was baptized, or whether the baptism was conferred validly, and this doubt remains after a serious investigation, then baptism should be administered conditionally. (Can. 869, §1) The formula for conditional baptism is: "If you are not baptized, I baptize you in the name of the Father and of the Son and of the Holy Spirit."

Those baptized in a non-Catholic ecclesial community are not to be baptized conditionally unless: (1) there is a serious reason for doubting the validity of the baptism; (2) this doubt remains after an examination of the matter and form used in the conferral of baptism as well as the intention of the adult who was baptized and the minister of baptism. (See can. 869, §2.)

If doubt remains whether the baptism was conferred or whether it was valid, baptism should not be administered until after the one being baptized, if he or she is an adult, has received instruction on the doctrine of the sacrament of baptism. Also the reasons for doubting the validity of the previous baptism should be explained to the person or, in the case of infant baptism, to the parents. (Can. 869, §3)

The rite of conditional baptism is to be celebrated privately and not in public. (See DE, 99d.) The local Ordinary is to decide in each case what rites are to be included or excluded in conferring conditional baptism. (See *Rite of Reception of Baptized Christians into the Full Communion of the Catholic Church* (RFC), 7; RCIA, US, 480.)

Confirmation. Those baptized in ecclesial communities which do not have valid orders and apostolic succession should be confirmed when they are being received into full communion with the Catholic Church. (See can. 888, 2° and RFC, 8; RCIA, US, 481.)

The reception of baptized Christians into full communion with the Catholic Church is treated in chapter three.

two

Eucharist, Penance, Anointing of the Sick

A. Reception from non-Catholic Ministers

As often as need requires it or true spiritual advantage recommends it, and provided that the danger of error or indifferentism is avoided, the faithful for whom it is physically or morally impossible to go to a Catholic minister may receive the sacraments of penance, Eucharist, and anointing of the sick from non-Catholic ministers in those churches in which these sacraments are valid. (Can. 844, §2)

> The general rule is that the Catholic faithful receive the sacraments from Catholic ministers. (See can. 844, §1.) The above law is an exception to the rule by which Catholics may receive the three sacraments mentioned under certain conditions.
>
> The principal condition is that these sacraments can be received only from ministers in whose churches these sacraments are valid. These are the "churches which have preserved the substance of the Eucharistic teaching, the sacrament of orders, and apostolic succession." (See Secretariat for Promoting Christian Unity, communication, Oct. 17, 1973, AAS 65 (1973) 616; CLD 8:471, n. 9.) This would include all Eastern non-Catholic churches, the Polish National Church, Old Catholics, Old Roman Catholics.
>
> A second condition is physical or moral impossibility of approaching a Catholic minister. Cases of physical impossibility would include any situations in which a person is unable to approach a Catholic minister as, e.g., when there is no Catholic church in the area. Moral impossibility means that a person is physically able to approach a Catholic minister, but cannot do so for some reason. For example, in a small town with only one

344

Catholic priest, a penitent who knows the priest well does not wish to confess to him for fear of recognition.

Another requirement is that of need or spiritual advantage. This can be interpreted broadly in keeping with the canonical axiom, "Burdens are to be restricted; favors are to be multiplied." (Boniface VIII, *De regulis iuris,* rule 15)

Finally, it is required that error and indifferentism be avoided. This refers to the erroneous and indifferent attitude that holds that there is no real difference between the churches and it does not matter to which church one belongs.

Since practice differs between Catholics and Eastern Christians in the matter of frequent Communion, confession before Communion and the Eucharistic fast, care must be taken to avoid scandal and suspicion among Eastern Christians through Catholics not following the Eastern usage. A Catholic who legitimately wishes to communicate with Eastern Christians must respect the Eastern discipline as much as possible and refrain from communicating if that church restricts sacramental Communion to its own members to the exclusion of others. (DE, 124)

Although a Catholic may have met all the requirements of canon law to receive the Eucharist, penance, or anointing of the sick from an Eastern non-Catholic (or equivalent) minister, the non-Catholic church might not admit of such reception. In the absence of local guidelines, permission from the non-Catholic minister should be obtained as an ecumenical courtesy before approaching the sacrament.

B. Reception by Non-Catholics

Eastern non-Catholic and equivalent churches. Catholic ministers may licitly administer the sacraments of penance, Eucharist, and anointing of the sick to members of the Eastern churches which do not have full communion with the Catholic Church, if these persons spontaneously ask for the sacrament and are properly disposed. This also applies to members of other churches which, in the judgment of the Apostolic See, are in a condition equal to the Eastern churches in reference to the sacraments. (Can. 844, §3)

This norm refers to a Catholic minister administering any of the three specified sacraments to a member of an Eastern non-Catholic church or some other equivalent church (Polish National Church, Old Catholic Church, Old Roman Catholic Church). Although the *Decree on Ecumenism* from Vatican II singled out the Anglican communion as having "a special place among those communions in which Catholic traditions and institutions in part continue to exist," there has not yet been a formal judgment published by the Apostolic See concerning the Anglican communion or other communions as a church or churches "in a condition equal to the Eastern churches." (See Vatican II, decree *Unitatis redintegratio,* AAS 57 (1965) 90–107, n. 13; CLSA Comm., 610.) However, if the church in question has preserved the substance of Eucharistic teaching, the sacrament of orders, and apostolic succession, it would be comparable to the Eastern churches and therefore its members would be eligible to receive the three specified sacraments in accord with the requirements of this law.

The requirement that the non-Catholic person in question "spontaneously ask" for the sacrament means that the person requests it on his or her own initiative and not at the suggestion of the minister. The minister ordinarily can presume the person has the proper disposition unless there is reason to doubt it as, e.g., when the person wishes to receive Communion and does not practice his or her own faith.

Ecclesial communities. If there is danger of death or, in the judgment of the diocesan bishop or the episcopal conference, there is some other serious need, Catholic ministers also licitly administer these same sacraments [penance, Eucharist, anointing of the sick] to other Christians who are not in full communion with the Catholic Church. This may be done when they are unable to go to a minister of their own community and they spontaneously ask for the sacrament, and provided they manifest Catholic faith concerning these sacraments and are properly disposed. (Can. 844, §4; DE, 130–131)

This law provides for Christians other than the Eastern non-Catholics and those who are in a condition equal to them. They must always be validly baptized Christians, because no one who is unbaptized can validly receive any other sacraments. (See can. 842, §1.)

For a person belonging to such an ecclesial community to receive any of the three specified sacraments from a Catholic minister, there must be danger of death or other serious need. In danger of death, Catholic ministers are free to administer any of the three sacraments to non-Catholics who fulfill the conditions of the law.

Regarding other cases of grave need, the *Directory for Ecumenism,* n. 130 states that Catholic ministers must observe the laws established by the diocesan bishop for verifying the other conditions of canon 844, §4. If there are no diocesan laws, the

Directory for Ecumenism itself should be observed. The previous Ecumenical Directory of 1967 gave two examples of serious need—during persecution and in prisons. (See n. 55.) A June 1, 1972 instruction of the Secretariat for Promoting Christian Unity mentioned another case of serious need, that of non-Catholic Christians who live in an area where they are unable to have access to their own ecclesial community. (See AAS 64 (1972) 518; CLD 7:590, n. 6.) Additionally, the 1993 *Directory for Ecumenism,* nn. 159-160 is open to the possibility of Eucharistic sharing with a non-Catholic party at a Catholic wedding Mass provided the diocesan bishop gives permission and the other conditions of the law are fulfilled.

One of the conditions of canon 844, §4 is that the non-Catholic person wishing to receive penance, Eucharist, or anointing of the sick must manifest Catholic faith in these sacraments. This does not mean that the person needs detailed knowledge about the theology of the sacrament in question, but only that the recipient believes in the essential meaning of the sacraments. For example, in reference to the reception of the Eucharist, it suffices that the recipients believe the consecrated bread and wine is spiritual food, the body and blood of the Lord. (See cans. 899, §1 and 913, §2.) For the anointing of the sick, it would be sufficient that they believe the sacrament is a spiritual means of promoting healing and comfort and, if necessary, the forgiveness of sins. (See RA, 6, 7, and 12.) For penance it would be sufficient that the penitents believe that the sacrament absolves them from their sins and this brings reconciliation with God and the Church. (See can. 959.)

D. Other Forms of Participation in Eucharistic Liturgies

Participation in Eastern non-Catholic liturgy. Since celebration of the Eucharist on the Lord's day is the foundation and center of the whole liturgical year, Catholics—but those of Eastern churches according to their own law—are obliged to attend Mass on that day and on days of precept. It is not advisable therefore to organize ecumenical services on Sundays, and it must be remembered that even when Catholics participate in ecumenical services or in services of other churches and ecclesial communities, the obligation of participating at Mass on these days remains. (DE, 115; see also can. 1247; CCEC can. 888, §1.)

Catholics may participate in the divine liturgy of separated Eastern churches but they may no longer fulfill the Sunday obligation there. The previous Ecumenical Directory of 1967, n. 47, had permitted Catholics to fulfill the Sunday obligation at the Eucharistic liturgy of a separated Eastern church.

Catholics may read the Scriptures at a sacramental liturgical celebration in the Eastern churches if they are invited to do so. An Eastern Christian may be invited to read the lessons at similar services in Catholic churches. (DE, 126)

With other Christians. The reading of Scripture during a Eucharistic celebration in a Catholic church is to be done by members of that church. On exceptional occasions and for a just cause, the bishop of the diocese may permit a member of another church or ecclesial community to take on the task of reader. (DE, 133)

> The bishop's permission is needed to invite a Protestant to read at Mass, but not someone from a separated Eastern church since the *Directory for Ecumenism,* n. 126 already permits this.

In the Catholic Eucharistic liturgy the homily, which forms part of the liturgy itself, is reserved to the priest or deacon since the homily presents the mysteries of faith and the norms of Christian living in accord with Catholic teaching and tradition. (DE, 134).

> Catholics are not prohibited from reading or giving a sermon at a non-Catholic liturgy, since this is excluded neither by the code nor by the *Directory for Ecumenism.*

Concelebration prohibited. Catholic priests are prohibited from concelebrating the Eucharist together with priests or ministers of churches or ecclesial communities that do not have full communion with the Catholic Church. (Can. 908)

> The reason for this prohibition is that Eucharistic concelebration is a visible manifestation of full communion in faith, worship, and community life of the Catholic Church, expressed by ministers of that church. (See DE, 104e.) This prohibition also includes priests from the Eastern non-Catholic churches.

Prayers for non-Catholics. Ancient Christian liturgical and ecclesiological tradition permits the specific mention in the Eucharistic prayer only of the names of persons who are in full communion with the church celebrating the Eucharist. (DE, 121) Non-Catholics, both living and deceased, may be prayed for during the prayers of the faithful at Mass. Likewise, a priest may also accept a Mass offering for the intention of a non-Catholic person, living or deceased. (See DE, 121; can. 901.)

E. Sharing of Church Buildings

For a just cause, with the express permission of the local Ordinary, and with scandal avoided, a priest may celebrate the Eucharist in the place of worship of another church or ecclesial community that does not have full communion with the Catholic Church. (Can. 933)

> Examples of a just cause include pastoral advantage and ecumenical good will. Since the canon requires permission of the local Ordinary to celebrate the Eucharist in non-Catholic *Christian* churches only, no permission is needed to celebrate in an interdenominational chapel or non-Christian church if there is a particular case of need. (See can. 932, §1.)

If priests, ministers, or communities not in full communion with the Catholic Church do not have a place or the liturgical objects necessary for celebrating worthily their religious ceremonies, the diocesan bishop may allow them the use of a church or a Catholic building and also lend them what may be necessary for their services. (DE, 137)

three
Liturgies of Marriage

A. Between a Catholic and an Eastern non-Catholic

In the Eastern churches. A Catholic minister may be present and take part in the celebration of a marriage that is properly celebrated between Eastern Christians or between a Catholic and an Eastern Christian in the Eastern church if invited to do so by the Eastern church authority. (See DE, 127.)

Witnesses. A member of an Eastern church may act as bridesmaid or best man at a wedding in a Catholic church; a Catholic also may be bridesmaid or best man at a marriage properly celebrated in an Eastern church. In all cases this practice must conform to the general discipline of both churches regarding the requirements for participating in such marriages. (DE, 128)

B. Between a Catholic and Another Christian

Witnesses. Members of other churches or ecclesial communities may be witnesses at the celebration of marriage in a Catholic church. Catholics may also be witnesses at marriages which are celebrated in other churches or ecclesial communities. (DE, 136)

> Although the *Directory for Ecumenism* does not explicitly state that these witnesses may be the best man and bridesmaid, this is not excluded and therefore is permitted in accord with established custom.

In the non-Catholic church. With the previous authorization of the local Ordinary, and if invited to do so, a Catholic priest or deacon may attend or participate in some way in the celebration of mixed marriages in situations where the dispensation from canonical form has been granted. In these cases there may be only one ceremony in which the presiding person receives the marriage vows. At the invitation of this celebrant, the Catholic priest or deacon may offer other appropriate prayers, read from the Scriptures, give a brief exhortation and bless the couple. (DE, 157)

In the Catholic church. Upon request of the couple, the local Ordinary may permit the Catholic priest to invite the minister of the party of the other church or ecclesial community to participate in the celebration of the marriage, to read from the Scriptures, give a brief exhortation and bless the couple. (DE, 158)

Because of problems concerning Eucharistic sharing which may arise from the presence of non-Catholic witnesses and guests, a mixed marriage celebrated according to the Catholic form ordinarily takes place outside the Eucharistic liturgy. For a just cause, however, the diocesan bishop may permit the celebration of the Eucharist. In the latter case, the decision as to whether the non-Catholic party of the marriage may be admitted to Eucharistic Communion is to be made in keeping with the general norms existing in the matter both for Eastern Christians and for other Christians [as seen above], taking into account the particular situation of the reception of the sacrament of Christian marriage by two baptized Christians. (DE, 159) Although the spouses in a mixed marriage share the sacraments of baptism and marriage, Eucharistic sharing can only be exceptional and the laws for sacramental sharing must be observed. (See DE, 160.)

For further treatment of mixed marriages, see chapters 8, 9, 11, and 12 above, especially the sections on the preparation for mixed marriage; the impediment of disparity of cult; dispensations from the form; the rite of marriage outside Mass, the rite of marriage of a Catholic and an unbaptized, and the place of marriage; and the dissolution of the bond.

four
Other Acts
of Divine Worship

A. Worship, Blessings and Prayers

Non-sacramental liturgical worship, such as morning and evening prayer, special vigils, prayer services, and so forth can take place between Catholics and non-Catholics. No special permission is required to participate in such non-sacramental forms of ecumenical worship, unless particular law states otherwise. (See DE, 116-19.)

Blessings can be given to Catholics in the first place and also to catechumens, and even to non-Catholics unless a prohibition of the Church prevents this. (Can. 1170; see also RB, 31; DE, 121.)

Prayer for the intention of Christian unity is recommended at all kinds of liturgies, including the prayers of the faithful at Mass. It is especially recommended during the annual week of Christian unity (January 18-25). (See DE, 62.)

Public prayer for other Christians, living or dead, and for the needs and intentions of other churches and ecclesial communities and their spiritual heads may be offered during the litanies and other invocations of a liturgical service, even at the Eucharist, but not during the Eucharistic prayer, as noted above. (See DE, 121.)

B. Funeral Rites for Non-Catholics

Catechumens are equated with the faithful in matters pertaining to funeral rites. (See can. 1183, §1.)

The local Ordinary can permit ecclesiastical funeral rites for *children who died before baptism* if their parents had intended to have them baptized. (Can. 1183, §2). Unless the local Ordinary has given general permission, this permission from the local Ordinary is required for each individual case. The *Roman Missal* contains a funeral Mass for a child who dies before baptism.

In the prudent judgment of the local Ordinary, ecclesiastical funeral rites can be granted to *baptized persons who belonged to some non-Catholic church or ecclesial community*, unless it is contrary to their own wishes and provided their own minister is unavailable. (Can. 1183, §3)

> The judgment of the local Ordinary must be made on a case by case basis. However, he could give general delegation to pastors to make this judgment. N.B. This permission cannot be given to those who were unbaptized or baptized invalidly.
>
> The inability to have the proper non-Catholic minister may result from moral as well as physical unavailability. Physical unavailability would be, e.g., when there is no minister of the non-Catholic deceased in the area. Moral unavailability would be, e.g., when there is a minister of the non-Catholic deceased in the area but the non-Catholic has not practiced his or her faith, and the practicing Catholic next of kin or other person responsible for the funeral would like to have the funeral in the Catholic church. If a non-Catholic had been regularly practicing his or her religion during life, it should be presumed that that individual would have wanted to have the funeral in his or her own church, and therefore it would be contrary to the wishes of the departed to have it in the Catholic church.

The diocesan bishop may permit non-Catholic Christian ministers the use of a Catholic church and a Catholic cemetery for funeral services and burial when they do not have a church or cemetery of their own. (See DE, 137.)

> *Burial of Catholic in non-Catholic cemetery, U.S.* In those situations in which a Catholic is to be interred in a non-Catholic cemetery, the priest [or other minister] after the liturgy in the church may conduct the committal service at the graveside. He should bless the individual grave and then follow the usual ritual for the burial of a Catholic. On those occasions when a non-Catholic is to be buried in a Catholic cemetery, the ordained minister of the church in which he shared belief or communion may conduct the committal service. (NCCC Guidelines, The Burial Rite, A, B, CLD 9:687).

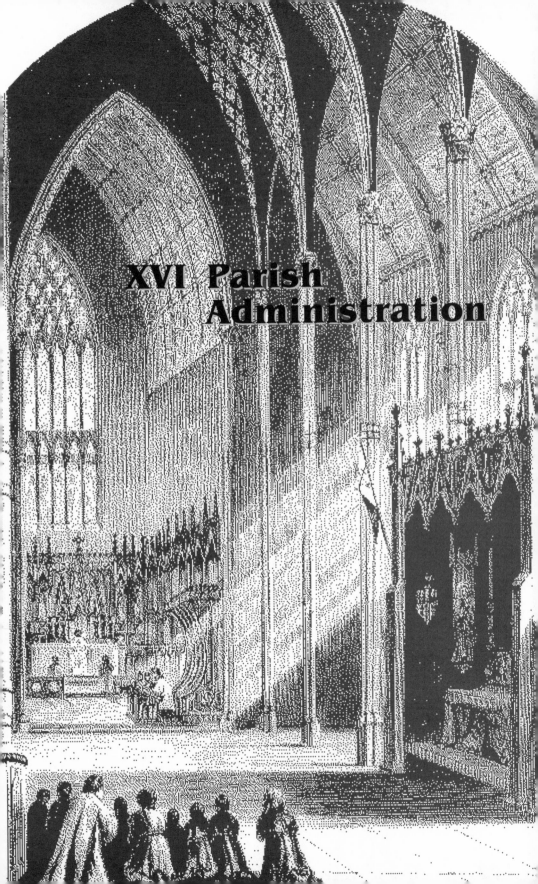

XVI Parish Administration

o n e

Pastors

A. Installation

The one who is promoted to carry out the pastoral care of a parish obtains that care and is bound to exercise it from the moment of taking possession of the parish. The local Ordinary or the priest delegated by him places the pastor in possession of the parish, observing the manner accepted by particular law or legitimate custom. However, for a just reason the same Ordinary can dispense from this procedure, in which case notification of the dispensation to the parish replaces the act of taking possession. (Can. 527, §§ 1, 2)

At the beginning of his term of office, the pastor is obliged to make a profession of faith personally, according to the formula approved by the Apostolic See, before the local Ordinary or his delegate. (See can. 833, 6'.) He is also obliged to make the oath of fidelity on assuming office.

> The approved English translation of the Profession of Faith and the Oath of Fidelity are found in Appendix I.
>
> *In the United States,* there is an approved "Order for the Installation of a Pastor" which is found in Appendix I of the *Book of Blessings.* If possible, the installation should take place at one of the Masses on the first Sunday that the pastor's appointment is effective. It may also take place during a celebration of the word of God, or during morning or evening prayer from the *Liturgy of the Hours.* The bishop is the usual celebrant, but he may delegate a priest to preside in his place, especially a vicar or a dean. (For further rules, see nn. 2012-21 of the *Book of Blessings.)*

B. Term of Office

The pastor must have stability in office and therefore is to be appointed for an indefinite time. He can be appointed for a definite term by the diocesan bishop only if this has been allowed by a decree of the episcopal conference. (Can. 522)

> *In the United States,* the diocesan bishops may appoint pastors for a six-year term which can be renewed. (See NCCB, decree, Sept. 24, 1984, CLD 11:80.) It is up to the bishop of each diocese to determine whether there is a term of office, whether it can be renewed, and how many times it can be renewed.

C. Cessation of Office

Retirement. When he completes his 75th year, the pastor is asked to submit to the diocesan bishop his resignation from office. The bishop should decide whether to accept or defer the resignation after considering all the circumstances of the person and the place. (See can. 538, §3.)

> The letter of resignation should be submitted on or before the day after the pastor's 75th birthday. The requirement also applies to a pastor who belongs to a religious institute or clerical society. If the superior wishes the pastor to remain in office after completing his 75th year, the superior should petition the bishop accordingly.

Completion of term. The office of pastor is lost by the completion of his term in accord with the prescriptions of particular law. (See can. 538, §1)

> At the end of the term, the bishop may reappoint the pastor to a new term or assign him elsewhere.

Transfer and removal. A diocesan pastor ceases from office by removal or transfer by the diocesan bishop done in accord with the norm of law. A pastor who is a member of a religious institute or a society of apostolic life is removed either by the diocesan bishop, having notified the superior, or by the superior, having notified the bishop; neither requires the consent of the other. (See cans. 538, §§ 1, 2 and 682, §2.)

> The procedures for the removal of diocesan pastors are found in canons 1740-1747, and for their transfer in canons 1748-1752.

Resignation. A pastor may resign for a just cause; the resignation, for validity, must be accepted by the diocesan bishop. (See can. 538, §1.)

Just causes for resignation would be poor health, inadequacy, retirement, etc. The pastor is not free to vacate the office unless the resignation is accepted by the bishop.

A pastor who is a member of a religious institute or clerical society, and who wishes to resign, should first submit his resignation to his competent superior.

D. Functions Especially Committed to Pastors

The following functions are especially committed to the pastor:

1) The administration of baptism.

If baptism was administered neither by the pastor nor in his presence, the minister of baptism, whoever the person is, must give notification of the conferral of baptism to the pastor of the parish in which the baptism was administered so that he may record the baptism in keeping with canon 877, §1. (Can. 878)

Except in a case of necessity, no one, without permission, may confer baptism in the territory of another, not even on his own subjects. (Can. 862)

2) The administration of the sacrament of confirmation to those who are in danger of death in accord with canon 883, n. 3.

> Canon 833, n. 3 permits not only the pastor but indeed any presbyter to confirm in danger of death.

3) The administration of Viaticum and the anointing of the sick, with due regard for canon 1003, §§ 2 and 3, and the imparting of the apostolic blessing.

> All priests who have been entrusted with an office of pastoral care have the duty and right to administer the anointing of the sick on behalf of the faithful committed to their pastoral office. For a reasonable cause, any other priest can administer this sacrament with at least the presumed consent of the priest entrusted with the pastoral office. (See can. 1003, §2.) Every priest may carry blessed oil so that, in a case of necessity, he may administer the sacrament of the anointing of the sick. (Can. 1003, §3)

4) Assistance at marriages and the nuptial blessing.

> Pastors have the faculty to assist at marriages in their parish in virtue of their office. (See cans. 1108, §1 and 1109.) If someone other than the pastor is to assist at the marriage and conducts the premarital investigations, that person should inform the pastor of the results as soon as possible by means of an authentic document. (See can. 1070.)

5)   The celebration of funerals.

6)   The blessing of the baptismal font in the Easter season, the leading of processions outside the church, and solemn blessings outside the church.

> The *Rite of Blessings* from the *Roman Ritual* specifies that the bishop should bless a new baptistery or baptismal font that is built in his diocese, or he may entrust this to another priest. (See RB, 839; US, 1087.) Thus, when the bishop does not bless a baptismal font that is built, the pastor would need his permission to do so; but the pastor does not need permission to bless a portable baptismal font. The blessing of baptismal fonts should take place on Sundays, especially in the Easter season, or on the feast of the Baptism of the Lord. It may not be celebrated on Ash Wednesday, during Holy Week, or on All Souls Day. (See RB, 840; US, 1088.)
>
> To have an outdoor procession for the veneration of the Eucharist, the permission of the diocesan bishop is required. (See can. 944.)
>
> The solemn blessings outside church would mainly be those found in Part II of the *Rite of Blessings*.

7)   The more solemn celebration of the Eucharist on Sundays and holy days of obligation.

> Canon 530 "especially commits" the functions listed above to the pastor. This does not mean that these functions are reserved exclusively to the pastor, but that he is entrusted with them in a special way. Some of the functions, since they are honorific, should more frequently be performed by the pastor, e.g., the blessing of the baptismal font during the Easter season, the leading of processions outside church, and the imparting of solemn blessings outside church. The other functions, insofar as they are regular pastoral responsibilities, can be performed by other priests or appropriate ministers at the pastor's discretion and ordinarily with his presumed permission.

E.   Residence, Vacations and Absences

The pastor must reside in the parish house near the church. Nevertheless, in particular cases, if there is a just reason, the local Ordinary can permit him to live elsewhere, especially in a house common to several presbyters, as long as there is proper and due provision for the performance of parochial functions.

Unless a serious reason prevents it, the pastor is allowed to be away from the parish on vacation each year for at most one continuous or intermittent month. Not counted in the vacation time are the days in which the pastor makes a retreat once a year. Moreover, the pastor, when he is to be absent from the parish for more than a week, is bound to notify the local Ordinary of this. (Can. 533, §§ 1, 2)

F. *Missa Pro Populo*

After taking possession of the parish, the pastor is obliged to apply a Mass for the people entrusted to him on every Sunday and holy day of obligation observed in his diocese. If he is legitimately impeded from this celebration, he should apply a Mass on these same days through another priest or he himself should do it on other days. A pastor who has the care of several parishes need apply only one Mass on Sundays and holy days for all the people entrusted to him. A pastor who has not satisfied these obligations shall as soon as possible apply as many Masses for the people as he has omitted. (See can. 534.)

A parochial vicar who acts as a substitute for the pastor is not bound to this obligation; a parochial administrator is bound. (See cans. 549 and 540, §1.)

G. Keeping Parish Registers, the Seal, Archives

In every parish there are to be parish registers for baptisms, marriages, deaths, and other registers in accord with the prescriptions of the episcopal conference and the diocesan bishop. The pastor should ensure that these books are accurately inscribed and diligently preserved. In the baptismal register there also should be recorded confirmations as well as those things which pertain to the canonical status of the faithful by reason of marriage, without prejudice to canon 1133, by reason of adoption, and likewise by reason of the reception of holy orders, perpetual profession in a religious institute, and a change of rite. These notations should always be mentioned on a baptismal certificate. (Can. 535, §§ 1, 2)

> Canon 1133 refers to the celebration of a marriage in secret which is recorded only in a special register kept in the secret archive of the diocesan curia.

Every parish should have its own seal. Testimonies which are given concerning the canonical status of the faithful, as well as all acts which may have juridical import, should be signed by the pastor himself or his delegate and sealed with the parish seal. (Can. 535, §3)

In every parish there should be a register or archive in which the parish books are kept together with letters of the bishops and other documents which must be preserved due to need or usefulness. At visitation or at another opportune time all these things are to be inspected by the diocesan bishop or his delegate. The pastor should take care lest these materials fall into the hands of outsiders. The older parish books should also be carefully kept in accord with the prescriptions of particular law. (Can. 535, §§ 4, 5)

G. Co-Pastors

Where circumstances require it, the pastoral care of a parish or of several parishes together can be entrusted to several priests jointly (*in solidum*). Nevertheless, one of them is to be appointed moderator for the exercise of pastoral care, namely, he should oversee the joint activity and is answerable for it before the bishop. (Can. 517, §1)

The priests who serve as co-pastors obtain the pastoral care only from the moment of taking possession of the parish. The moderator is placed in possession in the same way as the pastor in accord with canon 527, §2. For the other priests a profession of faith legitimately made replaces the taking of possession. (See can. 542, 3°.)

> Co-pastors should take the oath of fidelity on assuming office as well as the profession of faith.

If the pastoral care of some parish or several parishes together has been committed to priests jointly, each of them, in accord with an arrangement determined by themselves, are bound to fulfill the duties and functions of the pastor given in canons 528, 529, and 530. They all have the faculty to assist at marriages as well as all powers of dispensation granted by law to the pastor which, nevertheless, must be exercised under the direction of the moderator. (Can. 543, §1)

All the priests who belong to the group are bound to the obligation of residence. Through common agreement they should establish a rule whereby one of them celebrates the *Missa pro populo* in accord with canon 534. Only the moderator represents in juridic affairs the parish or parishes entrusted to the group. (Can. 543, §2)

When one of the priests from the group, or the moderator, ceases from office, or when one of them becomes incapable of exercising his pastoral duties, the parish or parishes, whose care is entrusted to the group, do not become vacant. However, the diocesan bishop is to appoint another moderator. Before another moderator is appointed by the bishop, the senior priest of the group by reason of appointment should fulfill this role. (See can. 544.)

> *The Eastern code's* treat of parishes and parish ministers is quite similar in substance to that of the Latin code.

$$t\ w\ o$$

Other Parish Ministries

A. Parochial Vicars and Administrators

Unless something else is expressly stated in the letter of the diocesan bishop, the parochial vicar is bound by reason of his office to assist in the entire parochial ministry, except for the application of the *Missa pro populo*, and likewise, if the case calls for it, to take the place of the pastor in accord with the norm of law. (Can. 548, §2)

> The parochial vicar is the canonical term for the office more commonly known as assistant pastor, associate pastor, or curate. Only a priest may validly be appointed parochial vicar. (See can. 546.) The diocesan bishop freely appoints the parochial vicar, without prejudice to the right of the major superiors of clerical religious institutes and societies of apostolic life to present the name to the bishop for appointment. (See cans. 547; 682, §1; and 738, §2.) A parochial vicar can be removed by the diocesan bishop or diocesan administrator for a just cause. A parochial vicar who is a member of a religious institute or society of apostolic life can be removed either by the major superior or the bishop, after each has notified the other. (See cans. 552 and 682, §2.)

The parochial vicar should report regularly to the pastor concerning prospective and existing pastoral undertakings. In this way the pastor and the vicar or vicars, through their joint efforts, can provide for the pastoral care of the parish for which they are together responsible. (Can. 548, §3)

The parochial vicar is bound to reside in the parish or, if he was appointed for several parishes together, he is bound to reside in one of them. Nevertheless, the local Ordinary, for a just reason, can permit him to live elsewhere, especially in a house common to several presbyters, provided no harm is done thereby to the performance of his pastoral duties. (Can. 550, §1)

The parochial vicar enjoys the same right as the pastor for a vacation. (Can. 550, §3)

> The parochial vicar may have an annual vacation of one month, whether continuous or interrupted, not counting the time spent away for his annual retreat. (See can. 533, §2.)

Concerning offerings given to the vicar by some member of the faithful on the occasion of his performing a pastoral ministry, the prescriptions of canon 531 are to be observed. (Can. 551)

> Canon 531 is presented below, page 369.

When the pastor is absent the parochial vicar is bound to all the obligations of the pastor except for the obligation of applying the *Missa pro populo.* (See can. 549.)

When the parish is vacant and likewise when the pastor is impeded from exercising his pastoral duty, the parochial vicar assumes the governance of the parish in the interim before a parochial administrator is appointed. If there are several parochial vicars, this is done by the one who is senior by appointment, or if there are no vicars, by a pastor specified in particular law. The one who has assumed the governance of the parish should immediately notify the local Ordinary of the vacancy of the parish. (See can. 541.)

> A parish is vacant when the pastor dies or when his office ceases due to the expiration of his term, resignation, transfer, or removal. The pastor is impeded when he is unable to function for a significant period of time for any reason. This is to be distinguished from a pastor who is merely absent temporarily for reason of vacation, retreat, etc., in which case no administrator will be appointed and the parochial vicar assumes the pastor's obligations.
>
> The parochial vicar who is senior by appointment is the one who was first assigned to the parish in question.

B. Deacons and Lay Ministers

If by reason of a scarcity of priests the diocesan bishop decides that a share in the exercise of the pastoral care of a parish is to be entrusted to a deacon, or some other person who is not a priest, or to a community of persons, he should appoint some priest who, endowed with the powers and faculties of a pastor, shall moderate the pastoral care. (Can. 517, §2)

> This law allows deacons and lay ministers, including a community of laypersons such as lay religious, to be appointed parish administrators in areas where there are not enough priests. This should not be confused with the canonical term "administrator" which is used of the priest who assumes the pastor's functions when the parish is vacant or the pastor is impeded. The priest who is appointed moderator of the pastoral care of a parish with a deacon or lay administrator need not reside in the parish.
>
> The section on parishes in the code says very little about the role of deacons and lay persons in parish ministry. The reader should consult other parts of this handbook, especially the parts on baptism, Eucharist, marriage, funeral rites, blessings, and the liturgy of the hours.
>
> *The Eastern code* does not mention deacons and lay persons as administrators in priestless parishes, but this in fact occurs in the Eastern churches when a resident pastor is not available. (See Pospishil, 189.)
>
> The ministry of the *pastoral associate,* which is a full-time parish pastoral ministry exercised by qualified deacons and lay persons, is a new office that exists in North America and elsewhere. It is not yet recognized in the universal law.

C. Parish Council

If it is opportune in the judgment of the diocesan bishop after consulting the presbyteral council, a pastoral council is to be established in each parish. The pastor presides over the council in which the faithful, together with those who in virtue of office participate in the pastoral care of the parish, offer their assistance in fostering pastoral action. The parish council enjoys a consultative vote only and is governed by norms enacted by the diocesan bishop. (Can. 536)

> Although the code does not require a parish council, it does permit the diocesan bishop to require it if he wishes. In the absence of a determination by the bishop, the pastor may decide whether to establish a parish council.

three
Financial Administration

A. The Pastor

In accord with the law, the pastor represents the parish in all juridical affairs. He should see to it that the goods of the parish are administered in accord with canons 1281-1288. (Can. 532)

The administration of ecclesiastical goods is the responsibility of the one who immediately governs the [juridic] person to which the same goods belong, unless something else is provided by particular law, statutes, or legitimate custom, and without prejudice to the right of the Ordinary to intervene in case of negligence by the administrator. (Can. 1279, §1)

B. The Finance Council

In each parish there is to be a council for financial affairs which, in addition to universal law, is regulated by norms established by the diocesan bishop. The faithful, selected for this council in accord with these same regulations, assist the pastor in the administration of the parish goods, with due regard for canon 532. (Can. 537)

> A finance council is mandatory for each parish. Since it is constitutive law, the diocesan bishop may not dispense from it. (See can. 86.) This requirement is a specification of the general law that states: Every juridic person should have its own council for financial affairs, or at least two advisers, who in accord with the norm of the statutes assist the administrator in fulfilling his or her duties. (Can. 1280)
>
> The finance council is distinct from the parish council,

although there is nothing to prevent certain members of the parish council from acting as a finance council provided this is not prohibited by diocesan statutes. On the other hand, if the diocesan statutes give the right to the pastor to choose the members of the finance council, he is not obliged to choose any members of the parish council. Since the term "faithful" includes baptized non-Catholics, they may be chosen members of the finance council, unless they are excluded by particular law.

The precise duties of the finance council should be spelled out in diocesan statutes. The competence of the council could extend to the preparing or reviewing of budgets and reports; advising on all acts of extraordinary administration, on contracts, salaries and benefits of parish employees, insurance, investments, loans, mortgages, leases, rents, fund raising, land and buildings and, in general, on any financial and legal matters within their competence as specified by particular law or as brought to their attention by the pastor.

C. General Duties of Administrators

All persons, whether cleric or lay, who by legitimate title take part in the administration of ecclesiastical goods, are bound to fulfill their duties in the name of the Church in accord with the norm of law. (Can. 1282)

Before administrators begin their duties they must take an oath before the Ordinary or his delegate that they will be good and faithful administrators. (Can. 1283, 1°)

> The pastor fulfills this law by his installation. Since the members of the finance council have a part in the financial administration of the parish, they too should take an oath in accord with this law.

All administrators are bound to fulfill their duties with the diligence of a good *paterfamilias.* Thus, they must:

1)   be vigilant that the goods entrusted to their care are not lost or damaged in any way; to this end, inasmuch as may be necessary, they are to take out insurance policies;

2)   see to it that the ownership of ecclesiastical goods is safeguarded in civilly valid ways;

3)   observe the regulations of canon and civil law, as well as regulations imposed by a founder or donor or by legitimate authority, and beware lest the non-observance of the civil law result in harm to the Church;

4)   collect income and profits promptly and in full, keep them

safe, and use them in accord with the intention of the founder or legitimate norms;

5)   pay the interest on a loan or mortgage at the time it is due and see to it that the capital debt itself is paid in due time;

6)   with the consent of the Ordinary, invest the money which is left over after expenses and which can be profitably allocated for the goals of the juridic person;

7)   keep well-ordered accounts of receipts and expenditures;

8)   prepare a report of their administration at the end of every year;

9)   keep in good order in the archives all documents and legal papers upon which depend the rights of the Church or the institution to its goods, and deposit authentic copies of all such papers in the archives of the curia when this can conveniently be done. (Can. 1284, §§ 1, 2)

Even though they may not be bound to administration by title of an ecclesiastical office, administrators may not arbitrarily relinquish the duties they have undertaken; if from their arbitrary neglect of duty any harm comes to the Church, they are bound to make restitution. (Can. 1289)

> Pastors are administrators by title of office. The members of the finance council participate in this administration even though they do not have the principal responsibility for finances; thus they are subject to this canon. Likewise bound to this canon are any employees or even volunteers in the parish who have any kind of financial responsibility. (See CLSA Comm., 878.)

D. Budget and Reports

It is highly recommended that administrators each year prepare budgets of income and expenses; however, it is left to particular law to require them and to determine more precisely the manner in which they are to be presented. (Can. 1284, §3)

Both clerical and lay administrators of any ecclesiastical goods whatsoever, which have not been legitimately exempted from the power of governance of the diocesan bishop, are obliged by their office to give a report every year to the local Ordinary, who shall present it to the [diocesan] finance council for examination. Any custom to the contrary is reprobated. (Can. 1287, §1)

> This law also applies to the property and funds of parishes administered by religious and members of societies of apostolic

life, but not the property, including the church, which is owned by the religious institute or clerical society.

Administrators should give an account to the faithful, according to the norms established in particular law, of the goods which are donated to the Church by the faithful. (Can. 1287, §2)

> The canon only requires the particular law to establish regulations for an accounting to the faithful for the donations made by the faithful, although particular law may require a more complete financial report to parishioners.

E. Duties Regarding Employees

In the employment of workers, administrators of goods must faithfully observe also the civil laws which pertain to work and social life, in accord with the principles handed down by the Church. They are to pay those who work for them under contract a just and honest wage so that they can appropriately provide for themselves and their dependents. (Can. 1286)

F. Inventory of Parish Goods

Before administrators begin their duties, they are to prepare an accurate and precise inventory, signed by themselves, of immoveable goods, moveable goods that are precious or of significant cultural value, and other goods, with a description and appraisal of them; after this is prepared, it should be reviewed. One copy of this inventory should be kept in the administration's archives, another in the archives of the curia. Any change that the patrimony may undergo should be recorded on both copies. (Can. 1283, 2°, 3°)

G. Offerings and Stole Fees

Although another person may have performed a certain parochial function, the offerings received on this occasion from the faithful are to be turned over to the parish fund, unless it is evident that it would be contrary to the will of the donor as far as voluntary donations are concerned. The diocesan bishop, having heard the presbyteral council, is competent to enact norms which provide for the allocation of these offerings as well as for the remuneration of the clerics who fulfill the same parochial function. (Can. 531)

Unless the law provides otherwise, the meeting of bishops of a province is competent to establish the amount of the offerings given on the occasion of the administration of sacraments and sacramentals. (Can. 1264, 2°)

In the absence of such a determination, diocesan law or custom is to be followed.

According to these laws, all stole fees and other voluntary offerings given to pastors, other priests, deacons, and lay ministers who perform parochial functions are to be turned over to a parish fund to be used for the purpose specified by the bishop. The established amount of an offering for any service is to go entirely to this fund, unless part of it is set aside for the payment for a particular service, e.g., organist, cantor, janitor, etc., as is sometimes the case with weddings, funerals, and the like. Any voluntary offering given over and above the established amount can be kept by the minister only if it is clear that this was the donor's intention. In doubt about the donor's intention, the offering goes entirely to the parish fund.

This provision does not apply to Mass offerings (stipends). Each priest has a right to keep Mass offerings in accord with the provisions of canons 945-958. In those places where the practice of the diocese is for priests to hand over all Mass offerings to the parish in exchange for a uniform salary, this diocesan practice would not apply to visiting priests who would be entitled by law to the Mass offerings for Sunday Masses, weddings, etc. in addition to any payment for their services to which they may be entitled. On the other hand, visiting priests are subject to the same rule governing stole fees and voluntary offerings as stated above, that is, they must turn them in to the parish fund unless a voluntary donation above the established amount was given to them personally.

Unless the contrary is established, offerings given to the superiors or administrators of any ecclesiastical juridic person, even a private one, are presumed to have been given to the juridic person itself. (Can. 1267, §1)

In the absence of any determination by the diocesan bishop concerning the allocation of the special fund for stole fees and offerings, the money should go into the general parish account in virtue of the law requiring offerings to go to the juridic person.

H. Acts of Extraordinary Administration

Unless they have obtained the prior written permission from the Ordinary, administrators invalidly place acts which exceed the limits and manner of ordinary administration, with due regard for the norms of the statutes. (Can. 1281, §1)

Ordinary administration includes the ordinary upkeep of

church property, paying bills, making necessary repairs, buying supplies, opening regular checking accounts, accepting ordinary donations, and the collection of debts, rents, interest, or dividends. Extraordinary administration covers acts which do not occur periodically or which by their nature are of greater importance, e.g., making long-term investments, changing investments, acts of alienation, the acceptance or refusal of major bequests, land purchases, construction of new buildings or extensive repairs on old buildings, leasing or renting property for an extended period, the opening of a cemetery, the establishment of a school, taking up special collections. (See CLSA Comm., 874.) Written permission from the Ordinary is needed for acts of extraordinary administration.

After he has consulted his finance council, the diocesan bishop is competent to determine the limits and procedures for acts of extraordinary administration by parish administrators (pastors, co-pastors, administrators in priestless parishes, etc.). (See can. 1281, §2.)

> Any act of extraordinary administration by a pastor or other parish administrator requires permission of the diocesan bishop who must consult his financial council.

The parish, as juridic person, is not held to answer for invalid acts of its administrators except and insofar as the invalid acts benefit the parish. The parish is responsible for acts which are illicit but valid, but it has the right to sue or to have recourse against administrators who have caused financial damage to the parish when they have acted illicitly. (See can. 1281, §3)

> If a pastor or other person charged with the financial administration of a parish exceeds the limits or does not follow procedures affecting validity, he or she acts invalidly. Even though a financial act is canonically invalid or illicit, this is not usually recognized by the civil law.

J.   Donations from the Parish

Within the limits of ordinary administration only, administrators are at liberty to make donations for purposes of piety or Christian charity from moveable goods which do not belong to the stable patrimony. (Can. 1285)

> Pastors may make donations from parish funds but not from any investments, property, etc. which belong to the stable patrimony. Such donations may not exceed the limits of ordinary

administration. This means that such donations should be budget-
ed, or at least not exceed the amount established by the diocesan
bishop for extraordinary expenses.

Moveable goods include investments, money, furnishings, art
objects, etc.; immoveable goods are land and buildings.
Immoveable goods belong to the stable patrimony. Moveable
goods which have great historical or artistic value, or which have
been invested for a specific purpose, also belong to the stable patrimony, e.g., a fund for a new church.

K. Contracts

Whatever the civil law establishes in the territory concerning contracts, both in general and in particular, and concerning their dissolution, is to be observed regarding matters subject to the Church's power
of governance with the same effects, unless it is contrary to the divine
law or canon law specifies something else, with due regard for canon
1547. (Can. 1290)

> This means that canon law defers to the civil law on all mat-
> ters governing legal contracts, except when the civil law is con-
> trary to divine law or when canon law makes other provision, as
> it does in canon 1547. Canon 1547 says that witnesses are a means
> of judicial proof. Hence, witnesses to a contract could establish
> proof of a contract in the absence of a written document, even if
> the civil law would not admit such evidence as conclusive.

L. Alienation

The permission of the authority competent by law is required for
the valid alienation of goods which by legitimate designation constitute the stable patrimony of a public juridic person and whose value
exceeds the amount defined by law. (Can. 1291)

> In the strict sense, "alienation" (also called "conveyance") is
> "any act by which the right to ownership of ecclesiastical proper-
> ty is transferred to another." In the broad sense, alienation is "any
> act by which the use of the right, or the right itself, of ownership
> is or could be diminished, restricted, or endangered." (See F.
> Morrisey, "The Conveyance of Ecclesiastical Goods," in *CLSA
> Proceedings of the 38th Annual Convention* (Washington: CLSA,
> 1976) 126-27.) The laws of alienation in canons 1291-1298 of the
> code apply to acts of alienation both in the strict and broad sense.
> Transactions involving the payment of money from free capital
> are not subject to the laws of alienation, but they are subject to the
> laws governing acts of extraordinary administration. Subject to

the laws of alienation are transactions involving sale, mortgage, lien, easement, option, compromise, settlement, renting and leasing of property, as well as expenditure of funds that are part of the parish's patrimony, i.e., its stable capital such as funds invested for a specific purpose. (See CLSA Comm., 879-80.)

The laws on alienation of goods in canons 1291-1294 apply also to any transaction through which the patrimonial condition of a juridic person can be worsened. (See can. 1295.)

> The patrimonial condition could be worsened by transactions such as granting an easement, usufruct, a protect lease, a mortgage, and turning over the administration of goods, especially if they are transferred in perpetuity. (See CCLA, 804.)

To alienate validly the goods of the parish whose value exceeds a certain minimal amount, the administrator is required to obtain permission of the diocesan bishop who must have the consent of his finance council and the college of consultors. (See can. 1292, §1.)

> The episcopal conference is authorized to establish this amount. In the absence of the determination by the episcopal conference, diocesan statutes prevail.

The permission of the Holy See is necessary to alienate goods whose value exceeds the maximal amount that the bishop can authorize. Permission is also necessary to alienate goods donated to the Church through a vow or goods which are especially valuable due to their artistic or historical value. (See can. 1292, §2.)

> *In the United States* the maximal value of an alienation that can be authorized by the diocesan bishop is three million dollars. For an alienation in excess of that amount, permission of the Apostolic See is necessary. (See NCCB, decree, May 21, 1993; *The Jurist* 53 (1993) 414.) If a religious institute owns a parish church or school and it wishes to alienate the property, e.g., by sale, the permission of the Holy See is necessary if the value of the property exceeds three million dollars. (This also applies to other acts of alienation, not just those involving parishes.)

Those who must take part in alienations through their counsel or consent are not to give counsel or consent unless they have first been precisely informed both of the economic status of the juridic person which is proposing to alienate goods as well as of alienations already made. (Can. 1292, §4)

Whenever ecclesiastical goods have been alienated without observing the canonical formalities, yet the alienation is civilly valid, it is up to the competent authority to decide, after mature consideration of all circumstances, whether and what kind of action, either personal or real, by whom and against whom, is to be taken to vindicate the rights of the Church. (Can. 1296)

If the thing to be alienated is divisible, one must mention all parts already alienated in the petition for permission for further alienation; otherwise the permission is invalid. (Can. 1292, §3)

To alienate goods whose value exceeds the minimum amount specified [by the episcopal conference], it is moreover required: (1) that there be a just cause, such as urgent necessity, evident usefulness, piety, charity, or another serious pastoral reason; (2) a written estimate by experts of the value of the thing to be alienated. Also other precautions prescribed by legitimate authority are to be observed to prevent harm to the Church. (Can. 1293)

An object ordinarily must not be alienated for a lower amount than that indicated by the estimate. The money gained from an alienation either should be carefully invested for the benefit of the Church or prudently spent in accord with the purposes of the alienation. (Can. 1294)

Unless an object is of minor importance, ecclesiastical goods must not be sold or leased to their administrators or to the administrators' relatives up to the fourth degree of consanguinity or affinity without special written permission from the competent authority. (Can. 1298)

> The competent authority in the case of parish administrators is the diocesan bishop.

M. Law Suits

Administrators are neither to begin a law suit in the name of a public juridic person nor act as a defendant against one in civil court unless they have obtained the written permission of their Ordinary. (Can. 1288)

> Parish administrators must have the written permission of the diocesan bishop before initiating a law suit in the name of the parish or even contesting a suit against the parish. If the parish is owned (as opposed to merely administered) by a religious institute or society of apostolic life of pontifical right, the major superior is the competent Ordinary to give this permission.

Appendices

The Profession of Faith and Oath of Fidelity

Canon 833, nn. 1-4 requires the following persons to make a profession of faith personally:

    1)   In the presence of its president or his delegate, all persons who take part with either a deliberative or consultative vote in an ecumenical or particular council, in a synod of bishops, or in a diocesan synod; the president takes it in the presence of the council or synod.

    2)   Those who are named cardinals in accord with the statutes of the college of cardinals.

    3)   In the presence of the delegate of the Apostolic See, all persons who are named bishops and those who are equivalent in law to the diocesan bishop.

    4)   In the presence of the college of consultors, a diocesan administrator.

Canon 833, nn. 5-8 requires the following persons to make a profession of faith personally; they are also obliged to make the oath of fidelity on assuming an office. (See CDF, *nota*, AAS 81 (1989) 104; *CLSA Roman Replies* (Washington: CLSA, 1991) 11-12.)

    1)   In the presence of the diocesan bishop or his delegate, vicars general, episcopal vicars, and vicars judicial.

    2)   In the presence of the local Ordinary or his delegate and at the beginning of their term of office, pastors, the rector of a seminary, professors of theology and philosophy in seminaries, and those to be promoted to the order of deacon.

    3)   In the presence of the grand chancellor or, in his absence, in

the presence of the local Ordinary, or in the presence of their delegates, the rector of an ecclesiastical or Catholic university at the beginning of the rector's term of office; in the presence of the rector, if the rector is a priest, or the local Ordinary, or their delegates and at the beginning of their term of office, teachers in any universities whatsoever who teach disciplines which deal with faith or morals.

4)   The superiors in clerical religious institutes and societies of apostolic life in accord with the norm of the constitutions. (Note the special formula for religious superiors in paragraphs four and five of the oath of fidelity.)

The following English translations are the versions submitted by the NCCB, approved by the Congregation for the Doctrine of the Faith in 1990, and published by the NCCB in 1991. Their use, however, is not restricted to the United States.

THE PROFESSION OF FAITH

I, N., with firm faith believe and profess each and everything that is contained in the symbol of faith, namely:

I believe in one God, the Father, the Almighty, maker of heaven and earth, of all that is seen and unseen. I believe in one Lord, Jesus Christ, the only Son of God, eternally begotten of the Father, God from God, Light from Light, true God from true God, begotten, not made, one in Being with the Father. Through him all things were made. For us men and for our salvation he came down from heaven: By the power of the Holy Spirit he was born of the Virgin Mary, and became man. For our sake he was crucified under Pontius Pilate; he suffered, died and was buried. On the third day he rose again in fulfillment of the Scriptures; he ascended into heaven and is seated at the right hand of the Father. He will come again in glory to judge the living and the dead, and his kingdom will have no end. I believe in the Holy Spirit, the Lord, the giver of life, who proceeds from the Father and the Son. With the Father and the Son he is worshiped and glorified. He has spoken through the Prophets. I believe in one, holy, catholic and apostolic Church. I acknowledge one baptism for the forgiveness of sins. I look for the resurrection of the dead, and the life of the world to come. Amen.

With firm faith I also believe everything contained in God's word, written or handed down in tradition and proposed by the Church, whether by way of solemn judgment or through the ordinary and universal magisterium, as divinely revealed and calling for faith.

I also firmly accept and hold each and everything that is proposed definitively by the Church regarding teaching on faith and morals.

Moreover, I adhere with religious submission of will and intellect to the teachings which either the Roman Pontiff or the College of bishops enunciate when they exercise the authentic magisterium, even if they proclaim those teachings by an act that is not definitive.

OATH OF FIDELITY ON ASSUMING AN OFFICE
TO BE EXERCISED IN THE NAME OF THE CHURCH

I, N., in assuming the office of _____, promise that both in my words and in my conduct I shall always preserve communion with the Catholic Church.

I shall carry out with the greatest care and fidelity the duties incumbent on me toward both the universal Church and the particular Church in which, according to the provisions of the law, I have been called to exercise my service.

In fulfilling the charge entrusted to me in the name of the Church, I shall hold fast to the deposit of faith in its entirety, I shall faithfully hand it on and explain it, and I shall avoid any teachings opposed to that faith.

I shall follow and foster the common discipline of the whole Church and I shall observe all ecclesiastical laws, especially those which are contained in the Code of Canon Law.

In Christian obedience I shall unite myself with what is declared by the bishops as authentic doctors and teachers of the faith or established by them as those responsible for the governance of the Church; I shall also faithfully assist the diocesan bishops, in order that the apostolic activity exercised in the name and by mandate of the Church may be carried out in the communion of the same Church.

So help me God, and God's holy Gospels, on which I place my hand.

For superiors in clerical religious institutes and societies of apostolic life, the following paragraphs replace the last three paragraphs of the above oath.

I shall foster the common discipline of the whole Church, and I shall insist on the observance of all ecclesiastical laws, especially those which are contained in the Code of Canon Law.

In Christian obedience I shall unite myself with what is declared by the bishops as authentic doctors and teachers of the faith or established by them as those responsible for the governance of the Church; I shall also cooperate fully with the diocesan bishops, in order that, without prejudice to the character and purpose of my own institute, the apostolic activity exercised in the name and by mandate of the Church may be carried out in the communion of the same Church.

So help me God, and God's holy Gospels, on which I place my hand.

two
Consultative and Legislative Offices and Bodies of the Roman Catholic Church

There are 22 churches *sui iuris* that comprise the Roman Catholic Church: the Latin church which observes the Roman rite, and 21 Eastern churches which observe various rites. In the diagrams that follow, the officials, councils, and synods in capital letters have legislative power and can enact true laws. The other offices, dignities, and structures are consultative and pastoral in nature.

I. THE UNIVERSAL CHURCH

Synod of bishops

COLLEGE OF BISHOPS

Roman curia

POPE

Cardinals

ECUMENICAL COUNCIL

Papal legates

The pope and the college of bishops have supreme power in the Church. However, the college of bishops traditionally exercises its supreme power only when meeting in an ecumenical council.

II. The Churches Sui Iuris

A. The Latin Catholic Church

Conference of Bishops
of a Region   PLENARY COUNCIL

Meetings of Bishops   Metropolitan   PROVINCIAL COUNCIL
of a Province

College of Consultors

Presbyteral Council

Diocesan Curia   DIOCESAN
                                  BISHOP   Diocesan Synod
Finance Council

Pastoral Council

The conference of bishops of a nation can make law only in cases permitted by law, and only when the law passes by two-thirds of the bishop members and is approved by the Holy See. The metropolitan, or
archbishop, can make laws only for his own archdiocese, not for his
suffragan sees. The diocesan synod can propose legislation, but the
diocesan bishop must approve and enact it into law since only the bishop has legislative power in the diocese.

B. The Eastern Catholic Patriarchal Churches

There are six Catholic patriarchal churches headed by a patriarch: the Coptic (Alexandrian rite), the Syrian and the Maronite (both Antiochene rite), the Armenian (Armenian rite), the Chaldean (Chaldean rite), and the Melkite (Byzantine rite). The various rites have to do with the church's distinct liturgical type, spirituality, and customs.

Permanent Synod

Patriarchal Assembly   Patriarch   SYNOD OF BISHOPS

Patriarchal Curia

The synod of bishops is the real legislative authority for the patriarchal church. However, the patriarch must promulgate the laws for them to go into effect. The patriarch's powers in the Eastern code are largely executive and pastoral, although a few powers are quasi-legislative in nature. (See CCEC, cans. 85, §§ 1, 3; 90; 96; 100; 112, §2.) He can, of course, make laws for his own eparchy (diocese). Liturgical laws enacted by the synod and promulgated by the patriarch are binding everywhere in the patriarchal church. Disciplinary laws have the force of law inside the territorial boundaries of the patriarchate; to have the force of law outside the territory, the eparchial bishop must attribute the force of law to them, or they must be approved by the Apostolic See. (See CCEC, can. 150.)

The patriarchal churches also have particular churches under the patriarch called eparchies, equivalent to dioceses, headed by an eparchial bishop. The outline that follows applies also to the eparchies of the other Eastern Catholic churches.

College of Consultors

Presbyteral Council

Eparchial Curia   EPARCHIAL   Eparchial Assembly
                          BISHOP

Pastoral Council

Finance Council

C. Eastern Catholic Major Archiepiscopal Churches

There are two major archiepiscopal churches: the Ukrainian (Byzantine rite) and the Syro-Malabar (Chaldean rite). The major archbishop presides over his church in the same way as a patriarch, but he lacks the patriarchal dignity. Unlike the patriarch, the election of the major archbishop by the synod must be confirmed by the pope. The synod of bishops is the legislative authority for the church; the major archbishop can only legislate for his own eparchy. The other consultative and pastoral structures for a patriarch are also to be understood as established for the major archbishop in accord with the principle enunciated in CCEC, canon 152 that the two churches are equivalent in law unless the law expressly provides otherwise or it is evident from the matter.

D. Eastern Catholic Metropolitan Churches

There are four metropolitan churches: the Ethiopian (Alexandrian rite), the Syro-Malankara (Antiochene rite), the Romanian and Ruthenian (both Byzantine rite). A metropolitan church is presided over by a metropolitan appointed by the pope. A council of hierarchs assists the metropolitan in governance. The council of hierarchs, consisting of all the bishops of the church in accord with CCEC, canon 164, is the legislator for the church, but its laws may not be promulgated by the metropolitan before he notifies the Apostolic See and receives written notice from the Apostolic See that it has received the acts of the council.

Metropolitan Assembly   Metropolitan   COUNCIL OF HIERARCHS

E. Other Eastern Catholic Churches

The other churches have small groups of faithful and are headed by a hierarch appointed by the pope, namely, an eparch, an exarch, or an apostolic administrator; usually they are bishops. There are four eparchial churches: Hungarian, Italo-Albanian, Slovak, and Krizevci (territories of the former Yugoslavia). Three churches are apostolic exarchates: the Belorussian, the Bulgarian, and the Greek; the Russian church has two exarchates. The Albanian church is an apostolic administration. All of these are in the Byzantine rite.

three
Principal Dicasteries of the Roman Curia

The descriptions of the various dicasteries are intended to give a general indication of the business handled, not a complete listing of all competencies.

I. Secretariat of State

Headed by a cardinal secretary, it consists of two sections:

> 1 The Section for General Affairs handles general ecclesiastical affairs such as communications, publications, statistics, major business.
>
> 2) The Section for Relations with States handles all matters with civil governments, including concordats and diplomatic relations.

II. The Congregations

The congregations are composed of cardinals and bishops appointed by the pope. The ordinary meetings consist only of the members living in Rome. In addition, each congregation holds plenary sessions usually once a year to treat major issues at which all members are to be present. A cardinal prefect presides over each congregation.

1. Congregation on the Doctrine of the Faith

It safeguards faith and morals for the universal Church. It reviews documents issued by other dicasteries that touch on faith and morals. It tries and punishes crimes against the faith, more serious crimes against morals, and more serious cases involving the celebration of the sacraments. It processes privilege of the faith cases for marital dissolution. It works with the Pontifical Biblical Commission and the International Theological Commission.

2. *Congregation for the Eastern Churches*

Its *de iure* members are the patriarchs and major archbishops of the Eastern Catholic churches and the president of the Council for Promoting Christian Unity. It has competence over matters pertaining to persons, discipline, or rites of the Eastern Catholic churches.

3. *Congregation on Divine Worship and the Discipline of the Sacraments*

It is responsible for the moderation and promotion of the Latin rite liturgy, especially the sacraments. It prepares liturgical texts in the Latin editions and reviews the vernacular translations of them. It approves particular calendars and feasts. It handles cases of dissolution of marriage due to non-consummation and nullity of ordination.

4. *Congregation on Causes of the Saints*

Its handles cases of beatification and canonization and the authentication of relics.

5. *Congregation for Bishops*

It has competence over the establishment, division, union, or suppression of particular churches; matters pertaining to military ordinariates and personal prelatures; the selection of bishops and matters pertaining to bishops. It works with the Pontifical Commission for Latin America.

6. *Congregation for the Evangelization of Peoples*

Its competence is matters pertaining to missions and missionaries. It has the same competence in mission territories as the Congregation for Bishops has for established dioceses.

7. *Congregation for the Clergy*

It handles matters affecting secular presbyters and deacons; catechetics; clerical life, discipline, rights and duties; the distribution of clergy; preaching and the apostolate; the administration of temporal goods. Its competence includes matters pertaining to presbyteral councils, colleges of consultors, chapters of canons, pastoral councils, parishes, churches, sanctuaries, clerical associations, ecclesiastical archives, Mass stipends, pious wills and pious foundations.

8. *Congregation for Institutes of Consecrated Life and Societies of Apostolic Life*

It has competence over religious and secular institutes and societies of apostolic life of pontifical right including their establishment, government, approval of constitutions, suppression, merger. It is also competent to handle matters pertaining to hermits and virgins, secular (third) orders, and related associations of the laity that might some day become institutes of consecrated life.

9. *Congregation for Seminaries and Institutes of Study*

It has competence over seminaries, Catholic universities, and other institutes of higher studies and Catholic schools.

III. Tribunals

1. *Apostolic Penitentiary*

It handles indulgences and matters of the internal forum such as absolutions from reserved censures, dispensations, commutations, sanations, condonations, and other favors.

2. *Supreme Tribunal of the Apostolic Signatura*

It hears appeals from sentences of the Roman Rota. It judges conflicts of competence between departments of the Holy See. It is the highest court for administrative recourse. It supervises tribunals and erects interdiocesan tribunals.

3. *Roman Rota*

A judicial court, it mainly handles marriage nullity cases from around the world on appeal, either in second or third instance. It may also try cases in first instance.

IV. Pontifical Councils

1. *Pontifical Council for the Laity*

Handles matters affecting the laity; approves or recognizes international lay associations.

2. *Pontifical Council to Promote the Unity of Christians*
Promotes ecumenism and dialogue with other Christians. It also has a special section for the Jewish religion.

3. *Pontifical Council for the Family*
Handles matters related to the family, marriage, parenthood, etc.

4. *Pontifical Council on Justice and Peace*
Promotes efforts for justice and peace in the world.

5. *Pontifical Council "Cor Unum"*
Coordinates efforts for relief and charitable assistance.

6. *Pontifical Council on the Pastoral Care of Migrants and Tourism*
Fosters care for migrants, immigrants, refugees, travellers by air and sea, circus employees.

7. *Pontifical Council on the Apostolate for the Care of the Sick*
Handles matters related to the sick and those who care for them; explains Church teachings on the spiritual and moral dimensions of illness.

8. *Pontifical Council on the Interpretation of Legal Texts*
Makes authentic interpretations of universal law; assists other dicasteries with the legal form of documents; reviews general decrees of episcopal conferences and synods. It can also give authentic interpretations of the *Code of Canons of the Eastern Churches*.

9. *Pontifical Council for Interreligious Dialogue*
Promotes dialogue with members of non-Christian religions; a special section deals with Islam.

10. *Pontifical Council on Culture*
Promotes the relationship of the Holy See with human culture, especially institutes of science and learning; in charge of dialogue with atheists and those who profess no religion; has periodic contacts with the Pontifical Commission for Preserving the Church's Patrimony of Art and History. It has two sections: (1) Faith and Culture and (2) Dialogue with Cultures.

11. *Pontifical Council on Social Communications*
Promotes a Christian presence in the media, including the press, cinema, radio, and television; oversees the Catholic media.

Sources: John Paul II, apostolic constitution *Pastor bonus,* June 28, 1988,

AAS 80 (1988) 841-932; *Origins* 23 (1993) 46-47; General Regulations of the Roman Curia, AAS 84 (1992) 201-67. See also James H. Provost, "*Pastor Bonus*: Reflections on the Reorganization of the Roman Curia," *The Jurist* 48 (1988) 499-535.

four
_____

Select Bibliography

I. Select Commentaries on the 1983 Code

ENGLISH

The Code of Canon Law: A Text and Commentary. Commissioned by the Canon Law
Society of America. Ed. James A. Coriden, Thomas J.Green, and Donald E.
Heintschel. New York/Mahway, NJ: Paulist, 1985.

Code of Canon Law Annotated. Translation of the fifth Spanish-language edition of
the commentary prepared under the responsibility of the Instituto Martín de
Azpilcueta. Ed. E. Caparros, M. Thériault, and J. Thorn. Montréal: Wilson &
Lafleur Limitée, 1993.

A Commentary on the New Code of Canon Law. By Thomas Pazhayampallil.
Bangalore, India: KJC Publications, 1985.

SPANISH

Código de Derecho Canónico, Edición anotada. Ed. Pedro Lombardia and Juan
Ignacio Arrieta. Pamplona: Ediciones Universidad de Navarra, S.A. (EUNSA),
1983.

Código de Derecho Canónico: Edición bilingüe comentada. Ed. Lamberto de
Echeverria. Madrid: Biblioteca de Autores Christianos, 5th edition revised, 1985.

Manual de Derecho Canonico. Ed. Instituto Martín de Azpilcueta. Pamplona: EUNSA,
1988.

FRENCH

Code de droit canonique: Edition bilingue et annotée. Traduction française établie à
partir de la 4 édition espagnole. Ed. E. Caparros, M. Thériault, J. Thorn.

Guide Pratique du Code de Droit Canonique: Notes pastorales. By Roger Paralieu et al.
Paris: Tardy, 1985.

GERMAN

Das Neue Kirchenrecht: Gesamtdarstellung. By Hugo Schwendenswein. Graz: Verlag
Styria, 1983.

Handbuch des katholischen Kirchenrechts. Ed. Joseph Listl, Hubert Müller, and
Heribert Schmitz. Regensburg: Verlag Friedrich Pustet, 1983.

Münsterischer Kommentar zum Codex Iuris Canonici, unter besonderer Berücksichtigung der Rechtslage in Deutschland, Österreich und der Schweiz. Ed. Klaus Lüdicke. Essen: Ludgerus Verlag, 1984- .

ITALIAN

Commento al Codice di Diritto Canonico. Ed. Pio Vito Pinto. Rome: Urbaniana University, 1985.

Il Codice di Diritto Canonico: Commento giuridico-pastorale, 2 vols. By Luigi Chiappetta. Naples: Edizioni Dehoniane, 1988.

Il diritto nella Chiesa mistero di communione: Compendio di diritto ecclesiale. By Gianfranco Ghirlanda. Rome: Edizioni Paoline, 1990.

II. Select Books and Articles in English

The publications have been selected on the basis of their appropriateness for the audience of and the matters treated in *The Pastoral Companion.* Given the vast literature on the canon law of marriage, only select books on that subject are listed, no articles.

The abbreviation "CLSA *Proceedings*" will be used in place of *Canon Law Society of America: Proceedings of the Annual Convention* (Washington: CLSA).

BACKGROUND STUDIES AND SELECT EDITED VOLUMES

Alesandro, John. "The Revision of the Code of Canon Law: A Background Study." *Studia Canonica* 24 (1990) 91-146.

Chicago Studies 23, no. 1 (April, 1984). [The entire issue is devoted to the 1983 code.]

Code, Community, Ministry: Selected Studies for the Parish Minister Introducing the Revised Code of Canon Law. Second revised edition. Ed. Edward G. Pfnausch. Washington: CLSA, 1992.

Coriden, James A. *An Introduction to Canon Law.* New York/Mahwah: Paulist, 1991.

Lynch, John. "Canon Law." *The New Dictionary of Theology.* Wilmington, DE: Michael Glazier, 1987.

The Ministry of Governance. Ed. James K. Mallett. Washington: CLSA, 1986.

Morrisey, Francis G. "*Decimo Anno ...* On the Tenth Anniversary of the *Code of Canon Law.*" *Studia Canonica* 28 (1994) 99-122.

New Law and Life. Ed. Elissa Rinere. Washington: CLSA, 1985.

Readings, Cases, Materials in Canon Law: A Textbook for Ministerial Students, revised edition. Ed. Jordan Hite and Daniel J. Ward. Collegeville: Liturgical Press, 1990.

Studies in Canon Law Presented to P.J.M. Huizing. Ed. James H. Provost and Knut Walf. Leuven: University Press, 1991.

THEOLOGY, INTERPRETATION OF LAW

Abbass, Jobe. "Canonical Interpretation by Recourse to 'Parallel Passages.'" *The Jurist* 51 (1991) 293-310.

The Art of Interpretation: Selected Studies on the Interpretation of Canon Law. Washington: CLSA, 1982.

Coriden, James A. "The Canonical Doctrine of Reception." *The Jurist* 50 (1990) 58-82.

Green, Thomas J. "The Revised Code of Canon Law: Some Theological Issues." *Theological Studies* 47 (1986) 617-52.

Huels, John. "The Interpretation of Liturgical Law." *Worship* 55 (1981) 218-37.

_____. "Interpreting Canon Law in Diverse Cultures." *The Jurist* 47 (1987) 249-93.

_____. "Non-Reception of Canon Law by the Community." *New Theology Review* 4 (May, 1991) 47-61.

_____. "From Law to Life." *Emmanuel*90 (1984) 143-49.

Koury, Joseph J. "*Ius Divinum* as a Canonical Problem: On the Interaction of Divine and Ecclesiastical Laws." *The Jurist*53 (1993) 104-31.

_____. "Hard and Soft Canons: Canonical Vocabulary for Legal Flexibility and Accommodation." *The Jurist*50 (1990) 459-87.

_____. "From Prohibited to Permitted: Transitions in the *Code of Canon Law*." *Studia Canonica* 24 (1990) 147-82.

Morrisey, Francis G. "Papal and Curial Pronouncements: Their Canonical Significance in Light of the 1983 Code of Canon Law." *The Jurist*50 (1990) 102-25.

Örsy, Ladislas. *Theology and Canon Law: New Horizons for Legislation and Interpretation.* Collegeville: Liturgical Press, 1992.

_____. "Interpretation in View of Action: A Quest for Clarity and Simplicity (Canon 96)." *The Jurist*52 (1992) 587-97.

Pottmeyer, Hermann J. "Reception and Submission." *The Jurist*51 (1991) 269-92.

Wijlens, Myriam. *Theology and Canon Law: The Theories of Klaus Mörsdorf and Eugenio Corecco.* Lanham, Maryland: University Press of America, 1992.

Wrenn, Lawrence G. *Authentic Interpretations on the 1983 Code.* Washington: CLSA, 1993.

THE LAITY, WOMEN IN CANON LAW

The entire issue of *The Jurist* 47 (1987):1 is devoted to studies on the laity in canon law. See also the studies in CLSA *Proceedings* 54 (1992).

Amos, John R. "A Legal History of Associations of the Christian Faithful." *Studia Canonica* 21 (1987) 271-97.

Huels, John. *The Faithful of Christ: The New Canon Law for the Laity.* Quincy, IL: Franciscan Press, 1983.

_____. "The Law on Lay Preaching: Interpretation and Implementation." CLSA *Proceedings*52 (1991) 61-79.

_____. "Women's Role in Church Law: Past and Present." *New Theology Review* 6 (May, 1993) 19-31.

Koury, Joseph J. "The Limits of Collaboration: The New Legal Language for the Laity." *Studia Canonica* 26 (1992) 415-36.

McDonough, Elizabeth. "Women and the New Church Law." *Concilium* 185 (1986) 73-81.

Morrisey, Francis. "The Laity in the New Code of Canon Law." *Studia Canonica* 17 (1983) 135-48.

_____. "The Rights of Parents in the Education of their Children (Canons 796-806)." *Studia Canonica*23 (1989) 429-44.

Perry, Joseph N. "Accessibility of Due Process for the Laity." CLSA *Proceedings*51 (1989) 65-82.

Provost, James H. "The Participation of the Laity in the Governance of the Church." *Studia Canonica*17 (1983) 417-48.

_____. "Lay Preaching in a Time of Transition." *Preaching and the Non-Ordained.* Collegeville: Liturgical Press, 1983, pages 134-58.

Richstatter, Thomas. "Instituted Lay Ministries: the History and Future of Canon 230." CLSA *Proceedings* 49 (1987) 35-44.

Smith, Rosemary. "Lay Persons in the Diocesan Curia: Legal Structures and Practical Issues." CLSA *Proceedings* 49 (1987) 35-44.

CLERGY

Donlon, James I. "Incardination and Excardination: The Rights and Obligations of the Cleric and of the Church—A Matter of Pastoral Justice." CLSA *Proceedings* 53 (1991) 124-53.

Garrity, Robert M. "Spiritual and Canonical Values in Mandatory Priestly Celibacy."
    Studia Canonica 27 (1993) 217-60.

Hynous, David. "Issues in Sacred Orders." CLSA *Proceedings* 49 (1987) 145-54.

Lyons, Richard L. "The Permanent Diaconate: A Commentary on Its Development
    from the End of the Second Vatican Council to the 1983 *Codex Iuris Canonici*."
    CLSA *Proceedings* 49 (1987) 77-100.

McKay, Gerard. "Spiritual Direction in the Diocesan Seminary: An Interpretation of the
    Canonical Norms." *Studia Canonica* 26 (1992) 401-14.

Mercês de Melo, Carlos. "Priests and Priestly Formation in the *Code of Canon Law*.
    Studia Canonica 27 (1993) 455-77.

Ombres, Robert. "Priests and Politics in Canon Law." *Clergy Review* 70 (1985) 180-83.

O'Reilly, Michael. "Recent Developments in the Laicization of Priests." *The Jurist* 52
    (1992) 684-96.

Pokusa, Joseph W. "The Diaconate: A History of Law Following Practice." *The Jurist* 45
    (1985) 95-135.

Provost, James H. "Permanent Deacons in the 1983 Code." CLSA *Proceedings* 46 (1984)
    175-91.

_____. "Clergy and Religious in Political Office: Canonical Comments in the
    American Context." *The Jurist* 44 (1984) 276-303.

PARISHES

Carlson, Robert. "The Parish According to the Revised Law." *Studia Canonica* 19 (1985)
    5-16.

Coriden, James A. "The Rights of Parishes." *Studia Canonica* 28 (1994) 293-309.

_____. "The Vindication of Parish Rights." *The Jurist* 54 (1994) 22-39.

Dalton, William. "Parish Councils or Parish Pastoral Councils?" *Studia Canonica* 22
    (1988) 169-85.

Doran, Thomas. "Rights and Duties of Pastors." CLSA *Proceedings* 45 (1983) 182-92.

Groves, Richard. "Priestless Parishes: Exploring Future Possibilities." CLSA *Proceedings*
    48 (1986) 54-60.

Huels, John. "Parish Life and the New Code." *Concilium* 185 (1986) 64-72.

Renken, John A. "The Canonical Implications of Canon 517 §2: Parishes Without
    Resident Pastors?" CLSA *Proceedings* 50 (1988) 249-63.

INTER-ECCLESIAL ISSUES AND EASTERN CATHOLIC CHURCHES

Faris, John D. "Synodal Governance in Eastern Catholic Churches." CLSA *Proceedings*
    49 (1987) 212-26.

_____. "Inter-Ritual Matters in the Revised Code of Canon Law." *Studia Canonica*
    17 (1983) 239-60.

Gallagher, Clarence. "Marriage and the Revised Canon Law for the Eastern Catholic
    Churches." *Studia Canonica* 24 (1990) 69-90.

Gallaro, George. "The Mystery of Crowning: An Interecclesial Perspective." CLSA
    Proceedings 51 (1989) 185-200. [The article is on Latin and Eastern law aspects of
    marriage.]

Green, Thomas J. "Reflections on the Eastern Code Revision Process." *The Jurist* 51
    (1991) 18-37.

Lynch, John E. "The Eastern Churches: Historical Background." *The Jurist* 51 (1991) 1-17.

McManus, Frederick R. "The Code of Canons of the Eastern Catholic Churches." *The
    Jurist* 53 (1993) 22-61.

Nedungatt, George. *The Spirit of the Eastern Code.* Rome: Centre for Indian and Inter-
    religious Studies, 1993.

_____, "Glossary of the Main Terms Used in the Code of Canons of the Eastern Churches." *The Jurist* 51 (1991) 451-59.

Pospishil, Victor J. *Eastern Catholic Church Law.* Brooklyn: Saint Maron Publications, 1993.

Pospishil, Victor J. and Faris, John D. *The New Code of Canon Law and Eastern Catholics.* Brooklyn: Diocese of Saint Maron, 1984.

Provost, James H. "Some Practical Issues for Latin Canon Lawyers from the Code of Canons of Eastern Churches." *The Jurist* 51 (1991) 38-66.

Thériault, Michel. "Canonical Questions Brought About by the Presence of Eastern Catholics in Latin Areas." *Canon Law Society of Great Britain and Ireland Newsletter,* no. 82 (June, 1990) 32-49.

Vadakumcherry, Joseph. "Marriage Laws in the *Code of Canon Law* and the *Code of Canons of the Eastern Churches.*" *Studia Canonica* 26 (1992) 437-60.

Walkowiak, David J. "Sacramental Law and the Code of Canons of the Eastern Churches: An Inter-Ecclesial Perspective." CLSA *Proceedings* 55 (1993) 214-33.

Wojnar, Melitius M. "Interritual Law in the Revised Code of Canon Law." *The Jurist* 43 (1983) 191-98.

LITURGY AND SACRAMENTS IN GENERAL

Doyle, Thomas P. "Sacramental Law in the New Code." *The Priest* 40 (Nov. 1984) 34-38; (Dec. 1984) 27-32.

Garrity, Robert M. "The Limits of Personal Accommodation in Sacramental Celebration." *The Jurist* 53 (1993) 284-300.

Green, Thomas. "The Church's Sanctifying Office: Reflections on Selected Canons in the Revised Code." *The Jurist* 44 (1984) 357-411.

_____. "Sacramental Law Revisited—Reflections on Selected Aspects of Book IV of the Revised Code: *De Ecclesiae munere sanctificandi.*" *Studia Canonica* 17 (1983) 277-330.

Huels, John. *Liturgical Law: An Introduction.* Washington: Pastoral Press, 1987.

_____. *Disputed Questions in the Liturgy Today.* Chicago: Liturgy Training Publications, 1988.

_____. "Participation by the Faithful in the Liturgy 1903-1962." *The Jurist* 48 (1988) 608-37.

_____. "Law, Liturgical." *The New Dictionary of Sacramental Worship,* ed. Peter E. Fink. Collegeville: Liturgical Press, 1990. Pages 661-69.

_____. "General Introduction" to *The Liturgy Documents: A Parish Resource,* 3rd ed. Chicago: Liturgy Training Publications, 1991.

_____. "The Ministry of the Divine Word (Canons 756-761)." *Studia Canonica* 23 (1989) 325-44.

_____. "Preparation for the Sacraments: Faith, Rights, Law." *Studia Canonica* 28 (1984) 33-58.

_____. "Canonical Rights to the Sacraments." In *Developmental Disabilities and Sacramental Access: New Paradigms for Sacramental Encounters.* Ed. Edward Foley. Collegeville: Liturgical Press, 1994. Pages 94-115.

McManus, Frederick. "Liturgical Books." *The New Dictionary of Sacramental Worship,* 687-91.

_____. "Reform, Liturgical, of Vatican II." *The New Dictionary of Sacramental Worship,* 1081-97.

_____. "The Church at Prayer: Going Beyond Rubrics to the Heart of the Church's Worship." *The Jurist* 53 (1993) 263-83.

Morrisey, Francis G. "Denial of Admission to the Sacraments." CLSA *Proceedings* 52 (1990) 170-86.

Quinlan, Michael R. "Parental Rights and Admission of Children to the Sacraments of Initiation." *Studia Canonica* 25 (1991) 385-402.

Richstatter, Thomas. *Liturgical Law: New Style, New Spirit.* Chicago: Franciscan Herald, 1977.

Seasoltz, R. Kevin. *New Liturgy, New Laws.* Collegeville: Liturgical Press, 1980.

_____. " The Sacred Liturgy: Development and Directions." *The Jurist* 43 (1983) 1-28. Also in *Remembering the Future: Vatican II and Tomorrow's Liturgical Agenda.* New York: Paulist, 1983. Pages 48-79.

SACRAMENTS OF INITIATION

Huels, John. *The Catechumenate and the Law: A Pastoral and Canonical Commentary for the Church in the United States.* Chicago: Liturgy Training Publications, 1994.

Jarrell, Lynn M. "Canonical Issues Surrounding the Sacraments of Initiation." CLSA *Proceedings* 55 (1993) 167-83.

Rehrauer, Ann. "Welcome In! Canonical Issues and the RCIA." CLSA *Proceedings* 52 (1990) 161-69.

Woestman, William H. *Sacraments: Initiation, Penance, Anointing of the Sick. Commentary on Canons 840-1007.* Ottawa: Faculty of Canon Law, St. Paul University, 1992.

BAPTISM

Counce, Paul D. "The Deferral of Infant Baptism According to Canon 868, §1, 2°." *Louvain Studies* 13 (1988) 322-40.

Cronin, James E. "The Juridical Status of Baptized Non-Catholics in the New Code." *Clergy Review* 70 (1985) 117-28.

Cox, Craig. "The Baptism of the Church of Jesus Christ of Latter-day Saints." *The Jurist* 49 (1989) 679-92.

Daly, Brendan. "Canonical Requirements of Parents in Cases of Infant Baptism According to the 1983 Code." *Studia Canonica* 20 (1986) 409-38.

Huels, John. "The Role and Qualifications of Godparents." *Catechumenate* 9 (September, 1987) 11-16. Revised and reprinted in *Finding and Forming Sponsors and Godparents.* Ed. James A. Wilde. Chicago: Liturgy Training Publications, 1988, pages 5-12.

Robertson, John W. "Canons 867 and 868 and Baptizing Infants Against the Will of Parents." *The Jurist* 45 (1985) 631-38.

CONFIRMATION

Balhoff, Michael. "Age for Confirmation: Canonical Evidence." *The Jurist* 45 (1985) 549-87.

Barrett, Richard J. "Confirmation: A Discipline Revisited." *The Jurist* 52 (1992) 697-714.

Huels, John. "The Age of Confirmation: A Canonist's View." *Catechumenate* 9 (November, 1987) 30-36.

EUCHARIST

Huels, John. *One Table, Many Laws: Essays on Catholic Eucharistic Practice.* Collegeville: Liturgical Press, 1986.

_____. "Use of Reason and Reception of Sacraments by the Mentally Handicapped." *The Jurist* 44 (1984) 209-19.

_____. "Bread and Wine." *Emmanuel* 90 (1984) 519-24.

_____. "Stipends in the New Code of Canon Law." *Worship* 57 (1983) 215-22.

Reprinted in *Living Bread, Saving Cup*. Ed. R. Kevin Seasoltz. Collegeville: Liturgical Press, 1987. Pages 347-56.

_____. "Stipend Intentions and the Eucharist." *Liturgy 80* 14 (October, 1983) 4-6.

_____. "Select Questions of Eucharistic Discipline." CLSA *Proceedings* 47 (1985) 48-65.

_____. "Eucharistic Reservation in Special Circumstances." *FDLC Newsletter* 16 (July-August, 1989) 1-4. Reprinted in *Emmanuel* 97 (1991) 284-89.

_____. "Options for Eucharistic Reservation." *FDLC Newsletter* 17 (May-June, 1990) 17-20. Reprinted in *Emmanuel* 98 (1992) 506-09, 512.

_____, and Willis, Thomas. "What Time for Anticipated Masses?" *Emmanuel* 96 (1990) 34-41.

_____. "Restrictions on Concelebration." *The Jurist* 47 (1987) 576-78.

_____. "Daily Mass: Law and Spirituality." *Review for Religious* 50 (1991) 572-78.

_____. "Should the Eucharist be Celebrated at Mixed Marriages?" *Liturgy 80* 18 (January, 1988) 12-15.

McSherry, Patrick J. *Wine as Sacramental Matter and the Use of Mustum.* Washington: National Clergy Council on Alcoholism, 1986.

Woestman, William H. "Daily Eucharist in the Postconciliar Church." *Studia Canonica* 23 (1989) 85-100.

PENANCE

Fahey, Patrick. "Reconciliation: Retrospect and Prospect." *Angelicum* 62 (1985) 168-93.

Huels, John. "Penance, Canon Law, and Pastoral Practice." *Liturgical Ministry* 4 (Winter, 1995) 31-36.

Malone, Richard K. "General Absolution and Pastoral Practice." *Chicago Studies* 24 (1985) 47-58.

O'Hara, Ellen. "Penance and Canon Law." In *Reconciliation: The Continuing Agenda.* Ed. Robert Kennedy. Collegeville: Liturgical Press, 1987.

Örsy, Ladislas. *The Evolving Church and the Sacrament of Penance.* Denville, NJ: Dimension Books, 1978.

_____. "General Absolution: New Law, Old Traditions, Some Questions," *Theological Studies* 45 (1984) 676-89.

_____. "The Sacrament of Penance: Problem Areas and Disputed Questions." CLSA *Proceedings* 48 (1986) 29-45.

Provost, James. "The Reception of First Penance." *The Jurist* 47 (1987) 294-340.

Robertson, John W. "Liturgical and Canonical Issues of Sacramental Celebration, Especially Reconciliation, Anointing of the Sick, and Orders." CLSA *Proceedings* 55 (1993) 192-213.

Stenson, Alex. "Penalties in the New Code: The Role of the Confessor." *The Jurist* 43 (1983) 406-21.

Woestman, William H. *Sacraments: Initiation, Penance, Anointing of the Sick. Commentary on Canons 840-1007.* Ottawa: Faculty of Canon Law, St. Paul University, 1992.

OTHER ACTS OF DIVINE WORSHIP, SACRED PLACES AND TIMES

Foster, Michael Smith. "The Violation of a Church (Canon 1211)." *The Jurist* 49 (1989) 693-703.

Fox, Joseph. "Notes on the Canonical Status of Shrines." *Notitiae* 28 (1992) 261-69.

Henchal, Michael. *Sunday Celebrations in the Absence of a Priest.* Washington: Federation of Diocesan Liturgical Commissions, 1992.

_____. "Sunday Celebrations in the Absence of a Priest." *The Jurist* 49 (1989) 607-31.

_____. "A Ministry for Gathering in Steadfast Faith: Lay Presiding." CLSA *Proceedings* 54 (1992) 130-46.

Huels, John. "Sunday Liturgies Without a Priest." *Worship* 64 (1990) 451-60.

_____. "The Liturgy of the Hours: Clerical Obligation, Prayer of the Whole Church." *Emmanuel* 97 (1991) 206-09, 224-25.

_____. "Canonical Comments on Concerts in Churches." *Worship* 62 (1988) 165-72. Reprinted in *The American Organist* 22 (1988) 44-46.

_____. "Preparing and Celebrating the Paschal Feasts." *Worship* 63 (1989) 71-79.

_____. "The Sunday Mass Obligation, Past and Present." *Chicago Studies* 29 (1990) 262-76.

McIntyre, John P. "An Apology for the 'Lesser Sacraments.'" *The Jurist* 51 (1991) 390-414.

III. Select Books on Marriage

Doogan, Hugh F., ed. *Catholic Tribunals: Marriage Annulment and Dissolution*. Newtown, Australia: E.J. Dwyer, 1990.

Mackin, Theodore. *Marriage in the Catholic Church: What is Marriage?* New York: Paulist, 1982.

_____. *Marriage in the Catholic Church: Divorce and Remarriage*. New York: Paulist, 1984.

Marriage Studies: Reflections in Canon Law and Theology. Vols. 1-3 edited by Thomas P. Doyle; vol. 4 edited by John A. Alesandro. Washington: CLSA, 1980, 1982, 1985, 1990.

Noonan, John T., Jr. *Power to Dissolve: Lawyers and Marriages in the Courts of the Roman Curia*. Cambridge, Mass.: The Belknap Press of Harvard Unversity Press, 1972.

Örsy, Ladislas. *Marriage in Canon Law*. Wilmington: Michael Glazier, 1986.

Rotal Anthology: An Annotated Index of Rotal Decisions from 1971 to 1988. Compiled by Augustine Mendonça. Washington: CLSA, 1992.

Stevenson, Kenneth W. *To Join Together: The Rite of Marriage*. New York: Pueblo, 1987.

Wrenn, Lawrence. *Annulments*, 5th ed. rev. Washington: CLSA, 1988.

_____. *Decisions*, 2nd ed. rev. Washington: CLSA, 1983.

Young, James J., ed. *Divorce Ministry and the Marriage Tribunal*. New York/Ramsey: Paulist Press, 1982.

_____, ed. *Ministering to the Divorced Catholic*. New York: Paulist, 1979.

For a General Audience

Lawler, Michael. *Ecumenical Marriage & Remarriage: Gifts and Challenges to the Churches*. Mystic, Connecticut: Twenty-Third Publications, 1990.

Robinson, Geoffrey. *Marriage, Divorce & Nullity: A Guide to the Annulment Process in the Catholic Church*. Collegeville: Liturgical Press, 1987.

Tierney, Terence E. and Campo, Joseph J. *Annulment: Do You Have a Case?* New York: Alba House, 1993.

Zwack, Joseph P. *Annulment: Your Chance to Remarry within the Catholic Church*. New York: Harper & Row, 1983.

five
Glossary of Canonical Terms

The canon number following a definition does not necessarily mean that the definition is taken directly from the code, whether Latin or Eastern. In many instances it may be only a reference to the place in the code where the canonical term is treated.

Abrogation. The revocation of a law in its totality. (Cans. 6, 20)

Administrative act (individual). A formal act given in writing by an executive authority that makes some determination, whether favorable or unfavorable, on behalf of an individual or individuals, e.g., an individual decree, a precept, or a rescript. (Cans. 35-47)

Adult. A person who is at least eighteen years of age. (Cans. 97, §1)

Advocate. An attorney who represents a party in an ecclesiastical proceeding. (Can. 1481)

Affinity. The in-law relationship that arises from a valid marriage and exists between a man and the blood relatives of his wife and between a woman and the blood relatives of her husband. (Can. 109)

Age of discretion. The age at which a person attains sufficient use of reason to commit a mortal sin, presumed to be at age seven. (Cans. 11; 97, §2; 989)

Alienation. The conveyance to another party, the encumbrance, or the placing in jeopardy of ecclesiastical property or goods that is part of a juridic person's stable patrimony. (Cans. 1291-96)

Annulment. The authoritative judgment, following procedures established in law, that a marriage is invalid.

Apostasy. The total repudiation of the Christian faith after the reception of baptism. (Can. 751)

Apostolic constitution. A formal, solemn document issued by the pope on matters of doctrinal and canonical importance for the universal Church.

Apostolic delegate. The representative of the Roman Pontiff to the Catholic Church in a country that does not have diplomatic relations with the Apostolic See. (Cans. 362-67)

Apostolic See. Also called the Holy See, the diocese of Rome. In canon law it is a generic term which includes the Roman Pontiff, the Secretariat of State, and the dicasteries of the Roman curia. (Can. 361)

Association of the faithful. A group of the faithful, distinct from institutes of consecrated life and societies of apostolic life, whether of a private or public nature, who are organized for a spiritual, charitable, or apostolic purpose. (Cans. 298-329)

Auditor. A tribunal official who assists the judge in the collection of proofs. (Can. 1428)

Authentic interpretation. An interpretation of the law given by the legislator or by the one to whom he has given the power to interpret his laws authoritatively. Authentic interpretations have the force of law. (Can. 16)

Auxiliary bishop. A bishop appointed to assist the diocesan bishop in the pastoral care of a diocese. (Cans. 403-11)

Canon law. Broadly, all the laws, both divine and ecclesiastical, universal and particular, of the Roman Catholic Church. More narrowly, the laws that appear in the form of canons in the *Code of Canon Law* and the *Code of Canons of the Eastern Churches.*

Canon penitentiary. The priest appointed as confessor with habitual faculties to remit automatic censures that have not been declared and are not reserved to the Apostolic See. In dioceses where there is no chapter of canons, he is called the priest penitentiary or penitentiary. (Cans. 508; 968)

Canonical form. The celebration of marriage before a priest or deacon who has the faculty to assist at marriages and before two witnesses. (Can. 1108)

Catechist (mission). A duly instructed lay person devoted to spreading the gospel and organizing liturgical functions and works of charity under the moderation of a missionary. (Can. 785)

Censure. A penalty which is either an excommunication, an interdict, or a suspension. (Cans. 1331-38)

Chancellor. An official whose principal task is to oversee the diocesan archives. Frequently chancellors are delegated other specific powers by the diocesan bishop. (Can. 482)

Chaplain. A priest to whom is entrusted in a stable manner the pastoral care, at least in part, of some community or particular group of the faithful. (Can. 564)

Chapter. An official, formal meeting of religious whether at the general, provincial, or conventual level.

Chrism, sacred. The oil consecrated by a bishop for use in the sacraments of baptism, confirmation, and holy orders. (Can. 880, §2)

Christian faithful (*christifidelis*). A person validly baptized. Collectively, the Christian faithful make up the Church, the community of baptized believers in Christ. (Can. 204)

Church (building). A building designated for divine worship to which the faithful have a right to go, especially for the celebration of the liturgy. (Can. 1214)

Church (community). A community of the baptized faithful of Christ that has maintained the substance of Christian doctrine, valid sacraments, and a hierarchy in apostolic succession, e.g. the Roman Catholic Church, the Eastern Orthodox Church, the Polish National Church.

Church *sui iuris*. A community of the faithful united by its own hierarchy in communion with the Roman Pontiff which is expressly or tacitly recognized by the supreme authority of the Church as autonomous, e.g. Latin, Ruthenian, Ukrainian, Maronite, Melkite, etc. (CCEC, can. 27) There are 22 such churches in the Roman Catholic Church.

Civil law. The laws of the secular state, as opposed to canon law. It may also refer to the legal system based on Roman law, as in continental Europe. See also Common law.

Cleric. An ordained member of the faithful; a deacon, presbyter, or bishop. (Cans. 265-93)

Coadjutor bishop. An auxiliary bishop with the right of succession to the diocesan bishop when the see becomes vacant. (Can. 403, §3)

College of bishops. The bishop of Rome and all the bishops in communion with him. (Can. 336)

College of consultors. A group of six to twelve priests, selected by the bishop from among the members of the presbyteral council, for the purpose of advising the bishop on certain matters determined in the law. (Can. 502)

Common law. The laws and legitimate customs that are common to all the Eastern Catholic churches as well as those common to the universal Church. (CCEC, can. 1493) The term is also used for the secular legal system originating in England and used in nations, including the United States and Canada, which had been English colonies.

Conditional consent. A ground for marital nullity if the condition concerns the future or, if it concerns the past or future, the subject matter of the condition is not fulfilled. (Can. 1102)

Conference of bishops. Also called the episcopal conference, it is a grouping of bishops of a given nation or a group of nations that jointly exercises certain pastoral functions on behalf of the faithful in their territory. (Can. 447)

Consanguinity. Relationship by blood. (Can. 108)

Consecrated life. Life consecrated by the profession of the evangelical counsels, including religious institutes, secular institutes, hermits, virgins, and other forms recognized by the Apostolic See. (Cans. 573, 605)

Consent (marital). The essence of marriage; the free choice between a man and a woman to choose to marry each other. (Can. 1057)

Consummation. The first act of sexual intercourse between a man and a woman, performed willingly and mutually, after entering a valid marriage. (Can. 1061)

Convalidation. A legal remedy by which a couple's marriage consent which was invalid is subsequently made valid. (Can. 1156)

Council. The group of advisors to a religious superior. (Can. 627) See also Ecumenical, Plenary, Provincial.

Crime. An impediment to marriage that arises when a person murders his or her spouse for the purpose of marrying another, or when a man and a woman have brought about the murder of the spouse of one of them by physical or moral cooperation in order to be free to marry each other. (Can. 1090)

Curia. Institutions and persons who furnish assistance to an ecclesiastical authority, especially the pope, Eastern patriarchs and major archbishops, and all diocesan bishops and eparchs and their canonical equivalents. Diocesan and papal curias have pastoral, administrative, and judicial functions. (Can. 469)

Custom. The unwritten law which is introduced and confirmed by the long, continued practices of the people and with the consent, at least tacit, of the competent authority. (Cans. 23–28)

Danger of death. The condition of being near death due to illness, injury, warfare, execution, or other proximate cause.

Days of penance. Days on which acts of penance are required or recommended, namely, on Ash Wednesday and all Fridays, unless they are solemnities. (Cans. 149–53)

Dean. Also called the vicar forane or archpriest, he is a priest in charge of a deanery (vicariate forane), which is a grouping of parishes in a diocese in territorial proximity. (Can. 553) In the Eastern churches *sui iuris*, he is called the protopresbyter. (CCEC, can. 276)

Decree (executory). Similar to a general decree, but issued by an executive rather than a legislative authority. Executory decrees are not laws, but are binding administrative norms that determine more precisely the methods to be observed in applying the law or themselves urge the observance of laws. (Cans. 31–32)

Decree (general). A document that is properly speaking a law, issued by a competent legislator for a community capable of receiving laws. A merely executive authority must have specific approval from a true legislator to issue a general decree. (Cans. 29–30)

Decree (individual). An administrative act issued by a competent executive authority in which a decision is given or provision is made in a particular case in accord with the norm of law; such decisions or provisions of their nature do not presuppose that a petition has been made by someone. (Can. 48)

Decree (judicial). An act of a judge that makes a binding determination on a matter pertaining to a trial. (Can. 1629)

Defender of the bond. A judicial official whose function is to propose and clarify everything which can be reasonably adduced against the nullity or dissolution of the bond of marriage. (Can. 1432)

Delegated power. Power of governance which is granted to a person, not by means of an office. (Can. 131, §1)

Delegation. The act of conferring a power by an authority who has this power upon someone who does not.

Delict. A crime; an offense for which a canonical punishment has been established in the law.

Derogation. The revocation of part of a law; an alteration in the law which does not change or abolish it completely.

Dicastery. A generic term for any of the departments of the Roman curia, including congregations, tribunals, pontifical councils, offices.

Dismissal. A penalty which for clerics results in the loss of the clerical state and for members of institutes of consecrated life and society of apostolic life results in loss of membership in their institute or society. (Cans. 290, 2°; 694; 729; 746)

Dimissorial. A letter written by one's Ordinary to the ordaining bishop attesting that a candidate for holy orders has met all the requirements for ordination. (Cans. 1050–52)

Diocesan bishop. A bishop in charge of a diocese. Equated in the law with diocesan bishops ordinarily are the heads of other local churches, namely, territorial prelatures, territorial abbacies, apostolic vicariates, apostolic prefectures, and apostolic administrations erected on a stable basis. (Can. 368)

Diocesan right. A kind of institute of consecrated life whose immediate ecclesiastical superior is the bishop of a diocese where, in general, the institute has its motherhouse or where it was founded. (Can. 594)

Diocesan synod. An assembly of priests and other members of the faithful from a particular church, convoked by the diocesan bishop, generally for the purpose of enacting diocesan laws and policies on various matters. (Can. 460)

Diriment impediment. Some fact, state, or condition that renders a person incapable of marrying validly in the Catholic Church. (Can. 1073)

Disparity of cult. An impediment to marriage between a Catholic and a non-baptized person. (Can. 1086)

Dispensation. A relaxation of a merely ecclesiastical law in a particular case given by someone who has the power to dispense. (Can. 85)

Dissolution. The act of legally ending the bond of marriage in non-consummation and privilege of the faith cases. (Cans. 1141-50)

Divine law. The law of God, whether positive or natural, that is binding on all human beings.

Divine liturgy. The term used by the Eastern churches for the celebration of the Eucharist.

Divine natural law. The body of laws and principles, known by human reason, as emanating from God and binding on all human beings.

Divine positive law. The laws of God that have been revealed in sacred scripture or declared as truths of the faith by the solemn magisterium of the Church.

Domicile. Permanent residence, established by residence with intent to remain in a place permanently unless called away, or by staying there five years. (Can. 102, §1)

Doubt. A state of mind that withholds assent between two contradictory propositions. (Can. 14)

Doubt of fact. The state of uncertainty arising when some fact is not conclusively demonstrated, e.g., a doubt about someone's age, or a doubt about the fact of baptism or its valid administration. (Can. 14)

Doubt of law. The state of uncertainty arising when the meaning of a law is uncertain due, not to the ignorance of the law's meaning, but to a defect in the law itself which allows more than one interpretation; the doubt can also pertain to an essential element of the law's effectiveness, e.g., its lawful promulgation, its binding force, its extension. Doubtful laws are not binding. (Can. 14)

Ecclesial community. A Christian denomination that is not recognized by the Roman Catholic Church as having all the essential criteria to constitute it as a church, used in canon law as a technical term for Protestant denominations. (See Church, community.)

Ecclesiastical law. A human law of the Church, as opposed to a divine law. (Can. 11)

Ecumenical council. A solemn assembly of the college of bishops which, in union with the pope, exercises supreme power and determines important doctrinal and disciplinary matters for the universal Church. (Cans. 337-41)

Enrollment (*ascriptio*). See **Incardination**. The term used in Eastern law for the incardination of a cleric. (CCEC, 357)

Eparch, eparchy. The terms used in the Eastern Catholic churches *sui iuris* that are equivalent to a diocesan bishop and a diocese in the Latin church. (CCEC, can. 177)

Episcopal vicar. A priest appointed by the diocesan bishop with the same powers as a vicar general but limited to a determined part of the diocese, or to a specific type of business, or to a specified group of persons. (Can. 476)

Error. Mistaken judgment. (Cans. 15; 126)

Error of person. A ground for marital nullity based on mistaken identity regarding one's intended spouse. (Can. 1097, §1)

Error of quality. A ground for marital nullity due to an error about a quality of a person, which quality was directly and principally intended. (Can. 1097, §2)

Evangelical counsels. The generic term for poverty, chastity, and obedience which are professed by all members of religious and secular institutes and hermits. (Can. 573)

Exarchy. A particular church of an Eastern Catholic church *sui iuris* which because of special circumstances is not erected as an eparchy. It is headed by an exarch whose powers are generally the same as those of an eparchical bishop. (CCEC, cans. 311-13)

Excardination. The process by which a cleric relinquishes his juridical attachment to a diocese, an institute of consecrated life, or some other society of clerics in order to incardinate in another. (Cans. 267-72)

Exclaustration. An indult granted to a religious in perpetual vows permitting him or her to live outside a house of the institute.

Excommunication. A censure which forbids a person from having any ministerial participation in the celebration of the liturgy; receiving the sacraments; discharging any ecclesiastical offices, ministries, or functions; and placing acts of governance. There are further effects if the excommunication has been imposed or declared. (Can. 1331)

Executive power. That power of governance which is broadly administrative, as opposed to legislative or judicial, exercised by a church official or body that has this power, e.g., diocesan bishop, vicar general, major superior, conference of bishops, Roman dicastery. (Can. 136)

Expiatory penalty. A category of penalties which are not censures and which may be inflicted perpetually, temporarily, or indefinitely. (Can. 1336)

External forum. As opposed to the internal forum, it is the forum of proofs, the public realm of observable, verifiable acts in which canon law generally operates and in which it can be enforced.

Extraordinary form. Marriage before two witnesses, without the active assistance of a priest or deacon who has the faculty to assist at marriage, in danger of death or outside the danger of death when it is foreseen that a qualified priest or deacon will be absent for a month. (Can. 1116)

Extraordinary minister. A minister of a sacrament or other liturgical rite who functions when the number of ordinary ministers is insufficient for pastoral needs. (Can. 230, §3)

Faculty. A certain power granted by law or delegation enabling the recipient of the faculty to perform a certain legal act validly and licitly.

Feast days. Sundays and holy days of obligation. (Cans. 1246-48)

Finance council. A group of the faithful at the diocesan or parish level who advise the bishop or pastor on financial matters. (Cans. 492, 537, 1280)

Force or fear. A ground for marital annulment when a marriage was entered due to force or grave fear inflicted from outside a person which compels the person to choose marriage in order to be free of it. (Can. 1103; see also can. 125.)

Form (canonical). The requirement that, for validity, a Catholic must be married in the presence of a priest or deacon who has the faculty to assist and marriages and two witness. (Can. 1108)

Form (sacramental). The essential words or formula necessary for the validity of a sacrament. (Can. 841)

Fraud (*dolus*). A ground for marital nullity based on error about a quality of one's spouse, which quality of its very nature may seriously disturb the marriage, and which was deliberately concealed by the other party in order to obtain consent. (Can. 1098)

Heresy. The obstinate denial after the reception of baptism of some truth which is to be believed as being of divine and catholic faith, or it is likewise an obstinate doubt concerning the same. (Can. 751)

Hermit. A man or woman who is consecrated to God by a public profession before the diocesan bishop of the three evangelical counsels and who observes his or her plan of life under the bishop's direction. (Can. 603, §2)

Hierarch. In Eastern law, a term roughly equivalent to an Ordinary.

Holy See. See Apostolic See.

Homily. A form of preaching by a cleric at liturgy. (Can. 767, §1)

House, religious. The place of residence of a religious community that has been lawfully erected, is under the authority of a superior, and has a church or oratory in which the Eucharist is celebrated and reserved. (Can. 608)

Ignorance. Lack of knowledge; also, a grounds for marital annulment if the ignorance concerns essential aspects of the nature of marriage. (Cans. 15; 126; 1096)

Impediment (marital). See Diriment impediment.

Impediment (orders). Some fact or condition that prohibits a man from being licitly ordained. (Cans. 1040–49)

Incardination. The act of a cleric's juridical attachment to a diocese, an institute of consecrated life, or other society of clerics; incardination occurs when one becomes a cleric at his ordination to the diaconate, or later by incardinating elsewhere according to the norm of law. (Cans. 265–72)

Indissolubility. An essential property of marriage requiring a permanent commitment of the spouses and no remarriage following divorce except after the death of the spouse. (Can. 1056)

Indulgence. The remission before God of the temporal punishment for sin which has already been forgiven which a member of the faithful obtains under the conditions specified in the *List of Indulgences.* (Can. 992)

Indult. A favor granted to someone by competent authority.

Indult of departure. A rescript granted by the competent authority that permits a perpetually professed or perpetually incorporated member of an institute of consecrated life or a definitively incorporated member of a society of apostolic life to leave the institute or society and cease being a member. (Cans. 691, 727, 743)

Infant. A person under the age of seven or one who habitually lacks the use of reason. (Cans. 97, §2; 99)

Institute of consecrated life. The generic term for a religious or secular institute. (Can. 573)

Instruction. A document which clarifies or elaborates on laws and determines the approach to be followed in implementing them. Instructions may not derogate from laws and cease to have force when the laws on which they are based are revoked. (Can. 34) An instruction (*instructio*) is not to be confused with the General Instruction (*institutio*) on the Roman Missal which is a legislative document.

Interdict. A censure which prohibits a person from having any ministerial participation in the liturgy or receiving the sacraments. (Can. 1332)

Internal forum. The forum of conscience, the private realm of a person's thoughts, sins, and actions that are not publicly known and the confidentiality and privacy of which must be strictly respected by confessors and spiritual directors. (Cans. 240; 630; 983-85; 1388)

Irregularity. A perpetual impediment to ordination. (Can. 1041)

Judicial vicar. Also known as the officialis, the priest who has ordinary power to judge cases in a diocese; he often is the chief administrator of the tribunal. (Can. 1420)

Juridic person. Aggregates of persons or things, whether public or private, established by law or by a competent ecclesiastical authority and ordered towards a purpose congruent with the mission of the Church and which transcends the purpose of the individuals who comprise it; a canonically established church corporation, e.g., a diocese, a province of a religious institute, a Catholic hospital, a charitable foundation. (Cans. 113-123)

Jurisdiction. See Power of governance.

Lack of due competence. The inability to consent validly to marriage due to the incapacity of assuming the essential obligations of marriage as a result of causes of a psychic nature. (Can. 1095, 3°)

Lack of due discretion. The inability to consent validly to marriage due to a grave lack of discretion of judgment concerning essential matrimonial rights and duties which are to be mutually given and accepted. (Can. 1095, 2°)

Lack of sufficient use of reason. The inability to consent validly to marriage due a lack of sufficient use of reason, e.g., as a result of severe mental retardation, insanity, etc. (Can. 1095, 1°)

Laicization. The loss of the clerical state by means of a rescript from the Holy See. (Can. 290, 3°)

Legal relationship. The relationship arising through legal adoption; it is an impediment to marriage in the direct line or in the second degree of the collateral line.

Legate (papal). A representative of the pope to a nation and/or episcopal conference; a nuncio or apostolic delegate. (Cans. 362-67)

Legislative power. The power of governance exercised by an authority who is competent to enact laws, e.g., the pope, the diocesan bishop, an ecumenical or particular council. (Can. 135, §2)

Liceity. Lawfulness, licitness; generally used of a law whose observance is not necessary for the validity of a legal act.

Liturgy. Worship carried out in the name of the Church by persons lawfully deputed and through acts approved by the authority of the Church, e.g. the sacraments, sacramentals, funeral rites, liturgy of the hours, benediction.

Local Ordinary. Also called Ordinary of the place, it is a generic term for the ecclesiastical authorities who exercise the power of governance territorially, namely, the pope, diocesan bishops, those equivalent to diocesan bishops in law (can. 368), vicars general, and episcopal vicars. (Can. 134, §2)

Major archbishop. The metropolitan of a see who presides over an entire Eastern church *sui iuris* which is not a patriarchate; his powers are generally equivalent to those of a patriarch. (CCEC, cans. 151, 152)

Major superior. Those who govern a religious institute, a province of an institute, a part equivalent to a province, an autonomous house, as well as their vicars. (Can. 620)

Mass obligation. The duty of a priest to celebrate a Mass for the specific intention for which he has accepted a Mass offering. (Cans. 949, 955-57, 1308-10)

Mass offering. A donation of money, usually of a fixed but small amount, for the celebration of Mass for a specific intention. (Cans. 954-54)

Matter (sacramental). The substance or essential sign of a sacrament, necessary for its validity. (Can. 841)

Metropolitan. Archbishop; the diocesan bishop who heads an archdiocese. (Can. 435) In Eastern Catholic law, one who heads a metropolitan church. (CCEC, can. 155)

Metropolitan church *sui iuris*. An Eastern Catholic church presided over by a metropolitan who is appointed by the pope. (CCEC, can. 155)

Minor. A person under eighteen years of age; also a person who habitually lacks the use of reason. (Cans. 97, 99)

Mixed marriage. A marriage between a Catholic and a non-Catholic, especially a baptized non-Catholic. (Can. 1124)

Motu proprio. Literally, "on his own initiative;" a term used for a document when it is issued on the legislator's own initiative and not at the request of another, as in an apostolic letter *motu proprio.*

Myron. The chrism or blessed oil used in the Eastern Catholic churches *sui iuris* for the sacrament of holy myron (confirmation). (CCEC, 693)

Notary. An official appointed to authenticate juridical acts in the administrative or judicial arena. (Cans. 483, 1437)

Novitiate. A period of not less than twelve months nor more than two years spent in a designated religious house in preparation for the profession of temporary vows in a religious institute. (Cans. 646-53)

Nuncio (papal). The ambassador of the Roman Pontiff to a country that has formal diplomatic relations with the Holy See. (Can. 365)

Oath. The invocation of the divine name as a witness to the truth which cannot be taken unless in behalf of truth, judgment, and justice. (Can. 1199)

Oath of fidelity. A formula, to be said after the profession of faith, by the faithful mentioned in canon 833, nn. 5-8. (Can. 833)

Office. A stable function established by divine or ecclesiastical law to be exercised for a spiritual purpose, e.g., the office of pope, diocesan bishop, major superior, vicar general, pastor. (Can. 145)

Oil of catechumens. The holy oil used to anoint adult catechumens during the catechumenate or infants during the celebration of baptism.

Oil of the sick. The holy oil used in the sacrament of the anointing of the sick; it is blessed by the bishop or, in necessity, by a priest during the celebration of the rite. (Can. 999)

Oratory. A place designated with the permission of the Ordinary for divine cult for the advantage of some community or assembly of the faithful who gather there. Other members of the faithful can also have access to it with the consent of the competent superior. (Can. 1223)

Ordinary. A generic term that includes all local Ordinaries as well as major superiors of clerical religious institutes of pontifical right and of clerical societies of apostolic life. (Can. 134, §1)

Ordinary power. Power of governance that is joined to a certain office by the law itself. (Can. 131, §1)

Parochial vicar. Also called an associate pastor or curate, he is a priest who assists the pastor in the pastoral ministry of a parish. (Can. 545)

Particular church. A generic term for the territorial units of the Latin church *sui iuris*, namely, dioceses, territorial prelatures, territorial abbacies, apostolic vicariates, apostolic prefectures, and apostolic administrations erected on a stable basis. (Can. 368)

Particular council. See Plenary council and Provincial council.

Particular law. As opposed to universal law, a law made for a particular territory or for a particular group of the faithful. (Can. 13)

Pastor (*parochus*). Also called parish priest; the priest who is entrusted with the pastoral care of a parish. (Can. 519)

Pastoral council. A group of the faithful at the diocesan or parish level who assist and advise the bishop or pastor especially in matters relating to pastoral work. (Cans. 511, 536)

Pastors of souls, or pastors (*pastores*). A generic term referring to bishops and presbyters who exercise the pastoral ministry.

Patriarch. A bishop who presides over a patriarchal church *sui iuris*. (CCEC, cans. 55–56)

Pauline privilege. The dissolution of a marriage between two unbaptized parties, one of whom is later baptized, provided the non-baptized party departs. (Cans. 1143–47)

Penal precept. A precept that threatens to impose a penalty. (Can. 1319) See Precept.

Penal remedy. A warning from the Ordinary to a person who is in the proximate occasion of committing an offense or who is suspected of having committed an offense, or a rebuke by the ordinary to a person from whose behavior there arises scandal or serious disturbance of order. (Can. 1339)

Penance (penal). Some work of religion, piety, or charity imposed by an Ordinary on a person who has committed some offense. (Can. 1340)

Personal law. A law made for a specific group of the faithful, e.g., the constitutions of a religious institute.

Personal prelature. An association of secular clergy governed by statutes approved by the Apostolic See having its own Ordinary who has the right to erect a seminary, incardinate the students, and promote them to orders under the title of service to the prelature; e.g., Opus Dei. (Cans. 294, 295)

Petitioner. The party who brings a case before a church tribunal, e.g., a spouse seeking an annulment of marriage. (Cans. 1476-80)

Petrine privilege. The dissolution of a marriage between a baptized and an unbaptized party given by the pope in favor of the faith of one of the parties.

Pious foundation. A trust or endowment established for a specific religious purpose, e.g., the celebration of Masses for a deceased person. (Cans. 1303-07)

Plenary council. A particular council, generally convoked for the purpose of enacting particular laws, for all the particular churches belonging to the same conference of bishops. (Can. 439)

Pontifical right. A kind of institute of consecrated life whose immediate ecclesiastical superior is the Apostolic See. (Can. 593)

Postulation. The election, by at least a two-thirds majority, of someone who is canonically impeded from being elected for some reason which can be and usually is dispensed. (Cans. 180-83)

Power of governance. Also known as jurisdiction, the power connected with ecclesiastical offices or granted to persons for the performance of specific legal acts. It is divided into legislative, executive, and judicial power of governance. (Cans. 129-44)

Precept. An individual decree by which a direct and legitimate injunction is placed upon a determined person or upon determined persons to do or to omit something, especially concerning the urging of the observance of a law. (Can. 49)

Presbyter. The second rank of the clergy; a priest who is not a bishop.

Presbyteral council. A group of priests chosen to represent all the priests of a diocese to aid the bishop in the governance of the diocese. (Can. 495)

Prescription. The process of acquiring or losing a subjective right or of freeing oneself from an obligation by means of exercising that right or not fulfilling that obligation over a long period of time as specified in the law. (Cans. 197-99; 1268, 1270)

Presentation. The exercise of the right of a person to present a name for an office to the authority who has the right of appointment to the office. (Cans. 158-63)

Priest (*sacerdos*). A generic term for both presbyters and bishops.

Prior bond. An impediment to marriage due to one or more previous marriages on the part of either or both parties. (Can. 1085)

Private chapel. A place designated for divine cult for the advantage of one or more physical persons, established with permission of the local Ordinary. (Can. 1226)

Privation. Removal from office as a penalty for an offense. (Can. 196)

Privilege. A favor made in behalf of certain persons, whether physical or juridic, by means of a special act. A privilege can be granted by the legislator as well as by an executive authority to which the legislator has granted this power. (Can. 76)

Procurator. Similar to an advocate, someone appointed to perform judicial business for a party in an ecclesiastical proceeding. (Can. 1481)

Profession. The act, whether by vow or other sacred bond, of a person assuming a life of poverty, chastity, and obedience in a religious or secular institute. (Cans. 573, 654, 712)

Profession of faith. A formula, approved by the Apostolic See, that must be uttered by certain officials and professors at the beginning of their term of office or appointment. (Can. 833)

Prohibition (*vetitum*). A decree of the local Ordinary or ecclesiastical court forbidding a party, Catholic or non-Catholic, to marry in church until certain specified requirements are met, e.g., professional counselling. (Can. 1077)

Promoter of justice. A diocesan judicial official appointed by the bishop for contentious cases in which the public good could be at stake and for penal cases. (Can. 1430)

Promulgation. The official act by which a new law is published. (Cans. 7–8)

Proper power. The ordinary power of governance exercised in one's own name, e.g., the power exercised by a diocesan bishop or a major superior. (Can. 131)

Protosyncellus. In Eastern Catholic law, the eparchial official corresponding to the vicar general in the Latin church. (CCEC, can. 245)

Province (ecclesiastical). A territorial unit consisting of all the particular churches in one area, namely, the metropolitan see and its suffragan sees. (Can. 431)

Provincial council. A particular council, generally held for the purpose of enacting particular laws, for all the particular churches of a province. (Can. 440)

Proxy marriage. A proxy marriage is the exchange of marital consent at which an absent spouse is represented by someone who has been mandated by the party for this duty. (Can. 1105.)

Public propriety. A relationship that arises from an invalid marriage after common life has been established or from notorious and public concubinage; it is an impediment to marriage in the first degree of the direct line between a man and the blood relatives of the woman, and vice-versa. (Can. 1093)

Putative marriage. An invalid marriage that has been celebrated in good faith by at least one of the parties, until both parties become certain of its nullity. (Can. 1061, §3)

Quasi-domicile. Temporary residence, acquired by intent to stay in a certain place at least three months unless called away, or by actually staying there for three months. (Can. 102, §2)

Radical sanation. The convalidation of an invalid marriage without the renewal of consent. (Can. 1161)

Ratified marriage. A valid marriage between the baptized; a sacramental marriage. (Can. 1061)

Recourse. An appeal against a decision made by a Church authority through an administrative, rather than a judicial, process. (Can. 1734 ff.)

Rector (of a church). A priest to whom is given the care of some church which is not parochial, capitular, or connected with a house of a religious community or a society of apostolic life. (Can. 556)

Rector (of a seminary). The person who presides over a seminary. (Can. 239)

Region (ecclesiastical). A grouping of neighboring provinces, e.g., all the provinces of a nation. (Can. 433)

Religious institute. The generic term for a religious order, congregation, or society. Religious institutes are characterized by members who take public vows of poverty, chastity, and obedience and live in common as brothers or sisters. (Can. 607)

Removal. The involuntary loss of office for grave reasons according to the procedures determined in law. (Cans. 192-95)

Rescript. An administrative act given in writing by a competent executive authority by which there is granted to someone requesting it a privilege, dispensation, or some other favor. (Can. 59)

Resignation. The voluntary renunciation of office by an office-holder for a just and proportionate reason. (Cans.187-89)

Respondent. In a church trial the party who is the defendant and responds to the charges made by the petitioner. (Cans. 1476-80)

Rite. The liturgical, theological, spiritual and disciplinary patrimony, culture and heritage of a church *sui iuris* that originated and developed in the ancient centers of Christendom. These rites are the Roman, Constantinopolitan (Byzantine), Alexandrian, Antiochene, Armenian, and Chaldean. (CCEC, can. 28)

Roman curia. The generic word for the various dicasteries of the Apostolic See. (Can. 360)

Rules of order. Rules or norms to be observed in assemblies of persons defining the constitution, moderation, and procedures of assemblies. (Can. 95)

Sacramentals. Sacred signs, somewhat in imitation of the sacraments, through which their effects, especially spiritual ones, are signified and are obtained by the intercession of the Church. (Can. 1166)

Schism. The refusal of submission to the Roman pontiff or of communion with the members of the Church subject to him. (Can. 751)

Seal of confession. The complete and inviolable obligation of secrecy and confidentiality required of confessors, interpreters in confession, or anyone who has knowledge of another's sacramental confession of sins. (Cans. 983, 1388)

Secular institute. A form of consecrated life, akin to religious, but which does not alter the member's proper canonical state as a cleric or layperson. (Can. 711)

See. A diocese or archdiocese.

Shrine. A church or other sacred place to which the faithful, with the approval of the local Ordinary, make pilgrimages for a particular pious reason. (Can. 1230)

Society of apostolic life. A group of the faithful organized for an apostolic purpose who, like religious, live in common as brothers or sisters but without taking religious vows. (Can. 731)

Spiritual relationship. The relationship between one who is baptized and his or her godparent and between the godparent and the parents of the baptized. It is an impediment to marriage in the Eastern Catholic churches. (CCEC, can. 811)

Statutes. The by-laws of a juridic person by which their purpose, constitution, government, and operation are defined. (Can. 94)

Suffragan. As opposed to the metropolitan, he is a diocesan bishop who is the head of a diocese which is not an archdiocese. (Can. 436)

Sui iuris. See **Church *sui iuris*.**

Supreme authority. The pope and the college of bishops.

Supreme moderator. A major superior of a religious institute who has power over the entire institute. (Can. 622)

Supreme power. The power exercised by the pope and the college of bishops, the highest authority in the Church, whose supreme power includes matters legislative, executive, and judicial. (Cans. 331, 336)

Suspension. A censure affecting only clergy that forbids the exercise of one or more of their powers, rights, or functions. (Can. 1333)

Syncellus. An eparchial official in an Eastern church corresponding to the episcopal vicar in the Latin church. (CCEC, can. 246)

Synod of bishops. A group of bishops, convoked by the pope, to advise him on issues affecting the universal Church in the case of a general synod, or for one or more regions of the Church in the case of a special synod. (Cans. 342–48) In Eastern law, an assembly of all the bishops of a patriarchal or major archiepiscopal church *sui iuris.* (CCEC, cans. 102, 152)

Transfer. The act of a competent authority that changes an office-holder from one office to a new one. (Cans. 190–91) It can also refer to the movement of a member of an institute of consecrated life or society of apostolic life to another such institute or society. (Cans. 684, 730, 744)

Transient (*vagus*). A person who lacks any domicile or quasi-domicile. (Can. 100)

Traveler (*peregrinus*). A person who is outside the place of domicile or quasi-domicile. (Can. 100)

Tribunal. A church court, especially for the processing of cases of marital nullity. (Cans. 1417–45)

Unity (marital). An essential property of marriage requiring monogamy and fidelity. (Can. 1056)

Universal law. A law binding everyone for whom it was made in the entire Latin Catholic church. (Can. 12, §§ 1, 2)

Use of reason. The intellectual and volitional capacity necessary to be subject to canon law, presumed to be attained at age seven. (Can. 11)

Validity. Legal efficacy. Laws affecting the validity of a legal act must be observed for the act to be juridically recognized as effective.

Viaticum. Holy Communion given to a person in danger of death. (Can. 921)

Vicar forane. See Dean.

Vicar general. A priest appointed by the diocesan bishop to assist him in the governance of the diocese; he is a local Ordinary and has executive power of governance for the entire diocese.

Vicarious power. Ordinary power of governance that is exercised in the name of another, e.g. the power of a vicar general or judicial vicar exercised in the name of the diocesan bishop. (Can. 131)

Virgin. A woman who consecrates her virginity to God and dedicates herself to the service of the Church in accord with a special liturgical rite presided over by the diocesan bishop. (Can. 604)

Visitation. The official visit of a diocesan bishop, major superior, or other official to institutions and persons subject to them at the time and in the manner prescribed by law. (Cans. 396–98; 436; 628; 683; 806; 1301, §2)

Vow. A deliberate and free promise made to God concerning a possible or better good and which must be fulfilled in virtue of religion. (Can. 1191)

Index of the
Canons of 1983 Code

General Index

423